Seventh Edition

Instructor's and Administrator's Guide

for *Career Choices* and My10yearPlan.com®

How to Implement a Freshman Transition Course
and School-wide Initiative that will
Increase High School and College Completion Rates

Written by Mindy Bingham

Editors and Contributors:

Tanja Easson
Kelly Gajewski

Contributions by:

Kenneth B. Hoyt, Ph.D.
Cathie Klein
Becky Simmons
Sandy Stryker
and the
generous Career Choices *instructors*
noted throughout this text

𝒜cademic Innovations
St. George, Utah

Copies of this book, along with any of the books or web sites in the *Career Choices* series are available from the publisher. Visit www.academicinnovations.com or call (800) 967-8016 for information.

Seventh Edition © 2013, © 2016 by Melinda Bingham and Associates, LLC
Sixth Edition © 2003 by Melinda Bingham
Fifth Edition © 2000 by Melinda Bingham
Fourth Edition © 1997 by Melinda Bingham and Sandy Stryker
Third Edition © 1995 by Melinda Bingham and Sandy Stryker
Second Edition © 1992 by Melinda Bingham and Sandy Stryker
First Edition © 1990 by Melinda Bingham and Sandy Stryker

ISBN 978-1-878787-39-2

Published by Academic Innovations

(800) 967-8016   FAX (800) 967-4027
www.academicinnovations.com
support@academicinnovations.com
My10yearPlan.com® is a registered trademark of Academic Innovations

25   24   23   22

Manufactured in the United States of America

Changing Attitudes,
Changing Lives…

In four words, that sums up the goal of the *Career Choices* curriculum. What began as a passion for author Mindy Bingham has grown into a mission for the 40 plus individuals who write, administer, support, and train in this curriculum.

To date, over 5,000 schools and programs with nearly two million students have used **Career Choices**. Throughout this manual you'll find the thoughts, ideas, and creative energies of some of the hundreds of educators who have embraced and championed the concept that every 8th or 9th grade student completes a comprehensive guidance course that culminates in a 10-year plan.

When **Career Choices** was first published in 1990, it was considered a cutting edge curriculum because it integrated the theme of career, life, and educational planning into the traditional subjects of English/ language arts, math, and social studies. Using an interdisciplinary approach grounded in real-life activities, students found the answer to the age-old question: "Why is education important?"

Now with the addition of technology-based enhancements and extensive online professional development, as well as public/private partnerships with the George Washington University's Freshman Transition Initiative and the **Get Focused...Stay Focused!**™ Initiative from developed at Santa Barbara City College, Academic Innovations continues to provide educators with the latest and best strategies for motivating and educating our young people.

If you want to make a major difference in the lives of your students, read on. Then pick up the phone and call our Curriculum and Technical Support department at (800) 967-8016. Our job does not stop when you order the textbooks or your online licenses; it only begins. We are devoted to your success and the success of your students.

Contents

Introduction

College and Career Readiness

> *The national conversation around education has shifted from baseline academic proficiency to preparation for the rigors of college and the workplace. This shift comes as many college faculty and employers note that students graduating from American high schools are not prepared for postsecondary education or workplace demands.*
>
> — The Alliance for Excellent Education, Washington, DC

Lack of college readiness is demonstrated by low college attendance rates, low college graduation rates, and high post-secondary remediation costs.

Yet by 2018, 62% of jobs are expected to require some level of post-secondary training, according to a 2009 study by the Georgetown University Center on Education and the Workforce. More students than ever are enrolling in college, but research reveals that an astonishing percentage of students drop out. According to a 2011 report released by the Pathways to Prosperity Project at the Harvard Graduate School of Education, only 56% of college students pursuing four-year degrees finish within six years, and only 29% of those who start two-year degrees complete them within three years.

Our country has long promoted the economic benefits of a college degree and touted college as a necessity for all students. Unfortunately, until recently not nearly enough attention has been focused on whether or not students actually finished college. As it turns out, we have failed to sufficiently prepare students for college, overlooking the skills, resources, and support necessary to ensure successful completion. Students have come to perceive getting into college as the ultimate goal but have no plan for how to succeed there, often not truly understanding why they are even in college. And, with an overemphasis on the four-year degree as the ideal option, we set many students up for failure when a two-year or technical program would serve them better.

As a result, college completion rates are abysmal.

Career and Education Plans: Critical to College Completion

Yet, according to "Advancing Student Success in the California Community Colleges" by the California Community Colleges Student Success Task Force:

> *Research from the Institute for Higher Education Leadership and Policy shows that students who entered a program [of study] in their first year were twice as likely to complete a certificate, degree or transfer as students who entered a program after their first year.*

The Student Success Task Force also found that guidance is essential for students to achieve their potential:

> The current matriculation model assumes that students will clarify their educational objective in the course of meeting with a counselor. However, many students never see a counselor... Helping students make informed choices about their education is a critical strategy to help increase student success...

The task force goes on to recommend that:

> Students who arrive without a clear goal need an education plan that allows them to systematically define their educational needs and objectives and explore their options... Expanded resources for career exploration are essential.

Why Wait—Start in Secondary School

We should all argue, why should students have to wait until entering college or post-secondary work to choose a major (program of study) or, for that matter, the best form of post-secondary education? After all, shouldn't these choices be explored prior to high school graduation to avoid the false starts, circuitous paths, or dead ends too many young people encounter on their educational journey?

A comprehensive guidance course using the proven methods of *Career Choices* and My10yearPlan.com® can make all the difference. Such a course empowers students to develop long-range 10-year career and education plans to carry them not only into—but through—college or post-secondary training and on to the workforce. And, as they build their career and life plans, the classroom-based guidance process students experience in your course provides the intrinsic motivation required to succeed.

Intrinsic Motivation: Vital to High School AND College Completion

Getting the unfocused, under-motivated student to embrace the rewards of education has long been a primary goal of education reform and redesign. The efforts of qualified, experienced instructors with quality instructional materials in well-funded programs are still stymied if students are unmotivated.

After all, **learning requires intrinsic motivation**, which is only possible when the learner internalizes the rewards inherent to a task and has a realistic expectation of success. Intrinsically motivated students are more likely to understand that academic achievement is not determined by luck and that they can control educational attainment by expending an appropriate amount of time and energy.

When students are immersed in a comprehensive guidance experience that helps them visualize, articulate, and plan for a productive future that matches their personality, goals, and dreams, the value of a good education becomes abundantly clear. Educators across the country have reported profound changes in motivation and, therefore, results, when using the *Career Choices* curriculum with their students. (See pages 1/27 to 1/30 for additional details.)

Common Core State Standards: An Opportunity for Change

With the advent of the Common Core State Standards, instructors across the country are meeting this challenge by "repackaging" traditional disciplines. By infusing real-world themes and issues, the core content is delivered with a fresher, more relevant slant. The Common Core State Standards require instructors to change not only the way they teach, but also what they teach. Old lesson plans must be retired in favor of new course material that, as reported in January 2012 by *Education Week*:

...focuses on the application of knowledge in authentic situations... Teachers will need to employ instructional strategies that integrate critical and creative thinking, collaboration, problem-solving, research and inquiry, and presentation and demonstration skills.

Freshman Transition Course and School-wide Initiative

This *Instructor's and Administrator's Guide* was designed to help instructors, school and district administrators, college partners, and state departments of education visualize, plan for, and implement a comprehensive college and career readiness program through a Freshman Transition course and school-wide initiative. After 23 years, this expanded seventh edition is not only for the instructor of the *Career Choices* course, but is equally useful for the administrator or program manager seeking to increase both high school and post-secondary graduation rates and transition students into productive and satisfying careers.

Proven, scalable, and cost-efficient, this rigorous course, followed by the periodic updating of students' 10-year Plans throughout high school and post-secondary education, will maximize the quantity and the quality of the guidance that students receive. Through the school-wide initiative model proposed by The George Washington University's Freshman Transition Initiative and expanded on by the *Get Focused...Stay Focused!* ™ Initiative developed at Santa Barbara City College, this program provides the foundation for a solid, whole-school redesign effort.

Implement this course and program with fidelity, using the resources and plans available in this guide (print and online) and through the online **Teachers' Lounge**, and you'll have a proven formula for helping students complete appropriate education and training in a field that will not only give them the greatest opportunity for lasting satisfaction but will also deliver the skills and aptitudes required to be competitive in today's workforce.

Read on. You're about to discover how *changing attitudes changes lives*.

How to Use this Guide

Your first thought after being handed this guide might be, oh my goodness, why is this so large? Do I need to know all this to teach this course? The answer is no.

This *Instructor's and Administrator's Guide*, along with the **new online edition**, was designed to provide comprehensive support to the instructors of the *Career Choices* curriculum, school and district administrators, program managers, and college partners interested in implementing a classroom guidance experience that will impact high school and college completion rates and. Coupled with instructional resources on the online Teachers' Lounge, this is probably the most comprehensive school-wide program available.

Naturally, you'll want to start by reviewing the table of contents. For a short narrative outlining the contents of this guide, see pages 1/11 to 1/14. Then focus on the sections providing information and resources applicable to your job or current tasks.

For Career Choices *Instructors*

We recommend that you carefully review the following sections throughout your preparation and implementation process:

Section 1: Quick Start

Section 2: Overview of the Curriculum

Section 4: Lesson Plan Suggestions for Each Activity

Section 6: Freshman Transition: Create a Vision of What is Possible

Section 9: My10yearPlan.com®

Section 10: Lesson Planning and Pacing

Section 11: Instructional Strategies

Section 14: Assessment

For Administrators or Program Managers

For those responsible for increasing graduation rates, we recommend a thorough review of the following sections:

START HERE --> Section 6: Freshman Transition: Create a Vision of What is Possible

Section 1: Quick Start

Section 3: Where to Use the Curriculum? Who Should Teach It?

Section 5: Getting Buy-in

Section 7: Program Planning Resources

Section 8: Integrating Academics and Technology

Section 12: Curriculum Support and Professional Development Options

Section 13: Getting Parents and the Community Involved

Section 15: Sustainability and Funding

More than a Course, It's a Program

This is more than an instructor's guide. It's a program-planning manual for a school-wide initiative built on the recommendations by The George Washington University's Freshman Transition Initiative. Over the past eight years, this program has grown in scope and in the resources developed. For more information, see Section 6.

Academic Innovations is also proud of its partnership over the past four years with the *Get Focused...Stay Focused!*™ Initiative developed at Santa Barbara City College. In the press release announcing the 2013 Aspen Prize for Community College Excellence, the Aspen Institute cited this incredible work:

> *Expanding student development efforts beyond its campus to local high schools, Santa Barbara City College has created the largest dual enrollment program—which allows high school students to take community college courses—among California's 112 community colleges. SBCC is also helping high-school students, many of whom may not be financially or academically prepared, develop long-term educational plans through college readiness and career counseling programs.*[1]

Working together, we will continue to develop and provide resources for a grade 8–14 program that spans middle school, high school, and into college. As we do, we'll provide updated announcements via the online version of this guide and **The Teachers' Lounge**. An overview of *Get Focused...Stay Focused!*™ is available on pages 6/22 to 6/30.

Online Instructor's Guide

New with this seventh print edition is an online edition that links directly to a variety of resources mentioned throughout this guide. The digital format opens up even more opportunities for you to fine-tune your planning and implementation, making it easier to expand your learning, increase your efficiency, and build your capacity.

You'll find this logo throughout this guide noting that additional information and resources can be found in the **Online Instructor's Guide**.

When you adopt the *Career Choices* curriculum and purchase this guide, you'll receive a code for the **Online Instructor's Guide**. Consult the inside cover of this guide for directions on how to activate your access to this incredible resource.

Curriculum and Technical Support

Academic Innovations believes that our responsibility only begins with your adoption of our course materials. To help ensure your success and the success of your students, we have created a variety of professional development options, curriculum support programs, and online resources.

You also have access to the most valuable of resources: Our dedicated staff, volunteer educators, and consultants who stand ready to support you via phone, email, or online meeting. A quick call to our office between 9:00 AM and 4:00 PM (Mountain time) will put you in touch with someone who can answer your unique question.

Curriculum and Technical Support
(800) 967-8016

---

1 Press release: March 19, 2013
2013 Aspen Prize for Community College Excellence Awarded to Santa Barbara City College and Walla Walla Community College

Section 1

Quick Start

Topics in this section include:

- Motivating students to increase the effort and attention given to school by helping them understand the relationship between mastery of their academic subjects and their future careers and life satisfaction.

- When used in middle or high school, *Career Choices* can impact college completion rates and help ensure college graduates have the skills needed to succeed in their chosen career.

- This *Instructor's Guide* as a resource for not only lesson planning and assessment but also for getting buy-in from your school and community partners.

- The valuable resources available through The Teachers' Lounge, from online training videos to lesson planning spreadsheets to a Professional Learning Community for *Career Choices* educators to motivational chapter introduction videos.

- Successful school models that have resulted in improved graduation rates, academic performance, and behavior markers.

A Quick Overview of the *Career Choices* Curriculum

What makes the *Career Choices* curriculum unique and effective? Quite simply, its effectiveness is the result of its careful design: **Academically-based and repackaged in a thematic format, it addresses the developmental needs of the early adolescent while delivering on the goals of the Common Core State Standards.** How?

- It teaches a critical decision-making process for evaluating life-defining choices.

- It culminates in the development of a 10-year career and education plan that helps young people envision a productive life of their own choosing.

- At the same time, it coaches students as they answer a pressing and crucial question: Why do I need a good education?

- It is different by design and, therefore, less threatening for all students.

- It melds high tech with high touch, an important component when seeking student buy-in of the content and concepts presented.

The bottom line: By changing attitudes, it changes lives!

Whether your students are headed for an Ivy League college or an entry-level job, they crave a clear sense of direction for their lives. A required class based on the Standards for a Freshman Transition Course from The George Washington University can help students develop a personalized, career-inclusive 10-year education plan. As they work through the coursework, students learn a self-discovery and planning process that culminates with a plan to:

- Make high school graduation a reality

- Enter and **complete** college or post-secondary education and training

- Transition into a productive and self-sufficient adulthood

This interactive course captures the attention of ALL students, because at its core are the issues of the greatest importance to teens: **themselves and their future**.

In addition, this semester or year-long course can include the integration of academics and technology, making personal mastery of these skills relevant to students' lives.

Known as the decade of transition, between age 14 and 24 is probably one of the most critical decision-making periods in anyone's life. High school freshmen start making choices that will impact the rest of their lives, often without realizing it. Some of these choices have far-reaching consequences: to stay in school or not; to become sexually active or not; to apply focused energy to school work or not.

When young people have a **productive vision of their future** that correlates with their goals, identity, aptitudes, lifestyle expectations, and passions AND a **10-year plan of their own making built around quantitative education and career goals**, the value of working hard in school and acquiring adequate education or training becomes abundantly clear. Essentially, the **process** taught in this standards-based course quantifies the **reason to learn**.

Key Strategies for Success

- Don't be fooled by the simplistic format of *Career Choices*. The lighthearted text and design are meant to trigger the self-discovery and contemplation needed to make the important and complex decisions students face.

- Start at the beginning and work sequentially through to the end. As students work through the book and My10yearPlan.com®, the concepts they master and the data they gather in the early chapters are used again and again as they make decisions, set goals, and develop their 10-year plan.

- Every student should leave the course with a comprehensive, meaningful, and personalized 10-year plan in their completed *Workbook and Portfolio* (specifically Chapter 12) and, in some cases, on My10yearPlan.com®.

- While students may be tempted to sit down and complete the activities in a few sittings, it is not recommended. As easy as they may seem, these are important questions that require reflection and thought. It is important that students take time to contemplate the issues and concepts presented and that instructors follow up with discussion and support as students process the information.

- It is not the purpose of this course to have students make a **final** career choice. In today's workplace, there is no such thing. However, they will learn a *process* for making career choices and life choices that will lead to a rewarding and satisfying future.

- You'll want to spend time prior to the first day of class developing your plan and creating your Pacing Guide. You'll find a variety of resources and suggestions throughout both the print and the expanded online version of the *Instructor's Guide*.

- In addition, we suggest you call Academic Innovation's Curriculum Support department and brainstorm your ideas and plans with one our technical assistance professionals. As a mission-oriented publisher, we are dedicated to you and your students success and know our job just begins when you adopt the *Career Choices* curriculum.

Your Quick Start Roadmap

The *Career Choices* curriculum is probably different than anything you've taught before. Just thumbing through the main textbook reiterates that fact. Based on the Socratic method of dialectic teaching where questioning, discussion, and self-discovery trumps didactic text or lecturing, it promotes higher-order thinking and reasoning while reinforcing the overarching goals of the Common Core State Standards.

The components of the *Career Choices* series are best taught in a classroom that gives priority to:

Active learning		passive listening
Socratic method of instruction	**V E R S U S**	didactic delivery
Higher order thinking (analysis, synthesis, & evaluation)		read and recall
Critical, creative, & strategic thinking		memorization
An interdisciplinary project-based culture		subject-centered isolation

The Common Core State Standards impact not only WHAT instructors teach but also HOW they teach. Old lesson plans have been retired in favor of new course material and strategies that, as reported by *Education Week* in January 2012:

> "…focuses on the application of knowledge in authentic situations… Teachers will need to employ instructional strategies that integrate critical and creative thinking, collaboration, problem-solving, research and inquiry, and presentation and demonstration skills."

This manual provides a wealth of information and support that will help you deliver the spirit of the Common Core.

Five-Step Quick Start

The five steps outlined on the following pages provide a comprehensive overview of key strategies for your course. Time spent reviewing and working through these resources will yield the foundation knowledge needed to launch a course that will change not only your students' lives but also your professional experience.

Step 1: This *Instructor's Guide*

This *Instructor's Guide* includes what you need to customize your course. It is a compilation of lessons learned and resources shared by educators we've worked with over more than two decades. Look to this guide as your first-stop resource for answering any of your questions about teaching a *Career Choices* course.

Step 2: Quick Start Checklist

This checklist provides a roadmap that includes all of the resources available to you through the different phases of implementation. You'll want to come back and review this often.

Step 3: Online Teachers' Lounge

As you develop your plans, visit this web-based resource repository. The Teachers' Lounge is where you'll find videos, sample lesson plans, and instructional resources that will save you hours and hours of prep time. Spend some time becoming familiar with what's available and plan to check back periodically since new resources are added as they become available.

Step 4: Self-Study Guide for a Quick Start

This self-directed professional development plan will prepare you to launch your course with the skills and confidence of a veteran *Career Choices* instructor. The online training videos, resources, and print materials allow you to invest in building your *Career Choices* capacity on your own schedule, at your own pace. The ideas and suggestions will enrich your teaching experience, and your resulting expertise will translate into motivated students who are proactive about their future.

Step 5: Professional Development Options

In addition to the online professional development videos and resources available through The Teachers' Lounge, we offer traditional, face-to-face, one- and two-day workshops around the country. We can also refer interested schools to certified trainers who are ready to assist with planning and implementation, make a site visit, or provide ongoing technical assistance. With a full complement of webinars and our annual Focus on Freshmen conference, there are a variety professional development options available. Details on current workshop offerings can be found at www.aiworkshops.com.

What do you stand to gain in exchange for the energy and work you'll devote to this instructional adventure? Turn to pages 1/24–1/30 for comments and results shared by schools and districts where this comprehensive guidance course has been implemented with fidelity.

Step 1: This *Instructor's Guide*

Your Daily Resource

This ***Instructor's Guide*** includes a variety of suggestions for planning and customizing your course, including sample lesson plans, discussion questions, and assessment tools. Look to this guide as your one-stop resource for answering any of your questions about teaching a ***Career Choices*** course.

The ***Career Choices*** curriculum is a flexible program that can be used in a variety of settings. Although this guide presents a number of possibilities, we encourage you to use your creativity to make the curriculum relevant and stimulating for your own classes.

Section 1: Quick Start

Start here! This section will get your preparations off the ground quickly! Get a brief overview of how to use this guide, checklists to streamline your planning and preparation, and information on an array of classroom resources Academic Innovations provides.

Section 2: Curriculum Overview

This section describes the unique format of ***Career Choices*** and explains how My10yearPlan.com® augments the text. It illuminates the goal of each of the three sections and summarizes each chapter in the book. For the best results with your class, you'll want to be very familiar not only with the course materials themselves but also with the pedagogy at its foundation.

Section 3: Where to Use the Curriculum? Who Should Teach It?

Career Choices has been proven successful in stand-alone Freshman Transition courses, integrated with English or technology, or in a wide variety of other courses. Let this section guide you as you look for the best home for ***Career Choices*** in your school.

Section 4: Lesson Plan Suggestions for Each Activity

First and foremost, this ***Instructor's Guide*** is designed to streamline not only your course planning process but also your daily or weekly prep. There is no need to reinvent the wheel and create your own lessons from scratch. Browse through this section and select the ideas that fit the goals of your class. The suggestions in this ***Instructor's Guide*** were designed to trigger your own creativity, so you can adapt them as you see fit.

We've identified six different phases of course planning and implementation. Sections 5 through 15 provide helpful information and resources for each phase.

The Buy-In Phase

Section 5: Getting Buy-in

Need help enlisting the necessary support to launch a Freshman Transition program or ***Career Choices*** course? You'll find resources here to get you started.

Section 6: Freshman Transition: Create a Vision of What's Possible

Freshman Transition is more than just a course; it has the potential to be the foundation of a school-wide redesign effort so all students are college and career ready.

The Planning Phase

Section 7: Program Planning Resources

Planning a program may seem overwhelming, but with this *Instructor's Guide*, you'll find all the help you need to make the preparation not only efficient but also very effective and rewarding. This section outlines the basics of the process you'll follow in planning your course.

Section 8: Integrating Academics and Technology

Career Choices helps to put academics and technology in context, so students have a vested interest in learning. Learn about the various academic supplements and technology enhancements as you discover techniques for supporting these important skills through your course.

Section 9: My10yearPlan.com®

While My10yearPlan.com® has an intuitive and user-friendly design, you'll want to be very familiar with it so you can answer students' questions. Why not work through your own "student" account as if you were choosing your next career or direction when you retire from education? The process is ageless.

Section 10: Lesson Planning and Pacing

By taking the time to plan prior to the start of your course, you'll reduce the prep time each class session requires. Take advantage of the pacing guide spreadsheets we've already created. These tools make it easy to plan ahead and "stay on track" so your students will have ample time for the creation of the 10-year plan in the final chapter. Sample pacing guides are included in this section and you can download editable copies from The Teachers' Lounge.

The Implementation Phase

Section 11: Instructional Strategies

This is probably unlike any course you've taught before, so you'll want to learn about the instructional strategies that are proven successful.

Section 12: Curriculum Support and Professional Development Options

While many instructors can jump right in and successfully teach this course with only the guidance in this *Instructor's Guide*, Academic Innovations also offers professional development and support resources to enhance your efforts and make your job as easy as possible. Many are outlined in this section. And, as questions arise, remember that curriculum support is available by phone from 9:00 AM to 4:00 PM (Mountain) by calling (800) 967-8016.

Section 13: Getting Parents and the Community Involved

This section will help you involve adults from your community so that they can lend support throughout students' decade of transition. Local business and service organizations have an interest in helping young people prepare for the future, so you can find willing partners for the important work ahead.

The Assessment Phase

Section 14: Assessment

Choose from a variety of options for assessing both individual students and the overall success of your course. For midterms and the course final, the emphasis is placed on authentic assessment. This allows you to gauge your students' growth in higher-order thinking skills as opposed to simply testing their recall of specific facts. If your school requires weekly assessments, you'll find short quizzes to audit students' recall and basic understanding of the material they read.

Sustainability

Section 15: Sustainability and Funding

Ensure that your program continues to benefit students for years to come with these strategies for maintaining support. Explore funding sources, publicity strategies, and the importance of documenting your program's results.

CREATING their own online 10-YEAR PLANS

using the Career Choices curriculum gives students practice with the

Critical Thinking Skills they'll require throughout their lives.

BLOOM'S REVISED TAXONOMY

Higher Order Thinking Skills

Creating
*Generating new ideas, products,
or ways of viewing things*
Designing, constructing, planning, producing, inventing

Evaluating
Justifying a decision or course of action
Checking, hypothesizing, critiquing, experimenting, judging

Analyzing
*Breaking information into parts to explore
understandings and relationships*
Comparing, organizing, deconstructing, interrogating, finding

vs.

Lower Order Thinking Skills

Applying
*Using information in another
familiar situation*
Implementing, carrying out, using, executing

Understanding
Explaining ideas or concepts
Interpreting, summarizing, paraphrasing, classifying, explaining

Remembering
Recalling information
Recognizing, listing, describing retrieving, naming, finding

My10yearPLAN.com ®
*Online 10-year Plan
& Portfolio*

Career Choices
A Guide for Teens and Young Adults
Who Am I?
What Do I Want?
How Do I Get It?

Project-based learning

Active and interactive

Socratic Method

Student-centered

Using critical, creative, and strategic thinking

Traditional
Didactic
Textbooks

"Flat"
online
enhancements

Knowledge-based learning

Read and recall

Lecture

Subject-centered

Memorization

For more information, call (800) 967-8016 or visit www.academicinnovations.com.

1/15

Step 2: Quick Start Checklist
Your Roadmap to an Efficient, Effective, and Rewarding Instructional Journey

Prior to the first day of class

In preparation for teaching this course:

- ☐ Complete your self-directed professional development using the Self-Study Guide for a Quick Start (pages 1/20–1/22).

- ☐ Activate accounts for the optional *Career Choices* online enhancements you'll be using (or make sure your administrator appoints a School Site Executive to handle this step).

  - CareerChoices.com and The Teachers' Lounge (www.careerchoices.com/lounge)
  - My10yearPlan.com®
  - LifestyleMath.com

- ☐ Use your Teachers' Lounge account to access the Quick Start training videos. You'll come away with tips and strategies to help you make decisions regarding the structure of your own course.

- ☐ Study My10yearPlan.com®. Visit the web site and use your populated trial account to review all the features available for students, teachers, and advisors.

  - At the time you or another member of your school or district activates your My10yearPlan.com® account, instructors qualify for access to their own blank student account on My10yearPlan.com®. If you have the time, consider completing your own online 10-year plan for the career you envision when you retire from education. You will understand the pedagogy better and have an example to share with your students.

- ☐ Learn from the experience of others: To get the desired results from *Career Choices* and My10yearPlan.com®, it is important to remember that your coursework:

  - Should be comprehensive and should integrate class discussion and active learning using the Socratic method
  - Must be sequential, beginning with Chapter 1 and proceeding through to the end of Chapter 12
  - Must culminate in the completion of a comprehensive, student-centered 10-year education and career plan

Finalize your lesson plans and pacing guide:

- ☐ Complete your lesson plan and pacing guide prior to the first day of class. We've made this easy for you.

- ☐ You'll find sample pacing guides on The Teachers' Lounge to use as your starting point. Select "Resource Cupboard" on the menu. The pacing guides are in the "Lesson Planning & Pacing" section. Choose the most appropriate pacing guide based on the time you have to complete your course. If you need assistance, call your Academic Innovations Educational Consultant or our Curriculum and Technical Support department at (800) 967-8016.

☐ Study the pacing guide spreadsheet you selected, reviewing each page in the *Career Choices* text and workbook with the corresponding activity at My10yearPlan.com®.

☐ Read through Section 4 of this guide, making notes or highlighting the ideas you want to use. At this point, you may want to edit and enhance the pacing guide spreadsheet based on your particular goals and your student population.

Optional coursework and resources:

☐ Study the CareerChoices.com links and determine how you want to incorporate this enhancement into your class.

☐ Review the pre- and post-surveys found in the Assessment section in this guide so you are ready to administer them at the appropriate times.

- The pre-survey should be completed before students are introduced to the content of the course.

- The post-survey is completed after students have finished their 10-year plans.

- The pre- and post-surveys can be enabled in My10yearPlan.com® if you would like student responses to be compiled automatically for easy storage, review, and reporting.

Once your class starts

First day of class:

☐ Have students complete the pre-survey during the first 15 minutes in class before you say much about the course at all. (See pages 14/9–14/14 of this guide for details.)

☐ Review the Help and FAQ sections on My10yearPlan.com® with your students. Remind them that they should be able to quickly find the answers to most questions about My10yearPlan.com®.

☐ As this is a comprehensive guidance course, it is important to set high expectations from the first day of class. You'll want to remind your students that this is a demanding class but that, as in life, the more they put into it, the more they'll get out of it.

Prior to each class:

☐ Prep for your course by reviewing your pacing guide spreadsheet.

☐ Turn to the corresponding pages in Section 4 of this guide and review the recommendations for that activity/exercise. Your *Instructor's Guide* is an important resource for this effort. The course is content-rich. Besides having relevance to your students' lives and helping them build relationships with themselves, others, and the world, it is rigorous. To complete the necessary lessons, you'll want to fine-tune your delivery and timing of activities.

- See yourself as a discussion leader, mentor, coach, and cheerleader, helping students explore and develop their own vision of a productive future. Use questioning and dialogue for instruction and content delivery rather than lecture.

☐ Assign homework at the end of each class session so students come to the next class prepared for discussion and group activities.

IMPORTANT: Homework assignments are vital to the success of the course.

- Homework should be assigned with the expectation that students come to class having read the text and prepared for that day's discussion. The homework assignment provides the opportunity to explore their own thoughts, goals, plans, and attitudes about the current topic. Class time can then focus on discussion, questions, clarification, energizers, brainstorming, and group activities as noted in this guide.

- Recommended homework assignments are noted on the pacing guide spreadsheets.

- At the end of each class, be sure to thoroughly review the homework assignment for the next class.

Throughout the course:

☐ Follow your pacing guide to ensure that you cover the material needed for students to create their personalized 10-year plans. If you get behind, assign additional homework.

☐ Assess student progress and mastery of the concepts. For a variety of ideas relating to grading, midterms, finals, or measuring your students' higher-order thinking skills, visit the Resource Cupboard of **The Teachers' Lounge**.

☐ Remember that Academic Innovations is ready to help! Contact your Educational Consultant or our Curriculum and Technical Support team at (800) 967-8016 or support@academicinnovations.com.

Final:

☐ At least two weeks before the end of your class, assign one or all of the following as the take-home final:

- All of Chapter 12

- The My 10-year Plan Summary Page on **My10yearPlan.com**®

- The online My 10-year Plan & Portfolio Report on **My10yearPlan Interactive**. You may assign all of it or just the last section. Students can turn this in as a printed report or by email attachment.

☐ Optional: Assign the post-survey after students complete their 10-year plans. Compare students' pre- and post-survey responses.

At the end of the course:

☐ Share your class experience with the staff of Academic Innovations by completing an online teacher survey at **www.academicinnovations.com/gettingstarted**. We take these evaluations seriously and use them to help us as we upgrade the services and materials we offer.

☐ Share your pre- and post-survey data reports with your department chair and at your next department meeting.

☐ CELEBRATE a job well done with both your students and your peers!

For an expanded Instructor Success Checklist, see pages 7/6–7/8.

Step 3: Online Teachers' Lounge
Your First Stop for Just-in-Time Resources

This online professional development web site for the *Career Choices* curriculum puts all of our resources right at your fingertips in one convenient place. It includes:

- ☐ Motivational chapter introduction videos hosted by Olympic Gold Medalist Dain Blanton
- ☐ Over 40 online training videos (with optional assessments)
- ☐ Online professional learning community of *Career Choices* teachers
- ☐ Video footage of Best Practice sessions presented by *Career Choices* educators from around the country
- ☐ An online evaluation tool for scoring students' pre-/post-surveys
- ☐ Grading resources and lesson planning materials to enhance your course
- ☐ Countless other tools and tips to ensure a successful *Career Choices* course

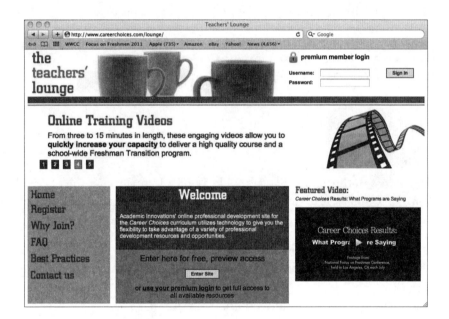

Basic membership is free and includes limited access to online training videos, lesson planning materials, funding, and buy-in resources. Premium membership is available with your school's CareerChoices.com membership and allows unlimited access to all Teachers' Lounge resources.

Your initial 12-month CareerChoices.com licensing fee is calculated on a sliding scale based on your order history. Annual orders are used to determine the licensing for subsequent years.

Please call (800) 967-8016 for a fee quote or complete the "Do I Qualify?" form at www.careerchoices.com/register and we'll contact you with the licensing information.

Step 4: Self-Study Guide for a Quick Start
Your Guide to Efficient, Productive, and Enjoyable Self-paced Capacity Building

Module 1: What is a Freshman Transition Initiative and Why is it Important?

Time required: 1 to 1.5 hours

Understanding the "big picture" is helpful to any effort. In this case, that means having a vision of the course, its goals, and the potential results.

> Visit www.whatworkscareerchoices.com/method.html and follow the steps outlined there. You may have seen some of the videos in our workshops, but we suggest that you watch them again. As you are starting your planning, this overview refresher will be helpful. If time is short, be sure to watch at least videos number 1, 2, and 4.

> Bookmark www.whatworkscareerchoices.com and, as you have time, peruse the resources found here. There are a variety of Best Practice resources along with videos of educators providing insights into their *Career Choices* programs' success.

> If interested, you might want to watch:
> **Why the *Career Choices* Curriculum was Developed**
> www.careerchoices.com/lounge/developed

Module 2: Curriculum Overview

Time required: 1.5 hours

Watch these five videos in this order. They provide a quick tour through the curriculum. You'll want to have your *Career Choices* textbook next to you as you watch. Each video is between 10 and 15 minutes long.

> *Career Choices*: **Why it Works**
> www.academicinnovations.com/whyitworks/
>
> **Who Am I?**
> www.careerchoices.com/lounge/whoami/
>
> **What Do I Want?**
> www.careerchoices.com/lounge/whatdoiwant/
>
> **How Do I Get It?**
> www.careerchoices.com/lounge/howdoigetit/
>
> **In-Depth Overview of My10yearPlan.com®**
> www.careerchoices.com/lounge/indepth
>
> For more information about My10yearPlan Interactive, visit
> www.my10yearplan.com/interactive

Module 3: Course Planning

A. Time required: 45 minutes to 1 hour

Watch these three videos (in this order):

Five Ingredients of a Successful *Career Choices* Course
www.careerchoices.com/lounge/success/

Instructor's Guide: Section 4
www.academicinnovations.com/igsection4

Customizing Lesson Plans Using Excel
www.careerchoices.com/lounge/excel/

B. Time required: 2 to 4 hours (depending on how deep you read)

Now read through Section 4 of this guide.

Once finished, you'll have a thorough understanding of the scope and sequence of the course and you'll be ready to start your own course planning. Remember it is imperative each student develops a 10-year plan. This step is key to having students who are not only college and career ready but are also motivated to complete their education.

As you read through this section, highlight the lesson ideas you find most helpful.

Module 4: Customizing Your Pacing Guide

Time required: 1 to 3 hours (depending on your adjustments to the template)

Having your own pacing guide ready for the first day of class is critical to success. For details, visit Section 10 of this guide. Sample pacing guides for courses varying in structure and total hours available can also be found in The Teachers' Lounge.

As you work to customize your pacing guide, remember that the *Career Choices* pages bearing a **graduation cap logo** have activities that make up the online 10-year plan. These activities should not be skipped.

If you don't have a password for The Teachers' Lounge, contact our Curriculum and Technical Support team at (800) 967-8016 or support@academicinnovations.com.

Module 5: Instructional Strategies

Time required: 1 hour

Watch the videos below (in order) for ideas on how to make this type of course engaging and enjoyable for you and your students.

Chapter 12: The Final Exam Option
www.careerchoices.com/lounge/classfinal/

Tips and Ideas to Create an Involved Learner
www.careerchoices.com/lounge/involved

Cooperative Learning and Team-building
www.careerchoices.com/lounge/cooperative

Strategies for Active Learning
www.careerchoices.com/lounge/active

Resources to Support Planning, Preparation, and Implementation

The Teachers' Lounge
www.careerchoices.com/lounge

You'll want to become familiar with all that The Teachers' Lounge has to offer. It will make your life easier and your class more rewarding for your students.

Join the Career Choices Online Professional Learning Community

Members can post questions, get feedback or share ideas with Career Choices educators across the country.
www.careerchoices.com/lounge/plc_home.html

TIPS—Teaching Insights, Practices, and Solutions Newsletter

Get wonderful suggestions and resources in each email edition from Curriculum and Instructional Support Advisor Georgette Phillips.

Step 5: Professional Development Options

Your First Stop for Optional Professional Development
www.aiworkshops.com

Providing the highest quality instructional materials is only a part of our mission. We are also committed to making sure new and experienced instructors have quality professional development resources to support their ongoing efforts.

- ☐ **Phone support** is available from our Curriculum and Technical Support team. They are ready to brainstorm, troubleshoot, and discuss any aspect of the curriculum and online enhancements.

- ☐ **Webinars** are provided on a variety of topics related to the implementation of the *Career Choices* curriculum and online enhancements. Hosted online by Academic Innovations, content is presented by our Curriculum and Technical Support team, *Career Choices* Certified Trainers, *Career Choices* Master Teachers, and other special guests.

- ☐ **The Teachers' Lounge** puts a variety of professional development resources at your fingertips, including more than 40 online training videos, archived webinars, Best Practices presentations from schools around the country, and the *Career Choices* online professional learning community.

- ☐ **Two-Day *Career Choices* Implementation Workshops** provide in-depth training on effective instructional strategies.

- ☐ **Onsite workshops** may be appropriate for schools or districts adopting *Career Choices* on a larger scale. Certified *Career Choices* Trainers can provide content tailored to address the specific needs of your instructional team.

- ☐ **Focus on Freshmen Conference**, held each July in Los Angeles, features several dynamic institutes, including the comprehensive *Career Choices* Lead Administrator and Lead Teacher Institute. With new institutes each year, **Focus on Freshmen** is fantastic for principals, administrators, and *Career Choices* teachers who attend individually or as a planning team.

- ☐ **Technical Assistance Contractors** who meet our exacting standards can be referred to schools and districts seeking ongoing support as they plan, implement, and improve their program.

For details, see Section 12 of this ***Instructor's Guide***.

Let Us Hear from You!

We are committed to your success, so our curriculum specialists are available to provide curriculum and technical support each step of the way. Do not hesitate to call (800) 967-8016 weekdays between 9:00 AM and 4:00 PM (Mountain) or email us at support@academicinnovations.com. We stand ready to help in any way we can.

Would you care to share your observations and ideas in future editions of this guide? What has worked well for you? What innovations have you made? What additional information or resources could we provide? Let our Curriculum and Technical Support department know what you think!

Here's What We're Hearing...

When all students have a 10-year plan that is used by all advisors, counselors, and instructors to personalize their guidance and advice, your campus culture can change before your eyes. Academic achievement improves when students can visualize a productive future, have a plan to realize that future, and understand the consequences of forfeiting their educational opportunities.

...from Educators

"One of the things that the curriculum does is it truthfully levels the playing field. It allows and encourages student accountability and parent accountability, but if we don't have the parent accountability in place, it allows the students to really determine what they want for their own lives."

— Brenda Deese, Curriculum Coordinator
Robeson County Public Schools, Robeson, NC

"So many parents say, 'I'm so happy that you're doing this because my child is understanding the difference between wants and needs and stops to think instead of badgering me for more money.'"

— Cathie Klein, College & Career Readiness Coordinator
Seaman Freshman Center, Topeka, KS

"Reality hit them when they hit the budget [in Chapter 4] and they realized how much money it would cost to live the way that they were thinking. It just opened their minds up. They didn't get depressed, they got mature. You could tell they were kind of slapped in the face by how much things were going to cost, and then they seemed to grow up."

— Chris Pulos, Teacher
North Valley Charter Academy, Granada Hills, CA

"It's given the students a lot more focus. It gives them a path to follow, whereas without the 10-year plan or the Success 101 class they're just coming to school, taking their classes, and moving on to their sophomore year... They're still freshmen, still 14 or 15 years old, but there's that sense of focus and maturity that they would not have without the class."

— Mark Brenner, Teacher
Indio High School, Indio, CA

"Students seem to be more connected to school, are here in the classroom more, and are just not getting in trouble as much. I think that relates to the Freshman Seminar course and what they're getting from the class—they understand that they need to be here and why their decisions [now] will affect them in the future."

— Erin Hansen, Teacher
Carpinteria High School, Carpinteria, CA

"Just seeing students in different places, they're mature, focused, they have a sense of direction, they have a plan. Those are the things they'll carry with them. They'll remember that connection you made with them."

— Margo McCormick, Assistant Principal
Indio High School, Indio, CA

"I received lots of positive feedback from students and parents. Most recently, a student of mine said, 'Mrs. Violante, because of your class last semester, I am enrolled in photography classes and have been shadowing a wedding planner every weekend. I had no idea what I wanted to do beyond high school, and now I have a goal! I can't wait!' The course is rewarding for both of us!"

— Sharon Violante, Teacher
Gardner Middle School, Temecula, CA

"I have been having a lot of fun working in the Career Choices *classroom. I can remember experiencing fear of the unknown future as a high school student. I believe* Career Choices *curriculum will help all our students not only dispel any fear, but energize them to be productive citizens and happy souls."*

— Kris Ann Lewis, Paraeducator
Meridian High School, Bellingham, WA

*"*Career Choices *helped our students begin to build their futures with concrete plans through critical thinking."*

— Krista Herrera, Principal
Summit Charter Collegiate Academy, Porterville, CA

"As I sit today and read all the great essays our kids submitted, tears of pride stream down my face. It is so cool to hear kids say that Transitions has actually changed their life…Our kids are saying it in almost every essay. Some say it directly. Others just say it by using the tools we have taught them in their thinking. The evidence is in their stories. So thank you yet again Career Choices, *for the opportunity to teach this class! I never knew how much it would change my view of our youth. They teach me just as much as I am teaching them."*

— Becky Simmons, Lead Teacher
Marquette Senior High School, Marquette, MI

"We had back to school night last night and I got such great responses from the parents. I gave them a heads up about Chapter 4 and let them know students might be coming home asking about $$ and why. They were very pleased we were offering such a 'practical' course!"

— Valerie Backus, CTE Teacher
Chaparral High School, Temecula, CA

"Our students are not just getting a better understanding of what courses they want to take in high school, but why they want to take them."

— Ben Keller, Assistant Principal
Wasco Union High School, Wasco, CA

...from Students

"Now I know how my parents feel when they have to pay bills. The budgets helped me realize that money doesn't grow on trees and it takes a lot of work to get, so don't take advantage of your parents' money. That's why I think it helps a lot."

— Michelle

"This class has helped me in realizing school is actually important. The section that helped me the most is the budget one. At first I was like, it's okay I can pay whatever. Then when we add the totals I was like, 'Dang! This is going to cost a lot.' That's when I noticed that school is really important. This class also showed me that a job isn't just something you have to do, it's something you like doing. I like building stuff and drawing, so I decided I would be an animator for the Walt Disney Co., or an architect, or an engineer. I think this class should be required for freshman. I really enjoy it!"

— Juan

"It has helped me to be organized and to set goals in life. For example, when I grow up I want a house in the city, so it's pretty expensive. Some research that we have done in class has helped me know what I need to do in life to get to have that house. Also it has helped me to be smart with my money because, to be honest, I'm one of those people that when I have money I go crazy and waste it on things I don't even need. But so far, since we had that lesson, I have been saving money even though it's been hard. That's what I have learned so far in freshman seminar."

— Evelyn

"This program has helped me a lot. It made me think that I could be somebody in life. When I was in middle school, I never wanted to go to college; I always thought it was a waste of time. But no, it is very important, and this class is not boring at all. I learn lots of things about life and it has changed me and I'm proud of that. Everything we do here is going to help us later on in our lives. ...everything seems so real and it makes you think that I could do something like that in my life."

— Jerrod

"This class has helped me a lot because I learned that everything is gained by hard work. I also learned about myself and where I am in life. It also helped me see what kind of money I would need in order to live the lifestyle I want to live. It helped me realize that all the rich and famous people didn't get rich or famous by just sitting down and playing video games or using the computer, they got where they are now by studying and working hard."

— Gerardo

Grace King High School (Metairie, Louisiana) took pride in being "the best" high school in the district, but Assistant Principal Pamela Pritchard was still appalled by the fact that only 76% of freshmen were being promoted to the 10th grade. She introduced the *Career Choices* curriculum and the concept that "Failure is Not an Option" as a part of the school's 9th grade redesign efforts.

The percentage of freshmen failing one or more classes dropped from 48.8% to 9% within one year.

The 9th grade dropout rate fell: 2.9% (2005-06) to 0.1% (2008-09).

The percentage of freshmen promoted to the 10th grade rose from 76% (2005-06) to 91% within one year and to 93% within three years, and suspension rates fell from 38.8% to 9.9% within one year and to 3.6% within three years.

You look for that panacea where every kid gets everything every day, this actually works.

- Pamela Pritchard, Assistant Principal
Grace King High School

Rahway High School (Rahway, New Jersey) had an achievement problem and sought to remedy it with a Freshman Seminar/Financial Literacy course utilizing the *Career Choices* curriculum.

Within one year of implementation, **the freshman failure rate dropped from 50% (2010-11) to 35% (2011-12).**

Suspension rates for freshmen fell from 10% to 5%.

Rahway High School was recognized by *New Jersey Monthly* magazine (August 2012) as **one of the top 10 most improved high schools in New Jersey.** Data related to this honor include: improved Advanced Placement, HSPA, SAT, and ACT scores; decreased failure rates; improved conduct; and an overall school setting built on an academic framework and supporting a college-going culture.

I don't have a dropout problem, I have an achievement problem...we took our failure rate from approximately 50% of our freshman class to 35%.

- John Farinella, Principal
Rahway High School

Most of the time when students, even good students, complete high school they still don't have a clear picture or focus about what they want to be or what their major should be. But students who come to college knowing what they want to be and having researched that are going to finish—and that's huge. That's why [Santa Barbara City College made] the investment in the 9th grade course.

- Dr. Diane Hollems, Dean, Educational Programs
Santa Barbara City College

Santa Barbara City College (Santa Barbara, California), home of a Dual Enrollment Freshman Transition (DEFT) course and founding college of the *Get Focused...Stay Focused!* ™ Initiative, was co-winner of the prestigious **2013 Aspen Prize for Community College Excellence**. In 2009, SBCC adopted *Career Choices* and My10yearPlan.com® as the curriculum for their DEFT course. The DEFT course and the *Get Focused...Stay Focused!* ™ innovations were cited in the announcement of SBCC's Aspen Prize:

"Expanding student development efforts beyond its campus to local high schools, Santa Barbara City College has created the largest dual enrollment program...among California's 112 community colleges. SBCC is also helping high school students, many of whom may not be financially or academically prepared, develop long-term education plans through college readiness and career counseling programs."

A 10-year career and education plan is required for graduation in the Santa Barbara Unified School District.

Carpinteria High School (Carpinteria, California), the first school to implement the DEFT course, reports:

- An increase in pass rates for courses required for acceptance to schools in the University of California or Cal State systems, **from 23.3% (2006-07) to 47.6% (2012-13).**
- An increase in **Academic Performance Index (API) score, from 710 (2006-07) to 778 (2012-13).**
- **A reduction in suspensions, from 137 (2006-07) to 47 (2012-13).**

Poughkeepsie High School (Poughkeepsie, New York) had been cited by the state as a consistently underachieving school, but a *Career Choices* course instituted in 2009 is showing promise.

The last cohort to graduate without *Career Choices* had a graduation rate of 59%.

The first graduating cohort to have the *Career Choices* class had a graduation rate of 63% (2011) and the second cohort achieved a graduation rate of 83% (2012).

Indio High School (Indio, California) was struggling with abysmal test scores. A freshman transition course using *Career Choices* (called Success 101) is continuing to transform the culture of this largely Hispanic school.

The number of freshmen with three or more Fs decreased by nearly a half from 29% in 2009 to 16% in 2010.

Freshmen were responsible for 49 of the school's 65-point Academic Performance Index (API) increase within that first year.

By the time the first class of freshmen became sophomores, 70 students had joined the CSF (California Scholarship Federation) versus 10 students from the previous class.

We wanted to do something about the school's academic culture starting with the freshman class. [In our second year,] we had a 38% drop [in freshmen with 3 or more Fs], and GPAs went up 15%.

- Rudy Ramirez, Principal
Indio High School

Carroll High School (Ozark, Alabama) introduced a Freshman Academy in 2011 to help freshmen make a successful transition into high school and build meaningful relationships. A key component of this academy was a *Career Choices* course. Compared with first-semester freshmen in 2010:

The number of students failing a class decreased by 50%.

The number of students who lost credit due to absences dropped by 35%.

A rural district, **Robeson County Public Schools** (Lumberton, North Carolina) introduced a mandatory Freshman Transition program using *Career Choices* in all seven high schools to help curb a serious dropout problem.

A 23% decrease in the number of dropouts was observed between 2010 and 2011.

...we've seen some very remarkable results. Our 2009 graduation rate hovered around 53%. ... The second cohort that was exposed to the Career Choices program, which graduated 2011-2012 school year, had an 83% graduation rate.

- Lynnette Williams, Lead Teacher
Poughkeepsie High School

When Bobby Cunningham started as principal of **McCormick High School** (McCormick, South Carolina), the school had one of the highest dropout rates in South Carolina. He chose to introduce *Career Choices* to all grades at once, and the results reported by Cunningham were staggering.

"After one year, [McCormick High School] moved from a 'below average' school to one of two 'excellent' schools in South Carolina."

The results from the second year were even more impressive:

The rate at which freshmen were retained fell from 10.8% in 2006 to 1.5% in 2008.

The percentage of students passing the High School Assessment Program (required for graduation in South Carolina) rose from 63.4% in 2006 to 78.6% in 2008.

The percentage of students enrolled in CTE classes jumped from 44.8% in 2006 to 67.3% in 2008.

The biggest surprise has been the brevity... it only took a year to make a major impact on our students.

- Bobby Cunningham, Principal
McCormick High School

McKay High School (Salem, Oregon) has seen major changes since the introduction of a *Career Choices* summer program for at-risk incoming freshmen in 2011. The summer program fosters relationships among students while providing the academic and study skills necessary to be successful in high school. McKay High School once had one of the highest dropout rates in Oregon, with 186 students dropping out (2002-03).

In 2011-12, only 3 students dropped out, making McKay's dropout rate the lowest in the state among schools with more than 750 students.

Career Choices received a Promising Intervention Award from the U.S. Department of Education in recognition of its effectiveness in reducing dropout rates and supporting higher achievement in reading and math.

- Association for Career and Technical Education's
Techniques magazine

High dropout rates, poor attendance, and low test scores prompted **Silverado High School** (Victorville, California) to implement small learning communities using the *Career Choices* curriculum.

A random sample group of **10th and 11th grade students who had been through the Freshman Academy increased their GPA by 69% from 2004-05 to 2007-08.**

Suspension rates for freshmen dropped from around 65% (2003-04) to around 10% (2006-07).

Tennessee implemented a statewide Freshman Transition Initiative entitled Career Management Success (2002-04). The vast majority of school districts adopted *Career Choices* to meet this new career education requirement.

Between 2002 and 2006, the state witnessed an 11.2 percentage point gain in high school graduation rates— greater than any increase of any other state during that period.

Duval County Public School District (Jacksonville, Florida) mandated a Freshman Transition course be implemented with over 9,000 freshmen in 19 high schools as part of a district-wide freshman initiative during the 2006-07 school year. In a presentation to the American Youth Policy Forum, Director of High Schools for the district, Beverly Strickland, reported:

The 9th grade promotion rate went from 51% to 82% after the first year.

I would like for teachers, administrators, and stakeholders to understand the rigor that is involved in this course. This is not a "fluff" course. This is a powerful course that causes students to think critically about themselves—now and in the future.

- Beverly Strickland, Director of High School Programs
Duval County Schools

The **Delaware School-To-Work Program** used the *Career Choices* curriculum in a 24-day summer program.

Of the 25 students completing the School-To-Work program in 2000, 20 showed overall improvement in reading, math, and language mechanics.

Analysis of the T-Test results of student gains states, *"While the 1999 program results were satisfactory, **the year 2000 results are spectacular**...There was only one replacement between 1999-2000. The utilization of the entire anthology of* Career Choices *by Academic Innovations..."*

The Denver Summer Youth Employment and Training Program used the *Career Choices* curriculum to provide academic enrichment services for 149 at-risk students. An independent evaluation of the 1996 program reported:

83% of students and 84% of staff believed the program would help the students in school during the coming year.

95% of students and 100% of staff believed the program would help students get a job.

95% of students and 68% of staff believed the program would help students be more independent.

90% of students and 74% of staff believed the program would help students become more responsible.

In addition, pre- and post-WRAT assessments (Wide Range Achievement Tests) showed **significant gains in reading scores among seven of eight groups and in math scores for five of the eight groups. All other groups showed positive gains.**

The **Havre Summer Youth Program** (Havre, Montana) targeted students with academic deficiencies for a culturally relevant remedial course. Students were tested before and after program participation.

The majority of students improved their reading and math skills by two grade levels. The skills of about 10% of students went up six grade levels.

> *I commend these materials for use in high school...*
> *I particularly like that the curriculum is grounded in a*
> *specific academic discipline and that it is competency-based.*
>
> — Dale Parnell , Author
> *The Neglected Majority*

In an effort to address a very high dropout rate, *Career Choices* became the backbone of a required course for all freshmen at **Coachella Valley High School** (Thermal, California) in 1992.

> Within one year, the dropout rate had fallen from 15.7% to 12.7%.

> **After the second year, the dropout rate fell to 3.8%.**

The **Boston Summer Youth Program** (Boston, Massachusetts) sought to link learning to real life in an immediate, tangible way. It clearly succeeded.

> **All students increased their math and reading skill by a half to one whole grade level.**

Then-Coordinator of **Delaware's Tech Prep Consortium** Dr. Jim Campbell was looking to add a guidance component to the program when he discovered the *Career Choices* curriculum in 1991. *Career Choices* was subsequently introduced in six districts in Delaware. A few years later, he reported the following:

Dropout rate decreases.

- Delaware Tech Prep students dropped out at rate of less than 1%, as compared to a statewide rate of 6%.

Math and language skill increased.

- Tech Prep students in seven high schools earned higher math and language scores on Iowa Basic Skills than non-Tech Prep students statewide.

Successful enrollment in postsecondary schools.

- Only 18% of students graduating from Tech Prep programs needed remediation, compared to the overall rate of 70%.
- Tech Prep graduates had a much higher retention rate for community colleges: 92%, as compared to 40% for non-Tech Prep students.

Project 17, a pilot program named for the graduation year of the 51 at-risk freshmen it served, was implemented at **South High School** (Bakersfield, California) in Kern High School District to combat spotty attendance, behavior issues, and low test scores. Using *Career Choices* to create 10-year plans, the aim was to motivate Project 17 students to improve academic achievement and increase the pass rate for courses required for acceptance to schools in the University of California or Cal State systems.

Despite testing below basic levels in English, Project 17 students were placed in college-prep English and all but 2 students passed.

Project 17 students started in remedial math, but 25 of the 51 students transferred to algebra during the first semester.

When evaluated against a similar group of 52 freshmen students who did not use *Career Choices*, Project 17 students demonstrated higher academic achievement.

- Project 17 students completed 27.5 credit units on average (the comparison group completed 23.5 credit units on average).
- Project 17 students had an average GPA of 2.2 (the average comparison group GPA was 1.9).

Project 17 students also had a lower dropout rate.

- Only 11% of the Project 17 group dropped out while 32% of students in the comparison group dropped out.

> *What really makes it all work is that students understand an important little secret about life, which is: Everyone has to work, and those who continue their education have a better chance to do interesting and rewarding work.*
>
> — Dr. Jim Campbell, Coordinator
> Delaware Tech Prep Consortium

Learn more about programs that have experienced success with these materials at

www.WhatWorksCareerChoices.com/bestpractices.html

Section 2

Overview of the Curriculum

Topics covered in this section include:

- *Career Choices* is a career- and life-planning course that demonstrates the vital role education plays in living an economically self-sufficient and personally fulfilling life.

- The format of this course is dialectic (i.e., discussion based) rather than didactic (i.e., lecture based).

- The culmination of this course is a meaningful and quantitative 10-year plan. Career and education plans are essential in encouraging both high school and post-secondary completion.

- The course teaches a powerful process for making life decisions that students can use throughout their lives. It also supports the development of critical thinking skills, which lecture-based classes often do not.

- My10yearPlan.com® stores student answers to activities in the text and compiles the data to format an online 10-year plan. Students can then use this plan to easily share their strengths, interests, achievements, and career aspirations.

- The supplemental text *Possibilities* features short literary works with themes relevant to *Career Choices*, demonstrating the relevance of literature as well as the importance of reading and writing skills.

- Another supplemental text, **Lifestyle Math**, extends the budget exercise of Chapter 4 in *Career Choices* to guide students through creating a comprehensive budget for their projected lifestyle at age 29 to personalize math and establish the need for mathematical fluency. It includes an online correction key, LifestyleMath.com.

- CareerChoices.com is a subscription-based site that provides online activities to enhance the curriculum while building Internet research and navigation skills.

Note: This section has text that will be helpful when writing your proposals for funding or support. Download a copy and edit to fit your programs and goals.

What is the *Career Choices* Curriculum?

How many times have you heard people say, wistfully, "I wish I would have known in school what I know now. I would have made different choices"? In a recent study on regret, what people in the United States most regretted in their lives was not getting enough education.

Career Choices is more than a career exploration course. It's really a career- and life-planning course that, in hindsight, would be more aptly named "Success 101" because it helps students make the connection between expectations, effort, and success. Helping students develop a vision of a productive, self-sufficient future by becoming career-focused is the key to success in both secondary and post-secondary educational settings.

Career Choices contains more than 100 student-centered exercises, leading students through a process that culminates in the development of a personalized career-inclusive 10-year education plan. This award-winning contextual learning curriculum presents life skills, career exploration, and education planning in a friendly, inviting format.

This curriculum is unique because:

- It provides a step-by-step workbook format, helping students discover for themselves the careers that match their passions, lifestyle aspirations, skills, and aptitudes.

- Rather than using didactic copy like many traditional career- and life-planning books, *Career Choices* asks students questions, opening the door to discovery and contemplation of their own unique qualities and desires.

- *Career Choices* introduces "a process" for education, career, and lifestyle decision-making that can be used over and over again, thereby empowering students to successfully navigate a lifetime of workplace and personal change.

Career Choices helps students develop a stronger sense of who they are and where they fit in the world of work as it relates to their own goals and plans. Students gain insights into which careers will help them realize their lifestyle aspirations because they have learned:

- How passions, values, and personality shape career decisions

- Techniques for building and updating their personalized career profiles

- How income expectations play a major role in career planning

- A step-by-step career research process using the Internet

- A systematic procedure for managing change in our rapidly evolving workplace

- The formula for writing and editing a workable life, career, and education plan

With the *Career Choices* curriculum, students quickly understand the consequences of not exerting the effort school requires. At the same time, they develop comprehensive and meaningful 10-year education and career plans. The results: they value education more, becoming self-motivated learners.

As students gain the wisdom necessary to form meaningful 10-year plans, they also build critical thinking skills. While many courses only expect students to *recall*, *understand*, and at best *apply* the information taught, the **Career Choices** program encourages students to *analyze* their strengths and desires, *evaluate* their options in life, and *create* new ideas. Students will benefit from these skills for the rest of their lives.

You'll find this curriculum ideal for a variety of classroom-based, hybrid, and distance learning opportunities, such as:

- Freshman Transition course
- Career planning and exploration course
- Introductory course for career academy or pathway
- Foundation course for a school-wide advisory program
- Integration of life skills into English/language arts course

Why an Academically-Based Comprehensive Guidance Course?

As the educational community struggles to determine what will improve our schools, research consistently points to the fact that *guidance is key to student success*. Students with access to quality guidance services perform better on standardized tests and are more likely to pursue post-secondary education. Alternatively, with the vast array of career paths available today and the differing levels of training required for each, students understandably struggle when forced to find their way on their own. Yet due to funding shortfalls, guidance services are often cut rather than expanded.

That's where a comprehensive guidance course using the ***Career Choices*** curriculum comes in. A course in which students develop plans to carry them through college and into the workforce gets students focused on the "big picture." They become that much more likely to complete their education in a field that will give them the greatest opportunity for lasting satisfaction. Proven, scalable, and cost-efficient, this is the best way to maximize the amount and quality of guidance that students receive. ***Career Choices*** works because:

1. ***It is classroom-based,*** providing between 45 and 180 hours of activities, discussion, and research opportunities in a sequential format.

2. ***It is integrated with academics,*** making it possible to provide quality career and educational guidance and maintain academic rigor for students at all levels of achievement.

3. ***It has scope and sequence,*** modeling a self-discovery and decision-making process students can use throughout their lives—whenever they make important decisions.

4. ***It helps students develop self-awareness*** by answering critical questions: Who am I? What do I want? How do I get it? And why do I need a good education? Students become "identity achieved;" learn progressive decision-making techniques and skills; become critical thinkers in relation to their future lives; complete quantitative plans; and discover reality-based options for their adult lives.

5. ***It exposes students to the skills of personal success:*** goal setting, decision-making, budgeting, resource management, and overcoming fears and personal resistance.

6. ***It exposes students to the realities and responsibilities of the adult world,*** providing opportunities to discuss and explore various aspects of adult life. Young people can then better define the kind of life they want and, as a result, make wise education decisions.

7. ***It helps students learn to project themselves into the future and understand the consequences of their actions today.*** Studies show that students who can visualize their futures and understand how today's choices impact future happiness are far less likely to drop out of school, become teen parents, or abuse drugs.

Career Choices: A Guide for Teens and Young Adults

A large, beautifully illustrated text, **Career Choices** is more journey than book. Masquerading as an attractive journal, **Career Choices** is actually a carefully designed, self-paced, easy-to-follow program that learners find visionary and logical—inspiring and, at the same time, matter-of-fact. In addition to helping learners set realistic goals, it contains a variety of questionnaires, self-evaluation quizzes, and exercises that empower individuals to think seriously about their aptitudes and inclinations.

The concept behind the **Career Choices** curriculum works because most adolescents have at least one thing in common: an avid interest in themselves and their futures. When classroom assignments help answer students' most urgent questions (Who am I? What do I want?), their attitudes toward writing, reading, and math assignments improve. Consequently, the motivation to practice these basic skills is elevated.

Career Choices has all of the expected career research information. It's the unexpected aspects that make this book exciting and unique. **Career Choices** augments traditional career planning topics with practical advice on overcoming obstacles and fears; solving problems; dealing with rejection and anxiety; and recognizing and using mentors.

This interactive book guides the reader toward greater self-knowledge, enabling them to make intelligent, well-thought-out decisions about their own futures. **Career Choices** helps students identify their own passions, values, personality styles, skills, and aptitudes. This knowledge then leads them to investigate careers that match their strengths and desires. As the "fit" becomes more apparent, so does the motivation to strive to prepare themselves for a desirable future.

Most importantly, **Career Choices** is a carefully crafted step-by-step process that, if learned, can be used over and over again throughout students' lives as they make important decisions. As they grow and mature, and as the world changes around them, this dynamic process will be one of their most meaningful life lessons.

The culmination of the process is the development of a workable 10-year plan for realizing their dreams. Equipped with their life vision and action plan, their chance of a successful transition to adulthood is greatly enhanced.

Teenagers may think they know all the answers because they haven't heard all the questions yet.

The *Workbook and Portfolio for Career Choices*

Ideally, every student would be given a copy of the *Career Choices* text to complete and take with them into the world. However, many schools simply don't have the funds to make this possible. For this reason, the *Workbook and Portfolio* was created. The *Workbook and Portfolio* is an inexpensive compilation of the activities contained within the *Career Choices* text, and it should be an integral part of any program.

What makes the *Workbook* so important?

1. The *Workbook and Portfolio* contains all the exercises found in *Career Choices*. Using the *Workbook*, young people can review the key concepts as they revise and refine their plans. The ultimate goal of *Career Choices* is not for students to create a final agenda for their lives, but for them to learn a process. Then, as their interests, abilities, and ambitions expand, or as new challenges or opportunities arise, they can repeat the process.

2. The *Workbook and Portfolio* grows with the student. Your students will grow and mature both intellectually and emotionally as they move through school (and life). The portfolio aspects of the *Workbook* allow students to review and re-visit the main concepts from *Career Choices* as their understanding of themselves and the world increases. For instance, learning to overcome stumbling blocks may not seem important to a teen that has faced few challenges. However, with their *Workbook and Portfolio* in hand, a student will have someplace to turn for help as obstacles arise.

3. The *Workbook* is a permanent record. How many of your students' notes are thorough enough to still make sense two months later, never mind two years later? This is precisely why providing each student with a *Workbook* is so important. Loose papers and notebooks are not viewed with the same importance and respect afforded a printed text. Furthermore, the *Workbook and Portfolio* is part book, part journal, so students tend to keep it and treasure it for years to come.

4. The *Workbook and Portfolio* can be extremely helpful to guidance counselors. The time counselors have with each student is often limited, and a completed *Workbook and Portfolio* quickly gives them insight into each student's aspirations, particularly if you are using My10yearPlan.com®. Counselors are then better able to steer students toward appropriate classes, programs, or colleges. Students who have been through a *Career Choices* program are more aware of their own needs and desires. Thus, they can articulate their own interests and plans more clearly and assertively and act as better advocates for themselves.

Are you considering omitting the *Workbook* because your budget is stretched? Before you make that decision, weigh the possibility of asking students to pay for their own copy. Because the *Workbook and Portfolio* is "consumable" (like an art project), many states allow for this arrangement. Teachers have succeeded using this strategy to help fund their *Career Choices* programs. Some have even found that students have more "ownership" in the program and are more devoted.

If student purchase is not a viable option, consider turning to the community for help. Often community service organizations or local businesses are happy to help out with this expense. See pages 15/16 to 15/17 and 13/5 to 13/9 for guidance on this process.

"Our freshmen were very excited to start putting their work in their workbooks. It's amazing what ownership they take over their work and how a workbook validates all their thoughts and efforts."

— Diane Goncalves, Assistant Superintendent
Region One School District, Falls Village, CT

Adapted Workbook and Portfolio *for Use with* Career Choices and Changes

A growing number of high schools are choosing to use the college text, *Career Choices and Changes*, in dual credit classes. As a result, an adapted workbook has been developed to accommodate these schools.

The adapted workbook includes the *Career Choices and Changes* chapters recommended for high school students: Chapters 1 through 10 and Chapters 14 and 15. (The topics in Chapters 11, 12, and 13 of *Career Choices and Changes* are covered in the *Get Focused…Stay Focused!* ™ Follow-up Modules designed for the 10th, 11th, and 12th grades.)

The activities in Chapters 1 to 10 are numbered the same in both *Career Choices* and *Career Choices and Changes*. Beginning on page 110 of the adapted workbook, an oval icon has been added to indicate the corresponding *Career Choices and Changes* textbook page.

My10yearPlan.com®

Personalization has been shown to be one of the most successful reform efforts in education today. How can we personalize education for all of our students and, in the process, help them develop a vision of a productive and attainable future? How can we act as advisors, using their dreams and plans to guide them to the greatest academic and personal success?

My10yearPlan.com® provides an online planning area where students can store, update, and save the data related to the development of their 10-year plans. When students share these plans, instructors and counselors are better equipped to advise students on their educational paths and provide support when academic effort doesn't match lifestyle aspirations.

How Does It Work?

It starts with the *Career Choices* text. As students work through the book sequentially, gathering the data and developing the understanding required for their 10-year plans, they go online, log into their own password-protected area of My10yearPlan.com®, and enter the information they've collected about themselves. The My10yearPlan.com® input pages mirror *Career Choices*, providing fields to hold all the information required for building their personal portfolio, Skills Inventory, and 10-year education and career plan online. This can be done in a school computer lab, in the library, or at home.

My10yearPlan Essentials

My10yearPlan Essentials provides a personal area online for students to store, review, and update their answers to the 25 keystone *Career Choices* activities that make up the 10-year plan. Once the learner inputs the information completed in *Career Choices*, the My10yearPlan.com® system uses it to create a My 10-year Plan Summary Page. This overview provides a snapshot of the key goals and plans the learner has set for their education, finances, and lifestyle choices over the next decade.

By putting the essential artifacts from the planning process online, the learner also has the core pieces of their 10-year plan in a digital format that can streamline the process of compiling, editing, and producing a career portfolio.

My10yearPlan Interactive

The level of access available with My10yearPlan Interactive takes the digital planning experience a step further by providing an online home for ALL of the activities in *Career Choices*. Each step of the learner's own unique self-discovery, decision-making, and personal planning process is outlined in My10yearPlan Interactive, so they have a complete, mobile record of who they are, what they want, and how they plan to get it.

My10yearPlan Interactive is more than just an electronic rendering of the planning process outlined in *Career Choices*. It is a comprehensive, Internet-based system delivering over 100 exercises, activities, and surveys that interact with the learner, facilitating a decision-making process that culminates in the development of a personalized 10-year plan that is not only quantitative but, more important, meaningful.

My10yearPlan Interactive is not a canned, one-size-fits-all experience where the learner has little control over or relationship with the outcome. Unlike those resources found on the web sites of the U.S. Department of Labor and commercial providers, My10yearPlan Interactive gives the computer a role that reaches beyond that of "tool" to something more akin to that of a coach, counselor, or mentor. The system gently guides, prompts, and, where necessary, prods the student through an in-depth decision-making process that often cannot be accomplished without this intense support.

Why Students Need Both the Workbook and the Online Experience

Students may be tempted to skip writing in their **Workbook and Portfolio** in favor of just entering their responses directly into the My10yearPlan.com® system. Urge them not to do so. To give them the best opportunity possible to create 10-year plans that will start them on the path of personal fulfillment and life satisfaction, an important two-step process was designed.

✓ **For in-depth learning:** This course was designed with a print version of the content as well as the online tool because this combination facilitates a deeper, more comprehensive understanding of this life-defining, multi-step process.

✓ **For ease of learning this life-defining complex process:** Making career, education, and lifestyle choices based on one's own goals, aptitudes, and attitudes is probably one of the most important yet complex skills anyone can develop. That is probably why so many people don't consciously make these choices and float from one job, relationship, or life situation to the next. Most learners would find it challenging to keep the required sequential, step-by-step process all in their heads without the ability to flip through a print copy to easily visualize these steps and understand where they've been and where they are going.

✓ **To be more user-friendly:** The online activities and worksheets were designed to be as user-friendly as possible. Adding all the content/text required for the background understanding of the concepts presented would have made the online experience too cumbersome and overwhelming.

✓ **To promote growth through contemplation, reflection, and adaptation:** This in-depth, personal reflection opportunity works best as a two-step process. As students read the content before completing the online activities, they'll want to jot down their initial thoughts in the **Workbook and Portfolio**. They should consider this their first draft. When they finally sit down to enter their work online, they'll have had a chance to think about their responses and they'll probably want to expand or even change their initial thoughts. Even if their feelings haven't changed, having their ideas already written out will make the data entry process much easier.

✓ **To encourage critical, creative, and strategic thinking:** Students will discover that going back and reviewing their choices multiple times will help to build confidence in the choices they are making. They'll want to give this two-step process the time and attention it deserves, because they are, after all, making one of the most important choices of their lives.

✓ **To provide support as students face changes and transitions throughout their lives:** This is one book students will want to keep on their shelf with their important papers so they can pick it up and refer to it again and again as they face life-altering decisions.

An important goal of this course is to help students develop a 10-year education and career plan. It's critical that they evaluate their choices based on what would make *them* feel successful. As we all know, success is a very individualized measurement. Personal success is simply the fulfillment of what makes you happiest.

In this process of developing a comprehensive 10-year plan, your students learn important strategies and formulas for a decision-making process that can be used when making any life-defining decisions. Because it's a systematic process, it's important to remember that the text follows a strict order. Information and data discovered in earlier chapters are used in later ones as students continue on the path to develop their *quantitative* and *meaningful* 10-year plans.

Quantitative, naturally, is something that is definable, usually associated with a measurement. When you review Chapter 12—where students compile all their data, information, and insights—you'll see that what they put together in the form of action plans are indeed measurable. After all, how else can success be determined?

Meaningful is an operative word. You and your students are about to invest over 100 hours of study, discussion, contemplation, and work on this self-discovery journey. Each student's resulting 10-year plan will be individualized, born out of their discoveries and "ah ha" moments. The carefully planned scope and sequence of the curriculum builds on earlier discoveries in a step-by-step process. Students systematically tackle issues and topics that most people learn about the hard way. As students develop a deeper self-knowledge, you'll introduce them to increasingly sophisticated concepts with which many adults still struggle.

Because the plan is personalized, of each student's own creation, they take ownership and are connected to its outcome. This is very important. Unlike a computer-based planning process that can appear to be "magical," using plans born out of their own efforts and analysis helps students understand at a gut level the rewards of following through. By completing **Career Choices**, they're also exposed to the consequences of *not* following through with their plans. This is important because, when the first roadblock inevitably presents itself, they're more likely to buckle down and do whatever is necessary to accomplish their goals instead of quitting or falling back to a safe position. Their motivation will be intrinsic, which is the best kind of motivation.

Speak of the 10-year plan with reverence in your class. By developing people who are long-range thinkers, you'll change your students' lives.

An important first step for your course is letting your students know from the very beginning that the culmination of the course—the product of their work—is the development of their own 10-year plan. This will become one of the most important documents they have.

We suggest that you enthusiastically introduce the 10-year plan by providing them with a vision of what it is and why it is important to their lives. Finally, ask your students to turn to Chapter 12 and let them know that everything they do throughout the course will be used in the development of their own 10-year plan, and that their 10-year plan will be their final exam for the course. Once they know that, there's no reason that everyone shouldn't get a good grade.

This textbook is different than others you've seen. Using a dialectic style (i.e., discussion) rather than didactic (i.e., lecturing) is the secret to success with **Career Choices**. Instead of reading great amounts of didactic text, students learn by reflection, analysis, and research as they come up with their own personalized answers to the questions in the activities and exercises.

Read below for a detailed outline of each chapter in this curriculum and the overarching concept behind its design. You can also watch overview videos online at **The Teachers' Lounge**.

Section 1: Chapters 1 and 2
Who Am I?

> "Know thyself."
> — Socrates

This is probably the most profound two-word statement in history. Individuals who have examined their passions, aptitudes, and attitudes are in a much better position to understand their own beliefs, dreams, and motivations. It is only then that one can make important choices that result in both happiness and life satisfaction.

In Chapters 1 and 2, students embark on this journey that culminates in a quantitative and meaningful 10-year plan.

Have a copy of the *Career Choices* textbook and this *Instructor's Guide* handy so you can refer to them as noted throughout this section.

Start by reviewing the table of contents for *Career Choices*. You'll see that the chapters are ordered into three sections:

Who Am I? What Do I Want? How Do I Get It?

Chapter 1—*Envisioning Your Future: How Do You Define Success?*

Chapter 1 opens with four fanciful stories about personalities known to your students. These fantasies are about the moment these individuals discovered their life's work. As the text on page 12 goes on to explain, planning your life based on luck or magic is probably not a good option. It is here your students are exposed, for the first time, to the formula for success:

Vision + Energy = Success

Post this formula in a prominent place in your classroom, if possible, so everyone can refer back to it often. It sums up what this course is all about: envisioning a productive and satisfying future and then creating the plans for achieving that vision so they know where to focus their energy.

On page 13, students articulate the visions of each of the celebrities (based on the story and what they know about them). Students then imagine what the celebrities did, the energy they expended both in school and at work, to accomplish their goals. This is the first of many times they will practice this life skill.

On page 14, they try to envision their own futures. For many, this is difficult. However, an important part of learning is first determining what you don't know. You'll learn a lot through your students' responses to this activity. The harder it is for them to detail a realistic future, the more at-risk that student is of dropping out of high school, college, or life. While you don't want to say that to them, keep that in mind as you individualize your work with each student.

It's a good idea to revisit the Envisioning Your Future activity again at the end of the course. Have your students write about their visions of the future once again and compare their responses. For most students, the difference should be profound.

Throughout the course, you'll be asking your students over and over again to expand their vision of the future in a variety of areas. The activities and exercises they're exposed to constantly prompt them to think into the future. Through case studies of others and personalized exercises, they're asked to stretch their focus to imagine their future lives.

Refer to your *Instructor's Guide* on a daily basis as you go through the balance of the chapter. The topics presented include:

- Why people work, where students discover it's about more than just money
- A rubric for defining success that helps students realize it's a personal definition and make their first attempt at defining success for themselves
- The different ways people make career choices; it becomes clear that having a rational process for making what could possibly be the second most important decision in their lives is the best way to go

As the text says on page 21, making choices that are right for each person is what the *Career Choices* curriculum is all about. Before you can choose what you want, you need to know who you are, which leads us to Chapter 2.

Chapter 2—*Your Personal Profile: Getting What You Want Starts with Knowing Who You Are*

This is a favorite chapter and one on which you'll want to spend sufficient time and energy. As Ralph Waldo Emerson once observed, "Self-trust is the first secret of success." Without a basic understanding of their own personality traits, values, skills, and passions, individuals can't hope to consistently make life decisions that are personally fulfilling.

You'll see a bull's eye chart on page 27, which is the Personal Profile chart that students will attempt to complete after reading the preceding pages. It will be difficult for most, but they'll soon discover that the activities that follow provide experiences to help them identify their traits, characteristics, and aptitudes.

As your students work through the various trigger activities, they'll learn to determine and articulate their passions, work values, personality and strengths, skills and aptitudes, and their roles. They'll gather important data about themselves that they'll use not only throughout the balance of the course but also throughout their lives.

Students discover and communicate the many layers that make up their unique identities. As they use that knowledge to make decisions throughout the course, they'll appreciate how empowering this information is. Reinforce that this is a life-long process because we all change. Throughout the course, refer students back to their bull's eye chart as they discover something new about themselves. If they get into the habit of periodically reviewing these activities and updating their bull's eye charts and 10-year plans, they will be much more likely to stay on track with what is most important to them.

Career Choices was developed around the high tech/high touch theory championed in the best-selling book *Megatrends* in 1982. Before the onset of the personal computer, author John Naisbitt identified the coming technological revolution. He warned at the time that, along with the high tech options we were soon to have, we should not lose sight of the "high touch" all people need in their lives.

His phrase high tech/high touch illustrated the need to seek understanding and harmony between technology and human interaction. He believed that every application of technology needed to be offset with an equal application of human touch or interaction. He wrote that when high touch is ignored in implementing technology, technology encounters resistance.

You'll want to be sure to bring this balance into your coursework. For the purpose of the *Career Choices* curriculum, high touch is the teaching style you'll want to adopt—one of facilitation, collaboration, questioning, and discussion.

The *Career Choices* curriculum and enhancements are built on the premise that brainpower is more valuable in the process of determining life-defining choices. The computer is a tool, not a crutch. To be truly successful in navigating the "slings and arrows" that life throws at us, we all need to be empowered to think on our feet and act or react appropriately and strategically. If we rely on computer-based surveys and personality tests to answer our most pressing questions about ourselves, we abdicate this most personal function.

By the end of Chapter 2, you'll observe a marked difference in many of your students. Having a better understanding of themselves and their motivation is very empowering to students. They are about to learn that this is the first step to taking in guesswork out of making choices.

Section 2: Chapters 3 to 7
What Do I Want?

You're probably thinking the answers to this question shouldn't be that hard to determine. Taco or hamburger? Blue shirt or black sweater? Easy, right? But when it comes to those big life decisions, it's a lot more difficult than we all care to admit.

Too many people rely on instinct or gut reactions to make decisions, or they simply avoid making choices, which, in the end, actually dictates the outcome.

If an individual is not comfortable making life-defining choices, this can have long-term ramifications. Therapists report that the majority of adults in mid-life crisis counseling can't articulate what they want out of life. The consequence of this inability hijacks careers and disrupts families.

In this section of *Career Choices*, students learn a decision-making process, not just applicable for career planning but for most of life's important choices. The goal of this section is to expose students to sophisticated concepts and tools to help them quantify important choices related to their own life planning.

Good decision-making is not instinctive; it takes research, exploring options, evaluating the pros and cons of each option, and determining the probability of success. In the five chapters in this section, students experience a variety of topics and strategies that help them make the choices needed to complete a quantitative and meaningful 10-year plan.

Chapter 3—Lifestyles of the Satisfied and Happy: Keeping Your Balance and Perspective

What comes first, career choice or lifestyle choice? Which did you choose first? Did your career dictate your lifestyle?

Taking a look at the different components of lifestyle, students start reviewing in general terms what decisions need to be made. This sets the stage for discoveries and choices made later in the course.

On pages 60–61, students make their first attempt at writing their own mission statement, articulating how they want to be remembered. They will come back to this activity throughout the course.

Using a modified version of Maslow's hierarchy of needs on pages 64–71, students experience a variety of issues that can impact their lifestyle and career choices. Using this model helps determine if their life is out of balance, a far too common problem in today's fast-paced world. Once an imbalance is identified, they're empowered to make the choices to get back on track.

Chapter 4—What Cost this Lifestyle? Every Career Choice Involves Sacrifices and Rewards

In this chapter, your students explore three different lifestyle costs: the financial costs, the emotional and psychological costs, and, finally, the commitment costs.

For over 20 years, the budget exercise has been one of the most powerful activities of this curriculum. Beginning on page 77, students plan a budget for the lifestyle they envision for themselves at age 29. The resulting figure provides another important piece of data as they plan their future. They now have a quantitative checkpoint for determining what level of commitment they want to make to their education.

You'll want to spend time working through each budget line item. The more these numbers reflect the student's vision of their future lifestyle, the more believable their total budget figure is to them. The number they come up with as their budget total is critical to their decision-making process. It's an important figure when later, in Chapter 6, they start researching careers and the education each one requires. They soon discover that compensation is usually tied directly to education level. You won't want to short-change this experience.

Now that students have their ideal budget figures, they're ready to analyze a variety of budgets. The more comfortable they are with the budgeting process, the more they'll use it. As they continue through Chapter 4, they experiment with a "hard times" budget, budgets for a variety of family types, and the realities of living in poverty. However, money isn't everything, as the next activities point out. Students find case studies and activities exploring the psychological rewards and sacrifices any career and lifestyle might present.

The chapter wraps up by pointing out another cost of lifestyle: the importance of making a commitment. Using the commitment to education as an example, students apply math formulas and rubrics to explore in quantitative ways how the choices they make right now impact their future happiness and life satisfaction.

Chapter 5—Your Ideal Career: There's More to Consider Than Just the Work

Through the various surveys, assessments, and activities in this chapter, students start describing their ideal career in general terms. By taking the assessments beginning on page 126, they understand how broad those choices are. Students explore:

- Physical settings
- Working conditions
- Relationships at work
- Psychological rewards of working
- Mixing career and family
- Financial rewards
- Job skills

In addition, they explore concepts like flexible hours, composite careers, entrepreneurship, and telecommuting. By the time they complete the questionnaires, assessments, and surveys, they can write a description of a work situation that they would find personally pleasing and motivating.

Here's what students have learned so far from the beginning of the course:

- They have started articulating a future they find exciting and satisfying.
- They have a better understanding of who they are—their passions, work behavioral style, work values, etc.
- They have started defining a lifestyle they find pleasing.
- They have a notion of the economic, emotional, and commitment costs associated with that particular lifestyle.
- They have constructed a general description of their ideal working situation.

Now they're ready to proceed to Chapter 6.

Chapter 6—Career Research: Reading About Careers Isn't Enough

After reviewing what they've learned about themselves in the first five chapters, students will conduct in-depth research on at least three careers they find appealing using a survey tool found on pages 150-151. This is a good time to turn to the Internet. See pages 148–149 for suggested web sites.

Just reading about and researching jobs using books and online resources isn't enough, though. After all: Tell me and I forget, show me and I remember, but involve me and I understand. The balance of this chapter presents activities that lead the student through more sophisticated ways of addressing the process of making a career choice. They envision what a day might be like in a particular job. You may also want to offer the option of shadowing someone at work.

In The Chemistry Test activity beginning on page 162, students draw on what they learned about themselves in Chapter 2. Using information they have gained about their own personality and strengths, students learn the sophisticated concept of matching work behavioral styles to different careers.

It makes sense to reiterate that the *Career Choices* course is not just about choosing a career; it's about learning a process. On the other hand, it's important for students to become career-committed and career-focused. Studies show that entering college freshmen who have a specific career in mind are much more likely to complete/graduate on time.

Don't forget to refer to Section 4 of this *Instructor's Guide* daily. You'll find academic and technological enhancement opportunities in each lesson.

Chapter 7—Decision Making: How to Choose What's Best for You

It's not the goal of this course to make a final career decision. After all, most people will have seven to ten different careers within their working life span. The goal is to help students create a vision of a future that they find appealing and, as a result, motivating. In the context of their 10-year plans, students are asked to focus their plan on one career area.

Be sure to remind them that this specific career choice will probably change at some point. By using the tools and strategies learned in this course, however, that decision-making process will be less stressful.

In Chapter 7, students are exposed incrementally to a systematic decision-making chart to help them with their career decisions and any other decisions they may make. Good decision-making is not instinctual; it takes knowledge, experience, and practice. Using the process and chart found on page 177, students learn a skill that will pay dividends in happiness and satisfaction throughout their lives.

Learning to determine and then articulate what we want is a complex yet very doable process. It is also critical to life satisfaction and success because, in the end, our lives are defined by the choices we make.

Section 3: Chapters 8 to 12
How Do I Get It?

Up until this point in the course, you and your students have spent the majority of your time collecting personal data and exploring issues that impact their futures. It is now time to start putting that data and their insights together to create a meaningful plan.

Achieving happiness requires action. Without an action plan for realizing dreams and desires, the path to a successful and satisfying life will probably be full of false starts and detours.

Because life is full of challenges, this section addresses particular challenges that impact planning and provides strategies to overcome them.

Chapter 8—Setting Goals and Solving Problems: Skills for Successful Living

This chapter opens with techniques for solving problems based on the writings of M. Scott Peck. For instance, the concept of delaying gratification is explored. As we know, for far too many people of all ages, the desire for instant gratification leads to trouble.

All good plans are quantitative, with measurable objectives that state what will be different, by how much or how many, and by when. In Chapter 8, your students learn one of the most important skills of any planning process: how to write quantitative goals and objectives. They diagram goals and objectives to make sure each statement has all three components and, by the end of the chapter, they're able to write measurable objectives for their own lifestyle goals.

The goals and objectives they write on page 190 are important. This is their first experience with creating an action plan, an empowering skill they'll use throughout the balance of the course and as they create their 10-year plan in Chapter 12.

Chapter 9—Avoiding Detours and Roadblocks: The Road to Success is Dotted with Many Tempting Parking Places

Life isn't easy and it isn't fair. Everyone, no matter how well they plan, faces barriers or problems at some time or another. How well they deal with these challenges determines how successful and therefore how happy they are in the long-term. You can do all the planning in the world, but if you hit a wall and can't get up, dust yourself off, and try again, you probably won't realize your most cherished goals.

The activities within this chapter help students explore and find strategies to address common problems that stymie people. The more at-risk your student population, the more time you want to spend on this chapter.

The chapter opens with a variety of exercises to assess and address self-limiting attitudes. The underlying message is that we all have to take responsibility for our own actions or, as the case may be, inactions. Using case studies, which are less threatening to students than discussing their own issues, they follow "friends" over a 15-year period and predict the outcomes based upon the effort and plans of each.

Students also look at the economic consequences of bad choices, whether it's dropping out of school or indulging in a bad habit. On pages 208-209, using the magic of compounding interest,

2/17

your students determine the economics of a possible bad habit. They calculate how much they would have at retirement if they were to put their cigarette, designer coffee, or impulse shopping money in a retirement savings account instead. The result of not planning is shockingly illustrated in a monetary figure of huge proportions.

In Chapter 9, students look at the costs of self-limiting notions, whether it's about giving up a dream or feeling undeserving of success. A young person can be the brightest individual in your class, but if they aren't able to cope with the fears that are sure to surface during this transitional time in their lives, it's highly unlikely they're going to stretch themselves to get the education and experience they need to make it in today's world. Learning to overcome anxieties that limit their ability to move forward is an important skill set.

Let's face it. Some students don't have the benefits that go with being born into a family with the resources to give them a "leg up" in life. They may have little support and even less money. On page 223, students create a 10-year plan for Yorik, a fictional character who has immigrated to the United States with nothing but his ambition. Starting with someone else's challenges helps make it less threatening when, in Chapter 12, they do the same for themselves.

Using the Career Alternatives chart on page 227, students are able to visualize various paths to career satisfaction. For instance, if they only have the resources to train to become a licensed vocational nurse, they can include strategies in their 10-year plan to move up the career ladder so they can realize their dream of being a registered nurse.

Students who work through these activities with your constant coaching and support are far less likely to be among those people who lament later in life, "If only someone would have told me what life was going to be like."

Chapter 10—Attitude is Everything: Learning to Accentuate the Positive

Success or failure is governed more by mental attitude than by mental capacity. If you think you can, you will. If you think you can't, you won't.

The best plans in the world can be sabotaged consciously or unconsciously by negative attitudes. Providing young people with the tools to evaluate, create, and maintain a positive attitude is critical to their future success in school and beyond.

In this chapter, students learn:

- How to use positive affirmations to push themselves to achieve cherished goals
- Strategies for achieving the highest standards of excellence
- Why a go-for-it attitude is critical to success
- How to recognize and reward a strong work ethic
- How to incorporate the skills and attitudes valued in the 21st century workplace
- Strategies for managing change

For many of your students, positive attitudinal shifts will be an important part of their growth process. The activities and exercises presented in this chapter will nudge them toward a more empowered mindset.

Chapter 11—Getting Experience: Finding your first job

In this chapter, students are exposed to the initial steps and strategies for getting a job. You'll want to encourage students to find a beginning job in a field in which they are interested, even if it just means running errands or manning the coffee cart. This provides an opportunity to be exposed to and experience the realities of work in their chosen industry. Most important, their experiences come at a time when students may still be able to make "course corrections" related to their education. For many, an entry-level job is also a powerful example of why further education is desirable. They'll see that jobs that require more education provide better rewards, both monetary and psychic.

Chapter 12—Where Do You Go from Here? Writing Your 10-year Plan

In Chapter 12, students take the data and insights they've gained in your course and put it all together for their 10-year plans. This complete chapter makes an ideal final examination. For details on how to do this, refer to the Section 14 of this guide.

As they complete their education 10-year plans, have them go online to My10yearPlan.com® for easy access to a wealth of college planning and post-secondary training resources readily available on the Internet.

Once your students have completed Chapter 12, have them enter the appropriate information from their *Career Choices* workbooks on My10yearPlan.com®. The online program then generates a summary of their 10-year plan and makes the information available to them for updating throughout high school.

When individuals are in the habit of evaluating who they are, what they want, and how to get it, particularly when making life's major decisions, the likelihood of long-term happiness and satisfaction is much higher.

If you are using the college edition, *Career Choices and Changes*, for a dual credit course, see pages 2/24–2/28 for details and chapter descriptions.

The *Instructor's Guide*: A Daily Resource

This *Instructor's Guide* includes a variety of suggestions for planning and customizing your course, including sample lesson plans, sample discussion questions, and assessment tools. Look to this guide as your one-stop resource for answering any of your questions about teaching a *Career Choices* course.

The *Career Choices* curriculum is a flexible program that can be used in a variety of settings. Although this guide presents a number of possibilities, we encourage you to use your creativity to make the curriculum relveant and stimulating for your own classes.

See the summaries of each section on pages 1/12–1/14.

Possibilities: A Supplemental Anthology for Career Choices

Career advice from John Updike and Robert Frost? Pep talks from Emily Dickinson and Albert Camus? Unusual, perhaps, but ideal when your goal is academic integration. When you combine *Career Choices* and *Possibilities*, a language arts class becomes an ideal place to teach problem solving, risk taking, and the work ethic.

Possibilities includes 50 essays, short stories, poems, speeches, and plays from poets, authors, and statesmen. Most of the literature contained in *Possibilities* appears on recommended reading lists across the country. However, the selections included in the anthology are flexible enough to be used in a variety of situations and with students of varying abilities.

The combination of *Career Choices* and *Possibilities* is effective because adolescents all have at least one thing in common: an avid interest in themselves and their futures. When reading and writing assignments help students find answers to their most urgent questions—"Who am I?" and "What do I want?"— and fictional characters are seen to be struggling with the same questions, literature takes on new meaning.

Discussion questions, activities, composition assignments, grammar, and vocabulary lessons support a literature-based approach to language arts while using the highly motivational themes of *Career Choices* to support the Common Core State Standards. Suddenly, the classics as well as the basic skills of reading, writing, and speaking are more relevant, which increases adolescent learners' motivation and academic performance.

Use *Career Choices* and *Possibilities* together as:

- A semester or year-long class in the English department

- A team teaching opportunity for the English department and the school counselor, career technician, or family and consumer sciences instructor

- A team teaching opportunity for the English department and the math and/or social studies department

- Two fully integrated classes (for example, a freshman transition course coupled with 9th grade English)

See the following pages of this manual for more detailed information about integrating *Career Choices* and *Possibilities* into the core English curriculum.

Career Choices/Possibilities *Cross Reference*

The *Career Choices/Possibilities* cross-reference guide was designed to assist you in deciding when to incorporate the stories, poems, essays, plays, or speeches found in *Possibilities* with the corresponding activities and exercise in *Career Choices*. See pages 8/11–8/14 for this sequential chart.

Lifestyle Math: Your Financial Planning Portfolio

Lifestyle Math is a wonderful way to personalize math. It effectively debunks many of the myths that hinder students in achieving math excellence. By making math exciting and pertinent, it proves to students that they can do math if they try. Perhaps most important, *Lifestyle Math* demonstrates to students the personal relevance math has in their daily lives—today and in the future. This, in turn, motivates them to apply themselves to their math studies.

Lifestyle Math is an extension of the budget exercise found in Chapter 4 of *Career Choices*. Working on the same premise, young people begin to think about and plan for the kind of life they want to have by age 29. As students move through a more detailed budgeting process, they build more than math skills. Step by step, the exercises increase motivation and commitment to prepare for the future by doing well in school today.

With *Lifestyle Math*, basic math practice comes in the guise of party planning, buying a dream car or home, and much more. Students find that math is important to their happiness and, with their newfound motivation, they realize that they can master math!

Lifestyle Math helps students by reducing the seemingly complicated life issues they'll face to the essential mathematical concepts they know. Students have the opportunity to practice addition, subtraction, multiplication, and division. They'll practice working with whole numbers, fractions, percentages, ratios, estimation, and graphing. They'll tackle real-life issues such as simple and compounded interest, affordability indexes, insurance deductibles, and more.

And *Lifestyle Math* is designed to be used as a supplementary activity for math classes at all levels.

- *Algebra:* Students can use it for enrichment, perhaps as a bonus activity after a weekly quiz. This activity will reinforce the need for more advanced math classes while, at the same time, teaching important life formulas.

- *Pre-Algebra:* Students can use it for supplemental activities to improve basic skills, increase problem solving and critical thinking and demonstrate the importance of math. It will be motivational to encourage a continuation of their math studies.

- *Basic Skills:* Students can be motivated to focus on higher achievement by seeing how math relates to many other aspects of their lives. This text, with supplemental instruction on basic computation skills, could form the basis for a basic math course.

I love this text. Lifestyle Math *presents down-to-earth material in a fashion that stimulates students to participate. It is the most practical, useful text we use in the BST class.*

— Sara L. Carter, Business Teacher
Garden City High School, Garden City, MI

LifestyleMath.com: The Online Correction Key

Because of the individualized nature of the *Lifestyle Math* workbook, correction and assessment can be challenging. To help make that task as easy as possible, we've created an optional technology component.

LifestyleMath.com is made up of 47 mathematical problems and activities from the *Lifestyle Math* workbook. Until now, math problems have needed to be uniformly designed with one answer for each problem so instructors could check student work against a written answer key. This web site allows students to quickly correct their own personalized math computations from their *Lifestyle Math* workbook.

LifestyleMath.com gives the dream of effortless correction embodiment, delivering a quick and easy tool for students to use at school or at home. After completing their computations the old-fashioned way (with paper and pencil in their workbook), students can go online with their password and check their answers digitally. Using the online correcting format, students are alerted to any errors and encouraged to rework their computations. Once students arrive at the correct solution, they can print out their work and turn it in to you for credit. For more information, see Section 8 of this guide.

*real intelligence   +   artificial intelligence   =   the workforce
of the
21st century*

[I particularly liked] the website [and] the practical math.

— Louis Fleming, Tech Teacher
Andrews High School, Andrews, TX

CareerChoices.com

With the launch of CareerChoices.com, we've made a daunting task easier for teachers and students. This easy-to-use web site can deliver exciting digital content to even the most novice computer user.

CareerChoices.com is a subscription site with over 80 web links tied directly to the *Career Choices* curriculum. The links we've chosen provide students with the means to take their research for the activities in *Career Choices* to a higher level, supporting the Common Core State Standards. Detailed instructions, learning objectives, and lesson plans for each web link are supplied for both teachers and students.

Career Choices and CareerChoices.com allow for virtually effortless integration of technology, career education, and core academics by providing:

- A ready-made Internet enhancement. CareerChoices.com has easy-to-follow lesson plans for teachers and step-by-step instructions for students. This Internet link allows for uncomplicated integration without endless Internet surfing.

- A proven guidance and career planning model for the academic teacher. Each activity in *Career Choices* and CareerChoices.com motivates students to excel by demonstrating the relationship between their present classroom studies and their future lives. As they practice reading, writing, and computation, students learn about themselves, build crucial life skills, and become competent Internet users.

- The best the Internet has to offer. CareerChoices.com was developed—and new activities are added—only after extensive research. It enhances the entire *Career Choices* experience, providing a safe environment in which to build critical skills—for students and teachers alike.

Whether you use this resource in English, math, or as a stand-alone career guidance component, *Career Choices* and CareerChoices.com will re-energize and re-focus the classroom experience. Students will:

- Explore vast career-related information

- Research college and post-secondary education opportunities

- Discover job-finding resources, from resume writing to interviewing techniques

- Use financial planning calculators to help quantify their lifestyle expectations

CareerChoices.com members also receive a license to The Teachers' Lounge, Academic Innovations' online professional development resource. Membership is only offered to schools currently using the *Career Choices* materials in the classroom.

Your initial 12-month licensing fee is calculated on a sliding scale based on your largest order to date. Annual re-orders are used to determine the licensing for subsequent years.

Please call (800) 967-8016 for a fee quote. Alternatively, complete the "Do I Qualify?" form at www.careerchoices.com/register.html to send us a fee quote request and we'll contact you.

Career Choices and Changes:
The College Version of *Career Choices*

Career Choices and Changes brings the same self-discovery process found in ***Career Choices*** to a more mature audience: college students, people re-entering the workforce, individuals changing careers—anyone wrestling with the important questions of identity, life satisfaction, and future planning.

Career Choices and Changes covers all the topics in ***Career Choices*** but is written for a more mature audience with age-appropriate stories and examples. ***Career Choices and Changes*** also includes three additional chapters and expanded content in the last chapters.

What are the differences between **Career Choices** *(high school) and* **Career Choices and Changes** *(college)?*

What you'll see is that Chapters 1 to 10 are nearly identical, because the decision-making process to that point is ageless and, therefore, the same. With the additional three chapters (Chapters 11, 12, and 13) and the expanded last two chapters, ***Career Choices and Changes*** is 100 pages longer than ***Career Choices***.

Chapter 11: Your Skills Inventory: The Precursor for Your Education Plan

Chapter 12: Study Skills for the Life-Long Learner: Developing Your Learning Plans

Chapter 13: Making Changes: The Inevitable Process

Chapter 14: Beginning the Job Search: Just Do It

Chapter 15: Where Do You Go from Here? Writing Your 10-year Action Plan

This last third of the college textbook emphasizes the development of a detailed Education Plan that is skills based, promoting not only traditional classroom learning but also the wide range of learning opportunities available.

In addition, ***Career Choices and Changes*** was designed to be used with My10yearPlan.com® Interactive.

Dual Enrollment Freshman Transition (DEFT)

If your school is interested in the Dual Enrollment Freshman Transition model created by Santa Barbara City College for the ***Get Focused...Stay Focused!***™ Initiative, you'll want to consider using ***Career Choices and Changes*** with your high school students.

For more information about this program see pages 3/13, 3/20, 4/170. and 6/24–6/30. You'll also want to visit **www.getfocusedstayfocused.org**.

Chapter 11—Your Skills Inventory: The Precursor for Your Education Plan

When you are applying for a new position, it often isn't as important what degrees you've earned or even what experience you have as it is what skills you have. The bottom line for many employers: Do you have the knowledge and skills necessary to be proficient at this job? In today's highly competitive job market, employers are allocating fewer resources toward training and requiring that new employees be capable of completing job responsibilities from day one.

This chapter coaches students to discover the skills they already have and catalog the skills they will need to obtain for their chosen careers. They will also designate two back-up careers and outline the skills those careers require. Students will create a Skills Inventory to keep track of all the skills they have and those they need to acquire. They will be encouraged to keep this list up to date and refer to it whenever they apply for a new position.

The chapter reinforces other requirements of the 21st century workplace, including the need to maintain an international perspective, keep up with new technology, and be flexible about career changes.

Chapter 12—Study Skills for the Life-long Learner: Developing your Learning Plans

This chapter builds on the previous one by guiding students through the development of Learning Plans to acquire the skills they will need in their chosen careers. Though these plans may include formal education, the focus is on self-directed learning. Students must be willing to take responsibility for learning new skills, and signing up for a class to learn each new skill would likely be time-consuming, costly, and, in some cases, unnecessary. Many students aren't aware of the myriad methods available for enhancing their skill set, so this chapter provides that exposure.

Ultimately, for any kind of true learning to take place, the learner must be intrinsically motivated, confident that they can learn, and familiar with the basic skills for learning and retaining information. After ensuring that the student is personally invested in learning and confident of a positive outcome, the chapter focuses on developing the most appropriate Learning Plan for each Learning Goal. It provides a wealth of resources from which students can choose as they pursue their Learning Goals, as well as tips for getting the best returns from each method. Different resources and study skills will work best for different individuals, so this chapter allows students to learn about their options and choose the methods that work best for them.

Chapter 13—Making Changes: The Inevitable Process

It is beneficial for students to designate an ideal career path. A single, focused path promotes degree completion and the development of job-specific skills. However, students must also be prepared for career changes. Most people will not have the luxury of moving up through the ranks at a single company from an entry-level start until retirement; change is now an unavoidable aspect of being a member of the workforce.

Change may be:

- **Personal** – the job reality may differ negatively from expectations, or priorities may change due to events such as starting a family

- **Company-specific** – one may seek advancement beyond what the current employer can or will provide, or desire a relocation

- **Structural** – new technology may make the job obsolete, or the company/industry may cease operations in this country

Regardless of the source of the change, individuals will eventually need to seek a different job. Many people will completely change careers and require retraining.

This chapter teaches students to take stock of their attitudes toward change, assess whether or not a change is necessary, and create a plan for accomplishing a change.

Chapter 14—Beginning the Job Search: Just Do It!

In this chapter, students are exposed to the initial steps and strategies for getting a job. Students are encouraged to find a beginning job in a field in which they are interested, even if it just means running errands or manning the coffee cart. This provides an opportunity to experience the realities of the work world, in general, and their chosen industry, in particular, at a time when students may still be able to make "course corrections" related to their education. For many, an entry-level job is also a powerful example of why further education is desirable. They'll see that jobs that require more education provide better rewards, both monetarily and psychically.

Chapter 15—Where Do You Go from Here? Writing Your 10-year Plan

In this final chapter, students take the data and insights they've gained and put it all together to create 10-year Plans. This chapter makes an ideal final examination. (For details on how to do this, refer to Section 14—Assessment.)

As students complete this final chapter, they should make sure the appropriate information from their *Career Choices and Changes* workbooks is included in their My10yearPlan.com® account. The online program can then generate a variety of dynamic documents, including 10-year Plan summary. The 10-year Plan information is available online and through a mobile app for updating throughout college.

When individuals are in the habit of evaluating who they are, what they want, and how to get it, particularly when making life's major decisions, the likelihood of long-term happiness and satisfaction is much higher.

Section 3

Where to Use the Curriculum? Who Should Teach It?

Topics covered in this section include:

- The lessons taught in *Career Choices* are essential for all students—from the college bound to those at risk of dropping out. All students need to go through the process of developing 10-year plans that encompass education, career, and lifestyle in order to have the best chance of living fulfilling, self-sufficient lives.

- Any enthusiastic teacher can teach this course—they don't need to have prior experience teaching a career guidance class.

- *Career Choices* can be used in myriad settings and interdisciplinary combinations, whether you envision a stand-alone course, an interdisciplinary approach, or daily advisories. Some options include a:

  - Freshman transition course for 8th or 9th grade

  - Launch course for career academies and pathways

  - Course to target dropout prevention

  - Course integrated with English, math, technology, etc.

  - Dual enrollment course

The Foundation Course for All Students

Whether your students are headed for an Ivy League college or an entry-level job, they crave a clear sense of direction for their lives. With the standards-based *Career Choices* curriculum, you can help them develop a personalized, career-inclusive 10-year education plan. Because the plan is both meaningful and informed, it will also be motivational.

With a proven track record for engaging students and teachers in an effective interactive learning process, *Career Choices* provides an interdisciplinary experience that is relevant, rigorous, and relationship-rich. Flexible enough to be used in a variety of classroom settings with students of varying abilities, the *Career Choices* curriculum teaches the self-awareness, career exploration, decision-making, and goal setting skills needed to build successful careers—and balanced, self-sufficient lives—in rapidly changing times.

When young people can project into the future and understand the consequences of their actions today, they are far more likely to choose a productive path to a self-sufficient and satisfying future. Armed with their carefully-thought-out 10-year plans, they'll have the tools to stay on track, graduate, and fulfill their personal goals. Along the way, they'll learn and explore skills, aptitudes, and attitudes that lead to personal success.

In this essential foundation course, they'll learn:

- ☐ A proven process for making good decisions
- ☐ How to set and achieve goals
- ☐ How to take personal responsibility for their own actions
- ☐ Strategies for overcoming obstacles
- ☐ Online career research and job search techniques
- ☐ How to set priorities and develop workable life and career plans

In addition, this comprehensive guidance course helps your students:

- ☐ Make the connection between expectations, effort, and success
- ☐ Understand the cost of living the lifestyle they aspire to
- ☐ Calculate the salary required to support a family
- ☐ Envision a future of self-sufficiency
- ☐ Learn to tolerate anxiety and push beyond it to meet their personal goals
- ☐ Understand and embrace a positive work ethic
- ☐ Experience practical uses for technology
- ☐ Value education and training, becoming self-motivated learners

Flexible for a Variety of Courses and Programs

Each school will need to determine the most appropriate way to deliver this course. Whether in language arts or life skills courses, in work readiness seminars or Freshman Transition courses, this *Instructor's Guide* offers enough suggestions that teachers can work with it creatively and comfortably, knowing they are meeting the needs of their students.

Used by 4,800+ schools over more than two decades in:

- ☐ Freshman Transition Courses
- ☐ Dropout Prevention Efforts
- ☐ Freshman Academies
- ☐ Academic Coaching & Advisory Programs
- ☐ Career Academies or Pathways
- ☐ Interdisciplinary Team Teaching Settings
- ☐ English/Language Arts Classrooms
- ☐ Smaller Learning Communities
- ☐ Tech Prep and School-to-Career
- ☐ Work Readiness and Career Exploration

Use *Career Choices* in a Variety of Course Structures

In use for over 20 years, *Career Choices* has been integrated into the course schedule a variety of ways. In the balance of this section, you'll learn about using it as:

- A stand-alone course in a variety of settings
- An academically integrated course to address the Common Core State Standards
- The curriculum for focused and effective daily advisories

The Career Choices *curriculum* offers many *integrated course structure* options

Career Choices and the Workbook and Portfolio is an ideal combination for:

- Freshman Transition courses
- Career education classes
- Freshman academies
- Foundation course for a career academy or cluster

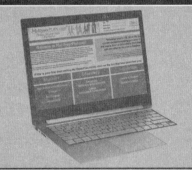

Use both Career Choices and Possibilities as:

- A semester or year-long class in the English department
- A team teaching opportunity for the English department and school counselors, careers instructors, or family and consumer sciences department
- Two integrated classes—a freshman transition class coupled with ninth-grade English

Use Career Choices, Possibilities, and Lifestyle Math as:

- A semester or year-long interdisciplinary course taught by the English, math, and social science departments
- A fully integrated academic course taught by one instructor within an academy, career pathway, or special populations program

Integrate Academics and Technology

Add these *optional* technology components to enhance any of the above winning combinations

My10yearPlan.com®

Unlike other online planning programs, My10yearPlan.com® supports students with a decision-making coach rather than a computerized crutch. As students complete the *Career Choices* coursework and record their responses in My10yearPlan.com®, the system saves and compiles the data so they can review, revise, and share their plans or easily produce a beautifully formatted 10-year Plan Portfolio report. This innovative advisory tool allows secure access for teachers, counselors, and advisors to review a student's 10-year career and education plan so they are better able to provide personalized support, help students stay on track, and reinforce their academic and life goals.

CareerChoices.com

Augment *Career Choices* with over 90 online lessons and demonstrate the power of the internet using real-life applications. Students learn to research careers, compare salaries, apply for financial aid, use various financial calculators, research college and training opportunities, and much more.

Go online to www.academicinnovations.com/internet_enhancements_overview.html

for details and examples of each of these exciting web-based tools.

Any Enthusiastic, Organized Instructor Can Teach this Course

When recruiting for this course, look for instructors who are:

Enthusiastic: This course is best taught by instructors who are enthusiastic. Teachers who **want** to teach this course, rather than being assigned this class, have the best results.

Organized: Because it is content-rich with a specific scope and sequence that culminates in the development of a quantitative 10-year plan, this class requires focused lesson plans and pacing to ensure students have ample time to complete Chapter 12.

Experienced: Teaching freshmen can be challenging—yet so rewarding—so recruit your best and most experienced teachers for this innovative course. This may include teachers who are newer to the classroom but have other experience outside of education.

Knowledgeable, using higher order teaching skills in their classroom: This interdisciplinary course is best taught by an instructor who practices inquiry-based learning. A Freshman Transition course based on the standards, delivering comprehensive guidance, and building higher-order thinking skills requires higher-order teaching skills:

- Student-centered versus subject-centered
- Socratic method of dialectic teaching versus didactic
- Cooperative learning versus lecture
- Active learning versus passive listening
- Project-based learning versus knowledge-based learning
- Higher-order thinking (analysis, synthesis, and evaluation) versus read and recall
- Critical, creative, and strategic thinking versus memorization

Used as a Stand-alone Class

Probably the most direct way to implement a comprehensive guidance course at your school is to find time in your school schedule for a stand-alone course. In either a semester (90 hours) or year-long class (180 hours), there are a variety ways to structure this course.

☐ Freshman transition course in the 8ᵗʰ or 9ᵗʰ grade

☐ Launch course for career academies and pathways

☐ Freshman seminar course for the core of your freshman academy

☐ Foundation course for your dropout prevention efforts

☐ Special program for college-bound and gifted students

☐ Career and life planning course

☐ Thematic English/language arts course

☐ First course for a dual enrollment *Get Focused…Stay Focused!*™ school-wide initiative

A Freshman Transition Course in 8ᵗʰ or 9ᵗʰ Grade

One of the most common ways this curriculum is used is as a semester- or year-long Freshman Transition class focusing on life skills and education and career planning. This is an ideal way to start incoming freshmen down the path to a successful high school career—and adult future. A standards-based Freshman Transition class will help students make informed selections as they plan their high school courses. In addition, they'll make better choices as they plan for their life beyond high school. While teaching important goal-setting and decision-making skills, *Career Choices* walks students through the step-by-step development of their own comprehensive 10-year plan that includes high school graduation, post-secondary completion, and successful entry into the workforce.

For details, visit Section 6 of this *Instructor's Guide*.

Indio High School in Indio, California, has transformed the culture of their school, improved on their attendance and failure rates, and increased the number of students participating in AP courses with a Freshman Transition course called Success 101. Watch their documentary to learn more about their program at www.whatworkscareerchoices.com/success101doc.html.

A Launch Course for Career Academies and Pathways

Career academies or pathways are a great way to help students get career-focused and start building specialized job skills early on. But how do students know which career pathway is right for them? Too many students are left to their own devices to make arbitrary decisions. Without exploring the reasons for pursuing a particular path, students may lack the motivation to perform up to their potential. Schools structured around different career tracks increase program effectiveness by requiring entering students to take a course using *Career Choices* before selecting the pathway they will pursue. This helps students to make informed decisions and gives them a strong incentive to excel.

Comprehensive guidance is a vital experience for students to have early in their high school career, especially if they will be entering an academy program. One way to ensure that all students receive the necessary career guidance is to require a first-semester career and life planning course using *Career Choices*. The insights provided by the in-depth career interest and aptitude surveys help reduce "lateral movement" between pathway offerings and ensure that students interest in pursuing post-secondary education or training increases.

This career academy launch course will help you:

- ☐ Direct students into college and certification programs. They'll enter focused, committed, and with a personal understanding of education's impact on life satisfaction.

- ☐ Create awareness of potential careers and appropriate workplace behaviors. In a short time, students' work maturity and career readiness skills will be of a level you have probably never experienced before.

- ☐ Expose young women to non-traditional (higher paying) occupations. Your female students will quickly understand that "playing it safe" by preparing for a low-skill, traditionally female career will cost them tens of thousands of dollars in future annual earnings.

- ☐ Cultivate a strong work ethic and build ambition as it combines guidance and employment skills.

- ☐ Support basic English/language arts and mathematics instruction through this academically integrated program. Suddenly reading, writing, and computation take on new meaning because assignments center on a topic of the utmost importance and interest: themselves.

- ☐ Introduce powerful Internet-based tools easily with CareerChoices.com and My10yearPlan.com®. The real-world applications accessed through these sites will pay dividends not only as students plan, prepare, and search for jobs but throughout their lives.

Dr. Jim Campbell, winner of the 1993 Parnell Tech Prep Award, pioneered a program that was successful in engaging and motivating students. However, Dr. Campbell found that many students still struggled when making an initial pathway selection, which caused problems with "lateral movement" between pathways. After implementing a transition program using *Career Choices* to guide freshmen through that selection process, fewer than 5% of students changed pathways. Read more about the program at www.whatworkscareerchoices.com/int17.html.

A Freshman Seminar Course to Anchor Your Freshman Academy

With a foundation course for a Freshman Academy, you can launch your students into high school with high expectations by:

- ☐ Effectively integrating academics, technology, and career guidance
- ☐ Demonstrating the relevance of education and, thereby, motivating teens to increase achievement
- ☐ Helping adolescents establish and consolidate identity
- ☐ Fostering ambitious—yet realistic—education and career plans
- ☐ Teaching the life, work, and technology skills necessary for success

This type of course might be the only opportunity your students will have to obtain the critical information they need to answer their three pressing developmental questions: Who am I? What do I want? How do I get it? With a proven track record for engaging students and teachers in an effective interactive learning process, *Career Choices* provides an interdisciplinary framework that is relevant, rigorous, and relationship-rich.

As either a semester (ideally during the first semester) or a year-long course, all students exit their freshman academy experience with a personalized 10-year plan that can be used in advisory, counseling, and academic coaching sessions throughout high school. See Section 6 for details.

A Freshman Seminar course using the *Career Choices* curriculum is the cornerstone of Seaman Freshman Center in Topeka, Kansas, a 9th-grade campus created to help ease students' transition into high school. "It's just one of those times in their lives that can be very impactful, socially and academically. We want to help them make that bridge and give them that support so they can begin their high school careers on a solid foundation," says teacher Cathie Klein. Read more at www.whatworkscareerchoices.com/intsea.html.

Course to Prevent High School *and* College Dropouts

If dropout prevention is a goal of your school redesign efforts, you'll want to institutionalize the creation of 10-year plans by every 8th or 9th grader in your system.

You may be asking yourself, "Why a 10-year plan? After all, our school already has each student complete a graduation plan. Isn't a four- or five-year plan enough?"

It is important that young people are able to envision and then plan a productive, self-sufficient future. Studies show that entering college freshmen who have a vision and plan for pursuing a specific career path are far more likely to graduate and successfully enter the workforce. Too often students enter with the vague notion that they "have to go to college" or they see themselves as "good students" and, therefore, college is the logical next step.

Think about it: A four-year plan, which is a common format for high schools, may get a student to high school graduation. But high school graduation is just not enough of an incentive to keep many students in school when they find it boring or irrelevant to their lives, as cited in *The Silent Epidemic: Perspectives of High School Dropouts*, a report funded by the Bill and Melinda Gates Foundation.

Without a vision of a productive future and, more important, an understanding of the consequences of not getting a good education, far too many will still drop out.

The U.S. Department of Education recognized *Career Choices* with a Promising Intervention Award for success in reducing dropout rates and supporting higher achievement in reading and math. The text effectively demonstrates the future benefits of completing high school and possibly post-secondary education. *Career Choices* also helps at-risk students understand that, despite individual challenges, they have the ability, resources, and responsibility to determine their own life patterns.

Coachella Valley High School in the desert of Southern California reduced their dropout rate from 12.7% to 3.8% in the first year of offering a Freshman Transition program. Read about this program's success at **www.whatworkscareerchoices.com/int22.html**.

Robeson County Public Schools in rural North Carolina achieved a 23% decrease in dropouts in the first year of implementing a Freshman Transition program at all seven high schools. Read about Robeson at **www.whatworkscareerchoices.com/introb.html**.

Most of the time, when students complete high school, they still don't have a clear picture of what they want to be or what their major should be. They often hear, "Just explore, you have all the time in the world, make up your mind later." Well, that doesn't work and it's not realistic. But students that come to college knowing what they want to be and having researched that are going to finish. And that's huge.

— Dr. Diane Hollems, Former Dean of Educational Programs (Retired)
Santa Barbara City College, Santa Barbara, CA
Co-founder, *Get Focused...Stay Focused!* ™ Inititative

For Use with College-Bound and Gifted Students

Career Choices allows instructors to bring personal relevance to the academic rigor of the language arts curriculum for gifted students. High achieving, academically motivated students are often as socially insecure, unhappy, and unsure about their future as other students. What's more, they may be reluctant to admit their insecurities and talented enough to conceal them.

Before you begin, you might want to hold a parents' meeting (with your principal's permission). Reassure the parents that you know the importance of the academic mission. These students, however, are probably capable of carrying on much of that work on their own. As parents and teachers, you want to be sure that they also have the personal skills they need to be happy and satisfied individuals. By discussing the importance of problem solving, decision making, and long-range planning with parents, you should be able to demonstrate that, while their children's academic talents will get them into college, these practical skills will equip them to stay there and thrive.

Studies clearly show that students who enter college with a specific career or career area in mind are far more likely to graduate four years later. It is the strongest indicator of success in college and in an individual's future work life.

Gifted students are often programmed to believe their talents should be applied in a particular direction. Or, because they are used to having things come easily to them, some may tend to give up at the first sign of difficulty. They may also be overwhelmed by the sheer number of choices available to them. It is very important, therefore, that they develop the skills and attitudes (decision making, anxiety tolerance, overcoming fears, and so on) needed to be their own best and happiest person.

Observing that many students struggled to choose a major in college, Vonore High School in Vonore, Tennessee, recognized the importance of providing career guidance to college-bound students and career and technical students. Teacher Priscilla Gregory also successfully facilitated a partnership with a local company that ultimately hired many graduating students and offered college-bound students the opportunity to interview for management positions after graduation. Read more about Vonore's program at **www.whatworkscareerchoices.com/int15.html**.

Career and Life Planning Course

The 21st century workplace demands employees who can effectively and efficiently navigate the challenges of a rapidly changing society. As a result, many schools are instituting career exploration and planning courses to build 21st century skills and provide their students with the best chance of achieving economic self-sufficiency.

With innovative features for building 21st century skills, *Career Choices*, the **Workbook and Portfolio**, and My10yearPlan.com® provide a solid framework for an effective career education course. The addition of *Possibilities* and/or *Lifestyle Math* can easily infuse academic relevancy.

☐ Support of core subjects and 21st century themes

- *Career Choices* motivates students to apply themselves by helping them recognize the role academic skills play in their lives outside of the classroom.

☐ Learning and innovation skills

- The planning process facilitated by *Career Choices* gives students practice with critical, creative, and strategic thinking—higher order thinking skills required for success in the 21st century workplace.

☐ Communication and collaboration

- *Career Choices* is designed to deliver a project-based learning experience that is student centered versus subject centered, dialectic versus didactic, and project based.

☐ Life and career skills

- *Career Choices* is effective in building the SCANS competencies—foundation skills, systems development, interpersonal skills, resource management, information management, and technology.

When the speech course requirement was removed at San Gabriel High School in California, the communications department reinvented their class as a career guidance course. Students were given the opportunity to explore their own unique values and dreams while developing valuable communication skills. Read more at www.whatworkscareerchoices.com/int12.html.

Thematic English/Languages Arts Course

Integration with English/Language Arts to Meet Common Core State Standards

When *Career Choices* is paired with *Possibilities*, there is a very natural fit for incorporating career guidance into students' regular language arts class. In fact, this approach is often used to help ensure that all students are exposed to the *Career Choices* materials.

Because the selections in *Possibilities* are drawn from recommended reading lists, English teachers can easily cover the required literature and add relevancy to class discussions. *Career Choices* and *Possibilities* also fulfill the Common Core State Standards for English/Language Arts (see the correlations at www.academicinnovations.com/standards.html).

The flexibility and variety of the *Career Choices* materials allow instructors to use *Career Choices* and *Possibilities* with general, honors, and even special education students.

Some schools choose to use the *Career Choices* curriculum in a course that combines English with career and technical offerings like business or family and consumer sciences. For details and strategies for this integrated course model, see pages 3/15 to 3/16 of this *Instructor's Guide*.

Career Guidance Integrated with English

Liz Lamatrice, a career coordinator, wanted career development integrated with all academic subjects. She was thrilled to discover the *Career Choices* curriculum at an Academic Innovations workshop in Columbus, Ohio. Liz took her full set of books and passed them on to Elizabeth Truax, a guidance counselor at Edison High School in Richmond, Ohio.

What timing! Edison needed a way to support the district-wide Individual Career Plan (ICP), a process that began in the 8th grade and culminated in the 12th grade with a Career Passport. Teachers wanted an emphasis on career exploration, decision-making, and self-awareness for 10th graders. Noting the curriculum's strong literature component, English teacher Cathy Miles saw the fit right away. "Having a proven curriculum like [*Career Choices*] gave us a foundation on which to build our own unique program." She and another English teacher, Rosann Lauri, developed a program and took it into the classroom for Tech Prep and college-bound students.

Edison High School graduated the first class to experience this model English program. Of the 221 graduates, 70% went on to pursue further education, generating over $1 million in academic scholarships (nearly double the amount of the year before). Cathy attributed the increase to a rise in ambition on the part of students who set goals for their futures while sophomores. Cathy and Rosann gave talks and workshops for other teachers, and their model program spread from school to school, with over 1,500 students receiving career guidance through academic classes.

For a complete profile of this effort, visit www.academicinnovations.com/library/howtoeng.pdf.

Dual Enrollment Freshman Transition (DEFT) Course for a
Get Focused…Stay Focused!™ Initiative

More and more, secondary schools and local colleges are partnering to develop programs that ensure all students graduate from high school career and college ready. One such progressive program was developed by Santa Barbara City College using the *Career Choices* curriculum. Their Dual Enrollment Freshman Transition semester course is required of all freshmen in the high schools of both the Santa Barbara and Carpinteria districts.

Why not collaborate with your local college to help students develop comprehensive 10-year plans with the *Career Choices* curriculum while reaping the added benefits of a rigorous dual enrollment freshman transition course? Dual enrollment encourages students to see themselves as college students, gives them the confidence that they can complete college-level work, and allows them to earn credits on their college transcripts, which studies show increases the likelihood that students will enroll in college after high school.

A dual enrollment freshman transition course also provides an excellent forum for starting students thinking about college options in their freshman year. By starting their planning early in high school, they can select appropriate courses and work to achieve or maintain the grades needed to be eligible for admission to the school of their choice.

Read about SBCC's pioneering efforts in developing this model based on The George Washington University's Freshman Transition Initiative at www.whatworkscareerchoices.com/deft.html, or visit the *Get Focused…Stay Focused!*™ Initiative web site at www.getfocusedstayfocused.org.

**Santa Barbara City College
was a co-winner of the
2013 Aspen Prize for Community College Excellence.**

The big picture is that if students as young as 14 years of age learn, in an informed way, what they want to do with the rest of their lives, the benefit is not only to those students but to parents, the high school, the college, and the community.

— Dr. Diane Hollems, Former Dean of Educational Programs (Retired)
Santa Barbara City College, Santa Barbara, CA
Co-founder, *Get Focused…Stay Focused!*™ Inititative

Used as an Academically Integrated Course
Flexible for a Variety of Interdisciplinary Models

Addressing the Common Core State Standards

For those who prefer a team teaching or interdisciplinary approach, the **Career Choices** program offers outstanding potential, both for structured schools and less traditional settings. And an academically integrated course is a wonderful way to support students' mastery of the Common Core State Standards while delivering essential 21st century skills.

The **Possibilities** anthology makes it easy for English teachers to partner with colleagues from many different disciplines. And, **Lifestyle Math** can be used in the math classroom as a supplemental text for all math levels, or by the consumer education, business, or economics instructor.

See pages 8/5–8/7 of this **Instructor's Guide** for additional detail on how **Career Choices** addresses the Common Core State Standards.

Easily Integrated with Literacy and Math Programs

Career Choices, used alone, can improve reading and math skills, often dramatically. If special attention is needed or desired in these areas, the optional companion texts **Possibilities** and **Lifestyle Math** make it easy.

The **Possibilities** anthology complements and expands on the themes in the main text. As these themes are of great personal interest to adolescents, this innovative formula makes literature suddenly relevant, even to students who have exhibited little desire to read in the past. Newly motivated, they apply themselves with enthusiasm to the task of upgrading their reading and writing skills. See pages 2/20 and 8/8–8/14 for details.

Similarly, **Lifestyle Math** motivates students to learn by making math relevant on a purely personal level. In addition to learning important math skills, they experience a process that helps them create a financial plan for their desired lifestyle. It makes math interesting and shows participants they can do it if they try. It also shows the relevance of math in their lives, today and in the future. See pages 2/21 and 8/15 for details.

Summer programs in Havre, Montana, and Denver, Colorado, used **Career Choices** to help students with severe academic deficiencies, and both programs witnessed amazing improvements in reading and math within a number of weeks.

Read about Havre's results at www.whatworkscareerchoices.com/int01.html and Denver's results at www.whatworkscareerchoices.com/int02.html.

Integrated with English/Language Arts

Prepare your students to make choices they never knew they had and learn strategies they never knew they could master using *Career Choices*, all while addressing the Common Core State Standards for English (see www.academicinnovations.com/standards.html for the correlations). Consider the other subjects that can be combined with English to add relevance and provide opportunities for "double dosing" to meet the standards.

English/Language Arts or Communications

In many of the schools using the *Career Choices* curriculum, it is the English teachers who teach the course. Some instructors use only the *Career Choices* text with the *Workbook and Portfolio*, and some supplement the *Career Choices* text with *Possibilities*.

Freshman Transition/Seminar and English/Language Arts

In collaboration, the Freshman Transition course instructor presents the *Career Choices* text along with the *Workbook and Portfolio,* and the English/language arts instructor teaches from *Possibilities*.

English/Language Arts and Guidance Department

Many English/language arts teachers have teamed up with the guidance department to enrich the curriculum by having a guidance counselor come in at appropriate points to lead the lesson for the day. Specific activities in Section 4 of this guide are noted. At the end of the course, students meet with their guidance counselor and use their 10-year plans as a starting point for the planning session.

Family and Consumer Sciences and English/Language Arts

Because of the life planning expertise of family and consumer sciences instructors, some schools have used this model. The family and consumer sciences teachers use the *Career Choices* text while the English teachers use *Possibilities*.

Business or Technology and English/Language Arts

Because communication and computer skills are integral to success in both post-secondary education and the workplace, these disciplines can be combined to form a powerful program for all students. The online course materials provide a meaningful application as students learn and practice using technology in real-world settings.

After the successful debut of a stand-alone *Career Choices* program in the home economics department, Lincoln High School English and keyboarding teachers realigned their curriculum to complement the Career Education class and stimulate a similar level of enthusiasm for their subjects (www.whatworkscareerchoices.com/int11.html).

You can read more stories about creative academic integration with *Career Choices* at www.whatworkscareerchoices.com/successstoriesai.html.

Interdisciplinary Programs for Freshman Academies or Career Academies

Helping students make considered, informed choices is a key component in the success of any academy. A comprehensive guidance course should be provided to all academy students during their first semester.

A Team of English/Language Arts, Math, and Social Studies Instructors

Schools using this format are usually divided into "houses" or clusters. The material in the *Career Choices* text is presented by the social studies instructor, *Possibilities* by the English teacher, and *Lifestyle Math* by the math teacher. This format is either a semester course or accomplished over a full school year.

Career Academies

Career Academies or Tech Prep programs are using the *Career Choices* texts as a foundation course to launch students. The course is designed to help students choose a career path, and instructors from a variety of career and technical disciplines could deliver the course successfully.

Business Education and English/Language Arts

Many business education instructors are right at home with the material in *Career Choices* and *Lifestyle Math*. Teaming with the English/language arts department to use *Possibilities* can provide an effective interdisciplinary approach to learning.

Tumwater High School in Tumwater, Washington, created an Applied English and Technology class and, ultimately, received the Washington Educators Association's "Leaders in Restructuring Award" for an innovative program developed "from the bottom up" in a site-based setting. Read more at www.whatworkscareerchoices.com/int16.html.

For more examples of how schools have used *Career Choices* is used in a variety of integrated and interdisciplinary settings, visit www.whatworkscareerchoices.com/successstoriesai.html.

The Career Choices *Curriculum*

Used as the Curriculum for Daily Advisories

As state and federal regulations mandate more personal and career guidance for all students, *Career Choices* allows already overworked counselors to provide high quality information and advice for every individual in their school. The curriculum meets all mandated requirements and can be used effectively in individual and group counseling programs, as well as in the classroom.

A Guidance Class: Counselor in the Classroom

In some schools, the counseling staff finds that one of the most efficient and effective ways to provide comprehensive guidance to students is in a classroom setting with a structured curriculum. Semester and year-long courses are designed and taught by the counselors. When counselors use *Career Choices* in the classroom, they become an important part of the teaching team.

Counselors at St. Marys High School in St. Mary's, Pennsylvania, had an easier time scheduling students in college-bound or Tech Prep pathways after they began teaching *Career Choices* course to help students make their decisions. The counselors were uniquely qualified to teach this course given their counseling degrees.

Read more at www.whatworkscareerchoices.com/int20.html.

Whole-School Advisory

Once schools discover the power of a comprehensive guidance program that culminates with an online education and career plan, they want to ensure that students in all grades have the same opportunity. Some schools take five minutes off each class period to create an extra 30- to 35-minute period each day. This period allows all students to focus on working through *Career Choices* and developing their 10-year plans.

A School-Wide Class: All Students Take the Course

At McCormick High School in McCormick, South Carolina, the whole school took the *Career Choices* course over a one-year period. Class periods were adjusted so that once each week, at the same time, every instructor in the school taught from the *Career Choices* text along with the *Workbook and Portfolio*. After that one year, McCormick had improved from having a South Carolina rating of "below average" to being rated one of two "excellent" schools in the state. Read the story at www.whatworkscareerchoices.com/mccormick.html.

Used as the Foundation Course of a School-wide Initiative to Ensure Career and College Readiness

Your school can transform its retention and graduation rates as well as campus culture by:

- mandating that all incoming students complete a *Career Choices* course and develop an online 10-year plan

- scheduling the periodic review and updating of 10th, 11th, and 12th grade students' 10-year plans, and

- training staff and students to use the 10-year plans as advisory and academic coaching tools throughout students' time in high school.

My10yearPlan.com® provides an online planning area where students can store, update, and save —for the duration of their time in school—the work and data related to the development of their 10-year plans. Quick and easy to access, it provides data-driven information about each student's future plans.

For advisory situations to function at the highest level, instructors, counselors, and advisors need quantitative information about each student as it relates to their education and career goals. Guidance is more effective when it's based on specific examples rather than general impressions or vague notions about the student. If advice and mentoring is founded in each student's identifiable goals and lifestyle expectations, it has more meaning. By having this information online, all appropriate stakeholders can quickly access this in-depth information, providing individual guidance easily and efficiently.

Storing the 10-year plan online means students can update their plans throughout their time in high school. When a student's 10-year plan is online and dynamic, any academic department can provide opportunities for students to rework and update their plans utilizing the knowledge students gather in their other courses.

You'll want to instruct all of your guidance staff on the use of My10yearPlan.com® to provide students with personalized academic counseling (see pages 9/2 and 9/6) and consider requiring that students meet with a counselor at least once a year. You'll want to train regular instructional staff on My10yearPlan.com® for use in advisory or academic coaching sessions or so they can develop tie-in activities related to their instruction.

This effort requires planning and coordination, but once this system of challenging students to revisit and update their 10-year plans is embedded into the culture of your school, you'll have more engaged students. Student education and career plans have more meaning and remind students of the consequences of not performing up to their personal best or leaving school without a degree.

The more students are asked to rethink and rework their plans, the more meaningful the plans will become and the more likely they are to value and strive to meet their stated education and career goals. As they continue to adjust their plans to reflect current dreams, hopes, and aspirations, ownership increases.

In addition, as students get in the habit of updating their plans, they become more comfortable with making decisions that involve change—which in itself is a crucial survival skill in the workplace of the 21st century. Why? Career stability is far less common due to globalization and technological advancements. Knowing how to navigate the ever-changing world of work is crucial. Those that fail to adapt to this new workforce reality could be condemned to subsistence living.

Finally, for those students considering dropping out (whether it's leaving school physically or emotionally) and, therefore, limiting their chances of achieving their full potential, this constant reminder of the consequences of dropping out will keep them in school. Because they have completed a *Career Choices* course, they understand the consequences of not following through with their education plans.

If you are interested in the school-wide model and want an easy-to-implement solution, you'll want to know about

The *Get Focused…Stay Focused!*™ Initiative

The Ultimate School-wide Initiative

Developed at Santa Barbara City College, the ***Get Focused…Stay Focused!***™ Initiative is a school-wide program that ensures students:

- ✓ Are college- and career-ready
- ✓ Have an informed declared major
- ✓ Have chosen a college or post-secondary path
- ✓ Have a meaningful 10-year Career and Education Plan

The founders of the ***Get Focused…Stay Focused!***™ Initiative are working to develop a national resource center to share their work with schools throughout the country. For details, visit www.getfocusedstayfocused.org.

Santa Barbara City College was a co-winner of the 2013 Aspen Prize for Community College Excellence.

Mission of the *Get Focused…Stay Focused!*™ National Resource Center

To promote the institutionalization of the *Get Focused…Stay Focused!*™ process that culminates with all students developing a meaningful and quantitative online 10-year plan in their freshman year of high school or college. In high school, the 10-year plan will be systematically updated in the 10th, 11th, and 12th grades and used for academic coaching and advisory efforts throughout high school and into college. The planning process will provide the impetus to motivate students to stay in school (high school and college) and achieve a self-sufficient and productive life.

The big picture is that if students as young as 14 years of age learn, in an informed way, what they want to do with the rest of their lives, the benefit is not only to those students but to parents, the high school, the college, and the community.

— Dr. Diane Hollems, Former Dean of Educational Programs (Retired)
Santa Barbara City College, Santa Barbara, CA
Co-founder, *Get Focused…Stay Focused!*™ Inititative

Section 4—The Most Important Section for Instructors

Lesson Plan Suggestions for Each Activity

- This section contains suggested lesson plans for each activity in the *Career Choices Series*, including a learning objective, presentation suggestions, and supplemental class activities and resources.

- We have provided more suggestions than you will have the time to implement, so take note of the ones you feel fit best with the main objectives of your particular course and your student population.

- Fit these lesson plans into your pacing guide (described in Section 10) with the ultimate goal of developing 10-year Plans.

These chapter-by-chapter, exercise-by-exercise classroom suggestions should be helpful as you develop your lesson plans. Each exercise has a learning objective with presentation suggestions. In addition, many have suggestions for optional activities, resources, and suggested reading and writing assignments along with the Common Core State Standards that are directly addressed in that lesson.

Make notes for yourself as you experiment with what works best with your students, and please remember to share your ideas so we can consider them for a future version of this *Instructor's Guide*.

Optional Course Enhancements:

You'll want to incorporate as many of the enhancements as you have time for. They include:

My10yearPlan Essentials or **Interactive**: See pages 2/8–2/9 and Section 9

The Motivational Introduction Videos: See page 4/2

CareerChoices.com: See pages 2/23 and Section 8

Possibilities: See pages 2/20, 3/12, 3/14,–3/16. and Section 8

Lifestyle Math and LifestyleMath.com: See pages 2/21–2/22, 3/14, 3/16, 4/49 and Section 8

Common Core State Standards:

Throughout this section and in Section 8 we'll point out the standards addressed in the activities. These new standards increase the depth with which students study certain topics, emphasize the use of more informational texts, and rely on higher order cognitive skills, requiring less memorization and more analyzing—all of which aligns beautifully with the overarching goals of *Career Choices*.

Course Introduction

Suggested Agenda for the First Class Session(s) to Introduce the Course and the 10-year Plan

Pre-course Survey:

In order to get the best data for course and individual assessment, have students complete the pre-course survey before any introductions about the course and it's goals. This can be done with paper and pencil or online at My10yearPlan.com (see pages 14/9–14/14).

Learning Objective: To motivate students to value their 10-year Plan and get excited about what they are going to learn about themselves.

Presentation Suggestions:

Introduction/Welcome: Ask students:

- *If you were asked what you would be doing in 10 years, what would your answer be?*
- *How many of you don't know or haven't thought about this?*
- *Why would this be good to know?*

Motivational Introduction Video: Show the video "Introduction to *Career Choices*" hosted by Dain Blanton and available on The Teachers' Lounge or on My10yearPlan.com®.

Introduce the 10-year Plan: Begin with the end in mind by showing students a sample of the product* they will produce—a 10-year plan.

- If using only the *Career Choices* textbook and *Workbook and Portfolio*, show students a fictional student's 10-year plan from Chapter 12
- If using My10yearPlan.com® Essentials, show students a fictional student's My 10-year Plan Summary Page
- If using My10yearPlan.com® Interactive, provide a printed copy of a fictional student's My 10-year Plan and Portfolio in a three-ring binder

Printable PDFs of these fictional plans can be found in the Resource Cupboard of The Teachers' Lounge.

Point out to students that they can share these documents with advisors and counselors, close friends, girlfriends/boyfriends, parents, and mentors. Their plans will be valuable and should be periodically reviewed and updated throughout their lives. The plan data will come in handy when interviewing for college admission or a job, and someday they'll want to share their plan with their own children.

Advise students now if you are going to use their 10-year plan as the course final (see pages 14/4–14/5).

My10yearPlan.com®: If your course utilizes My10yearPlan.com®, demonstrate how to log in to the site and remind students to take the pre-course survey (if you've enabled it). Using a demo student account, provide students with a live walk-through of the basic navigation and features (either projecting to a screen, interactive whiteboard, or through your online classroom).

- The drop-down menus under each chapter heading provide quick access to the activities in order.
- There is an introductory video for each chapter hosted by Dain Blanton. Watch the appropriate chapter video BEFORE you start working on each chapter.
- The HELP section on the side bar provides access to video tutorials and general troubleshooting hints

15-hour Interdisciplinary Lesson Plan for a Successful Launch can be found on the online version of this *Instructor's Guide*. See page 10/12 for details.

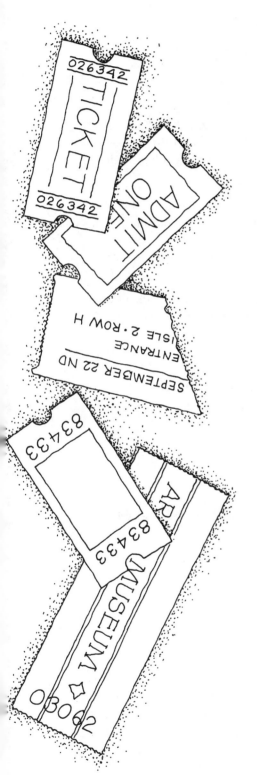

Section 1: Who Am I?

Chapter 1

Envisioning Your Future

As you move into Chapter 1, have students read the opening stories aloud.

The overall goal of this course is to help each student become aware of his or her own identity and ambitions, and to develop a 10-year action plan for realizing these dreams. The basic purpose of the first chapter is to get students to start thinking about an ideal future. It also provides some baseline information on how much thought students have given this topic and whether their ambitions are relatively high or low. This information should be taken into account as you plan the remainder of the course.

As you begin, be careful not to step on anyone's dreams. A goal may seem unrealistic for a particular student, but many, many people who demonstrate little potential even in college go on to excel in their future careers. You may need to remind some students from time to time that success requires action in addition to vision. It may also be appropriate to encourage some students to aim higher if you sense they lack confidence in their own capabilities.

Something That Flies

Before reading the text on pages 6–7 of *Career Choices*, ask students to partner up with another student and decide what they would bring back to class if they were given the assignment *"Bring something that flies"*. Student teams will record their ideas on a piece of paper. Have each team report out to the class.

Now read pages 6–7 aloud, emphasizing the last paragraph of the introduction: **It's not the purpose of the course to make a final career choice. Students will, however, learn a PROCESS for making rewarding choices in the future.**

Vision Plus Energy
Equals Success

Learning Objective:

To help students realize that success does not come just from daydreaming, but from combining a vision with appropriate and necessary actions.

Presentation Suggestions:

Discuss the difference between daydreaming and working toward a vision. Emphasize that daydreaming is an important first step, but that it must be followed by action if dreams are to become reality. Can students think of daydreams they've had that they did not work to realize? Did the daydreams come true?

After they work through the charts on page 13, ask the students to reflect on what they learned. While students can't know exactly what actions these people took, the class should be able to think of some reasonable steps based on their accomplishments.

Activities:

Ask the class to think of synonyms for the words *vision* (dream, imagination, conception, creation, inspiration, invention, fantasy, fabrication) and *energy* (activity, liveliness, spirit, vivacity, eagerness, zeal, vigor). What images do these terms suggest?

Chapter Introduction Video:

At the beginning of this chapter, consider showing the motivational chapter introduction video featuring Olympic Gold Medalist Dain Blanton (found on **The Teachers' Lounge**). Or, if your students are regularly using **My10yearPlan.com®**, have them watch the video online before starting their work in this chapter.

Common Core Standards for English

W.9-10.3. Write narratives to develop real or imagined experiences or events using effective technique, well-chosen details, and well-structured event sequences.

I invited a Native American artist to my class to teach my students how to make "DreamCatchers."

— Barbara Muir, Teacher
North High School, Minneapolis, MN

Distribute short magazine articles on the visions of famous people. (Newsweek online, Parade magazine, etc.) As a small group activity, have students write a phrase explaining the vision of each celebrity.

— Sharon Hurwitz, English Teacher/Technology Facilitator
Bethel High School, Hampton, VA

Common Core Standards for English

W.9-10.9. Draw evidence from literary or informational texts to support analysis, reflection, and research.

Optional

The Secret Life of Walter Mitty
by James Thurber

Page 11–18

Read after completing pages 10–13 in *Career Choices*

It is very important to begin this course by setting the tone properly. At Marquette Senior High School, teachers want students to understand that our year-long Transitions class is unlike any other class they have ever had, or will likely ever have in their future. Holly Warchock, Transitions teacher at MSHS created an activity that does just that. She adapted the idea from something she heard at the 2012 Focus on Freshmen conference held in Los Angeles, CA.

The lesson is taught on the first day of school. Students are greeted at the classroom door and given an invitation to graduate in four years with their peers. Pomp and Circumstance is played as students are handed a "future diploma" with their names on it and the signature of their Transitions teacher and the principal. The principal and assistant principals are in each classroom during the ceremonies to help create a ceremonial feeling. Statistics are shared regarding graduation rates and how income levels vary with levels of education. The students then sign their names onto a graduation gown using fabric paint. These gowns are displayed in the freshman hallway display case as a reminder of their promise to graduate in four years with their peers. The gowns will then be displayed at their graduation ceremony in four years.

*This activity is a great way to set the tone for a new year in a new school! We like to say, "Freshman year is a **fresh** start. You can be whomever you choose to be at our school!" This activity helps set a tone that the choices they make in high school greatly impact their future beyond our school doors. We also invited the local media to cover the event. It is so important to let your media know what is going on in your classroom. Having community support for your Transitions class helps the impact reach beyond the limited audience you have in your classroom each day.*

— Becky Simmons, Transitions Lesson Coordinator
Marquette Senior High School, Marquette, MI

Envisioning Your Future

Page 14   Page 6

Learning Objective:

To have students begin imagining the kind of future they would find most satisfying.

This provides baseline information that can be used to measure growth and learning.

Presentation Suggestions:

After reading the introductory material for this exercise, ask students to close their eyes and imagine their ideal future lives. Allow several minutes for the vision to appear, then have students write about what they imagined. You may want to have students share their visions as a way of getting to know each other better (and to help you know what their thoughts are at this point). You'll want to review everyone's description, whether it is shared with the class or not. This will help you gauge how much progress individuals are making as they proceed through the class.

This will be a difficult exercise for some people in the class. After they have attempted this task, reassure them that even if they had no vision at all, it's okay. They will develop a vision soon enough.

Refer again to the previous exercise, emphasizing that energy must match vision in order to achieve success.

This may be a good time to bring the school counselor into the class as a resource person and facilitator.

My10yearPlan.com® Essentials:

This is a keystone activity. Data will be extracted and used in each student's *My 10-year Plan Summary Page*. Direct students to enter their work from this activity on My10yearPlan.com® the next time they log on. For more information, see Section 9 of this guide.

> *I added musical selections to enhance my program. For example, for Martin Luther King's "I Have a Dream," I used Garth Brooks' "We Shall Be Free."*
>
> — Belinda Boyce, English Teacher
> Buckeye Local High School, Rayland, OH

Optional

A Psalm of Life
by Henry Wadsworth Longfellow

Dreams
by Langston Hughes

I Have a Dream… (speech)
by Martin Luther King, Jr.

Page 19–32

Read after completing page 14 in *Career Choices*

Common Core Standards for English

RI.9-10.6. Determine an author's point of view or purpose in a text and analyze how an author uses rhetoric to advance that point of view or purpose.

RI.9-10.9. Analyze seminal U.S. documents of historical and literary significance (e.g., Washington's Farewell Address, the Gettysburg Address, Roosevelt's Four Freedoms speech, King's "Letter from Birmingham Jail"), including how they address related themes and concepts.

Linda Paulson's "Visualizer" Activity

The idea for "visualizers" or "fantasy tuner-inners" came to Linda Paulson, 9th grade language arts teacher in Grafton, North Dakota, one day in class when students couldn't seem to grasp the meaning of James Thurber's story, "The Secret Life of Walter Mitty" (*Possibilities*, pages 11–18). Clearly, the students needed a way to get in touch with their hopes and dreams.

Paulson asked each student to bring a wire coat hanger (you may want to substitute pipe cleaners) to class the following day, and the first "visualizers" were born. The hangers were bent any way the students hose. The main requirement was that they be worn on their heads in order to receive visions of their futures.

Today, class members plan ahead and bring all sorts of materials to school to decorate their vision receivers, which have become much more sophisticated. Paulson's only stipulation is that only found objects can be used; nothing can be bought specifically for the project.

Students can wear their new head gear for an entire day (they get points for doing so). In Paulson's English class, they get time to fantasize about possibilities for their own lives — living somewhere else, holding a particular job, or whatever — and then write about that fantasy (*Career Choices*, page 14). In other classes, teachers allow five or ten minutes on that day to pose a question related to their subject, and students again imagine a solution and write it down. They receive credit for their work in every class.

Although the hats are formally used on this day, Paulson keeps them in her classroom. Students have permission to wear them "whenever they feel the need." It gives them "a right to be playful," Paulson says, and also breaks down barriers that can hold a young person's imagination in check.

What a wonderful way to help students begin to get in touch with their own visions of their future. Congratulations, Linda, on a fabulous idea!

Why People Work

Learning Objective:

To illustrate that work is not just a way to earn a living, but an important part of most people's identity.

Presentation Suggestions:

Review the reasons why people work listed in the book. Ask the class if they can think of other possible reasons. Why do they think their friends and family members work? Students will probably come to the conclusion that people work for a combination of all of these reasons.

When we studied "The Prophet," we divided our students into 6 groups with each group writing a section in their own words. As a large group we put all 6 parts together and the end result was fantastic!

— Lisa Demuth, Special Education Educator
Walnut Creek Campus, West Des Moines, IA

Optional

Work, an excerpt from *The Prophet*
by Kahlil Gibran

Page 33–36

Read after completing page 15 in *Career Choices*

Everybody Works

Page 17   Page 7

Learning Objective:

To help students recognize the scope and diversity of the things every individual accomplishes on a daily basis.

Presentation Suggestions:

Discuss work in terms of the things students do every day and ask them to answer the questions on page 17. Follow with class discussion. How do students feel about their accomplishments (proud, intelligent, resentful, satisfied, talented, lucky, relieved)?

Be sure to emphasize that everything we "do" is work. A student is a worker; unpaid, perhaps, but still a worker.

Activities:

Because students are going to be asked how they "feel" about something throughout this course, define emotions and feelings.

Brainstorm with the class a list of emotions and feelings. Are they adjectives or verbs? You might debate this issue. Noted psychologist Dr. William Glasser argues that emotions and feelings are verbs because you choose them (e.g., you choose to be angry).

As an activity for Chapter 1, I showed my class the music video for "I Believe I Can Fly" from the Space Jam soundtrack. My students made tent cards for their desks and decorated them as a part of "Defining Success," plus for the first five days during Chapter 1, I asked the students to write comments or questions on the back side of their tent cards as sort of a daily assessment.

—— Mark Reeves, Transition Teacher,
Oscar Smith High School, Chesapeake, VA

Defining Success
Your Definition of Success

Page 18–19   Page 8–9

Learning Objective:

To help students see that individuals have personal definitions of success and that the only one they need to meet is their own.

Presentation Suggestions:

In contemporary American society, success is often seen in terms of money, power, or material possessions. Assure students that while these things may make them appear successful to the rest of the world, they hardly guarantee a life of contentment. Everyone must define success personally. It is only by living up to that definition that people feel truly successful. Have students individually read the statements on the chart and mark whether they strongly agree, agree, are not sure, disagree, or strongly disagree with each definition. There are no right or wrong answers. The point is to help students sort out their own feelings on the topic. They should write their own definition of success on page 9 of their workbook and sign it.

Allow plenty of time for students to think about the quotations, or assign this exercise as homework. Emphasize in your discussion that their own definitions are likely to change depending on what's going on in their life. A new parent who formerly defined success as getting ahead at work may decide that raising a healthy, happy child is far more important. Someone taken seriously ill might redefine success as getting and staying well.

Activities:

Ask students how they think certain well-known individuals (Abraham Lincoln, Bill Gates, Dr. Phil, Steven Spielberg, Jennifer Lopez, J.K. Rowling, Venus Williams) would define success, based on their actions.

You may want to have students view the movie *Forrest Gump* for your first Video Book Club discussion (see listings on page 11/23–11/25). Did Forrest have a vision of success? What energy did he display? How does the class think he would define success for himself? Is Forrest a good role model for the class? Why or why not?

My10yearPlan.com® Essentials:

This is a keystone activity. Data will be extracted and used in each student's *My 10-year Plan Summary Page*. Direct students to enter their work from this activity on My10yearPlan.com® the next time they log on. For more information, see Section 9 of this guide.

Reading Assignment:

Bless the Beasts and the Children, by Glenden Swarthout

This book centers around a group of young "misfits" who have been sent to camp to be "straightened out." The group comes together as one by one they are rejected by the other groups in camp. The boys go on an unusual quest to see a herd of buffalo sentenced to a cruel death by the park service and, in so doing, find a measure of their own worth and freedom. This book is an excellent starting point for discussions on setting and achieving goals and defining and attaining personal success.

Course Wrap-Up

Ask students to write their own definitions of success entitled "Success Is…" Refer them to the Robert Louis Stevenson quotation at the bottom of page 283 in *Career Choices*. Throughout the course, there will be a great deal of discussion and debate as to what success is.

By the end of the course, each student should have a more complete personal definition. Allow at least a couple of days to complete the assignment; students will need time to think about it. This is not an activity that should be worked on as a group. Explain that the personal nature of the task requires individual contemplation.

Energizer:

Once they have completed their expanded definitions of success, have students turn them into an art project using computer printouts of their definitions, typeset similar to those in the book. Suggest the students "sign" their quotations similar to the style used for quotes in *Career Choices*. Once the projects are complete, post them around the room for everyone to share. If there are appropriate display areas in the school, why not share the project at a parent/teacher meeting, a school board meeting, or with other students?

At the time you make the assignment, why not share your own success quotation and art project?

The Stevenson quotation written in calligraphy with completed art would make a lovely classroom decoration. Collaborate with your art department on this or assign to a student interested in a career in visual arts.

Common Core Standards for English

SL.9-10.5. Make strategic use of digital media (e.g., textual, graphical, audio, visual, and interactive elements) in presentations to enhance understanding of findings, reasoning, and evidence and to add interest.

The writing activities were most appealing to the students. For example, writing the last page of Richard Cory's diary.

— Belinda Boyce, English Teacher
Buckeye Local High School, Rayland, OH

Optional

Richard Cory
by Edwin Arlington Robinson

Page 37–39

Read after completing pages 18–21 in *Career Choices*

Making Career Choices

Page 20–21   Page 9

Learning Objective:

To help students identify their own decision-making patterns and evaluate the effectiveness of these patterns.

Presentation Suggestions:

After students read the stories about the various decision-making patterns, ask them to evaluate and discuss:

- which patterns they use most often,

- which patterns are likely to lead to the most desirable results, and

- which patterns are likely to lead to the least desirable results.

Let students know they will learn much more about decision-making as they work through *Career Choices*.

While students are entering the room, have the Simon and Garfunkel song "Richard Cory" playing. Then have the students read the poem "Richard Cory" in Possibilities *and answer the questions following the work.*

— Sharon Hurwitz, English Teacher/Technology Facilitator
Bethel High School, Hampton, VA

Career Portfolio Notebook

My10yearPlan.com® gives your students online access to their career, education, and lifestyle data. Yet, for many individuals, having the information "in print" in a Career Portfolio Notebook is also desirable. Consider using this activity as a project to meet your Common Core Standards for English.

A career portfolio is an intentional collection of the records, work samples, and certificates that demonstrate an individual's qualifications, skills, experience, and achievements. The most effective portfolios are organized from a career development perspective. It is not only a product used to demonstrate competencies to a potential employer—it is also a process. A career portfolio is a way to track what an individual has accomplished and plan for the skills still needed—all in the context of the careers that will meet both an individual's emotional and financial needs.

How to Create a Career Portfolio Notebook

Instruct your students to select a three-ring binder with a two- or three-inch spine and a packet of tabbed notebook dividers. This format allows students to update and customize this notebook throughout their lifetime.

Sections 1 and 2 are the planning portions of their portfolio. Label the first tab *Career Exploration Activities* and the second tab *Professional Development Plan*. Include the documents listed below in the appropriate section.

Section 1—Career Exploration Activities

Activity	Career Choices Page	Workbook & Portfolio Page
Envisioning Your Future	14	6
Your Personal Profile bull's-eye chart	27	11
Components of Lifestyle	63	28
Your Budget Profile for your desired lifestyle in 10 years	92–93	42
Your Chart describing your ideal career characteristics	134	62
Career Interest Surveys	150–155	68–73
Career Decision-Making Chart	177	83

Section 2—Your Professional Development Plan

Activity	Career Choices Page	Workbook & Portfolio Page
Goal-Setting Chart	189–190	87
Transferable Skills Chart	begun on 246	101
Career Alternatives Ladder	227	109
Job Application and Interview Questions	257–259	112–113
Your Education and Training Plan	270–273	116–118
Your Plan – Goals for education/training, living arrangements, employment, and finances for the next 10 years	278–282	121–124

Section 3—Documentation of Competencies

In addition, have students create a tab sheet for each of the bulleted topics listed below. Review what should be included behind each tab and encourage students to make it a habit to place these important documents in their portfolio as they are completed or acquired. That way, when an opportunity arises for an important interview, the documents are readily available.

- Your resume

- Work or project samples

- Letters of recommendation

- Certificates, diplomas, awards

- Records of work experience (paid and unpaid)

Gathering the Documents for a Career Portfolio

Sections 1 and 2

Most of the documents listed are the keystone activities noted with the My10yearPlan.com® logo in their *Career Choices Workbook and Portfolio*. These documents can be downloaded directly from My10yearPlan.com® and then edited as needed. Students may either add these completed surveys, charts, and activities to their three-ring binder as they complete them or at the end of the course. Suggest they keep their completed *Workbook and Portfolio for Career Choices* in the back cover pocket of their three-ring binder for review in the future. Remind your students they will want to continually update these charts and surveys as they mature, gain experience, and change their goals.

Section 3

This will be an ongoing process over the course of their lives, and it is rewarding for an individual to watch this section grow. For instance, whenever they receive a letter of recommendation (from a teacher, counselor, employer, or community source) they'll want to keep a copy in their portfolio. The same is true for copies of certificates, diplomas, and awards. Employers and colleges like to see samples of an individual's writing and technical skills. Written reports or photographs of completed projects should also be included. A resume, work history, or curriculum vitae is a dynamic document that should be revised with each position, promotion, or volunteer activity.

How to Use the Career Portfolio

- *Career exploration and planning*—Encourage students to take their notebooks with them whenever they meet with their school counselors, mentors, instructors, and advisors.

- *Employment and college interviews*—Before an interview, the documents mentioned should be removed from the binder and placed in an appropriate professional-looking folder.

- *Career changes* — If future workplace conditions or personal desires dictate a career change, the notebook provides the framework for creating a new vision and plan for the future. Individuals will want to follow the *Career Choices* process and re-examine the questions: Who am I, what do I want, and how do I get it?

Section 1: Who Am I?

Chapter 2

Your Personal Profile

The purpose of this chapter is to help students answer the question "Who am I?" Without a basic understanding of their own personality, values, skills, and passions, they cannot hope to make wise career and life decisions. Yet, in most career exploration courses, the subject is touched on only superficially, if at all.

For the instructor, this material offers some unique opportunities and a few potential problems. Identity, after all, is a very personal matter. Some students will be reluctant to share their innermost thoughts and desires with the class. These feelings must be respected. It is much more important for the individual to discover his or her own unique qualities than it is for the class to hear about them.

On the other hand, some students may need to overcome a bit of discomfort in order to begin thinking about these important concepts. Many men, for example, may not be used to identifying and talking about their feelings at this level. Until they can articulate their emotional responses—either verbally or in writing—their lives are likely to be less satisfying.

You are in the best position to judge the activities that will best serve your class. Some groups will be open to lively class discussions. Others may feel more comfortable—or be more honest—in writing. In all cases, students should be assured of confidentiality, if they so desire.

The activities in Chapters 2, 3, 4, and 5 constitute a formal career interest and aptitude assessment. The information collected provides the personalized data necessary to begin researching career opportunities that match a student's traits and desires. With this information, they can analyze the effect personal interests and aptitudes have on educational and career planning.

Your Personal Profile
(Bull's Eye Chart)

Page 24–27   Page 11

Learning Objective:

To help students discover the many layers of qualities and characteristics that make up their unique identities, and to help them appreciate how knowing one's identity is a necessary and ongoing part of any rewarding life.

Presentation Suggestions:

Before you begin, review the definitions on page 26 with the class. Then, try to complete a chart together on the board. You may use yourself as the example if you are comfortable doing so. Or, you might try to make a chart for a celebrity or historic figure the class knows well (Examples: George Washington, Oprah Winfrey, Mark Zuckerberg, Michael Jordan, Jillian Michaels, Angelina Jolie).

Begin with the outer circles of the chart, working your way toward the center.

Activities:

Ask students to make a collage representing their own passions, values, personality traits, strengths, skills, and aptitudes, roles, occupations, and vocations. If you want to do this in class, bring in large pieces of paper or poster board, scissors, glue, and an assortment of recycled magazines. Have students find images they feel represent their own identity, cut them out, and glue them to the large pieces of paper. You may wish to assign this activity as homework.

If you want to infuse technology, have students "define" themselves audio-visually with a digital collage of photos, words, songs, or whatever comes to mind. Then, as a class, try to match the projects with the students that created them.

Energizer:

Ask students to complete their own charts but not to share them with anyone. Then have class members choose a partner they feel they know well and complete a chart for him or her. Ask them to compare the second-party chart with the original. In most cases, students will find it relatively easy to complete the outer rings of the chart. However, they are unlikely to do as well with the inner ring topics.

My10yearPlan.com® Essentials:

This is a keystone activity. Data will be extracted and used in each student's *My 10-year Plan Summary Page*. Direct students to enter their work from this activity on My10yearPlan.com® the next time they log on. For more information, see Section 9 of this guide.

Chapter Introduction Video:

At the beginning of this chapter, consider showing the motivational chapter introduction video featuring Olympic Gold Medalist Dain Blanton. Or, if students are regularly using My10yearPlan.com®, have them watch the video online before starting their work in this chapter.

Follow-up at the End of the Course:

When the class has completed the book or the course, ask students to go back and update page 11 of the workbooks with new information they have gained. These newly discovered qualities and traits should be entered in a different color ink. Then assign a one-page essay on the topic "Self-Discovery: A Lifelong Process." If students are willing to share, you might post charts and essays around the room or online. Then, allow time for students to read them and follow with a group discussion.

If your class is using My10yearPlan.com®, don't forget to have the students update their bull's eye chart online as well.

Reading Assignment:

The Diary of Anne Frank by Anne Frank

Common Core Standards for English

Throughout Chapter 2, as students complete the activities to discover their own unique personalities, traits, and skills, you will find a variety of opportunities to address the following English Common Core Standards:

W.9-10.3. Write narratives to develop real or imagined experiences or events using effective technique, well-chosen details, and well-structured event sequences.

W.9-10.6. Use technology, including the Internet, to produce, publish, and update individual or shared writing products, taking advantage of technology's capacity to link to other information and to display information flexibly and dynamically.

W.9-10.7. Conduct short as well as more sustained research projects to answer a question (including a self-generated question) or solve a problem; narrow or broaden the inquiry when appropriate; synthesize multiple sources on the subject, demonstrating understanding of the subject under investigation.

W.9-10.10. Write routinely over extended time frames (time for research, reflection, and revision) and shorter time frames (a single sitting or a day or two) for a range of tasks, purposes, and audiences.

RI.9-10.7. Analyze various accounts of a subject told in different mediums (e.g., a person's life story in both print and multimedia), determining which details are emphasized in each account.

SL.9-10.5. Make strategic use of digital media (e.g., textual, graphical, audio, visual, and interactive elements) in presentations to enhance understanding of findings, reasoning, and evidence and to add interest.

After discussing values, passions, roles, vocations, etc. [bull's eye chart, Chapter 2], I show the movie Mr. Holland's Opus. *Students can clearly see all of the concepts in that film.*

— Julie Gergen, Family and Consumer Science Teacher
Dover-Eyota High School, Eyota, MN

The Personality Profile helped them see themselves as well-rounded, complex, and unique individuals.

—Bonnie Morris, Business and Careers Instructor
Anacortes High School, Anacortes, WA

Chapter two was wonderful! The students enjoyed determining their values, passions, and work styles. The activities in the guide were fun and easy to incorporate into regular class discussion and activities. This chapter was a wonderful "ice breaker."

—Kyra Krause, Special Education Teacher
Lubbock-Cooper High School, Lubbock, TX

Identifying Your Passions

Page 28–29   Page 12

Learning Objective:

To help students learn to identify and articulate those things that are extremely important to them on an emotional level.

Presentation Suggestions:

We thought about substituting another word for *passion* but, after lengthy debate, decided it was the most appropriate term. You may get some snickering from a few students. Be prepared. Use the situation to demonstrate how the things that matter most to an individual can elicit feelings of excitement similar to those usually associated with romantic or sexual passion.

Begin by writing the two definitions on page 28 in **Career Choices** on the board. The dictionary defines passion as a *"powerful emotion; boundless enthusiasm; deep overwhelming feeling; or avid interest."*

> *Passion is the energy and enthusiasm wedded to a sense*
> *of purpose that gives life meaning and pleasure.*
>
> — Carl Goldberg, clinical psychologist and author

Then have students brainstorm and write their own definitions, sharing them with the class. If someone alludes to remarks on the romantic overtones in the term, ask him or her to describe the feeling. List these on the board and then use them to help the class identify other passions. "What else makes you grin? What other situations make your heart race? What else do you do that makes you lose track of time?" And so on.

Activities:

As a group, think of words that could be substituted for *passion* or that convey the same feelings. Examples: rapture, bliss, ecstasy, euphoria, exaltation, something that makes you go "aha!" Learning to recognize the objects, events, or situations that make you feel like this is an important step toward self-knowledge.

English/Language Arts:

Have students use the list of passions they identified on page 29 to write an essay on their ideal day—one that involves as many of their favorite experiences as possible. Letitia's day, for example, might include winning a political debate while wearing her red shoes; hearing "The Star-Spangled Banner" at the start of a Lakers' game; eating chocolate during a sad movie; and walking home in a thunderstorm.

Follow-up:

Occasionally, throughout the course, ask students at the beginning of class, "Did anyone discover a new passion recently?" Be prepared for blank stares and even giggles the first few times you ask this question. Share an experience or feeling you have had or someone has shared with you. You might start this conversation among colleagues or friends to gather stories and examples, just be sure to protect confidentiality. Soon students will start sharing their experiences and ideas. The importance of this is that they will start recognizing the feeling and evaluating what is happening at the time. This simple skill will contribute to lifelong happiness.

We start this lesson off by showing the students a video clip. I've used the clip showing Dain Blanton's Olympic story, available in The Teachers' Lounge. (Other appropriate videos are available on YouTube.) This video shows the moment Dain won the gold medal for beach volleyball at the 2000 Sydney games. At the end of the video, students are asked to sit quietly and think of one word that explains how the people in the video feel about volleyball or basketball (or whatever the subject presented in a clip). Then we ask them to say their word out loud at the same time. Every time the classes have shouted out "Passion." This is a great introduction to the lesson. You can then talk about passion being more than a feeling you have about a person, but it can be a force that drives your life choices! And we end by reminding them, "If you truly love what you do, you will never work a day in your life!"

— Becky Simmons, Transitions Lesson Coordinator
Marquette Senior High School, Marquette, MI

When students began to see themselves for what they wanted instead of what other people expected, it was remarkable.

— Lauren K. Delay, Family and Consumer Science Teacher
Conestoga Public School, Murray, NE

Optional

Excerpt from *Sonnets From the Portuguese* by Elizabeth Barrett Browning

Page 40–42

Read after completing pages 28–29 in *Career Choices*

Work Values Survey

Page 31–37   Page 13–16

Learning Objective:

To help students clarify which work values are most meaningful in their own lives.

Presentation Suggestions:

Read the directions on page 31 aloud. Allow about 45 minutes for students to complete the survey and score their answers. Stress the importance of answering from their own perspective since there are no right or wrong answers. Remind the class that values can change over the course of one's life. Periodic re-evaluations are helpful.

To make scoring easier, you may wish to prepare an answer sheet which will eliminate the need to turn pages back and forth.

After students have finished scoring their surveys, have class members identify their top three values. Review the definitions on pages 36 and 37. Remind students that a combination of their values must be considered when choosing a career.

Remind the class that values (what is important to you) can change over the course of one's life. Periodic re-evaluations are helpful.

Hint: When the survey is taken on **My10yearPlan.com**®, *the computer scores it for you.*

Gender Equity Activity:

Poll the class to see if there seems to be any relationship between gender stereotypes and values identification. How many males included helping others in their top three values? How many females? How many females had power as their top value versus the males? What about money?

If any trends are evident, discuss why this might be. Women, for example, are more likely than men to value helping others. And, quite often, men will be more comfortable saying they value power than will women. Why do students think this is so? Is it biological? Societal conditioning? Is there any relationship between power and helping others? Who would be in a better position to help people: a nurse's aide or a chief surgeon?

To carry this concept further, read the children's picture book *My Way Sally* to the class. Winner of the 1989 Ben Franklin Award, this story is an allegory in which a compassionate foxhound learns that power and leadership can be used to help others. The issues addressed in the Afterword on page 47 of *My Way Sally* would make for lively class discussion.

Follow-up:

Suggest that students have their family members and friends also take the Work Values Survey (on a separate piece of paper). Do they have the same work values? Different ones? This can open new fields of communication. It is also interesting to discuss in class how students' values compare to those of these "significant others." Quite often, brothers and sisters have very different work values, even though they were raised by the same parents in the same household. Why do students think this is so?

Students created "value totems" and then orally presented their belief systems. Many of the totems were works of art.

— John Fishburne, Teacher
Cascade High School, Leavenworth, WA

Of Special Note:

This Work Values Survey is an activity that helps students identify and evaluate the kinds of preferences they have in relationship to career or work choice. For instance, some students will find they value independence, while others may value security. The individuals who value independence will not want to work in an environment that is too restrictive or set in its ways. On the other hand, the student who values security would probably want to find a career where the work is steady and predictable. A Work Values Survey merely helps an individual measure his or her priorities, predilections, and inclinations.

If you are questioned about teaching "Values," the following quote from *Newsweek* magazine may be helpful:

For the ordinary citizen, virtue is easily confused with "values." Since personal values differ, Americans argue over whose values ought to be taught. But "values" is a morally neutral term that merely indicates preference and can be quite banal. To choose vanilla over chocolate is not the same as deciding how to raise children though both express values. A virtue, by contrast, is a quality of character by which individuals habitually recognize and do the right thing. "Instead of talking about family values," says James Wilson of UCLA, "everyone would be better off talking about virtues that a decent family tries to inculcate."

— Kenneth L. Woodward
Newsweek magazine, June 13, 1994

Strengths and Personality

Page 38–43   Page 17–19

Learning Objective:

To help students identify and understand their work behavioral style as an important trait to consider when evaluating their interests and career options.

Presentation Suggestions:

You may need to review the definitions on page 39 before students complete that exercise. A number are included in the vocabulary list for this chapter.

Once they have completed the exercises on pages 39, 41, and 42, ask each "style" to go to a different corner of the room. For example, all the students whose style is (a) are dominant, the (b)'s are influencing, etc. Then read the descriptions on page 43 together. Many students will nudge each other as they agree with these very basic descriptions.

Point out that the higher the number of responses in each of the letters the more prominent those characteristics might be. Also be sure to remind the students that there are 19 different profiles in this assessment system. Very few people are pure dominance or pure steadiness. Each person has varying degrees of each of these characteristics. Without taking the actual assessment tool (a self-scoring seven-minute activity), it would be hard to know just what your real profile is. The purpose of the activity is to introduce the student to another dimension of personality that should be taken into account when choosing a career and aiming for the highest level of life satisfaction.

For additional applications of this theory of personality, see pages 162–165 in *Career Choices* and the corresponding pages in this *Instructor's Guide*.

Resources:

William Moulton Marston, *Emotions of Normal People*. Persona Press, Inc. Minneapolis, MN.

House of Cards Activity: Divide students into groups of 4. Give each group a deck of cards. Allow students a 10-minute time frame to build a free standing house of cards. As students work on the task their work behavioral style will emerge. Celebrate the house that is the tallest. Then reinforce the four work behavioral styles by identifying the team's interaction when building their house of cards.

— Cathie Klein, College & Career Readiness Coordinator
Seaman High School, Topeka, KS

Author's Note

In 1983, I attended a week-long training seminar for community agency leaders. During that week, which was sponsored by the IBM Corporation, we were introduced to the latest systems and management techniques. These tools would help us better manage our charitable agencies. Of particular interest to me was the Personal Profile System assessment tool, which major corporations were using to help them determine what jobs employees fit best.

For more than 30 years, I have used this instrument with my staff, our local Junior League, and in various consulting and personal situations. It is one of the most usable and powerful assessments I have ever seen.

I was especially impressed by how people dissatisfied in their work were able to change either their job or job description to better fit their own work behavioral style. When this took place, I saw greater job satisfaction and, therefore, higher productivity.

Pretty soon, I became somewhat intuitive as to a person's style, which impacted who I hired for specific jobs in my agency. As I counseled young people on career choice, this factor was an important component when suggesting different careers for possible research.

It would be an understatement to say I was "excited" when the Carlson Corporation gave me permission to adapt their research into a simplified evaluation exercise. I feel that this information is extremely important to individuals and will give them another means of knowing themselves and making the right choices. Major corporations have used the assessment as an important management tool for 30 years; it is exciting to see it now available to young people.

I recommend that you consider giving the actual assessment to your students. Your career center is probably aware of them and they can be found online.

I would also like to recommend use of the Personal Profile System assessment tool (the one used by corporations) for staff development and team building activities with faculty and school personnel. It will be one of the most productive staff training and sharing sessions you have ever conducted. As your team begins understanding everyone's strengths (and weaknesses, too), task force assignments and committee work will become more productive and satisfying for everyone.

And, yes, I have a dream. It is my hope that once instructors learn their own personal style of working and communicating, they will use the assessment tool to identify the style of each of their students. Then, instructors will better understand how each student learns and works and, therefore, be better able to nurture and reward those individual strengths in the academic setting.

— Mindy Bingham
Author, *Career Choices*

Your Strengths

Page 44–45   Page 20

Learning Objective:

To help students identify their strengths and understand how those capabilities can be combined with the strengths of other individuals to create an effective team.

Presentation Suggestions:

Review the list of possible strengths and ask the class to add any other traits. Divide the class into groups of four, asking group members to help each other identify their strengths. Then have students individually complete the chart on page 45.

Activities:

Write the list of adjectives from page 44 of *Career Choices* on slips of paper with one word per piece of paper. Have each student draw three slips. Using each adjective, students complete the following statement (in writing):

I am _____ when I _____.
　　　　　(chosen adjective)

Examples:

I am decisive when I choose my wardrobe.

I am spontaneous when I play with my dog.

I am sensitive when I help my friends with a problem.

Ask students to share one of their statements at the next class meeting. This exercise should help them realize that, under various circumstances, they are capable of displaying almost any character trait. Knowing this will help build their confidence and self-esteem.

I had students ask adults at home to list their child's strengths and weaknesses, while I wrote each student a letter telling him or her what I thought their strengths and one of their weaknesses were—in a very positive vein, of course. The students seemed to appreciate the interest, and several had a chance for good interaction at home because of this activity.

— Mary Nan Johnson, 9th Grade English Teacher
Lake Brantley High School, Altamonte Springs, FL

Teamwork Energizer:

Divide the class into the same groups of four. Make copies of the Group Problem-Solving Exercise that follows in this guide and give one copy to each group. Ask them to choose one of the problems described. Then, based on their individual strengths, students must decide who would play what role and what their solution would be.

Ask each group to report back to the class.

This exercise should be useful for getting across the concepts of (1) how various kinds of strengths have different values and (2) the importance teamwork—and shared responsibility—play in occupations in our changing society.

Another Energizer:

Joyce Huff, School-to-Work Coordinator from Montgomery, Missouri, enhances her class discussion of teamwork with an activity known as the Egg Drop. The class is divided into teams and each team is directed to deliver a valuable product (an egg) to a customer. Their delivery company is located at the top of a ladder and the customer is located at the bottom. Each team is given the same resources and 10 minutes to prepare their product for delivery. After the activity, the class discusses the different delivery methods, the positive and negative team behaviors that are exhibited, and how teams might improve performance in addition to the probability of success.

After either of the above energizers, ask the class to brainstorm the characteristics of an effective team member and list these traits on the board. (Their list will grow throughout this course as they participate in the team-oriented activities).

Once the class finalizes this list, ask each student to evaluate their strengths and characteristics that match those from the list and complete an "effective team member" profile to place in their Career Portfolio. Employers are looking for individuals who are good "team members." This profile will come in handy when an employer asks the standard interview question: Describe your strengths.

Using the vocabulary words in Chapter 2 of the Workbook & Portfolio, *I had students identify at least five different super heroes and assign at least one trait to each. They then had to be able to defend their super hero choices in class when they shared their results. It was really fun to hear their perceptions and get them thinking outside the box. During that week (homecoming) some came to school dressed as their super hero.*

— Holly Warchock, Transitions Teacher
Marquette Senior High School, Marquette, MI

Using Langston Hughes's poem "Dreams," I have the students replace lines 3 and 4 and lines 7 and 8 with their own creations. Then after they've written their Acrostic Poem, I have them place them back-to-back on construction paper; attached to a wire coat hanger with red yarn and we hang them as mobiles around the room.

— Felicity Swerdlow, 9th Grade English Teacher
Duarte High School, CA

Optional

Alice in Wonderland
by Lewis Carroll

Page 43–46

Read after completing pages 28–45 in *Career Choices*

Group Problem-Solving Exercise

Before choosing a situation, review the four top strengths of each group member. Record below.

Name   Strengths

_____   _____

_____   _____

_____   _____

_____   _____

Choose one of the following situations then write a plan assigning tasks to the person whose strengths will match the job.

Situation 1

Your group is stranded behind enemy lines. You need to cross five miles of dangerous terrain in order to get back to your side. You are likely to be stopped. The enemy speaks English. What would your group do, and what roles would each group member play?

Situation 2

Your boss has assigned your group to develop a new product and a plan for selling it. What would the product be, and who would be in charge of what?

Situation 3

An industrial polluter is dumping the waste from its factory into the river that flows through the middle of your lovely city. Your group decides to expose the company's illegal activities and force it to stop poisoning the water supply. What would your group do, and what jobs would you assign to each group member?

Situation 4

Your group decides to hold a fundraiser for the new homeless shelter in your town. What would your group do, and what jobs would you assign to each group member?

Which situation did you choose? _____

Name That Skill

Learning Objective:

To help students begin identifying the skills they have developed and to begin the process of developing a Skills Inventory chart.

Presentation Suggestions:

Be sure that the class understands the difference between an aptitude, an interest, and a skill. An "aptitude" is best thought of as the potential for being able to do something. A "skill" is competence in doing something. An "interest" is a desire to do something. Some aptitudes, however, may not have been tapped. For example, a student may have an aptitude for math, but, if he or she has not taken the necessary classes, that aptitude is probably not yet a skill. An interest is something a person enjoys but does not necessarily involve an aptitude or skill. Millions of people, for example, have an interest in professional football, but few have the necessary aptitude or skills to take part.

Divide the class into small groups where individuals can help each other identify their skills following the exercise on page 47.

Students with low self-esteem may have trouble identifying any of their skills or accomplishments. As a class, identify things any class member could accomplish and break them down into the skills involved.

Also point out that each student does excel in some things.

> *Example*: Getting to school on time may involve coordinating a wardrobe, compiling books and papers, making breakfast or fixing lunch, and negotiating a ride with a friend.

If your class is mature and supportive enough, you might try a "hot seat" exercise in which class members take turns voicing the skills of a particular student. Unkind remarks—or deafening silence—can be devastating to the student's self-esteem, so judge your group carefully. It's also helpful to allow a few minutes for the class to consider its answers.

Throughout your course, encourage your students to add to their list of skills as they learn or discover something new. For instance, when you notice a particular skill in a student (someone has convinced you to change a B to an A), be sure to comment—i.e., *Amanda, you are a particularly good persuader. You'll want to add that skill to your skills list.*

This list will help your students develop their transferable skills chart (in chapter 10 of **Career Choices**), an important tool for their career exploration process and strategizing their education and training plan.

My10yearPlan.com® Essentials:

This is a keystone activity. Data will be extracted and used in each student's *My 10-year Plan Summary Page*. Direct students to enter their work from this activity on My10yearPlan.com® the next time they log on. For more information, see Section 9 of this guide.

Skills Identification

Page 48   Page 22

Learning Objective:

To help students identify and understand standard skills categories so they can

- group skills for the purpose of investigating career alternatives and
- identify transferable skills.

Presentation Suggestions:

Skills are the currency of the 21st century. Employers look for candidates who have skills to match their job openings. Therefore, in order to stay competitive in the job market, individuals need the right skills.

The concept of skills identification and skill development is interwoven throughout the balance of *Career Choices*. As your students complete the activities found in their *Workbook and Portfolio*, they will continue to identify the skills they have and more important, the skills they want to or need to acquire for their chosen career path.

Discuss the skills found on page 48 to make sure students understand the meaning of each term.

Have the class try to think of ways in which each of these skills might be used in a certain activity, such as throwing a party.

Once they understand the basic skills, have students follow the directions on page 48 to start determing the skills they have and those they want to acquire.

You might recommend students create an electronic spreadsheet of skills, grouping their skills based on the three categories: data, people, and things. That way, trends may become apparent that will help students narrow their search for the best careers for them.

To demonstrate that all skills are necessary and valuable, have the class consider all of the skills that go into a project: building a house or publishing a newspaper. The plumber and the painter are as essential as the architect. The reporters may get more glory, but where would they be without the typesetters, truck drivers, and press operators?

Remind the class that they will continue to acquire new skills throughout their lives.

Activities:

List the skills of several student volunteers on the board. Ask the class to brainstorm potential careers for someone with these skills.

Examples:

Drawing, computing, instructing, reading
Engineer, architect, designer, art teacher

Math, persuading, analyzing, playing the saxophone
Small business owner, music store sales associate, math/band teacher, real estate agent

Transferable Skills:

Transferable skills are those versatile skills that can be applied and used in a variety of careers. Transferable skills help guarantee resiliency in the job market over the long haul. For instance, keyboarding/typing is required in the majority of jobs. Therefore, typing 50 words per minute is a valuable skill to have. Because most jobs require teamwork, team building, and collaboration, these are also important skills to learn.

If you study the list of transferable skills found on the Internet or in **The Teachers' Lounge**, you'll see that the majority of these skills are taught in the academic classes of both high school and lower division work in college. So the next time a student asks, "When am I ever going to use this?" remind them of the importance of transferable skills and their value in the workforce.

In a rapidly changing workplace, understanding the application of transferable skills as it relates to career planning is important. Many workers will have sequential careers (a series of different careers throughout a lifetime). To demonstrate, share the following scenario with your students:

> Robin (the second student in the preceding example) was a sales associate in the local music store while working her way through college. Upon graduation, she took a job at the local high school as the music and band teacher. Unfortunately, the music program was cut due to budget deficits. Luckily, because of her excellent math skills, Robin was able to transfer into the math department. Upon retiring from education, she obtained a broker's license and started her own real estate company.

Look again at the students' brainstorming session. Choose one of the examples and ask small groups to create a scenario similar to the one above.

Follow-up:

After you have completed these exercises visit the U.S. Department of Labor's web site, O*NET Online for a variety of interest and aptitude surveys.

Roles, Occupations, and Vocations

Page 49   No Workbook Page

Learning Objective:

To help students identify and evaluate their roles, occupations, and vocations.

Presentation Suggestions:

With the class, review the definitions for roles, occupations, and vocations. Point out that this may be the easiest ring to complete on their charts since what you do is much more obvious than who you are.

Activities:

Divide the group into pairs and have them introduce each other to the class without using roles, occupations, or vocations. Instruct the rest of the class to respond with whistles or boos if any job titles (student, basketball player, song writer, athlete, or whatever) sneak into the introduction. It sounds easy, but it's not. When a hundred highly educated professionals came together and tried this experiment, they found it extremely frustrating. If it seems more appropriate in your classroom, you could have students introduce themselves instead of dividing into pairs.

Even though we usually define ourselves by what we do, it is important that students realize this is only a portion of who we are. It is a measure of self-esteem to be able to identify and value the traits that make us unique. Then, no matter what a person's occupation, he or she will feel confident of holding a special place in the world.

My10yearPlan.com® Essentials:

This is a keystone activity. Data will be extracted and used in each student's *My 10-year Plan Summary Page*. Direct students to enter their work from this activity on **My10yearPlan.com®** the next time they log on. For more information, see Section 9 of this guide.

I had students make a dream catcher to go along with chapter 2. They enjoyed this project and I learned a lot about their dreams and what is important to them.

— Kathy Yesensky, JTPA Coordinator
Camp Fire Boys and Girls, San Bernardino, CA

Chapter 2 Follow-up:

Once this exercise is complete, ask the students to turn back to page 27 in *Career Choices* and, in a different color ink, write the additional characteristics they've identified while working through Chapter 2.

As a homework assignment, ask each student to choose three heroes/heroines (present-day or historical figures). In class, ask them to complete a bull's eye chart for one figure they've chosen. When the chart is complete, ask the students to underline characteristics that parallel their own chart and to circle those characteristics on the hero's or heroine's chart they would like to acquire as they mature and gain experience.

Once this is done, write this statement on the board:

"The people we admire most are a reflection of our inner selves."—Joseph Campbell

Do your students agree or disagree with this statement? If many of the characteristics on their hero's or heroine's charts are either underlined or circled, this could be accurate.

I have students identify their heroes after the section on values. Then we compare to determine if their values coincide.

— Marianne Bryan, Science Teacher
Thomas Jefferson Middle School, Jefferson City, MO

With our theme, "Search for Identity," we use the mandala to show each student's "sun side" and "shadow side." After that search for self, they can better understand characters such as Mitty ("The Secret Life of Walter Mitty") and Loisel ("The Necklace"). Also, their identity poems were great and their poetry was so beautiful that some were published.

— Claudia Gerhardt, English Department Chair
Hillside Junior High School, Boise, ID

I had students create their visual representations of their bull's eye characteristics and their dream lives on an online poster site rather than using construction paper, markers, and magazine pictures. We used www.edu.glogster.com and it was a neat piece of technology for students to learn to use. We had to use the EDU version due to firewalls… We used this site for students to create visual representations of their dreams, lifestyles, and all the information on their bull's eye. At the end of the course, students presented their posters to the class.

— Valerie Hays, English Teacher
Moline High School, Moline, IL

Message Center

Learning Objective:

To help students become more aware of the messages—verbal and otherwise—they get from society and from significant people in their lives, and to help them understand how these messages can affect the way they feel about their future or their potential.

Presentation Suggestions:

If students become aware of the messages they are getting from their friends, family, or the world at large, they will be better able to base decisions about their future on their own desires and abilities. Discuss this concept and then ask students to complete the exercise on their own.

Activities:

Ask a school counselor or psychologist to speak with the class about this topic. The Message Center activity requires extra sensitivity so students don't reveal in class too much personal information. For discussions, focus on the bottom section of the activity: societies messages. Ask students to think about messages from music, television programs, movies, and commercials.

Invite a panel of professionals to complete the exercise. Then have the panel tell the class how the messages they were given had an impact on their career and life choices.

Discuss in class the messages society gives individuals based on their gender, race, age, physical appearance, physical ability, social status, economic status, intellectual capacity, and educational achievement.

Compositions:

"The Person Who Has Most Affected My Life" or *"The Brainwashing of the American Mind: How Media Impacts Our Culture."*

Debate:

"Does society still give females and males different messages?"
If you ask a group of students to debate this question, do not put all males on one side and all females on the other. Make sure each side is co-ed.

Ask students to write one of the messages they identified as limiting on a piece of colored paper. Then have students drop the limiting message into a document shredder and shout "I have endless potential" as the document shreds the limiting message. Save the shredded scraps and use them as confetti at a party celebrating your students.

— Tanja Easson, Curriculum Support
Academic innovations

Optional

Life
by Nan Terrell Reed

Read after completing page 52
in *Career Choices*

Excerpt from *Self-Reliance*
by Ralph Waldo Emerson

Page 61–68

Read after completing page 53 in *Career Choices*

Understanding Others

Learning Objective:

To help students learn to differentiate between individuals based upon their traits and motivations. At the same time, to help students understand that employers are evaluating them on these topics, as well.

Presentation Suggestions:

Success in the workforce requires understanding not only ourselves, but also the traits and motivations of others. Now that your students have completed an identity inventory for themselves, remind them they have the tools for evaluating friends and associates.

Activities:

Ask your students to brainstorm situations where the ability to evaluate traits and motivations is valuable.

> Hiring of employees
> Choosing a significant other
> Making committee assignments

We've included a Character Analysis Worksheet on the next pages. Suggest students use this as a prompt to help them get to know someone better. They'll want to ask questions and observe an individual's actions as they relate to the rings of the bull's eye chart and the six questions on page 4/35.

Energizer:

Divide the class into pairs. Ask each pair to role play a dialogue between two individuals considering going into business together. Point out that choosing the right business partner may be as important as selecting the right marriage partner. Suggest that students refer to the Character Analysis Worksheet for ideas about the type of questions to ask. You may want to brainstorm how the questions could be rephrased to elicit a certain response. This could be assigned as a written follow-up assignment.

Another Energizer:

Ask a mature student population to complete a Character Analysis Worksheet for a hypothetical drug dealer. When completed, review the worksheets in class and ask if this is the type of individual they want to have in their lives. Explain that while this is an extreme example, it is worth analyzing a negative and destructive personality to understand how to identify people that would best be avoided.

Optional

I Know Why the Caged Bird Sings
by Maya Angelou

Sympathy
by Paul Laurence Dunbar

Page 47–60
Read after completing page 28–53 in ***Career Choices***

Character Analysis

English/Language Arts:

Throughout the course, you might include the Character Analysis Worksheet on the following page with each reading assignment. It can be used in a variety of ways:

a. Ask students to complete the worksheet for their favorite character.

b. Choose three to five main characters. Divide the class into small groups to analyze one or all of them using the worksheet.

Writing Fiction:

When asking students to write fiction, suggest they use the worksheet to develop their character(s) before they begin to write.

For explanations of each of the concepts on the Character Analysis Worksheet, refer to the following pages in the text **Career Choices**:

> ***Bull's Eye Chart:*** *page 27*
>
> *Question 1: pages 15–16*   *Question 4: pages 66–71*
>
> *Question 2: pages 18–21*   *Question 5: pages 196–227*
>
> *Question 3: page 20*   *Question 6: pages 60–61*

For the author, character analysis is an essential task. Most great stories and screenplays have wonderful character development. However, remind students it is a vital skill for everyone to have as we choose our friends and associates.

Brainstorm relationships that require this in-depth analysis.

Examples:	Employer	Employee
	Spouse	Mentor
	Best friend	Business partner

We break the students into small groups and assign each group a biography of someone famous. We usually select a variety of people and use a web site like www.biography.com to find biographies that can be printed and assigned. The groups read their biography and then make a bull's-eye chart for that person. Then, the groups share their results with the class and their classmates ask them questions about any word entered that they found surprising. This assignment is fun because, through analyzing the person's values, passions, roles, etc., they usually discover interesting things about people that they didn't know anything about before. We provide them with an example chart before we start, most recently, Bill Gates. Many kids are surprised to discover certain things out about his personal life. It makes them see that famous people are just like them! Everyone can have their own unique bull's-eye chart!

— Becky Simmons, Transitions Lesson Coordinator
Marquette Senior High School, Marquette, MI

Common Core Standards for English

RI.9-10.1. Cite strong and thorough textual evidence to support analysis of what the text says explicitly as well as inferences drawn from the text.

Character Analysis Worksheet

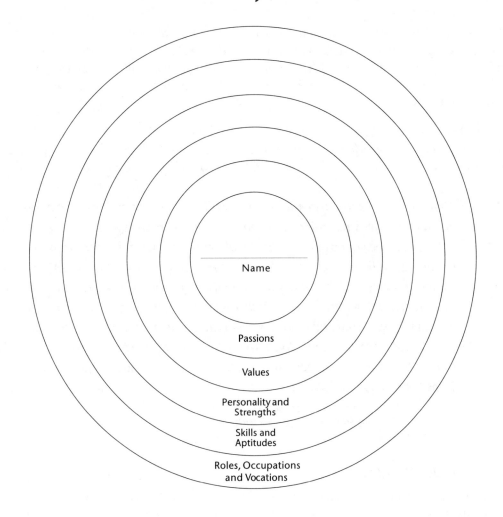

Name

Passions

Values

Personality and Strengths

Skills and Aptitudes

Roles, Occupations and Vocations

1. Why do they work? _____

2. How would they define success? _____

3. How would they make decisions? _____

4. How balanced is their lifestyle? _____

5. What limitations, either self-imposed or society-imposed, do they face? _____

_____

6. What is their mission in life? _____

_____

My10yearPlan.com® as an Advisory Tool

It is the end of the first section: Who Am I? If you haven't had your students log in to the optional My10yearPlan.com®, now would be a good time. After entering their work online, they will be able to print out a copy of their Personal Profile (a.k.a. bull's eye chart) and their essay "Envisioning My Future" (*Career Choices*, page 16), which can be shared with their parents, teachers, and advisors.

Note: Instructors report that students who arrive in the computer lab with all their work written in their *Workbook and Portfolio* have an easier time entering their data into My10yearPlan.com®. Those that have not completed a hard copy of their work ahead of time may struggle.

After the students complete their own charts in their z profiles, they print a copy and turn it in. We stress this assignment is a work in progress and, because it is online, it can be added to throughout high school as they discover more about themselves. I share this starting document with parents at the first parent/teacher conference session of the year. Many parents comment on how fun it is to see what their student's thoughts were about themselves. So often high school students are not willing to share things about themselves, and parents are left to judge them based on their actions alone. This activity often shows parents a side of their student that they had no idea existed. It also helps them understand what the Transitions course is all about.

—Becky Simmons, Transitions Lesson Coordinator
Marquette Senior High School, Marquette, MI

The School-wide Initiative

If you school has decided to follow the model set forth by The George Washington University Freshman Transition Initiative and later expanded on by *Get Focused...Stay Focused!*™ Initiative developed at Santa Barbara City College, start planting seeds with your colleagues throughout the school. Updating the 10-year plans in the 10th, 11th, and 12th grade is critical to the continued success of your students.

Your *Career Choices* course is the "Get Focused" portion of a school-wide effort. The process of having students update their 10-year plan in the 10th, 11th, and 12th grades is the "Stay Focused" element. For details, see pages 4/170 and 6/28–6/30 of this guide.

Chapter 3

Lifestyles of the Satisfied and Happy

The next five chapters of the book are meant to help students answer the question, "What do I want?" It's not an easy task. Perhaps that is why most career and life planning books devote more time to getting what you want than to determining what that is.

Establishing and consolidating identity, and then setting goals based on that identity, are essential parts of making career and life choices. Without these preliminary steps, it is impossible to choose wisely. Students are likely to base their decisions more on what their family or friends think they should do than on what they would actually find most satisfying.

In this chapter, students are asked to consider their ideal lifestyle. While career, family, leisure activities, friends, and spiritual concerns are part of everyone's lifestyle, each element's importance is something the individual must determine for him- or herself.

Career choice has a huge impact on the other aspects of lifestyle. In fact, for many people, lifestyle is determined in large part by career path. Therefore, we think it is essential that students give careful consideration to the way they want to live before deciding on a career and the educational path to qualify for that career.

TECHNICAL SUPPORT
For the *Career Choices* curriculum
(800) 967-8016 or
support@academicinnovations.com

Maslow's Triangle

Page 56–59   Page 26

Learning Objective:

To teach students Maslow's hierarchy of needs and help them understand its impact on their identity and self-esteem.

Presentation Suggestions:

Offer an overview of Maslow's triangle, explaining how survival needs must be met before a person can be concerned about safety; how people must feel safe before they can care about social needs; how they seek esteem when their social needs have been met; and how, finally, they can become self-actualized.

Discuss the difference between a *want* and a *need*. Many people, especially those with low self-esteem, do not see anything beyond the most basic means of survival as legitimate needs for themselves. Explain that everyone needs—and has a right to expect or ask for—respect, compassion, companionship, enjoyable experiences, and acceptance from others and from oneself.

Activities:

Have students complete the exercise on page 59 on their own. Once they have identified where they are on Maslow's triangle, ask them to begin thinking how they can continue to move up the triangle. What support can they seek? What action can they take? The rest of this course should help them identify possibilities.

Note of Caution:

If you are dealing with a population of at-risk students, it may become very apparent to the learners that they are stuck at the bottom rungs of the triangle. Take extra time with this group or these individuals. Talk about possible plans for feeling safe and secure, getting support, and gaining control over their lives. If appropriate, suggest privately that some students might like to see a school counselor.

Since this section has the potential to identify individuals who may need extra counseling and support, discuss how you should handle this with administrators and counselors ahead of time so you can respond to student needs immediately.

Chapter Introduction Video:

At the beginning of this chapter, consider showing the motivational chapter introduction video featuring Olympic Gold Medalist Dain Blanton. Or, if students are regularly using My10yearPlan.com®, have them watch the video online before starting their work in this chapter.

Reading Assignment:

Assign the fable *Pandora's Box*. Afterward, discuss how hope drives us to improve our lives.

How Do You Want to Be Remembered?

Career Choices Series
Page 60–61

Workbook and Portfolio
Page 27

Learning Objective:

To help students identify an overall goal or mission for their lives.

Presentation Suggestions:

Explain to the class that people have a strong need to be identified with something that is "bigger than themselves." Allow students some time to think about this assignment. It's something that requires some thought. Remind students that this is a very personal assignment, not something they should decide with a group of friends. Remind them, too, that their goal or mission may change over time.

Activities:

Invite three "self-actualizers" from the community—preferably senior citizens—to talk with the class about their mission in life: how and when they chose it; the sacrifices they've made as a result; and how they would advise someone just starting out. Be sure to tell the guests what you want them to talk about a few days ahead of time so they can be prepared. If possible, invite a variety of people as your guests: an activist; someone with a high profile in the community; a successful businessperson; and a private person with a satisfying personal life.

English/Language Arts:

Complete the Looking into the Future activity described on the next page. Ask for volunteers to share their letters. Take a poll. What percentage of students wrote about something they did or something they accomplished? What percentage wrote about an accomplishment in a career sense?

One success we have had is with "How Do You Want to be Remembered?" in Chapter 3. In addition to talking about the epitaphs, we have a picture of an ancient Memory Bottle that was discovered in China. After looking at the picture and trying to identify the items in the bottle, we discussed the different ways that different cultures have to remember themselves after their death. Students are then asked to reflect on what they would like their descendants to remember about them. After listing the items vertically on a sheet of paper, they are given the homework assignment to create a memory bottle (either visual or written)... The "bottles" brought in by most students were far beyond my expectations. Some students used arts and crafts tools to create a masterpiece.

— Sharon Hurwitz, English Teacher and Technology Facilitator
Bethel High School, Hampton, VA

Follow-up:

Students will be asked to reiterate their mission in life at the very end of the course. At that time, turn back and *again* administer the exercise that follows, Looking into the Future.

I began my unit, "My Dream: Why and How?" by doing a hands-on activity. My students developed huge collages or posters to represent their dreams for their lives, and because I do a unit on aging (using the poem "Warning" from When I Grow Old, I Shall Wear Purple as a springboard) I ask them to project dreams for an entire lifetime. I display these and refer back to them for the entire year. At the end of the year, we discuss these initial dreams and note any changes. The dreams are also identified in terms of the Maslow hierarchy. Are the students closer to self-actualization now? Usually, the answer is yes! My students' most common observation: "For the first time, I feel a class actually relates to me. I can use this 'stuff' in my life…"

— Sarah Marsh, 12th Grade Applied English Teacher
Burley High School, Burley, ID

In class today, we worked on creating message bottles. We had just finished working on the epitaph, describing how we would want to be remembered. The students created bottles and enclosed messages for their futures on what kind of legacy they would like to leave behind. Some of them created 3D bottles with scrolls inside and some just drew a picture of the bottle and included the details on the picture. They listed qualities and accomplishments they have now and ones they hope to achieve in the future!

— Jane Laughlin, Curriculum Specialist
Benson High School, Omaha, NE
sharing what teacher Angelina Gradel does in her GPS
(Goals and Pathways to Success) class

When using "I Shall Not Pass This Way Again" we had our students write their own version as suggested on page 73 of Possibilities. Then the students prepared illustrated posters with their poem and we put them up around the room to remind them of the goals they were setting for the year. We extended the activity by recognizing the uniqueness of each student and the student of the week program.

— Suzanne M. Reese, Teacher/Gifted Liaison
R.L. Turner High School, Carrollton, TX

Common Core Standards for English

W.9-10.7. Conduct short as well as more sustained research projects to answer a question (including a self-generated question) or solve a problem; narrow or broaden the inquiry when appropriate; synthesize multiple sources on the subject, demonstrating understanding of the subject under investigation.

W.9-10.9. Draw evidence from literary or informational texts to support analysis, reflection, and research.

Optional

Growing Older
by R.G. Wells

Read as an introduction to the activity on page 169 of this *Instructor's Guide*

Page 69–71   ### I Shall Not Pass This Way Again
Read after completing pages 60–61 in *Career Choices*

Looking into the Future

Do this activity after completing pages 60–61 in *Career Choices* and again at the end of your course.

Ask students to have their paper and pens or a laptop on their desks before you begin. Turn down the lights and close the doors and windows. If your room is unavoidably noisy, try to find a quieter one.

Speak slowly and quietly, pausing where indicated. Read the following script aloud:

> Relax and settle into your chair. Place your feet flat on the floor. Close your eyes. Clear your mind by imagining the space between your eyes. (Pause at least 15 seconds)
>
> Pay attention to your breathing. (Pause) Inhale slowly, filling your lungs with air. (Pause) Exhale slowly. (Pause) (Repeat two more times)
>
> Take a few slow, deep, deliberate breaths. As you exhale, tell yourself to relax and let go. (Pause long enough for three or four deep breaths)
>
> Feel your body relax (Pause) from your face all the way down to your legs and toes. (Pause) Feel the pleasant warm and tingly feeling of relaxed muscles. (Pause)
>
> Now project yourself into the future. (Pause) You see calendar pages flipping. (Pause) It's 2015. (Pause) 2020. (Pause) 2030. (Pause) 2040. (Pause) How old are you now?
>
> The calendar continues to flip. Stop the calendar at the year you plan to retire.
>
> You are there now. Take a look around. (Pause) Where are you? What is the setting? (Pause) Who is there with you? Who are the important people in your life? (Pause) Look in a mirror. What do you look like? (Longer pause)
>
> You hear the doorbell ring. When you go to the door, a mail carrier hands you a letter. You open the letter. It is from someone important to you, commending you, thanking you, and praising you. You feel very good about this letter. (Pause) You feel successful, (Pause) fulfilled, (Pause) and acknowledged. Enjoy that good feeling for a moment. (Pause 30–60 seconds)
>
> What does the letter say? (Pause a minute or two)
>
> Now open your eyes and, without saying a word, pick up your pen… (Wait until everyone picks up their pen) and write that letter. Begin now.

Note to Instructors:

Many authors and writers put themselves into a trancelike state in order to create. They become immersed in the time and place they are writing about, closely identifying with their characters. story, or topic. This exercise may provide your students their first experience with this "altered," creative state. After the students have turned in their letters, discuss this part of the creative process. Ask students how they felt during the exercise, and whether they have ever experienced this "altered," creative state before.

Components of Lifestyle

Page 62–63   Page 28

Learning Objective:

To teach students to project into the future and to recognize the wide variety of lifestyle options open to them.

Presentation Suggestions:

The necessity of projecting into the future and realizing how today's actions may have long-term consequences is a major theme of this curriculum. This ability has been shown to be a key factor in preventing a variety of problems, such as unplanned pregnancy, dropping out of school, and drug or alcohol abuse. The present exercise provides another opportunity for students to practice this skill.

Explain the importance of defining their desired lifestyle before choosing a career: careers can dictate lifestyles. This will not be an easy exercise for most students; explain this *after* they have attempted to complete it. Instruct them not to be frustrated if they cannot finish in one sitting. Students may need to come back to this as they work through the remainder of the book, adding elements or readjusting their plans. Stress, too, that it is a good idea to re-evaluate their lifestyle goals throughout their lives.

You may have to remind students that they'll need to draw on their fantasies and imaginations to complete this exercise. This is the first step in creating a vision. (Remember the formula for success: Vision plus Energy equals Success.)

Composition:

Once the chart on page 63 is complete, ask them to write an essay "*A Day in My Life in _____*" *(year)*. Have them choose a year sometime between 15 and 30 years into the future, when they will be in the middle of their careers.

Debate:

Which should come first—lifestyle choice or career choice?

My10yearPlan.com® Essentials:

This is a keystone activity. Data will be extracted and used in each student's *My 10-year Plan Summary Page*. Direct students to enter their work from this activity on My10yearPlan.com® the next time they log on. For more information, see Section 9 of this guide.

Common Core Standards for English

W.9-10.3. Write narratives to develop real or imagined experiences or events using effective technique, well-chosen details, and well-structured event sequences.

Happiness is a Balanced Lifestyle

Page 64–65

No Workbook
Page

Learning Objective:

To help students identify the components of a balanced lifestyle.

Presentation Suggestions:

Discuss the various concepts of a balanced lifestyle as described on pages 64 and 65.

Gender Equity Activity:

The class debates which worker would have the most options for parenting, someone in a structured job with specific hours or someone who is self-employed and directs their own hours.

Reading Assignment:

Having Our Say: The Delany Sisters' First 100 Years, by Sarah and A. Elizabeth Delany with Amy Hill Hearth, Dell Publishing, New York, NY 1994.

In *Having Our Say*, Bessie, age 101, and her sister Sadie, age 103, share humorous and poignant anecdotes of the previous 100 years. This inspiring memoir offers a rare glimpse into the early Civil Rights movement and the lives of women of achievement and wisdom.

The Modified Maslow Triangle

Page 66–69   Page 29

Learning Objective:

To help students understand and identify their needs and to appreciate the desirability of balancing internal and external, personal and professional, private and public lives.

Presentation Suggestions:

Present the modified triangle as described in the book. If students grasped the meaning of the Maslow triangle discussed earlier, this new concept should not be too difficult. Make sure they understand the difference between external and internal needs. Emphasize that it is quite possible to be at different levels on each side of the triangle. That, in fact, is how to determine if a life is out of balance.

Break the class into small groups. Ask each group to discuss Emma's and Isaac's problems and try to find solutions for them. Then have the groups evaluate Joanie's lifestyle, discuss what she might do to bring her life back into balance, and determine the trade-offs she might have to make.

> *We show the film* Rudy *and have students fill in a Modified Maslow Triangle for Rudy during the movie. Then, after the movie we discuss Rudy's triangle and how the input seemed to relate to his overall views about his life and his level of happiness. This helped students see how the triangle might apply to everyone's life.*
>
> — Becky Simmons, Transitions Lesson Coordinator
> Marquette Senior High School, Marquette, MI

For more movie ideas to share with your students, see pages 11/23–11/25

> *Throughout the curriculum we've adopted social studies lessons in anthropology, geography, sociology, psychology, etc. to enhance the text work. For example, in the "Who Am I?" unit, we explored personality theories in addition to the Maslow's Triangle activity.*
>
> — Mark Yanowsky, Social Studies/Careers Instructor
> North Monterey Co. High School, Castroville, CA

Optional

Red Geraniums
by Martha Haskell Clark

Page 74–75

Read after completing pages 66–69 in *Career Choices*

What About Your Life?

Page 70–71   Page 30

Learning Objective:

To personalize the balanced lifestyle evaluation process and help students realize the effect that outside forces can have on a person's life.

Presentation Suggestions:

Ask students to review the questions at the top of the page and write a paragraph about their perspective on their current situation before shading the triangle to represent the balance in their own lives.

Activities:

Have students interview an adult friend or colleague and then write a paragraph about this person's lifestyle before shading in a triangle to represent the balance.

As a class, talk about the chart for a homeless person. Obviously, he or she must be solely concerned with basic survival needs. What causes homelessness? There are both personal (drug abuse, emotional illness) and societal causes. Have the class discuss some examples of the latter.

Examples:

- Lack of educational opportunities
- Welfare "reform"
- Scarcity of unskilled jobs
- The minimum wage as it relates to the cost of housing
- Inadequate facilities or programs to deal with the chemically addicted or the emotionally ill
- Decreasing numbers of low-cost rooming houses because they are torn down to make room for office buildings

Can your class imagine how societal issues could have an impact on their lifestyles?

- What happens when a pregnant woman works for a company that does not offer extended maternity leave?
- What if a working single parent can't find affordable, competent child care?
- What happens if someone who can't afford or doesn't qualify for medical insurance becomes seriously ill?
- What if a person working at the best job he or she can find doesn't earn enough to rent an apartment?

English/Language Arts:

After the above discussions, ask students to write a fictional account in the first-person of a homeless individual's typical day.

Common Core Standards for English

W.9-10.2. Write informative/explanatory texts to examine and convey complex ideas, concepts, and information clearly and accurately through the effective selection, organization, and analysis of content.

Instructor's Notes:

Section 2: What Do I Want?

Chapter 4

What Cost This Lifestyle?

Students are likely to know that any given lifestyle has financial costs. Like many people, however, they have probably not considered the psychological costs, or the costs in terms of commitment to a given career. The goal of this chapter is to instill an understanding of *all three* costs. Emphasis should be on the importance of finding the balance best suited to each individual.

As they work through the exercises in this chapter, students should begin to see the relationships between these different aspects. For example, someone wanting a career that will support a lavish lifestyle must usually be willing to make huge commitments in terms of time and money for education and/or experience.

Similarly, a career that offers a great deal of psychological satisfaction may not always be the one with the biggest financial payoff. Many people find that financial success alone is not all it was promised to be.

Optional

The Mills of the Gods

Page 76–79

Read after reading Ivy Elms' story on pages 74–75 in **Career Choices**

Optional

Page 12–88

An expanded version of the budget exercise from **Career Choices** text (See pages 2/21 and Section8 for details)

Page 77–94   Page 32–43

Your Budget

Learning Objective:

Before they can make wise career and education decisions, students must take into account the cost of living. This exercise should give them a realistic view of the financial considerations that will be important when deciding on both a career path and an education plan. It should also start them thinking about their own financial priorities. Do they really want that expensive sports car? How important are exotic vacations? If they had to choose one or the other, which would it be? Are they willing to work hard enough to have either or both?

Presentation Suggestions:

This exercise can be approached in different ways. If you have the time, it is well worth doing a thorough, investigative job in which students come up with their own figures. If time is at a premium, however, students can simply use the charts provided in the book or online resources to come up with generally accurate figures.

Go over the exercise in class beforehand to make sure students understand what they should do and how to go about it. As an example, it may be helpful to complete the exercise as a class, creating a composite family, otherwise known as budget-by-consensus. To do this, complete each section, soliciting input from the class, and try to come up with figures that represent the average lifestyle expectations of the class.

Then, as students complete their own budget, you may want to review them section by section, stopping each time to discuss and brainstorm possibilities.

This is an extremely important assignment. Budgets are much more realistic and manageable when presented and communicated in written form. Once students have experienced this written activity, they will become much more adept at it as they mature.

If you do decide to take the more thorough route, you will probably want to bring in classified sections from local newspapers, catalogs from major department stores, utility bills, and other resources for class reference. Alternatively, you can direct students to online resources for these cost projections. They can use these resources to determine the cost of appropriate housing, transportation, equipment, furnishings, and the like. They may get other figures by asking parents or other adults and checking prices in stores. Having calculators available would also be helpful.

My10yearPlan.com® Essentials:

This is a keystone activity. Data will be extracted and used in each student's *My 10-year Plan Summary Page*. Direct students to enter their work from this activity on My10yearPlan.com® the next time they log on. Allow one or two computer lab sessions for this activity. For more information, see Section 9 of this guide.

Optional

For the most detailed version of the budget exercise, you will want to use *Lifestyle Math: Your Financial Planning Portfolio*.

Page 12–88

Lifestyle Math:
Your Financial Planning Portfolio

We hope you think this budget activity is a critical component to your course efforts. Educators and parents alike tell us this is a life-altering activity for most young people. Attitudes improve. Students become more focused and motivated. Math studies take on new meaning, and education as a whole becomes a desired and valued commodity. Your students will no longer have to wait to experience the costs of living on their own to understand how important a good education is today.

If you have the time and the resources, we recommend the addition of the workbook, *Lifestyle Math*, for each of your students. This expanded version of the budget exercise clearly demonstrates the link between education and life satisfaction, thus making math a relevant and essential subject that must be mastered. This one-hundred-page math problem walks students through the process of developing a budget for their desired lifestyle when they are 29 years old. Along the way, students learn important economic formulas and mathematical equations they will use throughout their lives.

You can team with the math department to present this important material or you can present it yourself. Instructors of all disciplines who teach *Career Choices* find they enjoy teaching this unit. They include:

- Careers educators
- Teachers of freshman orientation courses
- English language arts instructors
- Business and economics teachers
- Family and consumer science teachers
- Special populations instructors and program directors

For more details on *Lifestyle Math* and its online correction key LifestyleMath.com, turn to pages 2/21–2/22, 3/14, 3/16 as well as Section 8.

Lifestyle Math Contents

CareerChoices.com for Chapter 4

Internet Resources for the Budget Exercise

Better yet, on CareerChoices.com, you'll find a variety of resources that will help your students with their budget planning. This Internet enhancement to the *Career Choices* curriculum includes links and lessons for each of the following pages of the textbook:

Page 77—Where Do You Want to Live?
- *Calculator:* Cost of Living Comparison
- *Database:* Top 20 Cities

Page 78—Housing Options
- *Calculator:* Finding Current Mortgage Rates
- *Calculator:* Calculating Your Monthly Payment
- *Calculator:* Estimate of the Cost of Homeowners Insurance
- *Calculator:* Estimate of the Cost of Renters Insurance
- *Calculator:* Should You Buy a Home or Should You Rent?

Page 80—Transportation
- *Calculator:* Finding the Value of a Used Car
- *Table:* Comparison Car Shopping
- *Informational:* Weigh the Pros and Cons of a New vs. Used Car
- *Calculator:* Finding the Current Auto Loan Interest Rate
- *Calculator:* Calculating Your Monthly Car Payment
- *Table:* Operating Costs: Looking at Fuel Efficiency
- *Calculator:* Figuring Automobile Operating Costs
- *Interactive Quiz:* Auto Insurance Quiz

Page 83—Clothing
- *Database:* Children's Clothing
- *Database:* Pricing Appropriate Workplace Apparel

Page 88—Child Care
- *Calculator:* Calculate the Cost of Raising Kids: Birth to Age 18
- *Commentary:* USA *Today* Article on the Costs of Raising Kids: "You and Me and Baby Makes $197,700

Page 89—Health Care & Savings
- *Calculator:* Calculating Future College Costs
- *Calculator:* Calculating Savings Needed for Attending a Specific College
- *Calculator:* Saving for Retirement

Page 93—What Salary Will Support This Lifestyle?
- *Calculator:* Calculating Take-Home Pay
- *Table:* National Employment and Wage Data
- *Table:* State Employment and Wage Data

Page 116—An Investment in Education
- *Table:* The Link Between Earnings and Education

Page 120—Ask Someone Who's Been There
- *Database:* Interviewing Via E-Mail

And, best of all, students can use this site at school or at home—anywhere they can access a web browser. You'll want to check out the latest resources by visiting CareerChoices.com and signing in as a visitor. The index has over 80 lessons and activities. You'll find more detailed information beginning on page 2/23 and in Section 8 of this guide.

Throughout this section, you'll see this logo at the bottom of certain pages. This indicates enhancements are available on CareerChoices.com. As we find new and better resources, we add them to the site so the most current index will be found online. Go to the Visitor Section for information about membership and licensing fees.

Checklist of Resources for Budgeting Exercise

Depending on how extensive you want to make this exercise, the following items will help. If you don't have regular access to a computer lab:

☐ One complete classified section from the newspaper for each student in the class

☐ Sample utility bills, catalog, and print advertising for household items

☐ Catalogs of major department stores

☐ Sample weekly food bills for families of various sizes

☐ Vacation brochures

☐ Calculator(s)

☐ Internet access

If your students have laptops or you have access to a computer lab, all the above items can be easily found online by googling the topic statements. This is a great research project for your students. Divide them into groups of three, give each group one of the above topics, and delegate the task of finding the best two or three online resources for their assignment.

They will need to review multiple web sites and determine which ones are best for the research required. Suggest they first study the corresponding topics in their *Career Choices* textbook (pages 78 to 90). Ask them to defend the web sites they chose to recommend. Compile the recommendations and share that document with the whole class.

Our Career Advisory class has had a very interesting time working together to plan a budget for a family of four. We gave them a roll of butcher paper, markers/rulers, access to computers, and told them to "guestimate" what they thought they wanted/needed for one year. They did one "brainstorm" (with a focus on video games & makeup). We gave them NO teacher input. Then we asked some questions, such as "What are you going to do if someone gets sick? Who's buying the groceries?" They decided (amongst themselves) to re-do the whole thing. We have 15- to 17-year-olds in the class. It was remarkable to see how their second go-round differed from the first. It was sobering for them to realize THEY would be buying toilet paper and toothpaste!

— Leanne Soucek, Teacher
Arapahoe Ridge High School, Boulder, CO

Author's Note

Between 1976 and 1983, I taught evening classes at a local private college for soon-to-graduate seniors. One of the activities I used was a version of this budget exercise. I was always struck with the response I got from my students. It was usually one of shock and, because they were just completing a degree in a lower-paying helping profession, sometimes anger. "Why didn't someone do this with us before?" they'd ask, bewildered. They had just completed a degree, yet for many of them, the average salary of their chosen profession could not meet their lifestyle expectations.

This is one of the most critical exercises you can do with your students. Make it interesting, hands-on, and fun. Don't hurry through it. It will probably be one of the favorite activities of the course and, perhaps, one of the most important.

— Mindy Bingham
Author, *Career Choices*

Reality TV as a Resource for Your Budget Activities

Between HGTV, the Food Channel, and other lifestyle programming on television today, if you have adequate time (e.g., year-long course with 180 hours of instruction time), you'll find a variety of resources to record and show your students.

I have my students watch an episode of House Hunters *on HGTV when we are working on Chapter 4. We go through the entire process of purchasing a house and then watch an episode to solidify what we have learned.*

After each house is viewed, we pause and have a discussion on why this would make a good house for the particular people we are watching, and then relate it to their "fake life" (as I call it) and see if it would match all of their qualifications.

When the episode is over and the couple has selected their house, we have another discussion on why that was a good selection and how it would meet the needs of my students and their future lifestyle. At that point, they have to decide which house they would have chosen and then we discuss. It really makes the students think about the process of buying a home and seeing what all you want in a home and what you do not want in a home.

The students LOVE this assignment and beg to watch more. To end the housing assignment, we watch House Hunters International *and we view a million dollar home in another country. I think they like this episode more than one that is more relevant to most people's lifestyles. It is a fun project and a good way to end the week.*

— Rebecca Boyd, Teacher
Flour Bluff High School, Corpus Christi, TX

Common Core Standards for English (for the budget exercise)

W.9-10.6. Use technology, including the Internet, to produce, publish, and update individual or shared writing products, taking advantage of technology's capacity to link to other information and to display information flexibly and dynamically.

W.9-10.8. Gather relevant information from multiple authoritative print and digital sources, using advanced searches effectively; assess the usefulness of each source in answering the research question; integrate information into the text selectively to maintain the flow of ideas, avoiding plagiarism and following a standard format for citation.

SL.9-10.2. Integrate multiple sources of information presented in diverse media or formats (e.g., visually, quantitatively, orally) evaluating the credibility and accuracy of each source.

Family Profile

Page 77 Page 32

Before they begin to develop their budgets, students must project themselves into the future. After all, the exercise is intended to help them make career, educational, and lifestyle decisions. Emphasize that this budget should be based on the way they would like to live after they have completed their education and are working at the job of their choice. Students should imagine that they are at least 29 years old to calculate their budget.

The cost of living also depends to a large extent on the number of people in the household. Do the students plan to be married? Will they have children? How many? What ages?

Finally, since costs vary greatly depending on where they will be living (the budget of an executive in Manhattan, NYC, will be very different from that of a farmer in Manhattan, Kansas, for example), students must also consider this aspect of their future lives.

Encourage students to fantasize a bit here. They should consider the way of life they think would be most rewarding, not simply the lifestyle they think is most probable for someone in their circumstances. Where would they really like to live? What would be their ideal family? What kind of home would they have? Where would they vacation?

A word of caution before you begin. Because the lifestyles of the most visible individuals in the media tend to be lavish, try to encourage students to be somewhat realistic in their projections. At the same time, respect the students who insist they are going to have a lifestyle very different from their family's. One of the purposes of this total curriculum is to show how, with education, planning, and hard work, individuals can realize their dreams.

Once students decide on their future families, you may choose to introduce a hitch into the planning process. Tell them that, for whatever reason, they are suddenly single. In most cases, they will find themselves single parents. If they look at you aghast, remind students that nearly 50 percent of today's children are raised in single-parent families at some point in their lives.

This aspect of the exercise is of particular importance to the females in your class. Otherwise, many will complete the exercise assuming they will be married when, in reality, a high percentage will be the sole support of their families.

Chapter Introduction Video:

At the beginning of this chapter, consider showing the motivational chapter introduction video featuring Olympic Gold Medalist Dain Blanton (found on **The Teachers' Lounge**). Or, if your students are regularly using **My10yearPlan.com®**, have them watch the video online before starting their work in this chapter.

> *When starting the budget section, the kids picked out where they wanted to live in the U.S. (p. 77, Career Choices). Then they wrote to that city's Chamber of Commerce asking for info on that city. We went to the computer lab, they typed it up, and I mailed them. They loved receiving the responses. I loved it—it combined formal letter writing, computer skills, civics, and careers.*
>
> — Debra Kuperberg, Special Education Teacher
>   San Gabriel High School, San Gabriel, CA

Housing

Page 78   Page 33

Ask students to consider their ideal living situation. Would they own or rent? Have a mansion or a modest apartment? Once they've decided, have them go to the classified ads online to find something suitable and see how much it costs. The charts on page 79 of *Career Choices* will be helpful.

To figure utility costs, ask students to brainstorm with you all the expenses that fall into this category. As a homework assignment, ask them to bring in sample utility bills.

Sample utility categories:

Gas	Water	Heating fuel	Cable
Electric	Trash	Phone	Internet

CareerChoices.com:

You'll want to review the various online mortgage calculators and tables available through CareerChoices.com. Turn to page 4/50 and examine the list under *Page 78—Housing* for those available at the time of printing of this guide. To see the most current enhancements, you can sign in as a registered user or visitor. Once you sign in, select the image of the **Career Choices** textbook and click on the *Index to all lessons* link at the bottom of the screen.

Note the CareerChoices.com logo in the bottom corner of this page. You'll see these throughout the budget exercise (pages 4/55–64). When you do, review the available Internet resources on CareerChoices.com and build them into your lessons. This dynamic resource will not only motivate your students but also provide an important lesson on the availability of quality information on the Internet. Information is power!

Activities:

Invite a realtor or mortgage broker to speak to the class on the costs of housing in the community and how to finance the first-time purchase of a home.

We have students research two houses—one in a realistic price range for the area they want to live and the lifestyle they want, but the other could be a luxury home! By doing this they get to see two very different cost scenarios. For example, one of my students started by picking a 30-million-dollar home in Beverly Hills. That payment was well over $12,000 per month for the mortgage alone. Then, they found a 3-bedroom/2-bathroom home in a nearby neighborhood and found the payment to be $1,500 per month. This is a good way to show them how different your life can be, depending on how you choose to spend your money. Both houses provided them a solid place to live, but they had a very different impact on their monthly budget!

— Becky Simmons, Transitions Lesson Coordinator
Marquette Senior High School, Marquette, MI

Optional

Page 14–31

Transportation

Page 80   Page 34

Students should choose their desired mode of transportation, considering their living situation as well as their dreams. If they're planning to live in an area without much public transportation, for example, some kind of vehicle is probably necessary. City dwellers with access to taxis, buses, or subways, on the other hand, might not want or need to own a car.

If they feel the need to own a car, refer them once again to the Internet. Ask them to choose a make and model and figure the monthly payments.

What do they project will be their mileage per month? Once they have an idea of this figure, the chart on page 81 of *Career Choices* should help with estimating gas and maintenance costs.

If you are using iPads or iTouch, download the free app, Mortgage Rate (eRate). It is a simple mortgage calculator that students can use to figure financing for cars and homes.

— Cathie Klein, College & Career Readiness Coordinator
  Seaman High School, Topeka, KS

When we get to the lesson on choosing a vehicle to purchase, my students use the Internet to find the perfect one. Then, they create a PowerPoint slide on their vehicle with certain points—cost, description and color, MPG (city, highway, average), and why they chose this vehicle. Basically, the graphic is an advertisement for the vehicle that they chose.

— Patricia Evans, Teacher
  Hudson Middle School, Lufkin, TX

Today we worked on what it would take to buy a "real" car. (On a minimum wage income.) They were shocked! They are working in groups to define financial vocabulary such as equity, principal, down payment, etc., and we are talking with them about what it takes to buy property. I joined Charles Schwab so that our class could "buy" one share of Activision Blizzard Gaming stock, because they have new products coming out that should "storm" the market. . .We looked at trends of the big game companies…over the last five years. High-interest math!

— Leanne Soucek, Teacher
  Arapahoe Ridge High School, Boulder, CO

Optional

Page 32–42

We had loan officers from local banks take students through the loan process after they had chosen a car, house, and occupation they'd be interested in pursuing. This was extremely beneficial.

— Linda Wulff, Chairperson, Communication Department
  Waupun High School, Waupun, WI

Clothing

Students are probably more aware of clothing costs than they are of any other expense. However, their present wardrobes may not be appropriate for the kinds of jobs they hope to hold. They must take into consideration whether they'll need a uniform, special work clothes, or professional clothing. They may not have any idea how much children's clothing costs, or how quickly a child can outgrow a pair of shoes. You may be able to provide some of this information, or perhaps students with younger relatives can get figures to share with the class.

Remind students that they will not need to replace their entire wardrobe each year.

Activities:

This is an opportunity to talk about workplace dress codes, what is appropriate to wear to work, and what to wear to an interview. Business and professional magazines, along with online resources will provide examples for those working in offices and for interviews. You'll want to talk about personal grooming issues as well. Perhaps someone from a major department store can provide props or advice. There are also a variety of reality TV shows that deal with these topics.

After this discussion, schedule a day where everyone is encouraged to dress as they would for a job interview. Recognize those in class who have made particularly good choices.

Writing Assignment:

Ask students to break down their personal annual clothing budget item by item. Have them use either a current budget or their projected budget for this exercise.

We have students draw a picture of themselves in their favorite outfit and then label the drawing with the cost of each article of clothing. When done they total up the cost of that outfit. We then ask them how often they wear that same outfit? That helps them figure out how much they will need to spend on clothing to get the look they want. It also helps them understand why their parents say no to a few extra clothing items!

— Becky Simmons, Transitions Lesson Coordinator
Marquette Senior High School, Marquette, MI

Optional

Lifestyle Math Page 43–47

Food

Page 84   Page 36

Food costs vary widely depending on the size of the family, ages of children, and personal preferences. You might ask for volunteers that live with varying numbers of family members to bring in a week's worth of grocery receipts to share with the class.

Activities:

Ask students to plan a week's worth of menus for their fictional family. Then prepare a shopping list item by item. As a homework assignment, ask them to go to the store and price the items on their shopping list.

> *When students were preparing their budgets (p. 84, Career Choices), I brought in fliers from the local supermarkets. They first had to prepare a weekly menu, then price out the ingredients using the flyer (or, for some, a trip to the supermarket). Most appreciated their mother's efforts and many had to "pare down" their menu selections (steaks were replaced by Hamburger Helper).*
>
> — Sue Butler, English Teacher
> Branford High School, Branford, CT

Sundries

Variations are also possible in this category. You might ask students to consider how much they spend now for such items as deodorant, shampoo, makeup, and how often they get their hair cut. They might ask their parents how often they need to buy toilet paper, soap, laundry detergent, and other sundries.

Activities:

An activity similar to the one in the food section could be completed for sundries, with one change: ask students to complete it for a month's worth of supplies and services.

Optional

Page 48–63

Entertainment and Recreation

Page 86

Page 37

This item can be easily overlooked or carried to an extreme. Ask students to think seriously about the "extras" that they would find most satisfying. What are their hobbies? Their passions?

Optional

Page 64–67

We discuss the various food plans and costs in Career Choices *along with the cost of eating out vs. the cost of eating at home. Since many of my students eat out, I asked if they would like to learn to prepare some of the foods that they buy when eating out and of course they were very interested. So, I directed them to the CopyKat web site (www.copykat.com) to find foods to cook at home that they normally eat while dining out.*

— Patricia Evans, Teacher
Hudson Middle School, Lufkin, TX

Vacations

Page 87

Page 38

Around this point, students start becoming more cautious as their expense figures begin adding up. Many say, "We don't need a vacation!" This is the time to remind them that vacations are important for their physical and psychological health.

Activities:

Optional

Page 68–70

Ask a travel agent to visit the class and talk about vacation expenses.

Invite someone to speak to the class about how he or she went to Europe on $50 a day.

Brainstorm as a class ways to have economical vacations, such as:

Camping

Hostelling

House swapping

Visiting friends and relatives

Page 88   Page 39

Child Care

Ask students to research monthly costs for each of the child care arrangements listed on page 88 of *Career Choices*. You may want to divide the class up and give each small group a category to research.

It is important to point out that students should not assume "Grandma" will take care of their children. Failure to budget for this important expense could be disastrous.

Invite a panel of working parents to speak about their strategies for child care. One panel member should be single so students understand the unique child care challenges of one-parent households. Depending on the make-up of your class, you might find your panel among the parents of your students.

Optional

Page 71–72

Page 89   Page 40

Health Care

Because health insurance options are complicated and often in flux, for the sake of this exercise use the chart provided on **The Teachers' Lounge** for average health insurance costs. This is a good time to point out that budget line items can fluctuate from year to year. Health insurance and health care costs are just one of those items.

Invite an insurance agent in to discuss health care costs, pensions, and saving plans.

Many of my female students planned not to get married ("didn't want the commitment"), but they also planned children out of wedlock. After the budgeting exercise many said, "I don't think I can afford to have a baby."

— Linda Fraser, Instructor, Tech Prep Program
Edison High School, Minneapolis, MN

Optional

Page 74–75

Page 89   Page 40

Furnishings

Refer students to web sites of large department stores to get sample costs of furnishings. Students will want to add the electronic equipment they plan to own to this line item.

Activity:

This is a good time to discuss how each new electronic device adds a burden to household budgets. As a group, research and brainstorm the "must have" electronic appliances available in each decade in the last 60 years. Write the following dates on the board and by each date, write the electronics that *most* households had in that year. Invite an individual who is over 65 years old to help with this project.

1950	1960	1970	1980	1990	2000	2010
radio	radio					
	TV					
	Hi Fi					

Students will notice that the lists grow longer and longer as the years progress. What has this phenomenon done to household budgets? How have families compensated for the increase in costs? Could this be one of the reasons many households require two incomes to survive? Is there just too much to buy?

Savings

Refer to the charts on page 91 of *Career Choices*.

Important: Planning for retirement is important and should be encouraged for all ages of students. You will be doing your students a great service by spending time on this concept.

Activity:

You'll find the retirement calculators on **CareerChoices.com** particularly intriguing for your students (or yourself). The magic of compounding interest tax-free over 20, 30, 40 years is very motivational. Do your students a favor and devote some time to this important experience. Create a couple of scenarios for your students to research, varying when an individual starts making retirement account deposits, the rate of return, and the amount deposited each month.

The calculator can be accessed through the **My10yearPlan.com** activity for savings by clicking on CareerChoices.com Activity in the left navigation and then clicking Saving for Retirement. See also page 100 of *Lifestyle Math* for an example of what depositing $100 per month would earn.

Optional

Page 80–86

The Savings Book
by Gary Soto

Read after completing page 89
in *Career Choices*

Optional

Page 76–84

4/61

Recommended Reading:

The Millionaire Next Door: The Surprising Secrets of America's Wealthy by Thomas J. Stanley, Ph.D., and William D. Danko, Ph.D. Longstreet Press, 1996

This best seller is a fascinating study of the characteristics and behaviors displayed by individuals and families who are able to amass net assets of at least one million dollars. As to who these people are, the title says it all. Many "millionaires" in the United States don't necessarily live in luxury communities; they are our neighbors and friends, blue collar as well as white collar. The text is easy to read and chock full of interesting details students will love. It will be a launching point for lively discussions and energizing debates.

And don't be discouraged by the copyright date. The suggested strategies are just as valid today as they were over 15 years ago. You can find used copies on Amazon.com.

We show our students a savings calculator, using different scenarios. It is important for them to see how much can be saved, even if they are only putting in a small amount each month. We also discuss how savings can be critical to success, especially when unexpected expenses arise! Many students have come back and said they started a savings account after this class. They had no idea that saving $10 a week the entire time they were in high school could equal so much money at graduation!

— Becky Simmons, Transitions Lesson Coordinator
Marquette Senior High School, Marquette, MI

Miscellaneous

Page 90

Page 41

Ask the class to brainstorm other items that might go in this miscellaneous category. See page 84 of *Lifestyle Math* for examples.

My students play a simulation game called "Living On Your Own." They get a job, pay a deposit on an apartment, pay their deposit on utilities, etc. Students clock in each day. A class period is worth eight hours of work. They learn to budget their money because they must pay out-of-pocket, and emergencies each week along with monthly and weekly bills. We devote one day a week to this activity although my students would like to do it every day.

My students can't believe these activities are really English. I remind them that the skills learned in English (reading, writing, speaking, and listening) are the skills we are using.

— Linda Spriggs, English Department Chairperson
Lithia Springs High School, Lithia Springs, GA

Your Budget Profile

Page 92   Page 42

Students will total their figures from the previous pages to get the average monthly expenses for their desired lifestyle.

Writing Assignment:

Have students write a budget narrative describing, explaining, or justifying each of their line items. For example:

Housing:

The cost of a three-bedroom, two-bath home in a nice area of the city is $289,000. Amenities include fenced yard, fireplace, and large family room. It is located in one of the best school districts. Utilities are a moderate expense because of the conservation efforts of my family. The only high expense in this category is the gas bill because it gets cold in the winter.

Once these papers are complete, ask the students to share their budget figures (pages 92 and 93) and their budget narratives with their friends and family members. With this information, friends and family can reinforce the next phase of the course: how to prepare for a career that will support this lifestyle.

My favorite unit is Chapter Four, "What Cost This Lifestyle?" Your process is easy to understand with brief explanations, and I found your tables to be very realistic. Because this is an English class, I had the students write a paper at the end of the unit explaining what they had learned from the process. Some were wonderful!

— Dorette Kanengieter, 11th and 12th Grade English/Language Arts and Applied Communications Instructor
Owatona High School, Owatona, MN

Common Core Standards for English

W.9-10.6. Use technology, including the Internet, to produce, publish, and update individual or shared writing products, taking advantage of technology's capacity to link to other information and to display information flexibly and dynamically.

W.9-10.7. Conduct short as well as more sustained research projects to answer a question (including a self-generated question) or solve a problem; narrow or broaden the inquiry when appropriate; synthesize multiple sources on the subject, demonstrating understanding of the subject under investigation.

W.9-10.8. Gather relevant information from multiple authoritative print and digital sources, using advanced searches effectively; assess the usefulness of each source in answering the research question; integrate information into the text selectively to maintain the flow of ideas, avoiding plagiarism and following a standard format for citation.

W.9-10.9. Draw evidence from literary or informational texts to support analysis, reflection, and research.

Optional

Page 85

What Salary Will Support This Lifestyle?

Page 93   Page 42

Learning Objective:

To help students recognize the impact career choice has on personal lifestyle. This activity will help them begin selecting careers that match their personal lifestyle budget.

Presentation Suggestions:

One final step is required before monthly expenses can be transposed into the salary required to support this lifestyle: students must factor the tax withheld from their paycheck to arrive at their gross income. Gross income is the amount listed as the salary on career research sites. This figure will be very important as they continue the career research process.

Activity:

Spend one or two class periods conducting research at the career center or online. Students will need to compile a list of all the careers and jobs they can find that are interesting and also will support their desired lifestyle. They will want to add this list to their *Career Portfolio* notebook for reference.

What Careers Support Your Lifestyle?

Page 94   Page 43

Learning Objective:

To help students start matching career choice with income potential and to help students realize that most careers that provide enough income to support a family require post-secondary education or training.

Presentation Suggestions:

Ask students to read the text and follow the directions to find careers that match their income requirements. With an idea of the cost of the lifestyle they envision, their research will have more meaning and be more motivational.

Once they have completed this activity, have students examine the job titles they found and determine what they have in common. Because most students' lifestyle choices will reflect middle class (or higher) aspiration, they will better understand the need to prepare for college or post-secondary training in order to reach their lifestyle goals.

Optional

Page 86–91

I do a scenario unit. Students pick a real life situation from a hat which may involve a single parent, a dropout, a college student, or a lawyer. Each must locate a job in the employment listings of a newspaper, prepare a budget, and go through an interview with me. By starting with real life situations, students realize they don't want the handicap of being a single parent or high school dropout.

— Danah L. Mayers, English Teacher
Sequoyah Middle School, Edmond, OK

Hard Times Budget

Page 96

Page 43

Learning Objective:

To provide students with the experience of budgeting the most common way—by having a total income figure and then allocating available funds to cover budget line items. This also provides experience adjusting budgets when income is reduced.

Presentation Suggestions:

Learning to budget for subsistence is important for everyone, particularly for students who are planning for college or post-secondary training. Too many students fail to complete college because they can't figure out how to meet their daily expenses on a limited income, so learning to live on little is a survival skill that will help them stay in school. As life changes, lifestyle expectations can become disproportionate compared to earning potential. Learning to budget in a way that matches reality is very important.

Ask students to review the figure they arrived at on page 93. If this seems beyond what they think they will earn in a year, ask them to research that more appropriate figure and enter it on line (b). Now they must figure their net pay (take-home) from this figure. The formula is as follows:

$$\frac{\rule{3cm}{0.4pt}}{\text{annual salary}} \div 12 = \frac{\rule{3cm}{0.4pt}}{\text{(b) monthly salary}}$$

$$\frac{\rule{3cm}{0.4pt}}{\text{(b) monthly salary}} \times 80\% = \frac{\rule{3cm}{0.4pt}}{\text{net or take-home pay}}$$

Depending upon the population you are working with, you might choose to assign this exercise using the figures for the following:

- A person earning the minimum wage

- A single-parent family living on TANF (Temporary Assistance for Needy Families)

- A single-parent family living on unemployment insurance

Writing Assignment:

Have students write a budget narrative for this new minimalist budget. Additional direction is found on page 4/63 of this guide. After studying, analyzing, comparing, and contrasting their budget narratives (the one they completed from their work on page 92 of *Career Choices* and this new minimalist budget narrative), ask students to write an essay exploring strategies for "downsizing" their lifestyle because they lost their job when the company they worked for moved their position overseas.

Common Core Standards for English

Optional

W.9-10.2. Write informative/explanatory texts to examine and convey complex ideas, concepts, and information clearly and accurately through the effective selection, organization, and analysis of content.

W.9-10.3. Write narratives to develop real or imagined experiences or events using effective technique, well-chosen details, and well-structured event sequences.

W.9-10.5. Develop and strengthen writing as needed by planning, revising, editing, rewriting, or trying a new approach, focusing on addressing what is most significant for a specific purpose and audience.

Page 92–94

Some Sample Budgets

Page 97–101   Page 44–45

Learning Objective:

To have students learn to budget the way most do—by taking a given income and deciding how it should be allocated. An added observation will be the impact of career choice on lifestyle.

Presentation Suggestions:

The earlier budget exercise gave students a chance to dream about their future lifestyle, an extremely important thing for them to do. In the real world, though, budgets do not determine income. Instead, it is quite the opposite. In this exercise, students can begin doing something they are likely to become very familiar with later in their lives: deciding how to live within a fixed income. We have presented five stories, each representing a fairly common situation.

> Phyllis is a single parent supporting her two children and herself on her income alone.

> Will is a single person living in subsidized housing provided, in his case, by the military.

> Jeff and Francie are a typical blue-collar couple.

> Carl and Ruth head a double-income professional household.

> Ben and Lynn represent the two-parent, single-income family.

There are two ways to assign the exercise. You could ask students to complete it on their own, or you might break the class into groups and assign a particular budget to each. Group members can spend time discussing how the money should be allotted, and doing necessary research (don't forget the extensive resources on **CareerChoices.com**). Then, when the class comes back together, each group can present its budget to the class.

Follow-up:

This is a good time to talk about **dual-earner families** (both individuals work in low-skill jobs without a career plan) versus **dual-career families** (each individual has a career plan that focuses on the acquisition of additional skills to upgrade their desirability as an employee).

Common Core Standards for English

SL.9-10.1. Initiate and participate effectively in a range of collaborative discussions (one-on-one, in groups, and teacher-led) with diverse partners on grades 9–10 topics, texts, and issues, building on others' ideas and expressing their own clearly and persuasively.

The Hard Times Budget, reinforces the idea of "Wants" and "Needs". Most students will have a large portion of their budget dedicated to Entertainment, which can easily be eliminated from a budget when times are tough. I have my students do their "trimming back" on their own, then partner them up to "compare notes", which leads to a classroom discussion of personal choice of essential personal needs of a family and their wants.

— Cathie Klein, College & Career Readiness Coordinator
  Seaman High School, Topeka, KS

A Few Words About Poverty

Page 102–103   Page 46

Learning Objective:

To help students recognize the causes of poverty and to reduce their chances of becoming impoverished.

Presentation Suggestions:

Review the materials presented in the book in class. Then have students study the statistics on poverty. Ask them to select the statistic they found most startling and discuss why they think this condition exists. Have students share their thoughts with the class. On the board, list any statistic mentioned by a student in order to see if there is a consensus on which facts are most disturbing.

Ask students to discuss the questions on page 103 of *Career Choices*, "Could You Become a Poverty Statistic?"

A word of caution: Be particularly sensitive to students who may be living in poverty. If you think this might present a problem, ask a counselor to help facilitate this discussion. The important theme of this follow-up discussion should be that planning, energy, and a vision now while in school can enable individuals to work their way out of poverty.

Activities:

At the beginning of class, ask students to list the factors they think cause poverty. (Examples: lack of education, too few jobs, high cost of housing, inflation, the changing economy, lack of opportunity to succeed, inability to budget, or to live within one's means.)

Gender Equity Activity:

Ask a single parent on public assistance or a panel of single mothers living in poverty to talk with the class about what they thought they were going to be when they were growing up, how they got into their present situation, and, if appropriate, what their plans are for the future.

This activity could be especially powerful for young women in the class. Some may not think it's necessary to prepare for a career—there will always be someone else willing and able to support them. Students of both sexes may feel that poverty is something that happens to other people, never to anyone they know. This activity could be both a cautionary tale and a lesson in empathy.

Composition:

Poverty Is Only a Divorce Away: A National Crisis for Children.

After students research the topic and write up their findings, ask them to come up with recommended solutions.

After this assignment, brainstorm reasons women and men end up as poverty statistics. One example is that they are replaced in industry by automated machinery or robots. Another is drug or alcohol addiction.

Debate:

Do men and women experience poverty differently?

> *One student, who was doing the grocery shopping required for the budget, saw a woman with her child at the store. The student's scenario, chosen in class, seemed similar to this woman. As they both shopped for bargains, the student became aware that the scenario was real. The next day she shared the experience and cried in class. She described the clothing and attitude of the woman. She said she never wanted that scenario for herself, therefore she was never quitting school or having children too soon.*
>
> — Danah L. Mayers, English Teacher
> Sequoyah Middle School, Edmond, OK

Optional

Page 95–97

Optional

Miss Rosie
by Lucille Clifton

Christmas Day in the Workhouse
by George R. Sims

Page 87–94

Read after completing page 103 in **Career Choices**

Money Isn't Everything

Page 104–105   No Workbook
                              Page

Learning Objective:

To explore the myth that money will make you happy.

Presentation Suggestions:

It's a very common perception: life would be perfect if only one were rich. Statistics and anecdotal evidence, however, indicate that this is not so. Present the information to the class and have them discuss why they agree or disagree with the evidence. Ask students to list rich people or celebrities who have been in the news in recent years because of personal problems that would seem to indicate they are not entirely happy. Examples: Lindsay Lohan (numerous arrests, chemical dependency), Michael Jackson (divorce, chemical dependency death), Britney Spears (chemical dependency, suicide attempts, divorce), Mary-Kate Olsen (eating disorder), O.J. Simpson (numerous felonies, divorce), Amy Winehouse (alcoholism, death).

Activities:

Bring in newspaper or online articles or ask students to research and write a short paper based on a print or video interview with a wealthy person who has recently had problems. Have them share their reports in class. The same phrase will turn up repeatedly: money isn't everything.

If you know of a wealthy person in your community who has overcome personal tragedy, or who has given up "life in the fast lane" to do meaningful but unglamorous work, you might ask him or her to talk on this subject with the class.

Reading Assignment:

The Gift of the Magi, by O. Henry

After reading this story of a young couple who sacrifice their most precious possessions for each other, discuss how is happiness defined? Students will argue this one!

Optional

Gift of the Magi
by O. Henry

Page 95–102

Read before you assign *Money Isn't Everything* on pages 104–105 in *Career Choices*

Psychological Costs—
Sacrifices Versus Rewards

Page 106–110   Page 46–48

Learning Objective:

To help students learn that there are sacrifices and rewards associated with every job and every lifestyle. This exercise should help them evaluate both aspects of any career they are considering, and to decide whether or not it would be a wise choice.

Presentation Suggestions:

Discuss the material presented in *Career Choices*, using Bert's story as an example. Ask the class to add to the answers provided.

Then break the class into small groups and assign each to discuss Leon, Vincent, Sara, or Rosa's story answering the questions that follow. Bring the class back together, and have the groups summarize the story, and report their answers to the questions. Allow time for students to discuss as a group or to add to its answers.

In wrapping up, be sure to emphasize how important it is for each student to evaluate his or her own values in conjunction with the careers presented. Students should see that, depending on a person's values, some sacrifices would be devastating while others would not be too hard to accept. Similarly, some rewards would be well worth any sacrifice for certain individuals, while for others the same rewards would be less than satisfying.

Activities:

Ask students to write a paragraph about the situation of a well-known professional person in a position they know something about and answer the questions from this exercise for that individual. Suggested individuals might be the President of the United States, the governor of your state, or the mayor of your city. In the high tech world: Bill Gates (Microsoft), Mark Zuckerberg (Facebook), Marissa Mayer (Yahoo), or Meg Whitman (Hewlett-Packard).

Have a panel of community members in different professions discuss the rewards and sacrifices involved in their jobs and what values are reflected in both areas. Be sure to let your panelists know what you want them to talk about ahead of time. They may not have given this much thought.

Encourage students to watch some of the celebrity interview shows on TV, or bring in a DVD if you can. In-depth interviews with Barbara Walters or Piers Morgan often bring out this kind of information.

You Win Some, You Lose Some

Page 111   Page 49

Learning Objective:

To help students recognize the rewards and sacrifices of specific careers as they relate to their work values.

Presentation Suggestions:

Have students complete the exercise individually, or break the class into small groups to discuss and come to an agreement concerning which work values would be rewarded and which would be sacrificed in each of the careers listed. Follow with class discussion.

Then have students go back and circle any careers that are compatible with their own work values. A compatible career would be one in which at least one of their top values matches the rewards, while none of their top three is listed as a sacrifice.

Students are now beginning to relate their own work values to specific career choices.

Activities:

Have students list five careers they have considered for themselves in recent years, identifying which work values would be rewarded or sacrificed in each job.

> *The students are beginning to see that a career offers more than just an income. The psychological rewards are a new concept for many of them.*
>
> — Linda Poznanter, Careers Teacher
> Oasis High School, Fallbrook, CA

After-Hours Rewards

Page 112–113   Page 50

Learning Objective:

To demonstrate that values not satisfied on the job can be met with appropriate after-hours activities. This is an important concept, since few careers will be a perfect fit with all of a person's top work values.

Presentation Suggestions:

After presenting the material and going over the examples in *Career Choices*, have students complete the exercise individually or in pairs. Discuss as a class. There is likely to be some disagreement, and that's okay. An individual's perceptions are likely to be valid for him- or herself.

In the examples presented, a social worker would, of course, meet his or her need to help others. Creativity, too, would come into play through creative problem-solving in crisis situations. To meet a need for power, a social worker might consider being an officer in a community organization or political group.

A computer tech might feel secure about working in the high tech industry. He or she is likely to work with many potential friends. A need to directly help others might be met through community volunteer work.

A carpenter might satisfy a need for adventure with vacations in the wilderness or with hang gliding or similar sports as hobbies.

A traveling sales representative would need to make a point of being available to his or her family when home, calling nightly from the road, and perhaps taking family members along on a trip from time to time.

A homemaker might satisfy a need for power by taking a leading role in community activities.

A museum guide might find adventure spending a vacation working on an archaeological dig.

A professor might get recognition from publishing books and articles.

A farmer might find friendship in community or religious groups.

A psychologist might satisfy a need for aesthetics by collecting art or find adventure learning to pilot an airplane.

An accountant might find power by starting his or her own firm or find a creative outlet in painting or piano lessons.

A chemist might gain recognition by giving demonstrations to groups of school children.

A writer might find friendship in a writers' group or workshop.

A veterinarian could find power by leading a campaign to save an endangered species.

Activities:

Perhaps the same panel that spoke about rewards and sacrifices could address the question of how they meet some of their other values outside of the work setting. Discuss the concept that leisure activity is really work—unpaid work, perhaps—but work nevertheless. These endeavors meet the human need for meaningful work when that need isn't fully realized in paid employment.

Essay:

Ask students to choose a career that currently sounds interesting. Next have them review their top three work values based on their scores from their Work Values Survey in Chapter 2. (*Career Choices*, pages 34–35).

With this background information, students will write a one-page paper responding to the following questions:

Based on my work values, is this a good career choice for me? Why or why not? If this career doesn't meet all of my top values, what can I do outside of my work hours to fulfill my personal propensities?

Note: Students will use this higher order reasoning in Chapter 6 when they begin a formal career research project, so this preliminary practice is helpful in preparing them.

Common Core Standards for English

W.9-10.2. Write informative/explanatory texts to examine and convey complex ideas, concepts, and information clearly and accurately through the effective selection, organization, and analysis of content.

W.9-10.3. Write narratives to develop real or imagined experiences or events using effective technique, well-chosen details, and well-structured event sequences.

When we were talking about a balanced lifestyle, we talked about hobbies. Students brought in pictures or examples of their hobbies and did a quick five-minute presentation. The kids really enjoyed this. We talked about what needs or values their hobbies satisfied.

— Deb Plantz, Language Arts Teacher
South Tama County High School, Tama, IA

An Investment in Education Yields Dividends for a Lifetime

Page 116–117   Page 51–53

Learning Objective:

To demonstrate the financial payoff—over a lifetime—of an investment in education.

Presentation Suggestions:

Once students review the chart on page 116 ask this question: Does a common thread run through the data presented?

One obvious theme is that more education usually means increased earning potential. Be sure to remind the students that this is not a hard and fast rule—there are lots of exceptions—but, in the majority of circumstances, education and training usually correlate with earnings.

Ask students to complete the math on page 117. What is their response to these figures?

Example:

A student who expects to be in the workforce 38 years between the ages of 18 and 65 (taking time out for schooling and raising a family) and lives in a state with a minimum wage of $7.25 would have a chart like this:

$20,000 x 38 years in workforce = $760,000 lifetime earnings $30,000 x 38 years in workforce = $1,140,000 lifetime earnings

$50,000 x 38 years in workforce = $1,900,000 lifetime earnings $75,000 x 38 years in workforce = $2,850,000 lifetime earnings

$100,000 x 38 years in workforce = $3,800,000 lifetime earnings

What is the difference between a $20,000 and $30,000 annual salary over a lifetime? $190,000

What is the difference between a $20,000 and $50,000 annual salary over a lifetime? $380,000

What is the difference between a $20,000 and $75,000 annual salary over a lifetime? $2,090,000

What is the difference between a $20,000 and $100,000 annual salary over a lifetime? $3,040,000

What is the current minimum wage (rate per hour) in your state or city? $7.25

How much can a person earn per year at that hourly rate? $15,080

What does that equal over your lifetime? $573,040

You may also wish to direct students to view "The Link Between Earnings and Education," a chart of average earnings by educational attainment, by clicking on the CareerChoices.com Activity link in the left navigation of the "An Investment in Education" page within My10yearPlan.com®.

Visual Reminder:

Ask a digitally-savvy student to create a banner or poster for the classroom:

The More You Learn…The More You Earn!

At this point in the course, post this at the front of the room as a visual reminder. This course is not promoting the notion that you need to earn a lot of money to be happy, but is helping students understand that education and training are valuable assets and can be their ticket to a life of their choosing.

How Do You Want to Spend Your Time?

Page 118–119   Page 52–53

Beginning the Planning Process

Learning Objective:

To help students recognize that education and training pays off in life satisfaction. This awareness is a critical first step to their education and training plan.

Presentation Suggestions:

Have the students complete the Lifespan Graph on page 118 of *Career Choices*. What do their graphs show? Comments should suggest that time spent on the remainder of their education is short compared to the years they'll spend in the workforce.

Next ask the students to complete the worksheet on page 119 using the information from the Lifespan Graph.

Discuss the ratio between years spent in post-secondary education and years in the workforce. Do the energy and time spent in training seem worth it in the long run?

Portfolio Follow-up:

The charts found on pages 116–119 begin a process that will continue through the balance of the course. The information students are gathering and analyzing will culminate in completion of the Education and Training Plan on pages 270–273. These charts show each student's education plan from high school through post-secondary education and training programs and into the workforce.

Now is a good time to begin talking about education and training alternatives, particularly if you sense your students will struggle getting through college or trade school (for financial or academic reasons). Students can take different paths to their ultimate career choice as long as they keep their eye on the goal (vision) and are willing to do what is necessary to achieve that goal (energy).

Graphic Organizer:

On page 227 of *Career Choices*, students will have the opportunity to create a Career Back-up plan for an industry of interest. This chart will detail various careers within their area of interest based on the education and training levels. This alternative career ladder will graphically demonstrate how commitment to education and training pays off.

Optional

Careers are listed on index cards along with wages. Students are to calculate how many hours/weeks/months they must "work" to afford something on a "wish" list that they brought to class from the previous day. Later, they learn that the cards were color-coded by education levels. They quickly see that wages are directly proportional to education.

— Judy F. Miller, Teen Living Teacher
   Clinton Middle School, Clinton, TN

Page 98–99

Ask Someone
Who's Been There

Page 120

Page 54

Learning Objective:

To help students gain specific information about the costs and rewards of various careers from people they know through the interview process. This is likely to be more meaningful and to stick with them longer than any information they read in a book.

Presentation Suggestions:

While making the assignment, be sure to remind students of the etiquette of interviewing. When asking for the interview, they should clearly indicate its purpose and how much time it will take. If they are interviewing people outside their immediate family or visiting people on the job, it is essential to be punctual and not stay any longer than they said they would. After the interview, they should send a brief, handwritten [not email!] thank you note.

As in most interviews, the questions asked by the interviewer will usually solicit responses from the interviewee that take the conversation to other topics or areas. For instance, journalists are always looking for a new lead so they listen and let people talk. This type of interview provides the best and richest information. Encourage your students to ask each question on page 120 and then listen carefully, allowing the interviewee to go off on tangents if they choose. Remind students that the interviewee should be doing 90% of the talking. Because of the nature of these questions, they'll unearth information about a particular job or career that they wouldn't normally learn from simply reading about it.

When students have completed their interviews, ask them to share what they learned and add their written notes as a document in My Portfolio in My10yearPlan.com®.

Follow-up:

Encourage students to keep these questions in mind and to continue to ask them of individuals working in other fields as they proceed with their career planning process.

My10yearPlan.com®: Staying Organized with My Portfolio

To help them stay organized, students can upload up to 1 MB of documents to the My Portfolio area of their My10yearPlan.com® account. This gives them a consistent place to store resumes, letters of recommendation, PDFs of any PowerPoint or graphic design projects, and any writing samples that they may need for job interviews or post-secondary applications.

To add a document, students simply click "add new file" in the appropriate category. They then select a file from their computer, give it a title, and it's saved to their account. As is the case with the data they enter from their workbooks, the files students upload are accessible for all four years they are in high school.

Easier Said Than Done

Page 121   Page 55

Learning Objective:

To help students realize that, in order to meet long-term goals, they will have to make some short-term sacrifices. Additionally, to provide a decision-making model that will help them keep their goals in mind.

Presentation Suggestions:

As a class, discuss long-term and short-term goals in relation to the examples presented. In each case, ask students to circle the long-term goal and underline the short-term goal, and then to make a decision about the best course of action for each individual. Complete the chart at the bottom of the page.

Then ask students to turn back to page 63 and identify two or three of their own long-term lifestyle goals. Have them use the model provided to make some decisions about their own current activities.

Activities:

In class, consider what might have happened if certain historical figures had sacrificed their long-term goals in favor of the short term. First, you must decide what those long-term goals were. For example, what if Thomas Jefferson had decided to stay home and work in his garden instead of going to Philadelphia and writing the Declaration of Independence? (His long-term goal: to help his country gain independence. His possible short-term goal: to get rid of the crab grass.)

I have students write a lifestyle/budget essay to be shown to parent(s) at conference time after completing chapters 1–4 in Career Choices. *The essays are saved and taken home, to be kept and re-read in 20+ years.*

— Kathy Andersen, Journalism/Language Arts Teacher
Central High School, Aberdeen, SD

Optional

A Legacy for my Daughter
by James Webb

Page 103–107

Read after completing pages 114–121 in ***Career Choices***

Career Pathways

One way of integrating career/technical education and academics is through career pathways. The U.S. Department of Labor has outlined 16 pathways or clusters that "encompass virtually all occupations from entry through professional levels."

Agriculture, Food & Natural Resources	Architecture & Construction	Arts, A/V Technology, & Communications	Business & Administration
Veterinary Assistant Environmental Engineer Biochemist	Plumber Architect Heavy Equipment Operator	Actor Journalist Graphic Designer	Accountant International Trade Manager Entrepreneur
Education & Training	**Finance**	**Government & Public Administration**	**Health Science**
College Professor Teacher Assistant Corporate Trainer	Tax Preparer Tax Attorney Banker	Urban Planner Recreation Director Legislator	Doctor Physical Therapist Hospital Administrator
Hospitality & Tourism	**Human Services**	**Information Technology**	**Law, Public Safety, Corrections, & Security**
Chef Hotel Manager Travel Agent	Child Care Worker Social Worker Psychotherapist	Web Designer Software Engineer Technical Writer	Paramedic Attorney Police Officer
Manufacturing	**Retail/Wholesale Sales & Service**	**Science, Technology, Engineering, & Mathematics**	**Transportation, Distribution, & Logistics**
Machinist Automated Process Technician Production Engineer	Customer Service Representative Interior Designer Marketing Director	Oceanographer Laboratory Technician Chemical Engineer	Truck Driver Pilot Automotive Technician

Students can learn about occupations within each of the pathways listed above using O*NET Online (http://www.onetonline.org). Hover over the "Find Occupations" drop-down and select "Career Clusters" to locate information using the pathway name.

Pathways are not "tracks" designed to steer students into specific careers. Rather, they are a means by which academics and work-related activities can be integrated using a shared theme—that of a specific area of interest. All students in pathways study the same core academic subjects; however, the information is taught in context, demonstrating how academics are relevant to the world of work.

The emergence of pathway programs makes the surveys in Chapter 5 all the more vital. As your students explore what is important to them in a career (i.e., flexibility vs. security) they will be better able to identify a career with the characteristics they desire. Understanding who they are and what they want before they make a pathway selection will reduce "lateral movement" because they will already know where they want to go.

Section 2: What Do I Want?

Chapter 5

Your Ideal Career

It's important for students to take a look at the general characteristics they hope to find in a job before they begin considering a specific career. Since there are thousands of job titles to choose from, narrowing down those choices at the outset will save a great deal of time. In this chapter, students are asked to identify some important factors: the physical setting of a job, the working conditions, the kinds of relationships they would like to have in their career, the psychological rewards they hope to achieve, how they want their career to relate to their family responsibilities, the financial situation they would find most comfortable, and the types of skills they have or are capable of learning.

Preparing for a career takes a great deal of dedication and energy. People who can identify careers that meet their personal needs, values, interests, and aptitudes are more likely to commit the time and resources to staying in school and getting the education and training required.

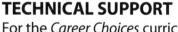

TECHNICAL SUPPORT
For the *Career Choices* curriculum
(800) 967-8016 or
support@academicinnovations.com

My Ideal Job

Page 126–134   Page 57–62

Learning Objective:

To help students narrow their career choice by first considering the general job characteristics that are most important to them, and then being creative in thinking of jobs that meet their requirements.

Presentation Suggestions:

In class, discuss each of the general classifications presented in this exercise to make sure everyone understands what is involved. Then have each student go through the lists, checking *all* the items they find appealing.

Once they have completed this process, ask them to go over their lists again, this time choosing only one or two items from each classification, those they think are most essential to career satisfaction.

Circle the boxes in front of these statements. When they have narrowed down their lists, have students enter their preferences on the chart on page 134, as illustrated by Gena's chart. Remind the class that this chart is important and that they should refer to it often as they consider different career options.

Initial Career Brainstorm:

After your students have completed their charts, begin brainstorming possible careers that meet their most essential career characteristics.

To get the class in a creative mood, discuss Gena's chart. Try to come up with as many other job titles as possible that fall within the range of her preferences (architect? advertising copy writer? public relations specialist?).

Encourage students to brainstorm careers that fit a variety of education training levels. Categories could include:

Master's or Doctorate Degree

Bachelor's Degree

Technical/Vocational school

High school graduate

Blue collar

White collar

Professional/Certified

Example: Gena might be a furniture refurnisher, antique restorer, art appraiser, cabinetmaker, art history professor, or office manager of a museum or gallery.

Break the class into focus groups of three or four students each. Have each student share his or her chart. Then instruct the group to brainstorm possible careers for each member. Students will always come up with the obvious, but encourage them to be as creative as possible. Bring the class back together and ask students to share their most creative ideas.

Energizer:

Offer a prize, extra credit points, or privileges to the group that comes up with the most creative ideas that fall within the range of its participants' charts. Let the class vote. This should encourage energy and creativity.

Resource:

Edward de Bono, *Lateral Thinking: Creativity Step by Step*. New York: Harper & Row, 1973.

My10yearPlan.com® Essentials:

This is a keystone activity. Data will be extracted and used in each student's *My 10-year Plan Summary Page*. Direct students to enter their work from this activity on My10yearPlan.com® the next time they log on. For more information, see Section 9 of this guide.

Chapter Introduction Video:

At the beginning of this chapter, consider showing the motivational chapter introduction video featuring Olympic Gold Medalist Dain Blanton (found on **The Teachers' Lounge**). Or, if your students are regularly using My10yearPlan.com®, have them watch the video online before starting their work in this chapter.

[One of my colleagues] has her classes create a PowerPoint for Chapter Five's "Your Ideal Career." She has students create a slide for each item of consideration: physical settings, working conditions, relationships at work, etc. Each PowerPoint is geared to each specific student's objectives in finding a job. It gives the students a guide for their careers or jobs, and definitely something to consider.

— Cindy Weems, AVID/Careers Teacher
Hudson Middle School, Lufkin, TX

A previous student, now at the community college, started the program wanting to be an auto mechanic but realized he didn't want the lifestyle and environment, so he has gone into computers because of the class.

— Jean Anne Conlon, English Teacher
South Tahoe High School, South Lake Tahoe, CA

Consider Your Options

Page 135–137   Page 63

Learning Objective:

To help students explore the employment options available in the changing workplace and analyze how best to match these with their personal levels of anxiety tolerance.

Presentation Suggestions:

Review the terms defined in the text to make sure students understand them. Then, as a class, list examples of jobs that fit each definition. Can the class think of individuals who have had composite careers? Sequential careers? (Examples: Emma Thompson has a composite career. She has won Academy Awards for her work as an actor and as a screenwriter. Former President George H. W. Bush's political career was sequential. He was a Congressman from Texas, Ambassador to China, Head of the CIA, Vice President, and President.)

Then ask students to circle the most appealing job characteristics on the chart provided. When they finish, bring up the topic of anxiety tolerance. This is an important issue that students may not have thought about before. Since anxiety is a part of everyone's life, learning to deal with and tolerate it is essential. That is not possible, however, until students can identify anxiety as a normal emotion.

Unless they can do that, they are likely to see this uneasy feeling as something to be avoided at all costs. Point out that running away from anxiety means denying themselves many of the things they hold most important in life. If something isn't important to a person, he or she is unlikely to feel anxious about it. For example, someone with low anxiety tolerance who dreams of attending a highly selective college probably would not even bother to apply for admission, because the fear or rejection would be so great. Similarly, the aspiring actor or actress will not audition for the community theater group if he or she thinks a knot in the stomach means it would be wise to reconsider that goal.

Discuss these and other examples with the class to make sure they thoroughly understand the topic. Then relate anxiety tolerance to job selection. As the chart shows, the most flexible careers, the ones offering the greatest amount of control and freedom, also call for more anxiety tolerance. Students need to be able to judge how comfortable they are with ambivalence and ambiguity in order to make a satisfying career choice in this regard. Point out, though, that with practice they can hope to increase their tolerance levels. Again, assure them the feeling is normal, but they must learn to trust themselves enough to go after what they really want.

Later, in Chapter 9 (*Career Choices*, pages 216–231), students will learn a strategy for developing anxiety tolerance.

Activities:

Ask a school counselor or psychologist to talk with the class about anxiety tolerance.

Employee or Employer?

Page 138–139   Page 64–65

Learning Objective:

To help students evaluate whether their attitudes, characteristics, and skills are more consistent with those of an employer or of an employee.

Presentation Suggestions:

Have students mark the checklist, score, and then discuss. Directions are on page 139 of *Career Choices*.

Point out that this is not a question of whether it is "better" to be an employee or an employer. It is simply a matter of what fits an individual's personality. Students should understand, too, that an employer can be anything from a self-employed individual to the owner of a huge corporation. Self-employed people don't necessarily have to invest a huge amount of money (another common misconception). Anyone with a skill that fills a need for someone else can do it. (Examples: carpenters, writers, child care providers, accountants, housekeepers, gardeners, hair stylists, caterers, plumbers, electricians, and physical trainers.)

Brainstorm the pros and cons of entrepreneurship. Students should realize that most people entering the workforce for the first time do not have the money or experience to start their own business. Point out that owning a business might be a future goal.

Activities:

Invite an entrepreneur to talk with the class. It's best if this is someone whose achievements are realistic enough for your class to identify with him or her.

The Small Business Plan—Ask students to complete this sentence in writing:

If I could start a business it would be a _____.

After reviewing the responses, form "entrepreneurial teams" of students with similar interests. Ask students to imagine they are partners and to write a business plan for a fictional business that they create.

They can start by writing a description of their business and naming it. They'll want to describe how their idea is unique and why it will succeed against the competition. How will they market their product or services? What are the start-up costs? Ask them to formulate a budget for the first six months of operations. How will they raise the capital?

The entrepreneurial committees will have a structured opportunity to write their job descriptions after they complete the activities on pages 162–165 of *Career Choices*.

Common Core Standards for English

W.9-10.3. Write narratives to develop real or imagined experiences or events using effective technique, well-chosen details, and well-structured event sequences.

What About Status?

Page 140–141   Page 65

Learning Objective:

To help students sort out their own feelings about status as it relates to job selection.

Presentation Suggestions:

Review the material presented and discuss the questions on pages 140-141. Then have students decide individually how they feel about the statements on page 141.

Debate:

Who should have more status, a teacher or a rock star?

Then ask your students to discuss if they would consider a career as a teacher, and why or why not.

Point out that in Japan, teaching is one of the highest paid and most respected professions. Also point out that, in past decades, teachers and professors were given higher status in the United States, as well.

Reading Assignment:

Goodbye, Mr. Chips, by James Hilton

> *My students interviewed a person who doesn't like his/her job so that they understand [the effect on a worker's morale and] what that can do to one's spirit over the years.*
>
> — Lynn Porter, Coordinator of High School Diploma Program
> Santa Monica-Malibu Unified School District, Santa Monica, CA

Optional

I Decline to Accept the End of Man
by William Faulkner

Page 108–111

Read after completing Chapter 5 in *Career Choices*

Section 2: What Do I Want?

Chapter 6

Career Research

In this chapter, students complete a three-step process as they begin researching a career choice that they will use for the remainder of the book. Be sure to emphasize that this is a *tentative* selection, one that will probably be changed a number of times, even during this course. There is no one perfect occupation. People entering the workforce today will change occupations several times throughout their lives.

The process we present in this chapter is based on the old saying "Tell me, I forget; show me, I remember; involve me, I understand." For many of us, career research involved only step one of this process. That stops far short of the goal: allowing students to get a real feeling for a career before they invest years of their lives preparing for it. Therefore, it is important to not only research a career with print or online resources, but to also experience it. Encourage students to take this extra step and visit, volunteer, or work within their career interest areas.

TV Worth Watching

It's not often we can recommend a TV show without reservation, but CBS's award-winning "Sunday Morning" is a treasure trove of materials you can use in your course. You'll find wonderfully written and produced segments on exceptional individuals working in the humanities and sciences. These are excellent resources for career exploration.

Check your local TV listing for the broadcast time in your area. The show runs for 90 minutes each week. You can find videos of selected segments from particular shows on their web site at **www.cbsnews.com/sundaymorning**.

Career Clusters

Page 145–146   Page 67

Learning Objective:

To help students understand the broad career interest areas and the types of jobs in each area. This will assist them in matching their own interests and aptitudes to specific career opportunities.

Presentation Suggestions:

Choosing a career path is probably the second-most important decision anyone makes. After all, most people spend at least fifty percent of their waking hours working—and that continues for up to 40 years. Taking the time to research and reflect on each career a student is contemplating is of critical importance. Getting appropriate education and training is needed to be competent and, therefore, competitive in your chosen career, but it requires a lot of resources: time, money, and energy. Preparing for a career that doesn't match your goals and personality is very costly.

Remind students that, yes, it takes time, but it will be the most productive time they'll spend in relation to their future happiness and life satisfaction. Having a career that matches their personality, dreams, life goals, and interests is, as they say, priceless.

The U.S. Department of Labor has outlined 16 Career Clusters that "encompass virtually all occupations from entry through professional levels." We've listed these clusters on pages 145–146 of *Career Choices*, along with sample occupations of each cluster. Students can locate information about occupations within each of the clusters using O*NET Online (see note below). Review each of the career interest groups presented and ask the class to think of additional careers that might fit in each category.

Chapter Introduction Video:

At the beginning of this chapter, consider showing the motivational chapter introduction video featuring Olympic Gold Medalist Dain Blanton (found on **The Teachers' Lounge**). Or, if your students are regularly using **My10yearPlan.com®**, have them watch the video online before starting their work in this chapter.

What is O*NET? www.onetonline.org

O*NET (Occupational Information Network), created and maintained by the U.S. Department of Labor, provides up-to-date, comprehensive information on thousands of jobs. The careers listed in each of the 16 Career Clusters share certain common characteristics. By investigating these family groups, students will come up with a number of career possibilities that might appeal to them.

Optional

The Boys' Ambition, excerpt from
Life on the Mississippi
by Mark Twain

Page 112–117

Read after reading page 146 in ***Career Choices***

Students enjoyed interviewing adults in the community who were already working in a career field of interest to them. Some were even offered part-time jobs or the opportunity to "shadow" an adult.

— Mary Turelia, 8th Grade English and Communications Teacher
North Royalton Middle School, North Royalton, OH

CareerChoices.com for Chapter 6

At the time of publication of this manual, the following activities were available on our web site CareerChoices.com for Chapter 6.*

Page 145–146—Career Research

- *Database:* Identifying Occupational Clusters

Page 148-149—Career Research

- *Database:* Interests: A Good Place to Start Your Career Search
- *Database:* Occupational Information by State
- *Database:* State Employment Climate Profiles
- *Database:* The U.S. Job Market

Page 150–155—Career Interest Survey

- *Database:* Searching the Occupational Outlook Handbook—Without Turning a Single Page

Page 158—The Shadow Program

- *Research Project:* Me and My Shadow

Page 159—The Shadow Program

- *Narrative/Instructional*: Writing a Business Letter

Page 160—Career Research

- *Directory:* Getting Experience — Volunteering

Page 209—The Economics of Bad Habits

- *Calculator:* Use Your Bad Habits to Fund Your Retirement
- *Interactive Quiz:* Investing Quiz
- *Calculator:* Everyday Savings Calculator

For detailed information and fee schedules, see pages 7/6–7/14 of this manual, or go online to the Visitor Section of **CareerChoices.com**.

You'll want to go online to see the most current index because of the growing and changing nature of the Internet. As we find new and better resources, we'll include them or substitute them for current lessons.

Bring In Your Identity

Page 147   Page 67

Learning Objective:

To help students select careers for further research based on the personal interests and aptitudes they discovered in Chapters 2, 3, 4, and 5 of *Career Choices*.

Presentation Suggestions:

At this point, students are ready to select some specific careers for more in-depth examination. Before they complete the exercise, make sure they understand that all of the work they have done up to this point must be considered in making these choices. A review of their data from chapters 2 through 5 is helpful now. In particular, have students review their bull's eye chart (page 27), their required annual salary (page 93), and their job characteristic chart (page 134).

The more careers studied, the greater the opportunity to find the best match. As you progress through the course, consider assigning additional *Career Interest Surveys* to research a STEM career, one career currently in high demand, and one career that experts predict will have a lot of job openings in the next 20 years.

Career Exploration Brainstorming Session (see page 13/9 for details)
You may want to contact a community service organization and solicit their help.

My 10-year Plan Summary Page:

If your students have been consistently entering their data from Chapters 1 to 5 onto their My10yearPlan.com® account, suggest they print their preliminary *My 10-year Plan Summary Page* to share with their team (use the print icon in the upper left corner of the Summary page). While this document will not be complete until the end of the course, by now it will have all of the information noted above. Plus, this simple act of reviewing what they have discovered so far will inspire your students, and they'll want to watch their 10-year plan grow. This can be very affirming for individuals.

Also at this point in the course, your students have enough information to be of value when meeting with a counselor or advisor. They can make their time more productive and quantitative by emailing their *My 10-year Plan Summary Page* before their appointment.

They can do this by opening the *My 10-year Plan Summary Page* and clicking on the email logo on the page that comes up. Naturally, they'll need to have the email address of the person they want to have review their plan.

And, yes, they can even share their plan with friends and family. Encourage them to solicit advice from as many trusted adults as they can to help them brainstorm careers that match their personality, goals, and strengths.

Optional

Possibilities

Lego
from
The New Yorker Magazine

Page 118–123
Read after completing page 147
in *Career Choices*

Common Core Standards for English

SL.9-10.4. Present information, findings, and supporting evidence clearly, concisely, and logically such that listeners can follow the line of reasoning and the organization, development, substance, and style are appropriate to purpose, audience, and task.

SL.9-10.5. Make strategic use of digital media (e.g., textual, graphical, audio, visual, and interactive elements) in presentations to enhance understanding of findings, reasoning, and evidence and to add interest.

Career Interest Survey

Learning Objective:

Page 150–155   Page 68–73

To help students begin an in-depth study of careers that match their aptitudes and interests. Students will learn to locate, analyze, and apply career information using print and online resources. They'll also gather preliminary education and training information specific to their chosen careers.

Presentation Suggestions:

Students will need to create a Career Interest Survey for each new career that is of interest to them. Using the survey they'll research what is required for competency in the field and evaluate whether the work conditions match their aptitudes, goals, and expectations for the lifestyle they envision. As they complete the survey questions, they'll need to go back to information they discovered about themselves earlier.

Mention that if they become interested in a career other than the three for which they are completing surveys, they will need to go back to complete a new Career Interest Survey. Explain that they must have this in-depth knowledge on any potential career before pursuing it. How awful to spend months or years preparing for a career only to discover it's not what you thought it would be.

This is an ideal opportunity to demonstrate different research techniques. Discuss basic career research methods and review the questions on the Career Interest Survey to make sure everyone understands. Students can do their research in the career center, at the library, and/or online.

Recruit your career center advisor to assist with this activity. There are excellent career research tools online; some of the best can be found through the U.S. Department of Labor web site.

My10yearPlan.com®:

If you are using My10yearPlan.com® in your course, you'll want to ensure that students understand how to complete their Career Interest Surveys on the site. There is a link to O*NET Online for easy access to this valuable research resource.

As students complete the surveys online, they can link back to activities in which they determined such things as their work behavioral style and salary requirements.

The My10yearPlan.com® program will not allow a student to randomly choose a career on which to build their 10-year plan. They must first complete a Career Interest Survey and work through the Decision-making Rubric (*Career Choices*, page 177). This will mitigate the misguided practice of building a plan around fantasized characteristics without doing the research to really understand the pros, cons, and possibilities of a career.

For more details about the Career Interest Survey functionality on My10yearPlan.com®, go to My10yearPlan.com® and click on FAQ in the left navigation.

My10yearPlan.com® Essentials:

This is a keystone activity. Data will be extracted and used in each student's *My 10-year Plan Summary Page*. Direct students to enter their work from this activity on My10yearPlan.com® the next time they log on. For more information, see Section 9 of this guide.

Activities:

Guest speakers can be very helpful at this point. Before choosing them, however, consider the careers of greatest interest to students. If no one seems to be a potential electrical engineer, for example, there's not much point in bringing one in to speak. Also, try to have a ratio of blue- and white-collar speakers consistent with the class's aspirations.

Ask speakers to discuss not only the tasks involved in their jobs, but also what they like and dislike about them, how they got interested in them, the necessary training, and so on. Allow time for questions from the class.

If you decide against having guest speakers, you might form committees of students interested in a particular career area and ask them to report on their research to the class.

Tomorrow's Jobs

Technological advances are changing the way we work. Job titles that are popular today may be very different in format or even defunct by the time your students complete their education and training.

At the end of each Career Interest Survey, students are asked to develop a timeline depicting the changes in that career over the last ten years and possible changes over the next ten years. In our swiftly changing society, this is a critical step in the career exploration process. Technology has already begun to prove its potential to automate jobs previously carried out by employees. Advanced telecommunications technology and the rapid industrialization of some of the world's largest developing countries have also made it possible for many jobs to be performed more cheaply in other countries. Manufacturing has already been largely outsourced, and even customer service can be provided by phone from countries on the other side of the globe. Students should, therefore carefully research their chosen careers to make sure they aren't expected to become obsolete in the U.S. in the near future. Instruct them to ask themselves, "Is this a job that could feasibly be accomplished by workers in another country?"

Occupations with the highest anticipated growth in the near term are those in health care, scientific, and technical services, though even service occupations could plausibly be outsourced. By education level, occupations that require some form of post-secondary education are projected to experience the greatest growth. Jobs requiring an associate degree are expected to grow the most, followed by jobs requiring a professional or master's degree. Jobs requiring only on-the-job training are expected to witness the least growth and consequently experience the greatest competition for jobs.

Also keep in mind that new technology will be sure to create jobs in the future that we can't even imagine today. Ultimately, students should be comfortable with the idea of change and seek to build skills that can be transferrable between various occupations.

The best place to start researching the outlook for particular occupations is at the Bureau of Labor Statistics web site (**www.bls.gov**) using the online version of the *Occupational Outlook Handbook* (**www.bls.gov/ooh**). Students will want to click on the link to "Overview of the Projections" at the bottom of the page and study the general societal trends affecting the workplace and employment. Students can also browse "Bright Outlook" careers—emerging careers and those that are expected to have a large number of job openings—at O*NET Online (**www.onetonline.org**) under the Find Occupations drop-down menu.

Activities:

Form groups with three students each. Using the data from the online article "Overview of the Projections" mentioned above, ask each group to list the five most "startling" statistics they found. Then ask each group to present their list, explaining why they found these statistics either intriguing or troubling.

Each group should review the three careers for which each member completed a Career Interest Survey. Ask the group to relate the information in the article to that particular career area or industry.

Using the complete *Occupational Outlook Handbook* online, each student should research the three careers in their survey in order to create the timeline. For each career, they'll find specific labor market information, societal and economic trends, and projections for the future.

Given their research, ask each student to rank their three choices, placing the one most likely to have the best future at the top of their list. While this may not be the career they ultimately choose when completing their plan in Chapter 12, at least students have evaluated this issue. By completing this step of the career exploration process, they understand how future workforce projections relate to job opportunity and job security.

Did any of your students discover their career choice might not be around by the time they finish their education and training? If so, work as a class to brainstorm some alternative careers with a strong prognosis for the future (taking the student's interests and aptitudes into account).

Common Core Standards for English

W.9-10.7. Conduct short as well as more sustained research projects to answer a question (including a self-generated question) or solve a problem; narrow or broaden the inquiry when appropriate; synthesize multiple sources on the subject, demonstrating understanding of the subject under investigation.

W.9-10.8. Gather relevant information from multiple authoritative print and digital sources, using advanced searches effectively; assess the usefulness of each source in answering the research question; integrate information into the text selectively to maintain the flow of ideas, avoiding plagiarism and following a standard format for citation.

Resources:

Jeremy Rifkin, *The End of Work: The Decline of the Global Labor Force and the Dawn of the Post-Market Era*. Tarcher/Putnam Books, 2004.

Rifkin's work is very interesting, well-written, and easy to read. This book will prepare you to answer your students' questions about the possibilities of the future workplace. It is an outstanding historical perspective of the transition of the worker from pre-industrial revolution, through the era of machines and mass production, to the advent of the information age in which he predicts there will be fewer and fewer workers required. His projections are insightful given the realities a decade later. Anyone interested in the dynamics of technology and globalization in the workforce will find this a fascinating read. His analysis seems hard to refute, yet he also offers some sensible ways in which society can adapt.

> *"Jeremy Rifkin addresses boldly and expertly a most important problem facing contemporary society, a problem most economists are reluctant to discuss… This is a very readable and important book."*
>
> — Wassily Leontief, Nobel Laureate, Professor of Economics
> New York University, NY

Seeing in the Mind's Eye*
Guided Visualization

Page 156–157   Page 73–74

Learning Objective:

To help students begin to think about—and actually experience—what it would be like to spend a typical day at the job of their choice.

Presentation Suggestions:

Review the concepts of visualization and "seeing in the mind's eye"* (SCANS) with the class, then guide students through the exercise using the script below. Ask them to choose one of the careers they researched for the Career Interest Survey. Have your students open their books to the exercise on page 157 in *Career Choices* or page 74 in their workbook and get out a pen before you begin.

Turn down the lights and close the doors and windows. If your room is unavoidably noisy, try to find a quieter one.

Speak slowly and quietly, pausing where indicated. Read the following script aloud.

> Relax and settle into your chair. Place your feet flat on the floor. Close your eyes. Clear your mind.
>
> Pay attention to your breathing. (Pause) Inhale slowly, filling your lungs with air. (Pause) Exhale slowly. (Pause)
>
> Take a few slow, deep, deliberate breaths. As you exhale, tell yourself to relax and let go. (Pause long enough for three or four deep breaths)
>
> Feel your body relax (Pause) from your face all the way down to your legs and toes. (Pause) Feel the pleasant warm and tingly feeling of relaxed muscles. (Pause)
>
> Now project yourself into the future. (Pause) You've completed your education. (Pause) You've found a job in the field of your choice. What is it? (Pause for 20–30 seconds) This is the beginning of a typical working day. (Pause) How do you feel as you get ready for work? (Pause) What are you wearing? (Pause) Are you looking forward to the day? (Pause)
>
> You're on your way to work. (Pause) Are you in a car or some type of public transportation? (Pause) Is it a long commute? (Pause) Or do you work at home? (Pause)
>
> You walk into your place of work. (Pause) What does it look like? (Pause) Who else is there? (Pause) How do they greet you? (Pause) How does your morning pass? (Pause) This is a typical day. What kinds of tasks do you see yourself doing? (Pause) Take a minute and do those tasks. (Pause for one minute)
>
> It's lunch time. (Pause) Where are you eating lunch? (Pause) Who is with you? (Pause)
>
> Back at work, you find some special challenges. What are they? (Pause) How do you deal with them? (Pause)

Work with those challenges for awhile. (Pause)

As you finish your day on the job, how do you feel? (Pause) What are you thinking about? (Pause) Do you have plans for this evening? (Pause) What are they? (Pause)

Now open your eyes and pick up your pen. Without saying anything, complete the exercise on page 74 in your workbook. Begin now. (Don't say anything more.)

Follow-up:

You might ask students to share any revelations they had during the exercise. For example, a future waiter or waitress may have realized how tired he or she would be by the end of the day. Suggest that students complete this type of exercise for each of the three careers they researched.

*One of the foundation skills recommended by SCANS is "seeing in the mind's eye." This skill is used by many successful people as they visualize how to complete a project at work or develop a new product.

The Shadow Program

Page 158–159   Page 75

Learning Objective:

To give students practice in writing a business letter and conducting an interview, and to allow them to see firsthand what it might be like to spend a day at a particular job.

Important note: In order to complete this exercise, students could miss an entire day of school. Check with your administration office and the students' parents for permission before proceeding. Solicit the support of your career counselor.

Presentation Suggestions:

This is an extremely valuable exercise, but it requires research on the part of the student to locate people who will consent to being "shadowed." We strongly urge that you get help from a volunteer. Many community or professional associations (Kiwanis, Lions, Soroptimists, Business and Professional Women) are supportive of such projects. These organizations are also a good starting point for locating the individuals who will take part in the exercise. Your Chamber of Commerce should have contact information for all the groups active in your community.

Don't be shy about calling. This is exactly the kind of program most professional and community organizations love to support. The secret is to ask up-front for a member to act as a liaison to organize and monitor the project. The right person will take 95 percent of the responsibility. All you need to do is supply him or her with complete copies of the student survey that follows, beginning on page 4/97.

Activity:

Make sure students understand that this is called the Shadow Program for a reason: shadows do not say anything, they do not do anything, they are just there. Emphasize the need for students to be as unobtrusive as possible, except during the agreed-upon interview time.

Use this exercise as an opportunity to review the components of a good business letter. Make the letter itself an assignment that will be graded on the basis of correct form, grammar, spelling, and neatness.

Over 150 students participated in Shadow Day at WRHS. Each student completed student profiles, wrote thank you notes, interviewed mentors, and conducted on-site evaluation forms… Students wrote reports on why people work and compiled graphic charts on their results.

— Marilyn D. Gattuso, English Teacher
Wahconah Regional High School, Dalton, MA

Energizer:

If the person shadowed is known to the student or is a family friend, it may be appropriate for some students to shadow their mentor beginning early in the morning at breakfast. It is a valuable lesson to observe a working parent and see how he or she mixes career and family.

English/Language Arts:

Use this exercise as an opportunity to review the components of a good business letter. Make the letter itself an assignment that will be graded on the basis of correct form, grammar, spelling, and neatness.

Ask students to write a short essay on what they learned from their day as a shadow and include it in their Career Resource File or online portfolio on My10YearPlan.com.

Common Core Standards for English

W.9-10.4. Produce clear and coherent writing in which the development, organization, and style are appropriate to task, purpose, and audience.

One girl (in our Career Choices *program) shadowed a medical surgeon into surgery, looked through a scope, then held some tissue… She's still talking about it two years later and has been accepted to nursing school!*

— Megan Schroeder, Vocational/Workplace Readiness Teacher
Cascade High School, Leavenworth, WA

TECHNICAL SUPPORT
For the *Career Choices* curriculum
(800) 967-8016 or
support@academicinnovations.com

Director of Mentors

The Director of Mentors position presents an opportunity to recruit a volunteer from the community. It is just the type of substantial assignment that involved, high-energy individuals want. Find the right person and let them do most of the work related to this effort.

How to Find Your "Director of Mentors"

Call the president of one of the service organizations whose members are career-oriented. Explain your project and ask for names of individuals who might be interested. Suggest you come and give a presentation at one of their meetings. This is ideal because you can generate a lot of interest and meet prospective volunteers. Be sure to take a couple of copies of *Career Choices* to pass around the audience as you speak. This visual prop will help them better understand what you are doing.

What to Look for in Your "Director of Mentors"

1. *Someone who has lived in your community long enough to have plenty of contacts.* A senior member of one of the professional service organizations mentioned earlier is ideal. A recently retired professional may have more time.

2. *Someone who likes to be responsible and follow through on a project from beginning to end.* The more the Director of Mentors does, the less responsibility you will have to assume. But remember that you have to let this person do his or her job. Give your Director of Mentors the necessary tools (completed, legible student surveys) and turn him or her loose. Provide support, praise, and appreciation!

This person could become a community liaison to your class. He or she could assist in finding guest speakers or perhaps be a guest speaker. Your volunteer might even be willing to mentor students with special needs. Many community members are vitally interested in working with young people. You can give them the opportunity to get involved. Be sure to share this *Instructor's Guide* and a copy of *Career Choices* with your volunteer. She or he might have great ideas.

Permission is granted to photocopy the surveys on page 4/97–4/100 of this guide.

Have each student complete the Shadow Program Student Survey. Pass these on so the Director of Mentors can begin the process of finding appropriate mentors.

Supply your volunteer with a copy of the Mentor Survey on pages 4/98 and 4/99 of this guide to use in locating mentors and matching students.

Hint: Ask the volunteer to share the completed Mentor Surveys with you. Keep a growing file for future years, along with a file of guest speakers.

Shadow Program Student Survey

Name _____ Age _____

High School _____ Grade _____

Teacher _____

Class Title _____ Period _____

Three careers of interest:

     1st choice _____

     2nd choice _____

     3rd choice _____

When I can shadow: (circle any restrictions)

     Any time   Evenings only

     Weekdays only   Weekends only

     Other _____

Explain any time restrictions such as employment or after-school activities from which you cannot be excused:

_____

_____

Do you plan to attend college?   Yes   No   Maybe   Undecided

Do you plan to attend trade school?   Yes   No   Maybe   Undecided

Why are you interested in these career areas? _____

_____

_____

_____

_____

Other considerations: _____

_____

_____

_____

Shadow Program Mentor Survey

We are seeking volunteers for a Student Career Shadow Program. This important activity links young people with someone in a career field in which they have expressed an interest. For a day or a portion of a day, the student will "shadow" that individual. They have been coached not to be obtrusive or to interrupt your work time. All we ask is that you grant 15-30 minutes for an interview at the end of the day.

If you are interested in allowing a student to "shadow" you for a day or a portion of a day, please complete the following survey and return to:

_____

_____

The student assigned to you will contact you directly by email, letter, and phone, so the two of you can arrange a convenient time.

Profession _____ Title _____

Name _____

Address _____

Day phone _____ Email _____

Evening phone _____ Fax _____

Company _____

Address _____

_____

A brief description of your job/duties _____

_____

_____

_____

Your educational background _____

_____

_____

_____

(Over)

Restrictions on shadowing times (days, times, etc.) _____

_____

Any preference on ability and motivation of student?   (check one)

_____ Please send me only motivated students.

_____ I am willing to work with an at-risk or under-motivated student.

_____ I am willing to work with a handicapped/learning disabled student.

_____ I would be especially good with _____

_____

_____ Undecided

Are you a working parent?   Yes   No

Optional: Would you consider allowing a student to come to your home an hour before you leave for work to observe how you mix career and family?   Yes   No   Perhaps

Optional: Would you consider speaking to a high school class on your area of career expertise or other professional experience?   Yes   No   Perhaps

Comments:

Shadow Program Referral Form

Referral for _____

Profession _____ Title _____

Name _____

Address _____

_____

Day phone _____ Evening phone _____

Email _____ Fax _____

Company _____

Address _____

_____

Restrictions on shadowing times _____

_____

Comments _____

_____

_____

_____

_____

If you have questions contact:

_____   _____
          Name   Day Phone

_____   _____
      Company Name   Email

                                 _____
                                       Evening Phone

Involve Me and I Understand

Page 160–161   Page 76

Learning Objective:

To allow students to observe people working in their chosen career field over a period of time through paid or unpaid employment.

Presentation Suggestions:

Review the material presented in the text and, as a class, try to think of paid and unpaid jobs for people wanting to work at the careers listed on page 160. Add to the list the careers students in your class are considering. Emphasize that the jobs may not be especially fun or interesting, and may offer little or no pay. The purpose is simply for the students to get into a position where they can observe people performing jobs that interest them and build experience that will look good on their resume. Instruct students to be especially observant of both what is happening around them and how they *feel*.

Have your students write a critique of each interview and experience (shadowing, interning, volunteering, beginning employment). They can use the questions on page 161 of *Career Choices* to stimulate their thinking. At the end of each critique they need to answer an important question: Is this a career that I should continue researching and pursuing? If they feel excited and stimulated by what they observe, then the answer should be yes!

My10yearPlan.com®:

Suggest students store their paid and unpaid work experience on My10yearPlan.com®. Direct them to the My Portfolio feature where they'll find categories for specific kinds of documents they can upload. For further details, see page 4/76 in this guide.

If some students aren't familiar with the basic process for browsing to find a file to upload or attach to an email, take time to walk them through the steps of this vital technology functionality. They'll use this skill in college and throughout their lives.

Follow-up:

Some students may want to do volunteer work with their shadow mentors. Please advise the students that it is not appropriate for them to ask about this on the day of their shadow assignment. Suggest that they follow up their visit with a thank you letter and a request for a volunteer position. It is not appropriate for them to mention a paid position unless it is offered by the mentor.

Again, your Director of Mentors can help. Finding these types of jobs, both paid and unpaid, usually takes someone with business or professional contacts.

Common Core Standards for English

W.9-10.6. Use technology, including the Internet, to produce, publish, and update individual or shared writing products, taking advantage of technology's capacity to link to other information and to display information flexibly and dynamically.

We used most of Chapter 6 during our Career Research paper assignment. In addition to writing a research paper, students are also required to present with a computer-generated multimedia presentation.

— Sharon Hurwitz, English Teacher and Technology Facilitator
Bethel High School, Hampton, VA

The Chemistry Test

Page 162–165   Page 77–78

Learning Objective:

To help students decide whether the careers they are considering are good matches for their personalities and working styles. To help them understand that matching individual strengths with job duties is an important step in effective team-building.

Presentation Suggestions:

Discuss the four personality styles described. This might be a good time to turn back to Chapter 2 (pages 38–43) for a quick review. If you are interested in providing your students with a more complete personal profile, you can order the official DiSC Profile assessment tool at www.discprofile.com.

Ask students to recall any occasions in the past few years when they've worked on a committee like the one described in the text. How did things work out? Can the students relate the results (either good or bad) to the personality styles of the people involved and the jobs they were assigned?

Have students complete the rest of the exercise individually or in small groups. Encourage students to come up with their own solutions before they look at the answers provided.

Energizer:

Student Team Project

Have students identify their work behavioral styles from either the exercise on pages 38–43 or using the actual Personal Profile Instrument. (Ask your career center if they have access to this tool.)

Forming heterogeneous groups that include at least one of each personality type:

Once they have identified their predominant style, ask all the Dominance (A) students to go to one corner of the room, Influencing (B) to another, Steadiness (C) to another, and Compliance (D) to another.

Ask each group to count off so that each group will have one 1, one 2, one 3, etc. Then ask the ones to form a group, the twos, the threes, and so on until you run out of numbers for the smallest group.

Assign the students who are left to the existing groups (which now have one of each of the personality types) so that each group has five to seven members. Be sure to have no more than two of each work style in a group.

The assignment for each group:

Design a company and assign job titles to each member of the group based upon the strengths and interests of the group.

Ask the group to review the exercises on pages 163 and 164. As a warm-up, choose one of the companies—for example, a factory—and list other jobs that each of the work styles might find matches their personality.

> *Example:*
>
> dominance (D)—union organizer, office manager, head custodian, plant manager
>
> influencing (I)—salesperson, trainer, personnel director, child care director, marketing director
>
> steadiness (S)—mechanic, heavy equipment operator, clerical worker, department specialist, computer technician
>
> compliance (C)—auditor, bookkeeper, research and development director, software author

Once you feel the groups understand the process, let them begin brainstorming. Provide them with an overview of the points they need to cover to best describe their business (see The Small Business Plan on page 4/83). At a minimum, they'll need to describe the business, its products and services, and how they'll market and deliver their goods.

It may be easiest to outline the assignment for them this way:

First—Identify an industry or company that everyone in the group finds of interest. The larger the company or industry, the better.

Second—Brainstorm all the possible job titles for each of the predominant work behavioral styles—Ds, Is, Ss, Cs—in that company or organization.

Third—Have each person choose a job title based on the charts they completed on pages 27 and 134 in *Career Choices*.

Fourth—As a group, write a job description for each person. Use the form on page 4/105 of this guide. The job description should include the following:

Job title:
Experience, skills, and training required:
Job duties:
Hours and working conditions:
Annual salary:

Ask the students to make the conditions as realistic as they can. For example, there should be no inflated salaries just to meet personal budget requirements.

Groups may need to spend time online researching this data.

Once the assignment is completed, ask the groups to present their projects to the class. After they have introduced their company and staff, open up the brainstorming to the rest of the class to complete the lists of possible job titles in that company. Then ask all members of the staff to make a presentation about their job, why they chose it, and how it fits their personality.

English/Language Arts:

Writing Job Descriptions

Writing job descriptions is a communication skill that will come in very handy later in life. Those that have some experience in writing job descriptions will impress their supervisors and, therefore, move up the ladder to supervision themselves. This career move brings more autonomy, responsibility, and higher pay. Ask all students to rewrite their job description from their notes.

Remind them that spelling, grammar, punctuation, and neatness are important.

Common Core Standards for English

W.9-10.2. Write informative/explanatory texts to examine and convey complex ideas, concepts, and information clearly and accurately through the effective selection, organization, and analysis of content.

Follow-up:

Small Business Plan

If your students are working on their own small business plans (as outlined on page 4/83 of this guide), they can use the information from this activity to write each partner's job description. Because their team was set up based on interest in an industry rather than work behavioral styles, they may find that all the members of the team have the same work behavioral style (i.e., they are all Ds or dominance). The challenge will be designing job descriptions that fit their styles, especially when they are all the same.

If you have a group in which this is the case, ask them to share with the class what they learned about team-building. A sophisticated concept? Most definitely! Is it important for effective teams to understand this concept? You bet! Can your students grasp the nuances? You'll be pleasantly surprised.

After reading and discussing "I Hear America Singing," the students, in groups of 3 to 4, rewrote the poem using occupations of today. They also made a collage to accompany their vision of the poem.

— Pam Wieters, English Teacher
Stratford High School, Goose Creek, SC

Optional

I Hear America Singing
by Walt Whitman

Page 124–126

Read after completing page 165 in *Career Choices*

Job Description for:

Name _____

Predominant work behavioral style is: (circle one)   D   I   S   C

Company/Industry/Organization: _____

Job title: _____

Experience, skills, and training required: _____

_____

_____

Job duties:

1. _____

     _____

2. _____

     _____

3. _____

     _____

4. _____

     _____

5. _____

     _____

6. _____

     _____

7. _____

     _____

8. _____

     _____

Hours and working conditions: _____

Annual Salary: _____

Career Wall

You may have a wealth of information about various careers right on your own campus. At your next faculty meeting, ask your colleagues to list all of the paid and unpaid jobs they have held. Your students might be surprised by the variety of jobs some of their teachers have held.

If you create a Google form or use an online survey tool to help gather names and jobs, the information can be exported to a spreadsheet for easy sorting. You might also ask your colleagues to identify the career cluster for each job they list. This will give you a way of easily categorizing the responses (beyond paid and unpaid).

Sort the list you generate by career cluster and post it on a wall in your room. Now you have a great point for reference during discussions.

- "Did you know Mr. Ramirez had his own business?"
- "It's unlikely that you will have only one job in your lifetime. Which teacher do you think has held the most different jobs?"

You might also decide to point students to the list as a resource for certain lessons or homework assignments. For instance, ask students to identify at least one person on campus who has worked in a job/career that they would also find interesting. Have students conduct a brief interview (no more than three questions) and write a brief summary of the responses.

Section 2: What Do I Want?

Chapter 7

Decision Making

The final step in choosing what you want is making a decision. As Anne Morrow Lindbergh said, "One cannot collect all the beautiful shells on the beach." Making a decision is difficult because choosing one thing inevitably means saying "no" to something else. For teens, this can be especially painful. It is essential, therefore, that students understand two points: that "not making a decision is still making a choice," and that "most decisions can be changed."

The Decision-making Rubric

The Decision-making Rubric (*Career Choices*, page 177) is a vital keystone activity in the 10-year planning process. After completing this rubric, students make the career choice that, unless changed in a later chapter (after again using this rubric), will be used for developing their 10-year plan.

As they complete their rubric, they'll compare and contrast up to four different careers that they researched earlier in Chapter 6 using the Career Interest Survey. After analyzing and reflecting on the data on the rubric, they'll make an initial career choice as their "chosen career."

Changing a career on a whim is never a good idea. It is important to research any potential career (*Career Choices*, pages 150–151) and compare it with other options using this decision-making graphic organizer. Only after careful consideration of the many factors they've learned about to this point in your course, should a student make the change.

If your students are using My10yearPlan.com®, the career title they choose populates the planning process for the balance of the course. The chosen career can always be changed, but the system will require students to return to the Decision-making Rubric to evaluate their choice.

TECHNICAL SUPPORT
For the *Career Choices* curriculum
(800) 967-8016 or
support@academicinnovations.com

Identifying Choices

  Page170

  Page 80

Learning Objective:

To help students discern the difference between long- and short-term goals and learn to take their plans for the future into account when making daily decisions.

Presentation Suggestions:

Ask a student to read Joyce's story aloud. Then have the class identify her two goals:

Becoming a doctor someday

Buying a car

What is Joyce's long-term goal? *Becoming a doctor.*

Right now, she is faced with deciding among three alternatives: getting a job so she can buy a car, becoming a hospital volunteer to get medical experience, or spending more time on her studies.

Activities:

List on the board and discuss the choices students face every day to help them realize that they are already quite adept at making short-term decisions. Students usually have no trouble identifying at least ten decisions they make every day: what time to get up, what clothes to put on, what to eat, whether or not to go to class, what friends to call, what music to listen to, what subject to study first, what TV show to watch, whether or not to exercise, what time to go to bed.

Ask them to list some longer-term decisions they will face in the next twelve months: what classes to take next year; whether to go out for a sport, get a part-time job, or join a particular school activity; when, and if, to date.

Brainstorm long-term (five years to life) decisions students need to start making.

* Which classes will I need for graduation and to prepare myself for college or trade school?

* Am I going to work or give priority to my studies?

* Am I going to stay in school?

* How will I make sure to keep up with the latest technology?

* How will I avoid abusing drugs and alcohol?

* Am I willing to start saving for the big expenses in life (e.g., college)?

* How will I avoid becoming a teen parent?

Ask students to discuss what kinds of choices are easiest to make and which are hardest. Why?

Chapter Introduction Video:

At the beginning of this chapter, consider showing the motivational chapter introduction video featuring Olympic Gold Medalist Dain Blanton (found on **The Teachers' Lounge**). Or, if your students are regularly using **My10yearPlan.com®**, have them watch the video online before starting their work in this chapter.

Learning to Think Critically, Creatively, and Strategically

Throughout this course your students will use the higher order thinking skills of analyzing, evaluating, and creating. For a graphic outlining Bloom's Taxonomy and the keystone products and projects developed in this course, refer to page 4/3.

The Decision-making Rubric (*Career Choices*, page 177) is an important tool that should be used throughout the balance of the course, particularly as students make increasingly complex choices related to their 10-year plan. This graphic organizer gives students in-depth practice with a systematic process for making meaningful and appropriate choices. It helps students analyze and evaluate life-defining options so, when they create their 10-year plans, they will have more meaning and will be therefore be more motivational.

As you work through this chapter with your students, you'll want to provide as many opportunities as you can to practice using this rubric so all students become proficient using this decision-making tool.

While this process may be intuitive to some students, for many others it may be the first time they've really thought about and analyzed a choice they are making at this depth. The more at-risk a student, the less prepared they may be for making informed, considered decisions. Therefore, if the population you are working with includes a large number of at-risk students, you'll want to make sure they are comfortable with the Decision-making Rubric. The more comfortable and confident they become the more they'll value the power behind its simplistic format. Then, throughout the balance of the course, find as many opportunities as you can to refer students collectively or individually to this rubric, both for class projects and personal choices.

Common Core Standards for English

W.9-10.7. Conduct short as well as more sustained research projects to answer a question (including a self-generated question) or solve a problem; narrow or broaden the inquiry when appropriate; synthesize multiple sources on the subject, demonstrating understanding of the subject under investigation.

Study: Many college students not learning to think critically

Academically Adrift: Limited Learning on College Campuses (Arum and Roksa, University of Chicago Press, 2011) reports on a four-year study of 2,322 traditional-age students. The study found that large numbers of students didn't learn the critical thinking, complex reasoning, and written communication skills that are widely assumed to be at the core of a college education.

The researchers examined testing data and student surveys at 24 U.S. colleges and universities ranging from the highly selective to the less selective. Forty-five percent of students made no significant improvement in their critical thinking, reasoning, or writing skills during the first two years of college, according to the study. After four years, 36 percent showed no significant gains in these so-called "higher order" thinking skills.

Gathering Information

Page 171　　　　　Page 80

Learning Objective:

To help students understand that before they can evaluate their choices, they need to discover the facts and determine the effect of these realities on the outcome for any of the options being considered.

Presentation Suggestions:

Review the material in the text and discuss in class. Other information that might be helpful to Joyce could include: whether the hospital would be willing to write a letter of recommendation to the medical school of Joyce's choice; whether she can borrow a friend's car on occasion or use a car-sharing service; whether her hours on the job or at the hospital would be flexible enough to let her study when she needs to; and how much time she needs to study each week in order to keep up her grades.

Emphasize the importance of being resourceful when making decisions. Thinking beyond the obvious choices often results in win/win solutions. If Joyce could find an alternative way to have access to a car, for example, she could satisfy her short-term goal without putting her long-term hopes at risk.

After reading and discussing pages 168-169, students need to see how decision making and problem solving are important in the business world as well as in their personal world. I split the class into small groups and assign them a section of the teachers' parking lot to examine. They are to identify the number of cars and their make so we can eventually determine how many are American-made, German-made, British-made, etc. Then the small groups share their numbers with the whole group until we know how many cars total were in the parking lot and how many are from other countries. We do a math lesson so students can create percentages! (Not a small feat in a Communications class!)

Next, we talk about the problems associated with so many cars being non-American. Then, students write a paragraph about their findings, including the importance of solving this problem in the marketplace. As students word process their paragraphs, they are also being taught how to convert their information into a spread sheet (we use the integrated package Microsoft Works), which will turn their percentages into a pie chart or bar graph. When students finish, they have a paragraph complete with pie chart showing the importance of companies solving problems in the workplace.

— Sharon Hurwitz, English Teacher and Technology Facilitator
Bethel High School, Hampton, VA

Evaluating Choices

Page 172–174   Page 81–82

Learning Objective:

To help students evaluate the pros and cons and the likelihood of success of different choices they may face.

Presentation Suggestions:

Continuing Joyce's story, have the class list the *pros, cons,* and *probability of success* if she doesn't work at all. (*Pros:* more time for study, more flexibility. *Cons:* no money, no car, no experience. *Probability of success:* moot point.)

After the class has worked through Joyce's example, break into groups of two or three to consider Jessica's and John's stories.

Jessica

Choice 1: To take Algebra I. Pros: keeps options for most majors and future careers open. Cons: more work, less time for other things. Probability of success: reasonably high for the class since she has done well at math in the past, and very high for her future career fulfillment since she will have a wide variety of options available to her.

Choice 2: To take basic math. Pros: easier, less work. Cons: fewer future options without advanced math. Probability of success: very high for the class since she has done well at math in the past, but only moderately high for her future career fulfillment since she won't have as many options available to her.

Choice 3: Not to take math. Pros: easy way out. Cons: future options severely limited. Probability of success: moot point.

John

Choice 1: Quit school and go to work. Pros: no more school, earn money. Cons: little chance for advancement, fewer options for future. Probability of success: lower without more education and skills.

Choice 2: Graduate and go to vocational school. Pros: good chance for rewarding work and good pay. Cons: more school. Probability of success: good, since he already knows a lot about graphic design.

Choice 3: Graduate and join the army. Pros: training with pay. Cons: must commit several years to military service. Probability of success: good, if he can receive written assurance from the recruiter that he will get the training he wants.

Choice 4: Graduate and attend college. Pros: better prospects for future earnings. Cons: must work hard to bring up grades so he can transfer, must commit time and money to future education. Probability of success: depends on how hard he's willing to work.

Bring the class back together and, as a group, brainstorm Jessica's and John's decisions. You might make a chart for each story on the board, listing all the alternatives thought of by students. Ask the students what they think are the best decisions for Jessica and John.

Decision-making Model

Page 175–176   Page 82

Learning Objective:

To help students understand the importance of reflective decision making and learn how to use the Decision-making Rubric graphic organizer (*Career Choices*, page 177).

Presentation Suggestions:

Review with your students the steps of the decision-making process listed on page 175 of *Career Choices*. Explain that if they start using the decision-making rubric (found on page 177) when making important decisions, these steps will become second nature to them. In the meantime, it is wise to memorize them so they can make sure they've addressed each of these when making long-term choices. This is a good mid-term question.

As a class discuss Gloria's chart on page 176. Note that a new element has been added to the process: considering Gloria's resources, wants, and needs. This is a step to take when making major decisions such as what career to pursue, whom to marry, and where to live. Can the class think of anything to add to Gloria's chart? What do they think Gloria should do?

Activity:

Brainstorm a list of choices that students would want to make where use of this rubric would help them identify the best choice. This list should include:

what career path to choose, where to live, if and when to get married, when and whom to date, where to go to college, what major to pursue, if and when to start a family, whether or not to acquire student loan debt, whether or not to drop out of high school or college

Ask the class if any of them are stumped by a choice they need to make. If a volunteer is willing, have them share the choice they need to make and ask the class to help them complete the chart. Explain and analyze each step so everyone is comfortable with the process. Emphasize that the final decision is up to the student involved, but that it's good to gather information, get input from others, and evaluate choices.

After the chart is complete, ask your students to pretend it's their choice. Without discussion, have them write down the choice that would seem best for them. Before you ask the class to share any of their choices, ask the person who shared their story what seems to be is the best choice for them. Then poll the class—how many chose option one, how many chose option 2, and so on.

Is there a consensus? Unless it's a really complex, individualized decision, there usually will be. Using this format, the best choices usually become pretty apparent.

Optional

The Monkey's Paw
A play based on the story by W.W. Jacobs

Page 127–138
Read after completing pages 168–174 in *Career Choices*

We showed the video Forrest Gump *to help students explore how choices depend on personal values. We asked students to recall three values that were held by characters in the film. One student focused on Forrest's love of life, and commented, "If you put love of life above all the bad things that can happen in life, you'll probably never commit suicide." He was thinking about a rock star (who recently committed suicide) and concluded that if the rock star had had Forrest's perspective, he would probably be alive today.*

— Doug Campbell, Communication Department
San Gabriel High School, San Gabriel, CA

Decision-making Rubric

Page 177   Page 83

Learning Objective:

To help students critically analyze and evaluate a career choice using the Decision-making Rubric. This choice will be used for the balance of the course.

Presentation Suggestions:

Once students have completed the process for Gloria, ask them to review their own resources (strengths, skills, and passions), values, wants, and needs. Have them enter these on the Decision-making Rubric (*Career Choices*, page 177). Their goal: To identify a career they would find satisfying.

To do this they will evaluate three or four possible career choices that they researched using the Career Interest Surveys. They will evaluate the pros, cons, and the probability of success related to each career. The work they have done to this point in the course will provide the data and insight to make a quantitative and meaningful choice.

Activity:

Consider breaking the class into small teams of three or four students. While each student must evaluate their own choices on their own chart, team members can support each other by sharing ideas, objectively evaluating their choices, and thinking of other options that align with the person's resources and desires. In the end, each student should make an individual choice. The group is just supporting their decision-making process.

My10yearPlan.com® Essentials:

This is a keystone activity. Data will be extracted and used on each student's *My 10-year Plan Summary Page*. Direct students to enter their work from this activity on My10yearPlan.com® the next time they log on. For more information about this process, see Section 9 of this guide and the FAQ link in the left navigation of My10yearPlan.com®.

Course Assessment: Suggestion for a Final Project

The Decision-making Rubric can be used for a variety of major life decisions, making it the most critical graphic organizer explored in this course. As such consider an assessment (mid-term or final) where students are asked to draw the rubric from memory and complete it to:

> Determine what to do immediately following graduation from high school.

Remind students to include their chosen career in the wants and needs area before determining their choices. For instance, an aspiring hotel manager might evaluate whether she or he wants to go to trade school, go to college, or get a job with a major hotel chain and work their way up.

If your students are using My10yearPlan.com®, have them print their *My 10-year Plan Summary Page*, review it, and attach that document to their rubric.

Optional

The Road Not Taken
by Robert Frost

When using "The Road Not Taken" we had students writing stories looking ahead into their own futures with two different scenarios.

— Suzanne M. Reese, Teacher/Gifted Liaison
R.L. Turner High School, Carrollton, TX

Page 139–141

Read after completing page 177 in *Career Choices*

Make a Decision

Page 178   Page 84

Learning Objective:

To help students assess the strengths and weaknesses of their decision-making strategies.

Presentation Suggestions:

Review the text on page 178, and ask students to check the box on the scale that best represents their decision-making behavior. There are no right or wrong tendencies. The purpose is to help students identify a range of decision-making characteristics and learn to recognize how and when they use them.

English/Language Arts:

Ask students to write a fictional short story about three siblings (*à la* "The Three Little Pigs") who must make an important decision. Each sibling has a different decision-making style: one tends to avoid decisions, another tends to make decisions too quickly, and the third has a more considered or moderate approach. Their choices could be autobiographical. Suggest that students review the words on page 178 and perhaps use them in their story. They might also review page 20 of **Career Choices**.

To reinforce the decision-making process, the following value exercise was used: The students were asked to choose between two groups. In one, they would get $5 a day just to show up to class. In the other, the first person who showed up would get $50, the second got $45, and so on down to zero for the 10th person and all those who followed.

Fifteen students chose the $5 group because they didn't want to compete. When asked what time the second group would arrive to class, one student said, "I'll show up an hour before to make sure I get in." The next said, "I'll show up two hours before." And a third said, "I'll sleep in the hallway!" They learned that if you pick a competitive field, someone will always "sleep in the hallway."

—— Doug Campbell, Communication Department
San Gabriel High School, San Gabriel, CA

Career Fair

Now that your students have narrowed their career interests to one career, it might be time to facilitate a student-directed career fair to be held later in the school year. The whole school should be invited. This can be a one-class, multiple-class, or whole school project.

Have students divide into committees by career interest areas. Each committee will choose a chairperson. Then they'll determine how to operate and communicate with each other. The following tasks will need to be assigned to members.

1. Inviting one or more appropriate representatives in their career interest area

2. Gathering additional information about the career area with pamphlets from professional organizations, books, online resources, etc.

3. Creating a fact sheet about the career that can be passed out at the fair

4. Display setup and cleanup

In addition, form an organizational committee of students. This committee should include an event chair or co-chair(s), school publicity chair, a facility chair, and the chair of each career interest committee (mentioned above).

After the Career Fair, ask each committee to meet and evaluate not only the success of the fair, but also the success of the committee. From this evaluation, brainstorm the traits of an effective team member. Then ask the group to brainstorm the strengths each person brings to a team. From this brainstorm, each student can prepare an inventory for inclusion in their Career Portfolio.

After reading Julius Caesar *by William Shakespeare, I ask, "Does Brutus make the right decision?" This is used as the culminating literary piece after studying the complete process of making decisions. Students then have to decide how they would have made a different decision than he did.*

— Sharon Hurwitz, English Teacher and Technology Facilitator
Bethel High School, Hampton, VA

Optional

To Build a Fire
by Jack London

Page 142–163

Read after reading page 179 in **Career Choices**

If you are using either My10yearPlan.com® Essentials *or* Interactive, *here are responses you can use when students ask these questions.*

Frequently Asked Questions:
The "Chosen Career" Designation in My10yearPlan.com®

Why am I limited to the careers in the drop-down menu of the Decision-making Rubric?

You'll note your choices in the drop-down list are limited to those careers you have studied and evaluated. To include a career among those available for comparison on the Decision-making Rubric, you first must complete a Career Interest Survey.

Why? This requires you to think through and reflect on this life-defining choice, and not just casually make a decision. During the process of creating a Career Interest Survey, you revisit a variety of important topics related to that specific career, including your personal profile (who you are), your lifestyle expectations and goals, and the characteristics of your ideal job (what you want). The chosen career used for your 10-year plan should be a carefully considered, internalized choice that you can be confident best meets your goals, personality, and lifestyle expectations.

How do I complete a Career Interest Survey for another career?

To complete an additional Career Interest Survey, click on the link within the **Gather** Information paragraph on the Decision-making Rubric, or return to the Career Interest Survey activity and click on the addition sign button to access a new input page.

Why do I have only four choices in the Decision-making Rubric?

It's difficult to compare too many choices at once. To avoid overwhelming your decision-making process, keep your chart limited to the four options you think are the best matches for you. Delete from the Decision-making Rubric any choices that either no longer appeal to you or for which the cons outweigh the pros.

How do I change my chosen career?

Circumstances and plans change, so it is important that your career choice remain dynamic. If you find another career that sounds even better than the one you've identified, you must:

- **First** complete a Career Interest Survey for that career

- **Then** work through the Decision-making Rubric to evelute that career

Remember, if you haven't completed a Career Interest Survey, carefully evaluated, and chosen a career using the Decision-making Rubric, it won't carry to the next steps in your 10-year planning process.

Why do I have to do all these steps?

Over the next decade, you will of invest a lot of time, energy, and money in getting the education and training required to prepare yourself for your career path. Only after research, analysis, and contemplation can you be certain that the career you've chosen matches your goals, your personality, and the lifestyle you envision for yourself. Think of this online program as your own digital best friend. It's not going to let you choose a career impulsively.

Can I use the Decision-making Rubric for other important decisions?

Absolutely. Get in the habit of using this rubric when making any important life-defining decisions: who and when to marry, if and when to have children, where to live, which job to take, if and when to change jobs, whether to get more education?

Section 3: How Do I Get It?

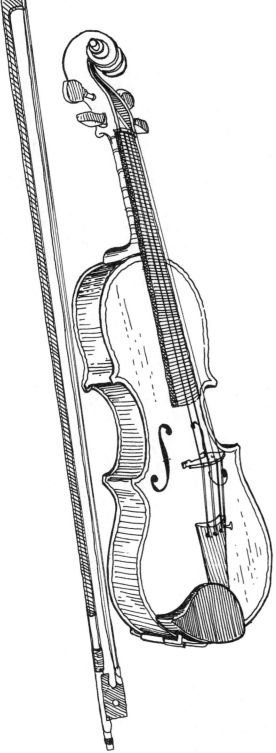

Chapter 8

Setting Goals and Solving Problems

Chapter 8 is the first of the "How to Get It" chapters that make up the remainder of the book. As students move through this final section, they will be making the plans, learning the skills, and acquiring the tools they will need to realize their dreams.

Solving problems and setting goals are two of the most important skills a person can learn. Fortunately, because new problems keep coming along and because there are always new goals to be set and achieved, everyone will have ample opportunities to practice these skills!

Optional

Uphill
by Christina Rossetti

Page 164–165

Read before beginning Chapter 8 in *Career Choices*

Tools for Solving Problems

Page 183–185   Page 86

Learning Objective:

To help students identify and apply the problem-solving techniques presented in the text.

Presentation Suggestions:

Discuss the way Hubert's problem relates to the four problem-solving tools: delaying gratification, accepting responsibility, dedication to truth or reality, and balancing. Then ask students to complete the exercise on page 185 individually or in small groups. Follow up with a class discussion.

Activities:

For further small group discussion, ask students to consider the following situations.

Jon has offered to lend his car to Pat for a weekend if Pat will let Jon copy his homework. Pat knows it's wrong to cheat, and that he could be suspended from his school if he's caught. But, he rationalizes, Jon isn't as good a student as he is, and the instructor really didn't explain the assignment well enough for him to understand.

> What is Pat risking if he gives Jon his homework?
>
> What is he sacrificing if he refuses?
>
> Who is responsible for solving Pat's problem? Jon's?
>
> What are the facts in the situation?
>
> What wishful thinking might enter Pat's decision-making process?
>
> What do you think Pat should do?

Lucy has been asked to go out drinking with a new group of friends on Friday night after work. Her friend, Debbie, plans to drive. Lucy knows it is illegal and dangerous to drink and drive, but Debbie assures her that she knows when she's had enough. Lucy doesn't want to be left out.

> What is Lucy risking if she goes with her friends?
>
> What is she sacrificing if she stays home?
>
> Who is responsible for Lucy's safety?
>
> What are the facts of the situation?
>
> What wishful thinking might enter Lucy's decision-making process?
>
> What do you think Lucy should do?

Assign the movie *Apollo 13* for your Video Book Club (see page 11/23 for more information). It includes excellent examples of problem solving and has the added advantage of demonstrating that jobs in math, science, and technology can be exciting, dramatic, and even heroic.

Chapter Introduction Video:

At the beginning of this chapter, consider showing the motivational chapter introduction video featuring Olympic Gold Medalist Dain Blanton (found on **The Teachers' Lounge**). Or, if students are regularly using **My10yearPlan.com®**, have them watch the video online before starting their work in this chapter.

Resources:

M. Scott Peck, *The Road Less Traveled*. A Touchstone Book, Simon and Schuster, Inc.

Reading Assignment:

Romeo and Juliet by William Shakespeare

Romeo and Juliet exemplifies the theme of fate versus free will. Did the lovers bring about their fate through their actions or was it just meant to be?

Once students have completed their reading ask them to rewrite the ending to *Romeo and Juliet* using Peck's four problem-solving components.

Common Core Standards for English (for the *optional* Shakespeare reading assignment and "The Myth of Sisyphus")

RI.9-10.4. Determine the meaning of words and phrases as they are used in a text, including figurative, connotative, and technical meanings; analyze the cumulative impact of specific word choices on meaning and tone (e.g., how the language of a court opinion differs from that of a newspaper).

RI.9-10.6. Determine an author's point of view or purpose in a text and analyze how an author uses rhetoric to advance that point of view or purpose.

Optional

The Myth of Sisyphus
by Albert Camus

Page 166–171

Read after completing pages 182–185 in ***Career Choices***

Setting Goals and Objectives

Page 186–190

Page 86

Learning Objective:

To introduce students to a process for writing quantitative goals and objectives.

Presentation Suggestions:

Setting goals and objectives is an extremely important skill, especially for those who tend to think in vague generalities. Make a presentation from the text, carefully working through the examples. It is essential that students become familiar with the three questions every goal statement must answer:

> What will be different?
>
> By how much or how many?
>
> By when?

Ask students to complete the exercises on pages 188 and 189 in *Career Choices* alone or in small groups. Ask a few volunteers to write and diagram their goals and objectives on the board.

You may want to provide additional practice by listing incomplete goal statements and having students indicate which component is missing. Examples:

Get a good job this summer.	*What will be different?*
Learn to speak Mandarin.	*By when?*
Get some new school clothes.	*How much or how many? By when?*
Learn to use a specific computer program.	*By when?*
Make some new friends.	*How many? By when?*

Activities:

Have students choose their most important goal for the next two weeks. Then ask them to write objectives for it. Ask them to keep this assignment readily available so they can glance at it over the next two weeks.

At the end of two weeks, have students share their goals and objectives in class discussion and report on how successful they were at meeting them.

When students have finished reporting, take a poll to see how many believe writing their goals and objectives down was helpful.

Note: If students are having trouble writing objectives for their goals, have them first identify the steps for reaching their goals. Then translate each step into quantitative objectives, with the three different components. It is helpful to list them in chronological order based on the date of completion.

Follow-up:

Encourage students to practice this skill by setting daily, weekly, and monthly goals and objectives. Suggest that they reward themselves for achieving their goals with small indulgences, such as a new music download or tickets for a special event.

Common Core Standards for English

W.9-10.10. Write routinely over extended time frames (time for research, reflection, and revision) and shorter time frames (a single sitting or a day or two) for a range of tasks, purposes, and audiences.

The students…are asked to set a personal goal for each day for 3 weeks. We discuss if they reached their goals, why or why not. As the year progresses, they are asked to make weekly, monthly, etc. goals. Most of my students stated that this has helped them to improve their grades and also to strengthen their organizational skills.

— Dee Hermann, English Teacher
Sandia High School, Albuquerque, NM

Optional

Page 102–110

Optional

 Excerpt from *The Prince of Tides*
by Pat Conroy

Page 178–211

Read after completing pages 182–191 in *Career Choices*

Your Lifestyle Goals

Page 190   Page 87

Learning Objective:

To help students develop the skill of writing quantitative goals and objectives related to their future plans. This is important preparation for writing their 10-year action plans in Chapter 12.

Presentation Suggestions:

Have students review the components of their envisioned lifestyle (first reported on page 63 of *Career Choices*). Are these still accurate? If not, now would be a good time to update that information.*

Direct students to identify three goals based on their lifestyle choices. Ideally, these will be goals they can accomplish in the next year that will contribute to acquisition of their desired lifestyle. Direct students to write their three goals on page 190. If some of your students still struggle with this concept, ask volunteers to share their lifestyle components and then, as a class, brainstorm potential goals for the next year that would further the realization of that lifestyle goal.

Now for each of the three goals, have students write and diagram three quantitative objectives. Remind your students that this is the format for developing action plans and the format for their 10-year action plan (*Career Choices*, pages 279–280) If you are using work from Chapter 12 as your final exam, this will be an important part of their grade, as well as being important to their future success and feelings of accomplishment.

My10yearPlan.com® Essentials:

This is a keystone activity. Data will be extracted and used on each student's *My 10-year Plan Summary Page*. Direct students to enter their work from this activity on My10yearPlan.com® the next time they log on. For more information, see Section 9 of this guide.

My10yearPlan.com® Archives:

* If students update their Components of Lifestyle in their **Workbook and Portfolio**, remind them to also update their online Components of Lifestyle in My10yearPlan.com®. This is a good time to point out the Archive feature built into My10yearPlan.com®. As students understand themselves and their abilities better, they will want to update different parts of their 10-year plans. That way they can always look back in the Archive section at the bottom of each activity to review what they once felt or thought about that particular topic. It is esteem building for them to watch themselves grow both in self-understanding and in skill levels.

Section 3: How Do I Get It?

Chapter 9

Avoiding Detours and Roadblocks

The fact that everyone has some degree of difficulty in his or her life comes as a surprise to most people. We tend to think that things should run smoothly—and that they do for everyone else. That idea makes it easier to give up when problems present themselves, or to turn to drugs or alcohol for relief from these difficulties. In this chapter, students should learn that problems are inevitable and must be faced head-on if they are to be overcome. Since they are responsible for their own lives, it is up to them to overcome any limitations they perceive.

In dealing with the issues of teen parenting, dropping out of school, and abusing substances, we ask students to imagine how short-range "solutions" can affect their lives in the long run. A number of exercises in this chapter, in fact, give students a chance to think about long-range planning.

Students may also feel pressured to give up their dreams. This pressure can be external (from parents, friends, society) or internal (based on irrational fears, anxiety, inability to take risks). Young women are especially prone to feelings of this sort. Review this material carefully, bringing in a school counselor or outside speaker if necessary. Remind students to turn back to this section any time in the future when they are discouraged and think they want to give up on a dream.

Optional

Mother to Son
by Langston Hughes

Page 214–215

Read after completing pages 196–197 in *Career Choices*

What's Your Excuse?

Page 197–199   Page 89

Learning Objective:

Students examine some of the reasons people use for not doing what they can and want to do, evaluate those excuses, and determine what might be done to avoid using them.

Presentation Suggestions:

Review the material on pages 197-199. Then ask students to check any "I can't do it because" statements which apply to them. After they have completed their charts, turn to page 199 and ask students to take turns reading items from the "They did it in spite of" chart. Discuss any additions that might be made to the chart.

Activities:

Invite someone who has overcome a significant handicap to address the class. Ask your guest to speak about both physical and emotional aspects: not just the physical obstacles encountered in not being able to walk, for example, but how the debilitation affected attitudes and self-esteem.

One excuse area not covered in the text is the "social excuse." Brainstorm with students different social excuses such as:

- I don't have time.
- None of my friends do it.
- My peers would object.

Evaluate those excuses. How inflexible are they? Are there situations where these excuses should not stand in the way?

If you are dealing with a population with a temporary problem (curable physical or emotional problems, incarceration, or chemical dependency), encourage students to carry or display photos of themselves before the problem developed. It is helpful for them to be able to see themselves as healthy, functioning, changing, free individuals.

Reading Assignment:

Ask students to read a biography or an autobiography of an individual who overcame an adversity. Brainstorm other individuals in addition to those mentioned on pages 198-199. One obvious choice is the biography of Helen Keller.

Chapter Introduction Video:

At the beginning of this chapter, consider showing the motivational chapter introduction video featuring Olympic Gold Medalist Dain Blanton (found on **The Teachers' Lounge**). Or, if your students are regularly using **My10yearPlan.com**®, have them watch the video online before starting their work in this chapter.

At the end of the school year we added an activity that helped students, faculty, and staff reflect on their year, and we found it to be a great fit. This idea involved collaboration between Lisa Jahnke, Holly Warchock, and myself. … When Olympic Gold Medalist Dain Blanton came to Marquette to speak to our students, he told our school, "You can be fueled by the obstacles you face."

We asked students in our Transitions course to state the biggest obstacle they faced over the past school year, in one or two words. We then asked them how that could be their "fuel." They also stated that in one or two words. We had them write their "obstacle" and "fuel" on sheets of white paper and then took photographs of them posing with each. We had faculty and staff take part in this activity at one of our final staff meetings for the year.

We then took the photos and made a collage and set it to music. We chose to use Kelly Clarkston's "Stronger" as our theme song. The video showed participants first showing their obstacle and then their fuel. This was a powerful statement that reinforced everything we had learned through our efforts in Transitions. We all face obstacles. The choice to let them be your fuel instead of your defeat is where you show the world your strength.

— Becky Simmons, Transitions Lesson Coordinator
Marquette Senior High School, Marquette, MI

For the past two years I've read the book entitled The Shark and the Goldfish *by Jon Gordon to my 8th grade classes. We relate it to changes that the 8th graders are/will be going through in their lives (ex. high school, college, workforce). My husband's work has training sessions using various books and this one caught my eye when he brought it home…*

It is perfect for this age group! Eighth graders still like to have story time whether they will admit it or not. We take notes from what the shark has to say along the way and then we answer some of the essay questions at the end after class discussions. Some of them are real thought provokers and you would be amazed at some of the essays that I have received from my students about their lives.

Each student also creates a poster, either using the computer or by hand to represent one of the points (rules) presented in the book. They kids love the book and talk about whether they are going to be a shark or a goldfish that day. Or, if they are having a bad day, I ask them if it is a "goldfish" or "shark" day.

— Patricia Evans, Teacher
Hudson Middle School, Lufkin, TX

To add an element of fun to the class and to control excuse-making, we made a list of excuses—some of them wild ("bad hair day")—posted them, and point to them when students haven't finished an assignment, are late, etc. This was a humorous extension of the activity on page 197.

— Lynn Porter, Coordinator of High School Diploma Program
Santa Monica-Malibu Unified School District, Santa Monica, CA

Optional

Hope
by Emily Dickinson

Page 172–177

Read after completing pages 194–199 in **Career Choices**

Taking Responsibility

Page 200   Page 90

Learning Objective:

To help students evaluate excuses and reframe them so that they are accepting the responsibility for their problems and simultaneously opening avenues for solving them.

Presentation Suggestions:

Ask students to write some excuses they've recently used to try to absolve themselves from responsibility for solving their problems. Then, individually or in small groups, ask them to reframe the excuses, this time *accepting* the responsibility.

As practice, reframe the following examples in a class brainstorming session:

I can't take a job because I don't have any way to get there.

I can't do my homework because it's too noisy at home.

I can't go to the party because I don't have the money for a new outfit.

I didn't make the team because the coach is out to get me.

I failed the test because the teacher expects too much.

Reframed examples:

I can't take a job because I haven't taken the time to investigate bus schedules or carpooling opportunities.

I can't do my homework because I don't want to go to the library.

I can't go to the party because I'm not imaginative enough to come up with something appropriate to wear.

I didn't make the team because I didn't practice hard enough.

I failed the test because I didn't seek out the extra help I needed.

Be sure to remind your students that although they are responsible for their own actions and decisions, many sources of help are available. Another step to solving problems should be to identify those sources of help and support, and determine when to use them. Refer to page 226 of *Career Choices*.

It is interesting to move from class to class to see the difference in the teachers' personalities and how they are unfolding Career Choices. *The common thread is that the students know that it is preparing them beyond high school and college. The program has already caused one young woman, who will be a junior next year, to rethink getting married at the end of her junior year."*

— Barbara Shannon, Ed.D., Teacher, Director, and Co-founder
Synergy Quantum Academy, Los Angeles, CA

Startling Statement Quiz

Page 201–202   Page 91

Learning Objective:

To expose students to some of the statistics relating to dropping out of school, substance abuse, and more.

Presentation Suggestions:

Quizzes like this one seem to have a lasting impact on students. Statistics that might be easily dismissed or forgotten in a text or lecture loom much larger in this context. Have students answer the questions to the best of their ability, then turn the page and review the correct statistics. When students have answered correctly, their impressions are reinforced. If they were wrong, the correct answer often has a deep impact. Follow with group discussion.

Activities:

Instead of having students take the quiz individually, divide the class into groups of three students and give them time to come to a consensus about which are the correct answers. The ensuing discussions can be valuable as students examine their own thoughts and where they came from, as well as those of their classmates. Follow with class discussion.

Offer a prize to the group that gets the most correct answers to the quiz. This approach further reinforces the learning process; students will try even harder to come up with the right answers. And if they don't answer correctly, the right answer is more likely to make a lasting impression.

For extra credit, have students research a topic of interest to the class. Ask them to write their own startling statement quiz using the statistics they uncover.

Energizer:

Have students create a startling statement quiz using the statistics they uncovered regarding the future trends of the workplace. Using the startling statistics found in the activity for "Tomorrow's Jobs" on page 4/90 of this guide, have each group write three or four startling statement questions (like those on page 201 of *Career Choices*), complete with the corresponding answers (as on page 202). Compile a quiz combining each group's best questions and answers.

This quiz can be shared in a variety of settings. The class can take the entire quiz, because they only know the answers to three or four of the questions. Why not have parents at the next open house take it? The students can submit it to the local newspaper for publication. Editors like quizzes that open their readers' eyes to societal trends.

Detours and Roadblocks

Page 203–206   Page 92–93

Learning Objective:

To allow students to examine some common problems and then project into the future to consider the possible long-term consequences of present actions.

Presentation Suggestions:

Ask the students to read the three stories. Follow with a discussion in class. Another alternative would be to break into groups of three students each and assign one of the problems to each group. Bring the class together and have the groups present their conclusions. If you have more than one group considering a particular story, compare answers to see how they differ and how they are alike.

Activity:

If you know someone who has dealt with one of the problems presented here, you might invite him or her to talk with the class and explain what he or she would do differently if given the chance to go back in time.

Find someone who has either:

- Quit high school or college

- Started a family young and was not able to finish their education

- Let substance abuse get in the way of their education

Ask your guest speaker:

If you could wave a magic wand, go back in time, and change the course of your life, what would you do differently?

One of the answers will most likely be, "Get a better education."

In a study of regret in the United States, when adults were asked what they regret most, the answer heard most often was: "Not getting enough education."

Common Core Standards for English

SL.9-10.1. Initiate and participate effectively in a range of collaborative discussions (one-on-one, in groups, and teacher-led) with diverse partners on grades 9–10 topics, texts, and issues, building on others' ideas and expressing their own clearly and persuasively.

The section on roadblocks and detours was very rewarding because the students realized they were using some of those excuses now.

— Hattie Burns, Business Education Teacher
Chesterfield Middle School, Chesterfield, SC

Is It Worth Staying in School?

Page 207

Page 94

Learning Objective:

To help students personalize the effect dropping out of school will have on their eventual job satisfaction.

Presentation Suggestions:

If members of your class are at a high risk of dropping out of school, you should place considerable emphasis on this activity. Complete the steps outlined in the text. Revisit the career center or have your students go online so they can complete the Career Interest Survey on page 150 for jobs that don't require a high school degree.

How many students found three careers that met all their personal requirements? There probably aren't many.

After the students finish answering the two questions at the bottom of page 207 of *Career Choices*, ask volunteers to share their responses.

Ask for a show of hands to the question: Which would you find more satisfying—a career from your first list (requiring at minimum a high school degree) or a career from your second list? Continue the discussion on why the majority (if not all) would choose a career that required at least a high school degree.

Using their budget requirements (pages 92–93) and the salaries of the "no degree required" careers they researched, have students factor their monthly and annual cash shortfall.

Activities:

Invite a panel of adults who dropped out of high school to speak to the class. One member of the panel should be someone who then went back to school to realize his or her dream.

This exercise is important even if your students are all college-bound. Dropping out of college can have devastating effects on their career and life satisfaction.

Writing Assignment:

Using the data students gathered in their research for this activity, have them write a persuasive essay using the following prompt:

Your younger brother is thinking of dropping out of school to work as a busboy at a local restaurant. Using the information you've learned write him a note aimed at dissuading him. Include evidence from your research relating to career opportunities for dropouts versus those who finish school.

Common Core Standards for English

W.9-10.1. Write arguments to support claims in an analysis of substantive topics or texts, using valid reasoning and relevant and sufficient evidence.

Students finally understood the cost of an upscale lifestyle and, most importantly, that education plays a major part in determining lifestyle.

— Dan Somrock, Social Studies Teacher
Cass Lake-Bena High School, Cass Lake, MN

The Economics of Bad Habits

Page 208–209   Page 95

Learning Objective:

To enable students to comprehend the financial costs of bad habits. The concrete evidence presented in this exercise may be more readily grasped than information about the physical or emotional costs, which can seem abstract.

Presentation Suggestions:

Review the material and then have students complete the exercise at the bottom of page 208 (mathematical answers are on page 209). What each student would do with the money, of course, will vary. Bring the class together for a group discussion. This is a good time to talk about retirement accounts, guaranteed incomes, and other investments. It may be difficult for most students to imagine that they will ever be of retirement age. You might ask them to think about some older people they know, preferably someone who has enough money to live comfortably and someone who just gets by. How do the lifestyles of these individuals differ? Who has more options for enjoying life? Who has more worries?

Break the class into small groups to consider the daily, weekly, and lifetime costs of nonproductive or even destructive habits. Use the chart at the bottom of page 209. Discuss the proactive nature of turning a negative activity (bad habit) into a positive one (saving for the future). How would that make them feel?

Activities:

Invite a guest speaker to discuss pensions and retirement accounts. Ask her or him to share charts that show how much income will be generated with different savings plans.

Ask a panel of senior citizens to speak to the class about their retirement planning and their current lifestyles. If possible, invite persons whose experiences range from satisfactory to struggling.

After they have calculated the costs per day and per year of their "bad habit," students can go to **CareerChoices.com**. There are several online calculators available to help students factor their own savings over a lifetime using the formula at the top of page 209. Moving from abstract totals (someone else's habit) to their own figures should have a strong impact on their motivation to quit. On page 4/131, find a sample portion of the lesson for this activity.

Our class completed the lesson on the economics of bad habits. One "hardcore" smoking student was so astounded by the overall cost of this habit that he quit! Health warnings and legal regulations had not fazed him—it was the money issue presented in this lesson that helped this student!

— Sara L. Carter, Business Education Teacher
Garden City High School, Garden City, MI

Sample Lesson from CareerChoices.com

This lesson is taken from the Teachers' Section for page 209

Lesson Objective:

To demonstrate quickly that there are economic costs tied to bad habits.

Directions:

After your students have completed the activity on p. 209 of **Career Choices**, have them use the money they would spend monthly on smoking as the amount deposited monthly into a retirement account and link to the online calculator. The figure that is computed will be VERY motivating. Do they want this amount to go up in smoke?

Extension Ideas:

Class activity: Is it reasonable to assume that a person would smoke one pack of cigarettes a day? Many people have a tendency to smoke more and more as the years go by. Why not rework the computations in **Career Choices** as a class using an ever-increasing number of packs?

Next, have your students brainstorm the average monthly costs of other detrimental habits (e.g., drinking). Encourage them to consider habits that aren't necessarily as costly physically, but that can take a toll financially.

- Shopping sprees at the mall
- Gambling
- Excessive driving (bad for your car and your wallet)
- Daily Extra Value Meals instead of packing a lunch
- Morning visits to Starbucks for your caffeine habit

You could throw some critical thinking at them, too. Are there physical downsides to any of these other habits?

- High cholesterol from too many French fries
- Stress from unpaid bills
- Broken legs because you can't pay your bookie
- Poor air quality from too much pollution
- The shakes and irritated mood from too much caffeine

Do your students know any adults with bad habits they are trying to kick? Suggest the student runs the numbers for them, given the yearly cost of the habit, their age, and the time until they are 65 (retirement age). The student, armed with the printout of the savings, should make a presentation to that individual. Take a poll three months later. Did anyone kick their habit?

Optional

Over the Hill to the Poor-House
by Will M. Carleton

Page 221–224

Read before completing pages 208–209 in **Career Choices**

If You're a Woman

Page 211–213   Page 96–98

Learning Objective:

To help students understand how flexibility and higher salary relate to mixing career and family, and to have young women recognize the advantages of careers not traditionally held by females.

Presentation Suggestions:

Young women who hope to have families often think that the best career options for them are the so-called traditional women's jobs: nursing, teaching, clerical work, retail sales, waitressing. On the surface, these choices seem reasonable. Nurses and secretaries can usually drop in and out of the workforce if they want to spend a few years at home with their children, and they can find work almost anywhere to accommodate a husband who may be transferred from place to place. Teachers share the same vacations as their children. Waitresses and sales clerks do not need to think about their jobs very much when they're off duty.

Upon closer examination, however, this reasoning falls apart. Today, most women work outside the home even when they have small children. In fact, more than half of all women with children under the age of one year are in the workforce. A staggering number of women are the *sole support* of their families. We have reached a point where it is less important to be able to move into and out of the workforce. Today's priorities are to earn a sufficient salary and to have the day-to-day flexibility required for responsible parenting, such as being able to take a few hours off to attend a child's soccer game or parent-teacher session.

The jobs that offer these benefits are likely to be those traditionally held by men, whether blue collar or professional. This exercise should help women see that preparing for this kind of career is as important for them as it is for the men in the class.

Review the instructions carefully, then have students complete the exercise on their own.

The amount needed for a woman and three children to live in minimum comfort will vary greatly from community to community. It might be a good idea to bring the class together to try to determine an appropriate figure for your community.

Activities:

Invite a woman who is successfully mixing career and family to speak with the class. Ask her to address her job, her training, and the reasons for choosing that field. Consider blue-collar workers as well as professionals.

On the board, list a number of jobs traditionally held by women (see above) and an equal number most often held by men. Discuss. What are the advantages and disadvantages of each? Which usually pay more? Which usually require more training? Is there anything about the work itself that makes it unsuitable or impossible for someone of the other sex to perform?

For a couple in which either partner is capable of supporting the family, brainstorm possible benefits: taking time off, going back to school, taking a lower-paying job that is more emotionally rewarding, and feeling less pressure. Discuss ways in which employers might make life easier for all working parents through job sharing, flexible hours, parental leave, child care facilities, and allowing people to work at home.

Writing Assignment:

Using the data students gathered in their research for this activity have them respond in writing to the following:

On page 213, the ***Career Choices*** authors claim that "The higher you go on the career ladder, the more flexibility you will have for parenting."

Do you agree? If so, support your position with facts drawn from what you've learned in this course. If you disagree, detail why.

Common Core Standards for English

RI.9-10.1. Cite strong and thorough textual evidence to support analysis of what the text says explicitly as well as inferences drawn from the text.

RI.9-10.8. Delineate and evaluate the argument and specific claims in a text, assessing whether the reasoning is valid and the evidence is relevant and sufficient; identify false statements and fallacious reasoning.

I think in the exploration of non-traditional careers, the female students have realized that there is a whole "new" world that is open to them!

— Catherine M. Fitzpatrick, Family and Consumer Science Teacher
Humbolt Security Complex, St. Paul, MN

I have seen former students enroll at Tech College because of what they learned in class.

— Janet Richards, Equity Teacher
Johnson High School, St. Paul, MN

Optional

Saving for Retirement

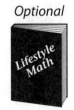

Page 100–101

Before You Give Up
Your Dream

Page 215

Page 99

Learning Objective:

To help students learn an evaluation technique to be used before acting rashly in abandoning a dream or plan.

Presentation Suggestions:

Ask for a volunteer to identify a dream he or she is considering giving up. Then in "fishbowl" fashion (see page 11/17 of this guide), work through the questions with that student. Ask the rest of the class to share problem-solving ideas they have with the student.

After reading "All I Really Need to Know I Learned in Kindergarten" and discussing it with students, they were allowed to illustrate one scene. They really enjoyed drawing the horror of walking into a spider web. Putting their words into picture form was a nice reverse activity.

— Rebecca Dunbar, Lead Teacher
Crossroads, Leavenworth, WA

One class made quilt squares using muslin and markers, illustrating their creeds. I stitched the squares to make a wall hanging.

— Nancy S. McKinney, English Teacher
Trigg County High School, Cadiz, KY

Optional

Page 212–220

A Dream Deferred
by Langston Hughes

Read after completing pages 214–215 in **Career Choices**

A Noiseless Patient Spider
by Walt Whitman

All I Really Need to Know I Learned in Kindergarten
by Robert Fulghum

Read after completing pages 216–217 in **Career Choices**

Conquering Your Fears
Developing Anxiety Tolerance

Page 216–217   Page 100

Learning Objective:

To help students overcome fears by seeing themselves achieve success at whatever makes them anxious through the process of guided visualization.

Presentation Suggestions:

Refer to Looking into the Future on page 4/41 of this guide for an example of guided visualizations and how they are administered.

Refer to Consider Your Options on page 4/82 of this guide for a review of the topic of anxiety tolerance.

Brainstorm with students a list of the kinds of situations that cause anxiety and therefore stop individuals from pursuing a desirable activity or goal. Without naming names, can they relate a story about someone whose anxiety stops them from being successful.

Ask students to identify an activity that makes them feel anxious and then, like Carlotta, break that activity down to its elements. Write a guided visualization that will help them become comfortable with the feeling, thereby defusing it.

A note on guided visualization: This technique is being used more and more by the established medical profession to control pain and anxiety and to promote healing and behavioral change. It should also be pointed out to students, however, that this technique is powerful and in the wrong hands can be used for brainwashing and manipulation.

Reading Assignment:

The Tell-Tale Heart, by Edgar Allen Poe

A wonderfully gruesome tale of fear controlling and destroying a man's sanity. This can lead to excellent discussion on fear and anxiety! Good reading with an excellent film and tape available.

Optional

Page 6–9

Your Courage Action Plan
One Step at a Time

Page 218–221   Page 101

Learning Objective:

To expose students to a hierarchical approach to conquering anxieties.

Presentation Suggestions:

Discuss Sally's story, what she did, and how she did it. How might her life have been different if she had not taken these steps? After brainstorming, ask the class to think of common fears and list them on the board.

Ask students individually to list some of their own fears, and then to rank them from the easiest to deal with to the hardest. Can they come up with a plan to overcome these fears? Some students may want to discuss this in small groups. Others may prefer to do this project privately. Respect those wishes. This might be a good time to bring in a guidance counselor for a class discussion.

Emphasize the importance of identifying the stress response and learning to tolerate that feeling. It helps to start with stress responses of a lesser degree and work up to stress responses of a greater degree.

A word of caution: While some phobic (severe stress reaction) responses can be cured in this fashion, it should not be attempted without the help of a trained professional. If you identify this potential in a student, be empathetic and supportive. Suggest that he or she seek help from the school or community counseling service. Check with your administration on school policy.

Reading Assignment:

I Am the Cheese, by Robert Cormier

This is a story of a boy seemingly lost in a circle of memories and forgetfulness resulting from a traumatic experience. As he continues his symbolic trip, he comes closer and closer to discovering the truth and, thereby, freeing himself from the prison of his own mind and his surroundings. To do this, he must face his fears. This book leads to perseverance, and the freedom of self-knowledge.

Optional

George Gray
by Edgar Lee Masters

Page 225–227

Read after completing pages 216–221 in *Career Choices*

Yorik's Story and 10-Year Plan

Page 222–223   Page 102

Learning Objective:

To give students an opportunity to make long-range plans for the success of someone who could reasonably be expected to fail. Since this is the classic American dream, we hope the exercise will allow students who see themselves as outside the mainstream of American society to view their own situation with more optimism and determination.

Presentation Suggestions:

Talk about anxiety! Yorik is facing some serious challenges. It is far easier to develop a long-range plan for someone else than for yourself, so this "third person" practice will help defuse any apprehension students might have.

This exercise could take up to two class periods. It's a very important first-step in preparing students to develop their own 10-year plan, which will also function as their final exam (Chapter 12). You may decide to complete the exercise in small groups or as a class. If you choose to do the exercise in class, begin with a review of setting goals and objectives. Remind students, too, that Yorik has both a vision (his goals) and the energy to realize it (his objectives or action plan). Vision plus energy equals success. Hint: It's often helpful to start with year 10 and work backward.

Ask individual students or teams to present their plan for Yorik in class. It will become obvious that there are a variety of ways for Yorik to meet his goal. As students present the plans in class, compile a chart of the alternative education and training paths available to Yorik. Discuss why having alternative plans is a good idea, particularly when preparing for a career through education and/or training.

Students will find the following time frames helpful as they complete their plans.

- Doctorate or Professional Degree (MD, JD, etc.)—2 to 6 years beyond bachelor's degree
- Master's Degree—1 to 3 years beyond bachelor's degree
- Post Baccalaureate Certification—1 to 3 years beyond bachelor's degree
- Bachelor's Degree—4 years or equivalent training/experience beyond high school
- Associate degree, technical certification, or equivalent training—1 to 3 years beyond high school
- High School Diploma—4 years (on average)

As they develop their own Career Back-up Plan (*Career Choices*, page 227), understanding the different levels of educational commitment will be helpful.

Common Core Standards for English

W.9-10.3. Write narratives to develop real or imagined experiences or events using effective technique, well-chosen details, and well-structured event sequences.

After reading Yorik's story aloud, I divide the class into groups of no more than 3, to write Yorik's plan. I allow students to be creative; however, he must accomplish or near completion of the goals he has set for himself. He may not win the lottery. Each group selects a representative to share their plan, which allows us to discuss working toward a goal, staying focused, and finding our own path to accomplish our desired result.

—Cathie Klein, College & Career Readiness Coordinator
Seaman High School, Topeka, KS

Taking Risks

Page 224–225   No Workbook
Page

Learning Objective:

To help students see that taking calculated risks is an important skill.

Presentation Suggestions:

Although the text contains no exercise on this topic, it's important to discuss it thoroughly. As the text states, taking a risk is a sort of cross between overcoming fears and making decisions. Review these concepts as part of your presentation.

Ask the class for examples of things they believe many people are afraid to do that are not life-threatening, such as public speaking, applying for a job, asking for a date, and introducing yourself to a stranger at a party. List these on the board. Discuss possible outcomes for someone taking these risks. What is the worst that could happen? The best thing? Could it be worthwhile to take this risk?

Activities:

Ask students how they would complete the sentence "If I could do anything I wanted, I would…" Is this action desirable? Is it risky? Have the class evaluate the risks involved.

Ask students to give examples of times they took a risk. Did it pay off?

Brainstorm ways in which students could motivate themselves to take a calculated risk. They might break the action down into more manageable parts or offer themselves a reward.

Invite someone who has taken a major risk to address the class. Consider asking someone who started their own business.

Getting Back on Track
If You've Derailed
Career Back-up Plan

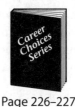

Page 226–227   Page 101

Learning Objective:

To help students understand how to find education and training alternatives, particularly if they have to take a less-than-direct path toward their career and life goals.

Presentation Suggestions:

Your students will leave your class with a comprehensive plan for achieving their education and career goals (see Chapter 12 of *Career Choices*). They'll feel empowered, energized, and focused. Encourage these feelings.

However, the path to success is often a winding one. Even people with the most comprehensive plans sometimes get sidetracked. The causes are varied: financial, health, family, or personal problems, societal changes, etc. Any of these can derail your students in the coming years. Therefore, it is important they develop contingency plans before they are needed. If something happens that takes a person off track, a contingency plan gives them confidence to know that, with time and energy, they can continue to follow their dream. The chart on page 227 will help them develop a vision of what is possible.

Before you talk about these issues, assign the completion of the Alternative Career Ladder chart on page 227. Students will classify employment opportunities based on the education and training requirements of jobs within their chosen career interest area or industry. At the same time, this chart outlines median salaries for these jobs. Students will research and fill in the final columns using their own career interest areas. This can be assigned to individuals or to teams of students interested in the same industry.

Students may need help coming up with enough jobs in their interest area to fill each of the education/training levels. Suggest they start with the U.S. Department of Labor's online Occupational Outlook Handbook found at **www.bls.gov/ooh**. For a high-interest research project that will engender student ownership, see page 4/140 of this guide.

If they don't have My10yearPlan.com® Interactive access, students can create their own electronic spreadsheets, which will allow them to update their plans and add additional columns (industries or interest areas) as they change. To start, use the first column printed in *Career Choices*, along with the top three rows.

Once completed, ask students to interpret the data on their chart. Responses may include:

- Generally, the more education and/or training, the higher the salary.

- There is a substantial jump in wages between on-the-job training and vocational certification.

- With each increase in education level attained, salaries rise substantially.

Ask students to consider the job they listed as their ideal. Given the information gathered, have they changed their plans? If so, how? Some students may decide to make a commitment to more education and/or training. Others may discover they can qualify for a desirable job primarily through training with few or no classroom requirements.

This activity can help students whose visions may be limited. By researching and reviewing the opportunities in a career interest area or industry they find intriguing, especially as this relates to the commitment to education and training, they just might realize that a few more years of preparation is worth it for a lifetime of satisfaction (review pages 118–119 of *Career Choices*).

Ask students to look back at their salary requirements on page 93 of *Career Choices*. Have them indicate the jobs that meet those requirements. If their ideal career does not pay enough to meet their desired lifestyle projections, have them list a variety of strategies to address this situation. These should include:

- Reworking their budget to bring it in line with their future salary range
- Dual earner families—having a spouse that will also work
- Continuing education throughout their working life to increase skills and wages
- Committing to higher educational goals

My10yearPlan.com® Essentials:

This is a keystone activity. Data will be extracted and used in each student's *My 10-year Plan Summary Page*. Direct students to enter their work from this activity on My10yearPlan.com® the next time they log on. For more information, see Section 9 of this guide.

Team Research Project:

(This could also be assigned as an individual project.)

The *Occupational Outlook Handbook* (OOH) is a very powerful tool that students use throughout their lives. Being a proficient user of the OOH opens a door to current information, data, and knowledge required to navigate the ever-changing workforce.

Divide the class into teams of no more than four based on Occupation Groups of interest. Without giving any further direction, challenge each group to complete the chart on page 227 using the OOH and the U.S. Department of Labor's O*NET web site (www.onetonline.org).

Presentation of Research:

Ask each group to present their findings (their completed chart) and, just as important, explain how they came up with their data. Did some groups take a different path but arrive at the same information? Which group(s) had the most direct and efficient research path? To enrich this experience, incorporate components of the following Common Core Standards for English in your project directions and instruction.

Common Core Standards for English

W.9-10.6. Use technology, including the Internet, to produce, publish, and update individual or shared writing products, taking advantage of technology's capacity to link to other information and to display information flexibly and dynamically.

W.9-10.7. Conduct short as well as more sustained research projects to answer a question (including a self-generated question) or solve a problem; narrow or broaden the inquiry when appropriate; synthesize multiple sources on the subject, demonstrating understanding of the subject under investigation.

SL.9-10.4. Present information, findings, and supporting evidence clearly, concisely, and logically such that listeners can follow the line of reasoning and the organization, development, substance, and style are appropriate to purpose, audience, and task.

SL.9-10.5. Make strategic use of digital media (e.g., textual, graphical, audio, visual, and interactive elements) in presentations to enhance understanding of findings, reasoning, and evidence and to add interest.

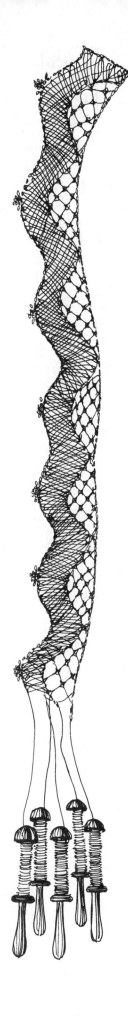

Section 3: How Do I Get It?

Chapter 10

Attitude Is Everything

Attitudes can be empowering—or limiting. To paraphrase the old adage, "You are what you think you are." In this chapter, we try to instill the attitudes that lead to success, as defined by each individual.

We have identified four areas of attitude for discussion here: attitudes toward excellence; toward work ethic; toward a changing world; and, most important, attitudes that make any chosen career a dignified and noble pursuit.

TECHNICAL SUPPORT
For the *Career Choices* curriculum
(800) 967-8016 or
support@academicinnovations.com

Affirmations Promote Action

Page 231   Page 104

Learning Objective:

To help students understand the power of affirmations in changing self-limiting attitudes.

Presentation Suggestions:

Affirmations have been shown to be a powerful tool in changing attitudes. Before discussing this topic with students, review the text on affirmations (*Career Choices*, page 231).

Suggest students review the voicemail messages from significant people and society that they imagined on page 52 of *Career Choices* and the positive messages on page 53 that counter balance the negative messages. In their *Workbook and Portfolio* (page 104), have students write an affirmation to support those positive messages to themselves.

Ask students to think of attitudes they have that may damage their potential for future success: I'm too shy. I'm too dumb. I'm too lazy. I'm too poor. I'm too uncoordinated. Then have them write affirmations to help change these attitudes:

I, (*their name*), am a confident person.

I, (*their name*), am a good student.

I, (*their name*), am willing to work hard for what I want.

Activity:

Provide 3 x 5 cards on which students can write their affirmations. Or, they can print out the affirmations from their My10yearPlan.com® account.

Advise them to take these home and tape them to their bedroom or bathroom mirror so they can be repeated every time they comb their hair or brush their teeth.

Follow-up:

Periodically, remind students to keep repeating their affirmations. Several weeks after they've begun, ask if any have noticed a difference in their behavior or thought patterns about themselves.

Chapter Introduction Video:

At the beginning of this chapter, consider showing the motivational chapter introduction video featuring Olympic Gold Medalist Dain Blanton (found on The Teachers' Lounge). Or, if your students are regularly using My10yearPlan.com®, have them watch the video online before starting their work in this chapter.

The Six Es of Excellence

Page 232–235   No Workbook Page

Learning Objective:

To recognize and evaluate the characteristics and attitudes of excellence in themselves or as part of a team.

Presentation Suggestions:

Discuss the concept of excellence with the class. This idea goes beyond the "vision plus energy equals success" equation; excellence requires added effort. Ask students if they can recall an instance in which they truly excelled at something, or can think of some part of their lives for which they must meet particularly high standards (playing a musical instrument or sport, for example). Then discuss the six Es as presented in the text, asking students to consider what part each of these characteristics plays in their own interest area. Emphasize that, although performance is often judged by others, only the individuals concerned know for sure whether they gave it their best shot.

Activities:

Ask students to write a paper about something they have done or would like to do, relating how each of the six Es plays a part in this activity.

Or ask the class to write about different activities in which they display each of the six Es of excellence (expecting to be a good student, having enthusiasm for basketball, putting energy into making friends).

Choosing the task of being a first-rate student, ask them to write affirmations that support excellence. For instance:

I, _____*(their name)*_____ , am enthusiastic about algebra; it is fun.

I, _____*(their name)*_____ , put my best energy into my schoolwork.

This activity is especially important for people who do not view themselves as particularly good students. If you get resistance, have them turn back to their charts and plans from page 227 and review their findings. Remind them the more you learn the more you earn.

Using your class's experience with teamwork over this course, discuss how the six characteristics and attitudes of excellence are beneficial to a group accomplishing a task. Add these traits to the list of effective team member traits begun in the activity explained on page 4/25 of this guide.

Writing Assignment:

Ask volunteers to share stories about individuals they know who exemplify excellence, giving examples of how that person personifies each of the six traits. Then ask the students to write a thank you note to one or two individuals they know who they feel embody the traits of excellence. In their letter, have them comment on specific instances where each trait was demonstrated. It will be one of the most substantial thank you notes they have ever written. Encourage them to send it; they'll make someone's day.

Striving for Excellence: An Indicator of Success

Understanding the concept of striving for excellence will help students set themselves apart throughout their decade of transition—from high school to college to the workforce. College admissions officers or workforce personnel directors report that one of the important things they review on applications is an individual's propensity for striving for excellence. Does that person do something really well? Whether it is in the world of academics or sports, work or community leadership positions, or a passion for a hobby they've taken to an exceptional level. For instance, their stamp collection has been recognized by their local historical museum or their "hotrod" has won an area car show.

Writing Assignment:

Recognizing excellence is the first step to pursuing it. Have students revisit their Personal Profile Chart (*Workbook and Portfolio* or My10yearPlan.com®, page 11) and imagine situations where one of their passions, skills, roles, occupations, or vocations could present an opportunity to demonstrate excellence.

Once chosen, direct them to write a narrative detailing their expertise (real or imagined).

Then challenge your students to work to make that scenario a reality so when the time comes to complete either college or job applications, they'll be able to include this description or something similar on their resume or college application.

Recognizing excellence is the first step to pursuing it.

Reading Assignment:

To Kill a Mockingbird by Harper Lee

This classic novel opens up many wonderful areas of discussion on overcoming adversity and striving for what is right. The book deals with prejudice in a small Southern town and one man's courage to do the right thing. The excellent movie based on the novel can be shown.

The Necklace by Guy de Maupassant

A young woman dooms herself to years of hard labor and poverty because of her inability to admit to her friend that she lost a necklace she borrowed to attend a special ball one evening. Years later, she meets her friend and explains to her that she appears old and worn out "because of her." Ironically, the friend reveals that the necklace had been a fake. Excellent story, excellent departure point for a discussion on "facing up to the truth" and dealing honestly with problems.

Common Core Standards for English

W.9-10.3. Write narratives to develop real or imagined experiences or events using effective technique, well-chosen details, and well-structured event sequences.

Optional

The Necklace
by Guy De Maupassant

Page 228–239

Read after completing pages 232–235
in *Career Choices*

I teach the steps of proper negotiating (Communications 2000, module 8 & module 7). Then I have the students read "The Necklace"... [and] write an essay on how negotiating could have saved Madame Loisel years of grief. [The students] must include some of the steps of negotiating when they discuss Mme. Loisel's problem.

— Lela Fay Roy, English Teacher
Somerset High School, Somerset, KY

Going for It…
Work Is an Aggressive Act

Page 236–237   Page 104

Learning Objective:

To help students realize that action is necessary to achieve any goal. They will also learn to evaluate positive and negative behaviors on the job.

Presentation Suggestions:

The correct answers are obvious, and student reaction should help reinforce the lesson to be learned. Women, especially, should be assured that aggressive acts are often required at work in order to achieve excellence.

Activities:

Suggest students read business or industry-specific magazines or blogs that relate to their career interest area. As they read they'll probably come up with a series of terms, phrases, or adjectives used to describe work or situations related to work in that field.

Ask students to suggest aggressive words and phrases often used in the context of work and list them on the board. Examples: organize, manipulate, control, wrestle, grapple, make a killing, break a leg, knock 'em dead, sock it to 'em, whip into shape, take a beating, make a pitch, or score points.

Repeat the same activity with words that connote excellence, noting how they also imply aggression. Examples: superiority, supremacy, advantage, the height of, unsurpassed, overriding, transcending, unequaled, paramount, preeminent.

There is no *work* without *effort*—and *effort* requires aggressiveness.

Be sure to point out that the word *aggressive*, when used in the context of work, does not mean overbearing, uncivil, cruel, arrogant, domineering, rude, or dictatorial. If an individual is described as any of these adjectives, they are unlikely to hold a job for long. They'll be fired.

Ask students to write workplace scenarios (similar to those on page 236) about employees they've worked with or about customer service representatives they've encountered who:

a) personified the positive trait of aggressiveness and

b) embodied the negative traits discussed above.

After completing the next activity, You're the Boss, come back to their scenarios. How might they deal with the individuals with negative behaviors?

Common Core Standards for English

RI.9-10.4. Determine the meaning of words and phrases as they are used in a text, including figurative, connotative, and technical meanings; analyze the cumulative impact of specific word choices on meaning and tone (e.g., how the language of a court opinion differs from that of a newspaper).

You're the Boss

Page 238–241   Page 105–107

Learning Objective:

Through job scenarios, interviews, and other activities, help students understand the importance of a positive work ethic, productive work habits, and a can-do attitude. They will also learn how to recognize negative behaviors and develop plans to change.

Presentation Suggestions:

Read the introductory paragraph to the class. Help students identify with Chris so, as they evaluate the employees, they can understand the employer's point of view. This person has made a large personal and financial investment in the business. If students were the employer, how would they feel about the people described in this exercise? Discuss individual employees in small groups. Have students identify the problem exhibited by each employee and design an objective to help him or her overcome it. What about Tim? What productive work habits does he exhibit? (Examples: dependable, helpful, creative, easy to get along with, honest and thoughtful, hard working.)

Brainstorm other productive work habits:

- Doing your best
- Finishing a task that you've begun
- Cooperating with fellow employees
- Respect for authority
- Teamwork toward the common goal
- Promptness

Activities:

Ask students with jobs whether their co-workers exhibit any of these negative or positive work traits (no names, please). Which type of co-worker is the most enjoyable to work with? In teams, ask students to create scenarios (similar to those on pages 238-240), choosing two of the negative work traits and two of the positive work traits around which to build their stories.

Discuss the term *work ethic*. *Work ethic* refers to something you do because you feel obligated to do so. In contrast, the term *work values* implies something you choose to do.

Have students interview three local employers to find out what they value and expect of their employees. Once the interviewee has shared their thoughts on this topic, have the students then ask them to rank the characteristics they look for in order of importance.

We tried to make our work environment in class as much like a work situation as possible. We used teams, projects, due dates set in advance, bonuses, etc.

— Linda Neef, 9th Grade English teacher
Pardeeville High School, Pardeeville, WI

Compile the employers' responses into a report: What employers in our community look for in employees. Suggest your class publish their findings in the school newspaper and online.

Now ask your students to evaluate their own work habits. Those that don't have jobs should apply these concepts to their schoolwork and other responsibilities.

Common Core Standards for English

W.9-10.6. Use technology, including the Internet, to produce, publish, and update individual or shared writing products, taking advantage of technology's capacity to link to other information and to display information flexibly and dynamically.

W.9-10.7. Conduct short as well as more sustained research projects to answer a question (including a self-generated question) or solve a problem; narrow or broaden the inquiry when appropriate; synthesize multiple sources on the subject, demonstrating understanding of the subject under investigation.

A Word about Interviewing:

Although face-to-face interviewing is ideal, employers are busy and may not be able to devote more than 10 or 15 minutes to meet with a student. Phone interviews may be the best option.

Recommend that students offer email as an option. If the interviewee is enthusiastic about this option, advise students to send only two or three questions at a time rather than the whole interview. Otherwise, it may be overwhelming and the responses less thought out. One of the advantages of email is the student can save the text responses in a word processing program.

For safety, advise students not to meet with someone they don't know outside of that person's place of employment.

*When students look at situations involving others, it helps
them to address those same problems with themselves.*

— Karen Michael, English Teacher
Bronson Junior-Senior High School, Bronson, MI

Optional

To Be of Use
by Marge Piercy

Page 249–251

Read after completing pages 238–241 in *Career Choices*

The Employee of the Twenty-First Century

Page 242–245   Page 108–109

Learning Objective:

To discuss and analyze the attitudes and skills most in demand in today's rapidly changing workplace. This activity will help students understand the skills, aptitudes, and attitudes required to manage their career trajectory as they face technological, global, and industry changes.

Presentation Suggestions:

After reading the introduction, ask students to take the self-evaluation quiz and score their answers. Follow with class discussion, brainstorming objectives that can be used to adjust attitudes that may need improvement.

Activities:

Discuss the technological advances most responsible for bringing about change in the way people work today (jet travel, online conferencing, mobile apps, wide area networks, smart phones, etc.)

Team project: Divide the class into groups of three to five. Ask each group to invent an item or service that doesn't exist today and present their design to the class. They should answer the following questions: Why is it needed? Will it create new career opportunities or eliminate old ones? If so, what types of careers? What skills will the workers need? What impact will it have on the future? Some examples include:

- Interactive online videos for at-home education
- Cure for the common cold
- At-home desalination machines
- Servant robots
- Gas-less or driver-less automobiles
- Nylon stockings that don't run

In completing this activity, did students discover any new skills that will make them more competitive in the workforce of the next decade? If so, remind them to update their list of skills they have and skills want to learn.

Energizer:

Read to the class *Tonia the Tree*, by Sandy Stryker, the 1989 winner of the Merit Award of Friends of American Writers. This charming allegory about a tree that must be uprooted and moved in order to grow will launch great class discussion concerning dealing with change.

Writing Assignment:

Divide the class into small groups to brainstorm possible story lines about the following concepts and then write an allegory based on one of these concepts:

- Embracing change
- Valuing people different from you
- Curiosity and valuing learning

Optional

Page 240–248

Tonia the Tree
by Sandy Stryker

Read after completing pages 242–245 in *Career Choices*

Be the Best of Whatever You Are
by Douglas Malloch

Read after reading page 246 in *Career Choices*

Skills Inventory Chart: The Foundation for a Quantitative Education Plan

My Skills Inventory: Transferable Skills, a dynamic chart on My10yearPlan.com®, tracks the skills students have identified as:

- Skills they have
- Skills they'd like to learn

Students can link skills to specific careers of interest and easily sort them by clicking on the column heading for a particular career title. From this data an Education Plan will evolve so they'll want to share this chart with counselors and advisors.

Employers look at a candidate's skills when hiring. The more skills relating to an industry, the more employable a person will be. As students develop their Education Plan, the goal should be to acquire skills matching their career focus. Once they identify the necessary skills for their chosen and back-up career(s), they can focus on getting the training/education needed to master those skills.

Remind your students that their Skills Inventory will continue to grow throughout their life. When they identify a skill they need for their chosen career or they learn a new skill, they'll want to add it to their My Skills Inventory chart under the appropriate category.

The "My Skills Inventory" link becomes available in the left menu as students identify and add skills. For My10yearPlan Interactive users, this process starts in Chapter 2; for My10yearPlan Essentials users, this happens in Chapter 10.

Populating My Skills Inventory on My10yearPlan.com® Essentials:*

Students identify skills in Chapter 2 (pages 44–48), Chapter 5 (page 132), on their Career Interest Surveys (pages 150–155). They will want to add these to the My Skills Inventory chart when it becomes available in Chapter 10.

Populating the Skills Boxes:

Add skills to your list by typing in the appropriate input field at the top of the chart.

- Add a skill you already have
- Add a skill you want to have

Click on the "Add" button beside the box to add that particular skill to the appropriate list.

Important Points:

Students have to go back to Make a Career Choice (**Career Choices**, page 177) if they want to change their "Chosen Career." They don't want to make this important choice on a whim.

Their Back-up Careers can be chosen and prioritized using the existing Career Interest Survey job titles listing in the drop-down menus.

If they've discover a new career they want on their chart, they must first complete a Career Interest Survey to determine if it matches their lifestyle expectations, personality, and educational commitment.

*Directions for My10yearPlan.com® Interactive are slightly different. Refer to the FAQ and Help sections online.

Managing Change

Page 246   Page 109

Learning Objective:

To help students learn to recognize and manage the inevitable changes in the workplace.

Presentation Suggestions:

In class, review the points made on page 246. Stress that technological and international changes cause shifts in the workplace. As a job changes so do the skills required to remain competitive in that occupation. Because technology will make certain tasks redundant, students may even have to completely change careers.

Activities:

Brainstorm with students to create a list of the workplace changes they've learned about during this course. You'll want to review material covered in:

- *Career Choices*, pages 135–137, 150–155, 211–213, 242–246

- Activities found in this guide on pages 4/90–4/91 and 4/127

In groups of two or three (or individually) compose a report explaining the positive and negative aspects of one example of societal change. Encourage your students to interview friends, relatives, and mentors, asking their opinions on the pros and cons of their chosen topic.

Students should keep the planning documents recommended on page 246 in their *Career Portfolio* notebook or My10yearPlan.com Portfolio. They include:

- An inventory of the computer equipment and software they master, along with any other high tech equipment. They should add these skills to their skills chart and to their resume.

- A periodic update of all the skills they are acquiring. Remind them to review the list on page 48 of *Career Choices* and update their skills inventory started at that time or use the Skill Inventory on My10yearPlan.com®.

- An annual audit of the health of the industry and job title they are pursuing. They will want to update their ten-year timeline periodically (see page 151 of *Career Choices* and 4/90–4/91 of this guide).

- The *Transferable Skills Chart* (as explained on page 31 of *Career Choices* and shown on page 109 of the *Workbook and Portfolio* for *Career Choices*). By using an electronic spreadsheet program, they can easily update this chart as their skill list expands and their career choices change. This will become an important planning document, so they'll want to keep it in their *Career Portfolio* notebook. Or use the Skills Inventory Chart on My10yearPlan.com®

My10yearPlan.com® Essentials:

This is a keystone activity. Data will be extracted and used in each student's *My 10-year Plan Summary Page*. Direct students to enter their work from this activity on My10yearPlan.com® the next time they log on. For more information, see Section 9 of this guide.

Section 3: How Do I Get It?

Chapter 11

Getting Experience

This chapter introduces students to some of the most basic job-hunting skills: writing resumes, locating jobs, informational interviews, filling out applications, and job interviews. Included also are the job seeking strategies of the online and technological realities of today.

Because so much information is already available on these topics, we have not covered them in depth, but an overview of this topic is an important part of helping individuals to visualize their futures. You may want to refer students to online resources or library research if the materials provided are not sufficient for the needs of your class.

Career Choices and Changes *Lesson Extensions*

Some secondary schools use the post-secondary edition of the *Career Choices* series, *Career Choices and Changes*, particularly if their course offers dual enrollment credit (see pages 6/25-6/29).

Career Choices and Changes has three chapters not found in *Career Choices*. Beginning with Chapter 11, you'll find lesson suggestions for these additional *Career Choices and Changes* chapters on the online version of this *Instructor's Guide*.

The final chapters of *Career Choices and Changes* (Chapters 14 and 15) are similar in content to the final chapters of *Career Choices* (Chapters 11 and 12). Suggestions regarding any additional topics in the last two chapters of *Career Choices and Changes* can also be found on the online version of this *Instructor's Guide*.

Your Resume

Page 250–253   Page 312   Page 111

Learning Objective:

To teach students the features of a professional resume and to give students experience in writing a personal resume in the format they determine is best for them.

Presentation Suggestions:

Review the information and example in the text on pages 250–253 before students complete and turn in their own resumes. There are numerous web sites devoted to this topic, so if students are starting the job seeking process, suggest that they go online to research resumes in detail.

Activities:

Have students select a job from an online posting and practice writing a cover letter for that position.

Cover letter checklist:

- Title of position identified
- How you found out about the vacancy
- Brief highlights of your resume related to the job requirements
- Examples of tasks this job requires that you have experience with
- How the results of your efforts benefited your former employers
- How and when you can be contacted
- Closure

If you know someone who works in a personnel office, check to see if you can get copies of about 20 resumes, ranging from very good to very bad, with all personal information blacked out to assure privacy. You can also find countless sample resumes online. Divide the class into small "Personnel Department" groups to evaluate the resumes and decide on five to interview. Ask them to articulate the reasons for their choices.

When they are finished, ask these very important questions: "What impact did the neatness and the correctness (spelling, grammar, punctuation, and so on) have on your impression of the applicant? Did you eliminate any individuals from the interview process because their resumes were not complete, readable, and free of errors?"

At this point, it should become clear to students how writing skills can have an impact on their lives and their futures.

The type of resume students prepare for this activity (pages 250–253 of *Career Choices*) is ideal for a student applying for their first job or volunteer position in an industry in which they are interested.

I had the students watch Indiana Jones and the Temple of Doom *and fill out a complete resume for the main characters.*

— Tammy T. Schofield, Social Studies Teacher
Walterboro High School, Walterboro, SC

A Resume for the Future:

To give students a chance to prepare a more professional resume (even though they haven't had a lot of experience yet), have students craft their "ideal" resume for their current career choice. This will be the resume they'd have if they could wave a magic wand. For this exercise, they need to create a fictional resume that assumes they:

- Have completed their education and training for the position they are seeking
- Have acquired all the skills required for their chosen career, and
- Have had internships, entry-level jobs, and/or volunteer experience in this field.

Resources Available on CareerChoices.com and Other Web Sites:

After students create their first draft using the outline on page 251 of *Career Choices*, they'll want to access resources to help them create their first "professional" resume. There are many online resources available, and this is probably the most direct way to accomplish the task. If Internet access is not available, have students get books and pamphlets on how to write a resume from the library or career center.

Online, they can also view resumes of individuals who are currently applying for positions in their chosen area of interest. This will provide ideas for their own "ideal" resume.

To gather the data required, ask students to review their Career Interest Survey and 10-year timeline for the career they've chosen. If the position requires specific education or training, skills, attributes, etc., be sure those are listed on this new resume.

- Once they determine what kind of education and/or training they require, students need to decide what school(s) or apprenticeship programs they "attended."
- What are the skills that would demonstrate to an employer that the student would be an excellent candidate for this job? List the skills they have mastered.
- Next, they'll want to fabricate some experiences—whether paid or volunteer—and list those along with their specific duties (all made up, of course).

They'll continue visualizing their ideal resume as they work through the topics required. Once complete, suggest students include this futuristic resume in their Career Portfolio Notebook or online portfolio. It will function as a "checklist" as they create their education plans for the next four to ten years and prepare for their chosen career.

My10yearPlan.com® Essentials:

This is a keystone activity. Data will be extracted and used in each student's *My 10-year Plan Summary Page*. Direct students to enter their work from this activity on My10yearPlan.com® the next time they log on. For more information, see Section 9 of this guide.

Chapter Introduction Video:

At the beginning of this chapter, consider showing the motivational chapter introduction video featuring Olympic Gold Medalist Dain Blanton (found on The Teachers' Lounge). Or, if your students are regularly using My10yearPlan.com®, have them watch the video online before starting their work in this chapter.

CareerChoices.com for Chapter 11

At the time of publication of this manual, the following activities relating to Chapter 11 of *Career Choices* were available on CareerChoices.com. See page 2/23 for detailed information about CareerChoices.com.

Page 253—Your Resume

- *Interactive Writing Activity:* Your Resume—From a Global Perspective
- *Instructional:* First Contact: The Cover Letter

Page 254—Finding a Job

- *Database:* Search a National Database for Jobs Across the Country
- *Database:* Jobs by State or Major City
- *Database:* Search the Job Listings of the Federal Government

Page 255—Finding a Job

- *Informational:* Conducting an Informational Interview

Page 256—Job Applications

- *Downloadable Form:* Getting a Social Security Card Application
- *Directory:* Finding your Local Social Security Office
- *Directory/Instructions:* Get a Certified Copy of your Birth Certificate

Page 258—Getting the Education and Training You Need

- *Informational:* Interview Preparation Tips
- *Informational:* Interview Follow-Up: The Thank-You Note
- *Informational:* Practice and Coaching with Common Interview Questions

Page 261—Accepting a Job

- *Tutorial:* Learn About Income Tax Withholding and Form W-4

Common Core Standards for English

As students complete A Resume for the Future (page 4/153), the online activities mentioned above, and the balance of this chapter, they'll:

W.9-10.4. Produce clear and coherent writing in which the development, organization, and style are appropriate to task, purpose, and audience.

W.9-10.6. Use technology, including the Internet, to produce, publish, and update individual or shared writing products, taking advantage of technology's capacity to link to other information and to display information flexibly and dynamically.

Finding a Job… Conduct an Informational Interview

Page 254–255   Page 320–324   No Workbook Page

Learning Objective:

To give students experience in using various methods for finding an entry-level job and to familiarize them with techniques for conducting informational interviews

Presentation Suggestions:

Review the information on pages 254–255 in *Career Choices* in class. Discuss and suggest students use the proactive approach below for finding a job rather than just reviewing online job postings.

Step 1: Choose the industry in which you wish to work.

Step 2: Choose the top four or five companies in this industry in the area you live or one you are willing to relocate to.

Step 3: Contact those employers to find out about available positions and to express your interest in working for them.

Ask for a student volunteer and brainstorm as a class the kinds of workplaces in your community affiliated with that particular student's chosen career. Review the information on pages 160–161 of *Career Choices* with your class for ideas.

See page 4/94–100 in this guide, the Shadow Program, for hints on finding people willing to be interviewed. Review the information in the text, including proper etiquette before students conduct their interviews.

Activities:

Ask students to write a paper about what they learned from their interviews.

Our 10th graders do a "Career Portfolio"—complete with actual resume and model application form—to present to parents at our Spring Open House. Its purpose is for students to use when applying for summer jobs, as well as to demonstrate growth and achievement toward personal goals over the course of the year. It begins with a student letter to parents about "me in 1 to 5 years."

— Andree Liscoscos, English Department Chair
Santa Maria High School, Santa Maria, CA

We do take field trips to the Workforce Development Center (Job Service) to see what jobs are available.

— Jean Granger, Careers Teacher
School Age Parents Program, Waukesha, WI

Job Applications

Page 256–257   Page 330   Page 112

Learning Objective:

For students to gain experience by practicing filling out job applications and gathering the information they'll need.

Presentation Suggestions:

Review the material in *Career Choices*. Ask students to obtain any information they need and answer the questions on page 256. Remind them to bring this information along whenever they apply for a job.

Activities:

Go to a local bank or other large employer in the community. Ask for copies of their application forms so students can get experience filling out an actual application. You may also be able to find a sample form online. When they have completed the forms, break the class into small groups and ask students to evaluate each other's applications. Would they hire this person? Since most won't have much job experience, the evaluations will center around neatness and completeness.

For practice in business writing, students can write to an employer in their career interest area and request a copy of their standard job application.

Note: Small businesses rarely use an application form. They rely on the information provided on the resume.

My10yearPlan.com® Essentials:

This is a keystone activity. Data will be extracted and used in each student's *My 10-year Plan Summary Page*. Direct students to enter their work from this activity on My10yearPlan.com® the next time they log on. For more information, see Section 9 of this guide.

Common Core Standards for English

W.9-10.4. Produce clear and coherent writing in which the development, organization, and style are appropriate to task, purpose, and audience.

The Job Interview

Page 258–259   Page 326   Page 113

Learning Objective:

To provide students with information and practice in preparation for job interviewing.

Presentation Suggestions:

Review the information in this activity and have students gather the data required for the questionnaire on page 257. They'll use this information for any interview they do in the future, so remind them to update it periodically and include it in their Career Portfolio Notebook or online portfolio.

Have students role-play the interview process by taking turns "interviewing" for a job in their area of interest. You can also invite a local employer to conduct mock interviews with student volunteers as the class watches and critiques.

Energizer:

If you or someone in the class has video recording equipment, record the interviews and play them back so that individuals can judge their own performances. Perhaps a professional interviewer or career coach would be willing to watch with the students and offer hints for improvements. This is a high anxiety situation for most people, but it can be very valuable. You may want to get assistance from the vocational counselor or someone else in the school who has had experience with this type of activity.

Job Interview Night—Turn to page 13/9 of this guide. You may want to contact a community service organization and solicit their help. (See pages 13/6–13/7 of this guide for strategies.) You can also turn the project of organizing this session over to a committee of motivated students or a parent/student committee. Ask students if any of their parents belong to the groups listed (or similar groups) on page 13/6 of the guide.

My10yearPlan.com® Essentials

This is a keystone activity. Data will be extracted and used in each student's *My 10-year Plan Summary Page*. Direct students to enter their work from this activity on My10yearPlan.com® the next time they log on. For more information, see Section 9 of this guide.

Common Core Standards for English

SL.9-10.4. Present information, findings, and supporting evidence clearly, concisely, and logically such that listeners can follow the line of reasoning and the organization, development, substance, and style are appropriate to purpose, audience, and task.

The interviewing helps them to realize how important it is to present themselves appropriately for an interview.

— Ann Barber, Business Education Teacher
Lenox Memorial High School, Lenox, MA

Optional

 Looking for Work
by Gary Soto

Page 254–261

Read after completing pages 250–259 in *Career Choices*

Dealing with Rejection and Accepting a Job

Page 260–261   Page 332–333   No Workbook Page

Learning Objective:

To help students obtain information on how to deal with these two important facets of a job search.

Presentation Suggestions:

Review the materials in the text. Share your experiences and those of individuals you know. Some students may wish to share their experiences.

Activity:

Invite a human resources director or owner of a small business to speak on these topics. Role-playing with an expert would also be helpful.

This chapter is most effective when I take at least two weeks. My students are required to fill out job applications and compose a working resume. After this is accomplished, we set appointments for a mock interview. The students are required to dress professionally and prepare for their interview. The interviews are videotaped. After completion, we view the results in class. Students can see their strengths as well as get tips on how to improve. Everyone learns something; it is a very positive experience.

— Stephanie Born-Mathieu, Business Teacher
Edison High School, Minneapolis, MN

Making Connections

Page 262–263   Page 334   Page 114

Learning Objective:

To help students aquire an understanding of mentoring and encourage them to seek out opportunities to have or be a mentor.

Presentation Suggestions:

Discuss the material in the text. Then review the questions on page 263 individually, in small groups, or as a class. Ask students to share their own experiences as mentors.

Activities:

When guest speakers come to class, ask them about their own mentors.

You might have students write a paper about an experience they've had as a mentor. If they don't think they've ever been a mentor, try to jog their memories. Have they ever instructed a younger brother or sister? Helped a new student find his or her way around? Tutored a classmate? Helped their parent with technology?

Reading Assignment:

Authors as Mentors

Ask each student to read and report on a book whose major theme centers around one of their career interest areas. It could be fiction, biography, or autobiography. This is an ideal time to reinforce library research skills. Be sure to demonstrate the use of *Books in Print: Subject Directory*, along with the search engines of large online bookstores such as Amazon.com.

Common Core Standards for English

I.9-10.6. Determine an author's point of view or purpose in a text and analyze how an author uses rhetoric to advance that point of view or purpose.

RI.9-10.8. Delineate and evaluate the argument and specific claims in a text, assessing whether the reasoning is valid and the evidence is relevant and sufficient; identify false statements and fallacious reasoning.

Dance students were mentored by our community dance companies, and students founded their own dance companies. They worked on grants, budgets, jobs, dates, etc.

— Jeannette Van Dorn, STW Implementor
Milwaukee High School of the Arts, Milwaukee, WI

We had students write thank you notes to someone who helped mentor them after reading "The Bridge Builder."

— Suzanne M. Reese, Teacher/Gifted Liaison
R.L. Turner High School, Carrollton, TX

Optional

The Bridge Builder
by Will Allen Gromgoole

Thank You, M'am
by Langston Hughes

Page 262–269
Read after completing pages 262–263 in *Career Choices*

Instructor's Notes:

Section 3: How Do I Get It?

Chapter 12

Where Do You Go From Here?

We've now reached the point in the course where students use the information they've gained and the skills they've developed to write their own plan of action. As they begin, remind them again that this is a tentative plan. It can—and probably will—be changed. The process, however, can be repeated as often as necessary.

This material can also be used by school counselors to advise individual students. Recommend that students take their *Workbook and Portfolio for Career Choices*, their Career Portfolio, and/or a printout of their *My 10-year Plan Summary Page* to any counseling appointments. If a computer is available in a counseling session, they can go online and share their 10-year plan on the screen.

Final Exam

This whole chapter could be assigned as a take-home final examination. Allow at least one week as several assignments require research and contemplation to be completed accurately and thoroughly. It is probably a good idea to let your students know from the first day of class that this will be their final (or a portion of their final grade).

Common Core Standards for English

As students work through the process of creating and articulating their 10-year plan outlined in this chapter they'll:

W.9-10.2. Write informative/explanatory texts to examine and convey complex ideas, concepts, and information clearly and accurately through the effective selection, organization, and analysis of content.

W.9-10.3. Write narratives to develop real or imagined experiences or events using effective technique, well-chosen details, and well-structured event sequences.

W.9-10.5. Develop and strengthen writing as needed by planning, revising, editing, rewriting, or trying a new approach, focusing on addressing what is most significant for a specific purpose and audience.

W.9-10.6. Use technology, including the Internet, to produce, publish, and update individual or shared writing products, taking advantage of technology's capacity to link to other information and to display information flexibly and dynamically.

W.9-10.7. Conduct short as well as more sustained research projects to answer a question (including a self-generated question) or solve a problem; narrow or broaden the inquiry when appropriate; synthesize multiple sources on the subject, demonstrating understanding of the subject under investigation.

W.9-10.10. Write routinely over extended time frames (time for research, reflection, and revision) and shorter time frames (a single sitting or a day or two) for a range of tasks, purposes, and audiences.

Getting the Education or Training You Need

Page 267–269   Page 339   No Workbook Page

Learning Objective:

To help students understand the various education and training alternatives available to them. This will enable them to complete comprehensive education and/or training plans based upon their career interest areas.

Presentation Suggestions:

Review and expand on available education and training opportunities. This is also a good time to bring in various speakers: career counselors, vocational/technical counselors, college placement officers, employment development workers, and military recruiters.

Ask students to refer to their Career Alternative Ladder from page 227 of *Career Choices* and review the education and training alternatives in their career interest areas. Suggest that students go online to investigate their options in more detail.

Activities:

Ask students to imagine a point in the future when they have completed all education or training necessary for their chosen career. They have worked in this career for five years when the occupation suddenly becomes obsolete, perhaps due to outsourcing or new technology. They are forced to make a career change.

Have students begin by identifying career alternatives and consulting their Skills Inventory chart, then, create a five- to ten-minute presentation detailing what skills from their now-defunct career would be transferable to their new career. How were these skills used in their former career? How will they be applied to their new career? They will also want to explain what skills they will need to acquire in order to qualify for their new career. Will there be additional education or training involved?

Resources:

Review the list on page 4/163 of this guide that details the resources available on **CareerChoices.com**. These web sites will provide up-to-date information for most major education and training institutions within the United States. If students are planning on industry specific accreditation or certification, they'll want to start by visiting the industry association's web site.

Chapter Introduction Video:

At the beginning of this chapter, consider showing the motivational chapter introduction video featuring Olympic Gold Medalist Dain Blanton (found on **The Teachers' Lounge**). Or, if your students are regularly using **My10yearPlan.com®**, have them watch the video online before starting their work in this chapter.

One student, when asked why he was flunking math even when he said he needed it for his future job, paused then said, "Because I never thought of it like this before, that it would help me for my career."

— Debra Kuperberg, Special Education Teacher
San Gabriel High School, San Gabriel, CA

CareerChoices.com for Chapter 12

At the time of publication of this manual, the following activities relating to Chapter 12 of *Career Choices* were available on CareerChoices.com. See page 2/23 for detailed information about CareerChoices.com.

Page 267—Getting the Education or Training You Need

- *Informational:* The GED

Page 268—Getting the Education or Training You Need

- Community or Junior Colleges
  - *Informational:* A Good Alternative: The Two-year College
  - *Directory:* Two-year Colleges Listed by State
- Four-Year Colleges and Universities
  - *Directory:* Finding a College to Match Your Needs
  - *Directory:* What to Look for in a College
  - *Calculator:* Financial Aide – How Big of a Student Loan Can Your Career Support
  - College Bargains

Page 269—Getting the Education and Training You Need

- The Military
  - *Databases:* Military Recruitment
    - U.S. Army
    - U.S. Air Force
    - U.S. Navy
    - U.S. Marine Corps
    - U.S. Coast Guard
  - *Databases:* Military Academies
    - U.S. Military Academy – West Point
    - U.S. Air Force Academy
    - U.S. Naval Academy
    - U.S. Coast Guard Academy
- Vocational Schools
  - *Databases:* Public and Private Vocational Schools

Page 271—Preparing for the SAT and ACT

- *Database:* SAT Information and Registration
- *Instructional:* Hints on Preparing for the SAT
- *Database:* ACT Information and Registration
- *Instructional:* ACT Preparation Strategies

What Is Your Committment to Your Education?

Page 270–271   Page 346   Page 116–118

Your Education and Training 10-Year Plan

Learning Objective:

To help students select high school and post-secondary courses related to a specific career choice in the student's interest area. As they finalize their plans, students should also consider alternative education and training paths.

Presentation Suggestions:

Your Education and Training 10-year Plan: Students affirm their current career choice and, using the Career Interest Survey for that career, indicate the education needed and the duration of training. Some careers have several training options—technical school, apprenticeship, military, or college. Urge students to weigh the pros and cons of all options before making a choice.

The chart in *Career Choices* on pages 270–271 requires additional research; allow ample time for this essential activity. Suggest students review their Career Interest Surveys. If they are using My10yearPlan.com®, they should also review My Skills Inventory, incorporating the skills needed for their chosen career to help identify the courses and experiences needed. Encourage students to consult counselors or advisors.

My10yearPlan.com® Essentials:

This is a keystone activity. Data will be extracted and used in each student's *My 10-year Plan Summary Page*. Direct students to enter their work from this activity on My10yearPlan.com® the next time they log on. For more information, see Section 9 of this guide.

Updating Student's 10-year Plans throughout High School:

The *Get Focused…Stay Focused!*™ modules support the updating of student's 10-year plans in the 10th, 11th, and 12th grades with a systematic process. With the *Get Focused…Stay Focused!*™ process, students hone—and maintain progress on—their quantitative and meaningful education plan through 16 annual sessions. Designed for academic integration (e.g., in English), the modules prompt students to research opportunities in science, technology, engineering, and math (STEM) fields and other fast-growing sectors. Students learn the process for researching and applying to appropriate post-secondary institutions, and explore other considerations, including financial aid. By the time they graduate from high school, students are truly college and career ready—armed with a meaningful, up-to-date 10-year Career and Education Plan and an informed, declared major for their college or post-secondary path.

For details, see page 4/170 and Section 6/22–6/30.

Optional

If
by Rudyard Kipling

Page 270–272

Life-long Learning Graph

Page 273   Page 348   Page 118

Learning Objective:

To help students visualize the long-range educational plan of a life-long learner by graphically building a visual model.

Presentation Suggestions:

Knowing what is needed to accomplish a career goal helps students set priorities and make plans, now and in the future. Even so, the thought of spending another 10 to 15 years preparing for and getting established in a job may seem overwhelming. To help students visualize their commitment to life-long learning, have them complete the graph on page 273. Then, to put this time frame in perspective with the balance of their life, have them turn back to the graph on page 118 of *Career Choices*. What's 10 to 15 years over an average 80-year lifetime?

My10yearPlan.com® Essentials:

This is a keystone activity. Data will be extracted and used in each student's *My 10-year Plan Summary Page*. Direct students to enter their work from this activity on My10yearPlan.com® the next time they log on. For more information, see Section 9 of this guide.

Delaying Gratification

Page 274–275   Page 350   Page 119–120

Learning Objective:

To personalize delaying gratification by identifying the sacrifices and commitments required to follow their plans.

Presentation Suggestions:

Break the class into small groups based on individual career plans, type and duration of training required, or general career field—whatever seems most appropriate. Since training for any career involves some type of delayed gratification, it should be fairly easy for groups to identify the types of sacrifices they will probably need to make. Having done this, they can help each other complete the questions on page 275.

Facing Fears and Anxieties

Page 276–277   Page 352   Page 120–121

Learning Objective:

To personalize the issue of facing fears and anxieties so students can take this into account when they write their own plans.

Presentation Suggestions:

Ask students to review the material on overcoming anxieties in Chapter 9 before completing the exercises on pages 276 and 277. You might use yourself or a student volunteer as an example and run through the exercise as a class.

Your Action Plan for the Next Ten Years

Page 279–280   Page 354   Page 121–123

Learning Objective:

The students prepare education, career, and lifestyle plans for a career within their interest areas. These plans begin where they currently are in school and continue through post-secondary education or training and into their first career-related jobs. The complete plans will cover at least 10 years.

Presentation Suggestions:

Depending upon the level of the class, this segment of the chapter might be used as the final exam. A more advanced or gifted class should be given the whole chapter as an exam. A class with lower abilities may need the assistance of class discussion in the previous exercises.

You'll want to suggest students review the key planning documents listed in the charts on page 125 of their *Workbook and Portfolio for* **Career Choices**. This data will help them make their plans with confidence.

If you choose to use this as the final, we suggest making it a take-home exam and allowing at least a week for its completion. Statements should be written as measurable objectives with all three components: What will be different? By how much or how many? By when? Review this material in class, if necessary. You should also evaluate the plans according to how realistic they are, the amount of time and thought students have given them, and the accuracy of planning.

For an example of a rubric to use when scoring this activity, see page 4/14.

My10yearPlan.com® Essentials:

This is a keystone activity. Data will be extracted and used in each student's *My 10-year Plan Summary Page*. Direct students to enter their work from this activity on **My10yearPlan.com®** the next time they log on. For more information, see Section 9 of this guide.

Many of my students got really excited about creating their plan. I even received a few letters from parents.

— John Fishburne, Teacher
Cascade High School, Leavenworth, WA

Optional

Ex-Basketball Player
by John Updike
Read before beginning to work on "Your Plan" in **Career Choices**

Page 273–283   ***25th High School Reunion***
by Linda Pastan

Read after completing "Your Plan" in **Career Choices**

When we read "25th High School Reunion," it inspired the students to create a scrapbook that could be carried throughout their high school years so that they would have it for their 25th reunion. Also, they began work on a time capsule.

— Janet Sinclair, English I Teacher
Hancock High School, Kiln, MS

Mission in Life

Page 282   Page 358   Page 124

Learning Objective:

To help students re-evaluate and clarify their personal mission statements as well as their definitions of success, and to understand the importance of this valuable process.

Presentation Suggestions:

It may be beneficial to re-do the guided visualization on page 4/41 of this guide. Preface this with a simple statement that, considering the growth and change students have likely undergone as a result of their experiences articulating their dreams and goals during this course, it makes sense to look at what is important to them **now**.

Once they've completed their new letters and vision, ask them to re-write both their mission statement and their definitions of success based on any new feelings, insights, or thoughts. Have they changed their mission from what they indicated earlier on page 61 of *Career Choices*?

If students are willing to share their mission statements, you might want to post them around the room or provide the information to the yearbook editor. Be sure to respect any wishes for privacy.

My10yearPlan.com® Essentials:

This is a keystone activity. Data will be extracted and used in each student's *My 10-year Plan Summary Page*. Direct students to enter their work from this activity on My10yearPlan.com® the next time they log on. For more information, see Section 9 of this guide.

Assessment and Evaluation:

If assessment and/or evaluation is a critical element of your program, be sure to review your options on the following pages of this guide:

Pages in this guide	Description of Assessment
4/169	Post Assessment Activity using *Envisioning Your Future* Activity
Section 14	Assessment and Evaluation
14/15	Teacher Survey and Evaluation
5/2	Sample Measurable Goals and Objectives for the *Career Choices* curriculum

As a Portfolio assignment at the end of the year, students read "We Are a Success" and wrote about how they have been successful over the year.

— Suzanne M. Reese, Teacher/Gifted Liaison
R.L. Turner High School Carrollton, TX

My students worked in groups to produce bulletin boards throughout the school depicting themes learned in their class.

— Janet Richards, Teacher
Johnson High School, St. Paul, MN

Back to the Future

Letters Remembering Your Dreams and Goals

Students will have a clearer sense of themselves and their dreams for the future as they finish their *Career Choices* course. This vision should be captured for a future time when it might trigger renewed enthusiasm.

Have your students write two letters to themselves about their dreams and goals for their future. Tell them they will receive one letter in two years and the other in five years. Ask them to attach a copy of their 10-year plan and with a copy of the most current letter written from the activity "Seeing in the Mind's Eye," on page 4/41 in this guide.

Ask each student to bring two self-addressed envelopes to school, each bearing "forever" first-class postage (to take into account any rate increases). The envelopes should be addressed to the students, in care of someone in their family who they feel is not likely to move. The return address should be that of a second relative who is also likely to stay at the same address. This doubles their chances of receiving the letters.

After they have written and sealed their letters, box them up and store them for mailing. You'll want to label the boxes with the year they are to be sent. Then each year (perhaps with the new year) you'll deliver the appropriate envelopes to the post office.

Your students' letters just might arrive at a critical moment when they are considering giving up a cherished dream or goal. It could rekindle a passion or remind them of the benefits of staying on course and pursuing a goal.

Once they've completed their new letters and vision, ask them to re-write both their mission statement and their definitions of success based on any new feelings or thoughts. Have they changed their mission from what they indicated earlier on page 61 of *Career Choices*? For those that have ask them to share their reasons with the class.

We do graduate surveys two years and five years after graduation. Students consistently rank this class as one of their favorites.

— Steve Rzeka, Counselor
South Park High School, Fairplay, CO

Post Assessment Essay

At this time, the exercise "Envisioning Your Future" on page 14 of *Career Choices* should be administered again. Compare this version with the one completed at the beginning of the course. Do you see any growth in the students? Have their horizons been broadened? Perhaps their goals are more realistic for their capabilities and commitment. Have young women considered non-traditional careers? Do you sense better self-knowledge? Do their plans include post-secondary education?

If appropriate, share these two assessments with the school counselor. They could also be included in the students' school files, if appropriate and legal.

Turn back to the exercise "Defining Success" on page 4/10–11 of this guide. You may be interested in doing the course wrap-up activity recommended there.

> During the last ten minutes on the final day of the course, we recommend reading aloud *Oh! The Places You'll Go!* By Dr. Seuss. This is a wonderful book for people of all ages, filled with many of the messages imparted in *Career Choices*. Published by Random House, New York, ISBN 0-6779-80523-3, it should be available online and in most bookstores. The summary provided by the Library of Congress is as follows: Advice in rhyme for proceeding in life; weathering fear, loneliness, and confusion; and being in charge of your actions.

A Capstone activity that was fun was creating a game similar to "Life," "Bingo," and "Jeopardy." Students had to use vocabulary, goals, and Envisioning Your Future information we have studied to make a game. One team of girls created a very clever and fun game similar to Life. All the students wanted to play it and it was very creative and practically made.

— Sharon McElroy, Career Center Coordinator
R.A. Long High School, Longview, WA

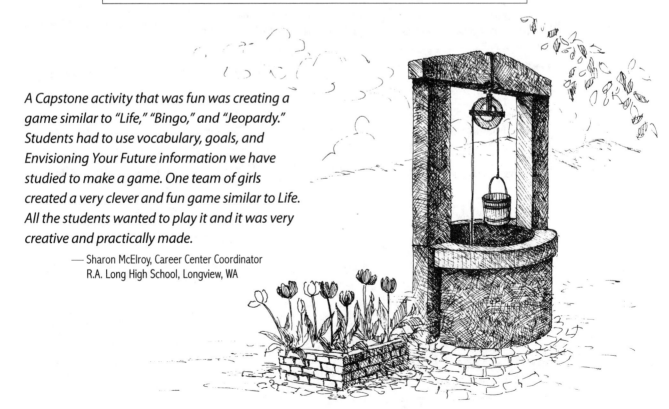

Get Focused…Stay Focused!™ Outline for Updating the 10-year Plan

Lesson #	Follow-up Module 1: *Developing Attitudes & Aptitudes that Promote College & Career Readiness*	Follow-up Module 2: *Determining Your Informed Major & Post-Secondary Education Path*	Follow-up Module 3: *Preparing to Act on Your 10-Year Education & Career Plan*
1	Reviewing Your 10-year Plan & Analyzing How You've Changed	Reviewing Your 10-year Plan & Analyzing How You've Changed	Updating Your 10-year Plan & Your Education Plan
2	Updating the 10-year Plan to Bring into Perspective Who You are Today	Revisiting Keystone Topics: My Skills Inventory & Counseling with Your 10-year Plan	Building a Skills-based Education Plan: A Road Map for Self-directed Learners
3	Which Careers Will Have the Highest Demand in the Next Decade?	Learn about STEM-related Careers on the Department of Labor Web Sites	Back-up Plans: Critical to Navigating Your Education & Career
4	Creating a Career Interest Survey for a High-Demand Career of Interest	Creating a Career Interest Survey for a STEM Career & Reaffirming Your Chosen Career Path	Time to Take Action: Developing Your Action Plan Checklists
5	Writing an Education Plan for a High-Demand Career	Your Education Plan & Transferable Skills	Developing Your College Planning Timeline & Action Plan
6	Developing an Education Plan & Course Schedule for a High-Demand Career	Choosing a Major to Match Your Chosen Career	Seeking Letters of Recommendation
7	Writing the Autobiographical Statement for Your 25th High School Reunion	Choosing a College to Match Your Chosen Career	Finalizing Your Application Essay
8	*Lesson 7 continued* Presentation of autobiographical statements	Examining Colleges that Offer Your Chosen Major & are Close to Home	Research Scholarships Online
9	*Lesson 8 continued* Presentation of autobiographical statements	Examining Colleges that Offer Your Chosen Major & are Within Your Budget	Apply for Financial Aid & Scholarships
10	Which Post-Secondary Option is Right for You? Starting Your Education Plan	Comparing Colleges to Find the Right Match	Complete College Applications
11	How to Conduct Online Research for College & Post-secondary Options	Getting Ready for the Application Process & the College Acceptance Probability Worksheet	Writing Your Resume, Cover Letters, & Thank-you Letters
12	*Lesson 11 continued*	Writing the College or Scholarship Essay: Your Outline	College or Career? It's Not an Either/Or Choice
13	How to Afford College Regardless of Individual Circumstance	Writing the College or Scholarship Essay: Your First Draft	Write a Student Education Plan (SEP)
14	Do You Have the Preparation to Get into the College or Job of Your Choice?	Creating a Timeline for Applying to College, Financial Aid, and Scholarships	Apply for Jobs and Prepare for Interviews
15	Online Research of Post-secondary Schools' Admission Requirements	Updating Your Resume for Applying to College, Scholarships, & Summer Jobs	Build a College Schedule
16	Update Your Online 10-year Plan to Guide You in Making the Best Life Choices	Updating My 10-year Plan and Portfolio	Your Portfolio for Success: Updating Your 10-year Plan, Now and in the Future

See pages 6/28 to 6/30 for details.

Section 5

Getting Buy-in

Topics covered in this section include strategies for:

- Meeting with the decision makers at your school or district individually and in groups to talk about starting a new program.

- Developing measurable goals from the outset for implementing the program and for what the program is to accomplish.

- Getting access to a number of videos and other helpful resources to assist you in creating buy-in. You can find most of them on **The Teachers' Lounge**.

Getting Started

Starting a new program offers a variety of challenges. Here are the main steps needed to turn your goals into reality.

1. ***Identify Your Goals***

   The first step with any new project is to identify your goals and objectives. You might want to review the system presented in Chapter 8 of the *Career Choices* textbook. This tried and true format will help you articulate your plan and write it as quantitative goals and objectives, providing deadlines and metrics that are measurable. This beginning roadmap will help you explain your plan to your peers and funding sources. See pages 5/12 for suggestions.

2. ***Create Buy-In Within Your School and Community***

   It is critical that you get all stakeholders within your school community to buy in to your new Freshman Transition effort. After you identify your stakeholders, this section provides some step-by-step strategies that have worked for other educational innovators. Also see Section 13 for community involvement strategies.

3. ***Identify and Secure Funding***

   A critical and important step, Section 15 demystifies the process of getting the funds you require to make your plan a reality. You'll want to review the federal, state, and local mandates that support your goals to gauge the feasibility of funding your efforts through those sources.

Sample Measurable Goals and Objectives

for the **Career Choices** *Curriculum*

The following measurable goals and objectives are the kind funding sources (from private foundations to school boards) require. You may want to choose the most appropriate two or three for your project and edit accordingly. Include a copy of your assessment tool(s) with your proposal. See Section 13 of this guide for a pre- and post-survey for students and other suggested assessment strategies.

- Upon completion of the **Career Choices** curriculum, ____ % of students will have raised their career goals and expectations as demonstrated by pre- and post-surveys.

- Upon completion of the **Career Choices** curriculum, ____ % of students who at the beginning of the class had not planned any further education or training after high school will have changed their minds and will be preparing for post-secondary education or training.

- Upon completion of the **Career Choices** curriculum, ____ % of the students in the course will have changed their attitude towards and, therefore, increased their effort in their academic subjects, as evaluated by pre- and post-surveys of their other teachers.

- Upon completion of the **Career Choices** curriculum, each student will have a realistic education and career plan for the next ten years. They will also be able to demonstrate the goal setting, analytical, and decision-making skills necessary to adapt that plan as they mature.

- Upon completion of the **Career Choices** curriculum, all females will be able to articulate, in a quantitative way, why becoming a teen parent is not a good plan. Females who were ambivalent about teen pregnancy at the beginning of the course will have a strong opinion and attitude against teen parenting.

- Students completing this course will be less likely to drop out of high school. This will be demonstrated by decreasing the dropout rate among the graduates of this program from ____ % (current school average or average of similar ability students) to ____ %.

- Test scores within academic subjects (define which ones) will increase by ____ within one year of completing this course.

- In post- surveys, ____ % of graduates' parents will report a positive impact on their child due to this classroom experience.

As compared with data from the three years prior to the course introduction, after completion of the **Career Choices** course, among the completers:

- The attendance rate will increase by ____%

- Suspension rates will decrease by at least ____%

- Expulsion rates will decrease by at least ____%

- The state required (test name) pass rate will increase by ____%

- Average GPAs will increase by ____%

- The percentage of students promoted to the next grade of ____ will increase by at least ____%

Long-range Goals for Students Entering Post-secondary Education

- The rate at which entering college freshman require remediation will decrease ____%.

- The completion rates (associate degree, certification, or transfer to a four-year college) will increase by ____%/

- The length of time to complete the above degree or certification will decrease by ____%.

Getting Buy-in from All Stakeholders

For any new program to be successful, it must have the buy-in of all stakeholders. Your stakeholders for your Freshman Transition course include:

> Faculty
> Parents
> District administrators
> The community
> Post-secondary partners
> Students

Generating support for your *Career Choices* program from these stakeholders is usually the principal's most important task.

Let's start by addressing some common concerns you are likely to hear.

> ***Most of our students are going to college. Why would they need a course like this?***

50% of students drop out of college or do not graduate within six years. That statistic alone should convince stakeholders that something has to change.

In addition, studies show that students who are career-focused and career-committed are far more likely to graduate from college and transition into the workforce at the level for which their post-secondary education prepared them.

Today, 20% of 26-year-olds live at home or are not economically independent of their parents. A recent CNN Poll showed that 48% of college graduates return home after college, and one year later 44% are still there.

Addressing the issue at it relates to economic self-sufficiency requires that students understand the necessity for a career focus and have a vision in the form of a 10-year plan to help guide them through their decade of transition—from high school, through post-secondary training or college, and into the workforce as a fully self-sufficient adult.

> ***How do we convince parents who insist "My students don't need this. They are going to college!" of the necessity of this type of course for their teenagers?***

In the United States, young adults who require economic support from their parents (past their schooling years) are known as Twixters according to a *Time* magazine article.

In Great Britain, they are known as KIPPERS, which is an acronym for:

Kids **I**n **P**arents **P**ockets **E**roding **R**etirement **S**avings

Next time you are with a group of parents who might question the importance of this type of course, ask how many of them know families whose adult children returned home after graduating from college because they couldn't find a job that would support them. Watch the hands go up and the heads nod!

Our school uses a software program or online tool to help students choose a career. Isn't that enough?

For the top 20–30% of students, perhaps; those are students who receive this information and exploration at home or observe it within their family. For them, a couple of hours with a software program might be enough.

But for the balance of students, the ones who do not see the relevance in education and cannot envision a productive future with plans to realize their dreams, a couple of hours behind a computer screen is just not enough to set them on the path to making the second most important decision of their lives: how they'll spend 40 hours per week for up to 40 years. Without an understanding of why they need to prepare vigorously for a career, you'll lose them.

In addition, it is important for ALL students to have the skills and information necessary so they can modify their plans when they are forced to or choose to change careers. Rather than rely on software programs that are unavailable once they graduate, students will have the confidence to plot their own productive work-life course if they learn the **process** for research and decision-making. By using the real-world applications readily available on U.S. Department of Labor-sponsored web sites, they'll learn where to go to get the help they'll need throughout their lives.

They'll be empowered with the skills to chart the trajectory of their own career after they leave school and will not have to rely on commercial online tools that "magically" come up with career options or directions once a survey is completed.

Encouraging the Faculty at Your School

Once you've addressed these concerns, you'll want to start orienting faculty on the advantages of every student having a 10-year plan and the online strategies for maximizing its potential. You'll need buy-in from your faculty if you hope to institutionalize the use of this tool for personalization in advisory situations. Plus, each academic department will need to buy into the notion of helping students update their 10-year plans in the 10th, 11th, and 12th grades as they learn more about themselves and the world around them.

If you have a group that is still not convinced of the need for this type of information for your students, take a look at pages 5/7 of this *Instructor's Guide* for a suggested agenda and brainstorming option.

An involved individual will be a committed individual. Find ways for everyone to get involved.

- Hold brainstorming sessions with all stakeholders
- Form department committees to plan for the school-wide initiative
- Bring the counseling staff in to provide training and support for the advisory functions of the teachers
- Schedule staff development sessions for the whole school
- Ask parents to become mentors
- Invite district administrators and board members to students' presentations of their 10-year plans
- Get the education reporter for the local newspaper to cover your efforts over the year, starting with an article that covers the questions at the beginning of this module

Spending time on the process of getting buy-in is critical to the success of any new project. For resources, visit **The Teachers' Lounge** or call Academic Innovations at (800) 967-8016.

Creating Buy-In for Your Course

Vision and teamwork are critical elements in any restructuring or redesign effort. However you plan to use the *Career Choices* curriculum, you will probably have to change some of the things you've done in the past, and change is uncomfortable for everyone.

The first step toward positive and lasting change is getting the buy-in of the individuals involved. If you plan a class where you are the only instructor, you will need to get buy-in from the administration and, perhaps, a school improvement committee (parents and community members). If you are planning an interdisciplinary curriculum, you will also need to get active buy-in from all teachers working with you, including the other instructors that touch your students' lives at some level.

You'll need to lobby for your project. Studies on the process of change suggest that the best way to get people to accept a transition is through one-on-one discussions. Meet with individuals over lunch or coffee and present your idea. Use this time to listen for any discomfort or concern expressed by your colleagues. You will want to address their concerns or provide possible solutions right then. If this isn't possible, get back to the individual with more information quickly. Once you have addressed any concerns and you have a team of individuals willing to explore the possibilities, it is time to call a meeting.

Buy-in & Planning Resources to Share with Your Team Members Via Email

Below is a list of videos available on **The Teachers' Lounge** (www.careerchoices.com/lounge.) If you don't have time for one-to-one meetings let the videos assist in generating buy-in and launching the planning needed for your Freshman Transition, dropout prevention, and/or college readiness efforts. Use these videos for staff meetings, presentations, and to provide data required by funding sources.

The videos listed below are production quality, so they can be shown to large audiences.

Video Resources to Use in Buy-in Meetings

These can be found online on the home page of **www.whatworkscareerchoices.com**

- The Key to Success for Dropout Prevention
- What is a Freshman Transition Initiative?
- Documentary: Success 101: A Prerequisite for Life
- *Career Choices*: Why it Works
- The School-wide Initiative
- My10yearPlan Interactive introduced by Dain Blanton

A School-wide Meeting

Introducing Your Career Choices *Course, the 10-year Plan, and the Freshman Transition Initiative to the Entire Faculty*

Use this meeting to generate interest in the course and school-wide effort. This is a good recruiting tool for course instructors and committee members.

Equipment or Props

- Computer, LCD projector, speakers, and screen
- Flip chart on an easel and felt tip marker
- Sets of the *Career Choices* curriculum (at least one per table)
  - Consider showing complete sets of the curriculum (five textbooks) even if you are only using the main *Career Choices* text and the *Workbook and Portfolio*. This will get academic instructors thinking about how they can integrate the concepts thematically into their classrooms.
- DVD with training videos
  - The Key to Dropout Prevention
  - The School-Wide Initiative

Handouts for Participants

- Photocopies of pages 5/13–5/14 of this *Instructor's Guide*
  - These two pages need to be printed two-sided (back to back) to facilitate the exercise. You want to make sure the horizontal dark lines on both sides match up.
- Copies of your measurable goals and objectives for your *Career Choices* program
- Form for collecting feedback
- Copies of the article "A Personalized Plan for Life" by Dr. Rebecca Dedmond

Room Set-up

- Participants at round tables in small groups to facilitate discussion and brainstorming activities.

Lead Teacher Prep

- Read pages Section 5 of this *Instructor's Guide*

Time Allotment for Workshop

- 45 to 90 minutes

Excerpted from the Career Choices Lead Administrator and Lead Teacher Manual and reprinted with permission.

School-wide Meeting Agenda

Group Brainstorm (5 to 8 minutes)

Ask your audience to respond to the question below by calling out their answers. This is best done as the whole group. You'll want to have an assistant to write the responses on the flip chart.

If you could wave a magic wand and give your students any characteristics, attitudes, or skills, what would they be?

Show Training Video (10 minutes)

The Key to Dropout Prevention: Why a 10-year Plan?

Introduce *Career Choices* Textbooks (15 to 40 minutes)

- Share copies of the **Career Choices** curriculum at each table

- Provide an overview of the curriculum

- Use the video entitled *Career Choices: Why It Works* (found at **The Teachers' Lounge**)

- *Optional: If you have the time, show these three short training videos*
    Who Am I: Chapters 1–2 (8 minutes)
    What Do I Want: Chapters 3–7 (7 minutes)
    How Do I Get It? Chapters 8–12 (6 minutes)

- Handout the photocopies of pages 5/13–5/14 of the **Instructor's Guide**

    - Ask each table to decide on a topic of interest from the group brainstorm, take a few minutes, and locate where in **Career Choices** that is addressed. This allows participants to get into and study the course material. If you already have your **Career Choices** textbooks, consider providing each participant with a copy to review during the workshop. The textbook itself is a good recruiting tool.

Create a Vision (10 to 30 minutes)

- Provide an overview of the process so participants begin to form their own understanding of what is possible when using the 10-year plan as an advisory tool

- Show the video *The School-wide Initiative* (9 minutes)

- Hand out copies of your own measurable goals and objectives for the **Career Choices** course. Choose three or four objectives from the example on page 5/2 of the **Instructor's Guide** or write your own.

- If you have time you can start the process of the whole school setting goals and objectives, particularly if your ultimate goal is to institute a School-wide Initiative such as the **Get Focused...Stay Focused!** ™ Initiative model that continues through the 10th, 11th, and 12th grade (**www.getfocusedstayfocused.org**).

Questions, Comments, and Commitments

Prior to the school-wide meeting, recruit support for your course and your efforts from a few key faculty members who are considered leaders and are particularly well respected. Do this in one-to-one meetings. At the end of the workshop, ask these individuals to share their thoughts and to outline their or commitment to the School-wide Initiative.

Parent's Meeting

Introducing Your Career Choices Course and the Freshman Transition Initiative to Parents and Community Partners

Use this meeting to generate interest in the course and school-wide effort. The support of parents and community members is critical to any lasting change within a school.

Equipment or Props

- Computer, LCD projector, speakers, and screen
- Flip chart on an easel and felt tip marker
- Sets of the *Career Choices* curriculum (at least one per table)

  Note: Consider showing complete sets of the curriculum (five textbooks) even if you are only using the main Career Choices text and the Workbook and Portfolio.

- DVD with training videos
  - The Key to Dropout Prevention
  - The School-Wide Initiative

Handouts for Participants

- Photocopies of pages 5/13–5/14 of this *Instructor's Guide*
  - These two pages need to be printed double-sided to facilitate the exercise. You want to make sure the horizontal dark lines on both sides match up.
- Copies of your measurable goals and objectives for your *Career Choices* program
- Form for collecting feedback
- Copies of the article "A Personalized Plan for Life" by Dr. Rebecca Dedmond

Room Set-up

- Participants at round tables in small groups to facilitate discussion and brainstorming activities.

Lead Teacher Prep

- Read pages Section 5 of the *Instructor's Guide*

Time Allotment for Workshop

- 45 to 90 minutes

Invitees

Invite parents, but be sure to also ask the local newspaper reporter for education, school board members, district office personnel, and members of community service organizations who support your school's efforts.

Parent's Meeting Agenda

Group Brainstorm (5 to 8 minutes)

Ask your audience to respond to the question below by calling out their answers. This is best done as the whole group. You'll want to have an assistant to write the responses on the flip chart.

If you could wave a magic wand and give your students any characteristics, attitudes, or skills, what would they be?

Show Training Video (12 minutes)

The Key to Dropout Prevention

Introduce *Career Choices* Textbooks (20–30 minutes)

- Share copies of the **Career Choices** curriculum at each table
- Provide an overview of the curriculum*
- Use the video entitled *Career Choices: Why It Works*
- Hand out the photocopies of pages 5/13–5/14 of the **Instructor's Guide**
  *You won't have time to provide the same amount of information you did in the school-wide meeting.

Review the Expected Outcomes (10 minutes)

- A 10-year plan that is updated yearly in academic classes
- Comprehensive academic plans that are tied to the student's life goals and dreams
- Regular advisory opportunities with all their teachers
- A young person who understands the consequences of not getting a good education
- More questions about jobs and life planning
- A more connected and enthusiastic student who becomes a consumer of education

Create a Vision (10 minutes)

- Discuss how parents and community partners can support students in the development and updating of their 10-year plans
- Hand out copies of your own measurable goals and objectives for the **Career Choices** course. Choose three or four objectives from the example on page 5/2 of the **Instructor's Guide** or write your own.

Small Group Brainstorm (10 minutes for brainstorm and sharing)

How can parents and/or community partners support students and the school-wide program?

- Handout – 12 Ways Parents Can Support Students in the Freshman Transition Program (found in the Freshman Transition Leadership Manual)
- Ask a guidance counselor to address this topic in relation to the opportunities created by the Freshman Transition effort

Questions & Answers

Notes as You Plan Your Meetings:

Strategies for Creating Buy-In
The Student-Centered Model

THE TRADITIONAL ORGANIZATIONAL MODEL	
Organization | | | \\/	The ORGANIZATION of education… (class periods that were X minutes long held between 8 AM and 3 PM five days per week; English, math, science, social studies departments; classrooms with desks in rows, lecture format leading to easily scored tests; etc.)
Curriculum | | | \\/	dictated the CURRICULUM and (50-minute lessons, broken into specific disciplines for students in a structured classroom studying for a test)
Needs of students	the CURRICULUM defined the "NEEDS OF STUDENTS."
In the past, many organizations, including public education, were structured after the above model. Industry eventually recognized that the needs of customers—not the organization—must come first. This concept drove the restructuring many companies experienced in the 1980s and 1990s. Today, education, too, is finding it must restructure to better serve its "customers"—the students.	

THE PROGRESSIVE STUDENT-CENTERED MODEL	
Needs of students | | \\/	The first step is to articulate the educational NEEDS OF STUDENTS,
Curriculum | | \\/	after which an appropriate CURRICULUM can be designed
Organization	Once a CURRICULUM is designed to meet students' needs, an ORGANIZATIONAL STRUCTURE to deliver that curriculum must be put in place (See Section 3 of this guide.)
The future of public education will likely be both exciting and challenging. The more support and information you have in your restructuring efforts, the better your chances of success. Toward that end, we have included a variety of optional resources and suggestions that you may find helpful as you and your colleagues restructure your school and district.	

Academic Innovations is committed to helping you provide your students with the best and most relevant education possible. Please don't hesitate to contact our Curriculum and Technical Support department as you work to implement the *Career Choices* curriculum (800) 967-8016.

Creating a Shared Vision: Group Activity

Include this activity in your meetings to get buy-in and support.

See pages 5/7 and 5/9 for sample meeting agendas.

We suggest opening your meeting after only a word or two of welcome with the following group brainstorm:

> *If you could wave a magic wand and give your students any characteristics, attitudes, or skills, what would they be?*

Have available a large pad of paper and easel, a whiteboard, or a computer attached to an LCD projector, so you can take notes for future reference. Following the rules of brainstorming (page 11/14 of this guide), identify the needs of students. Once you have completed this exercise, present the concept of The Progressive Model (page 5/11).

Start a discussion with your audience about what kinds of characteristics, attitudes, and traits you'd like your teens to develop. You'll likely come up with a list similar to ours found on page 5/13.

Line this list up with the list of pages in *Career Choices* that address them and your audience will quickly see the benefits of a freshman transition course.

Other Resourses to Share

Enlighten your colleagues on the benefits of the student-centered educational model over the typical organizational model with our helpful graphic found on page 5/11.

Funding sources like private foundations and school boards require measurable goals. We've developed a guideline for metrics you may want to target at your school. For examples see page 5/2.

> Hint: Before you even begin lobbying, we recommend you call Academic Innovations for curriculum support. Not only can we give you ideas and examples of how other schools with your demographic profile are using the curriculum, we can also provide you with resources such as short videos and presentations that will make your meeting planning easier.

Visit www.whatworkscareerchoices.com to access a series of short buy-in videos that can be used for this purpose.

What Are the Needs of Students?

This list was created by 36 teachers and administrators during a brainstorming session at the beginning of one of our two-day workshops.

Would your list look similar?

Once you have read this list, fold back along the dotted line. →

Once you have read this list, fold back along the dotted line. →

What characteristics, attitudes, and skills do we want for the teens we teach?

Critical thinking skills
Interpersonal skills
Pride in who they are
Adaptability to change
Value the educational system
Enthusiasm
Tolerance of people/cultures
Pride in workmanship
Ability to plan for the future
Setting goals/Planning
Stick-to-itiveness
Follow through
Risk taking
Good decision-making skills
Respect for others and self
Indulge creativity
Ability to handle stress
Initiative
Personal responsibility
Pursuit of excellence
Feeling entitled
Sense of humor
Good role models
Seek out mentors
Find out aptitudes/interests/strengths
Career exploration
Communication skills
Vocational skills
Empowerment
Introspection and self-evaluation
Being in charge of their destiny
Visionary
Access information

You'll want to evaluate any curriculum materials you choose for your program, based on the "needs of students" list you produce at your meeting.

Where Career Choices *Addresses These Issues*
Infused throughout activities
Practiced in group activities
Chapter 2
Pages 242–245
Pages 116–119; 266–273
Page 233
Pages 242–245
Pages 238–241
Chapter 12
Chapter 8
Pages 114–121
From Chapter 1 on
Pages 224–225
Chapter 7
Chapters 2, 9, 10
Encouraged in all activities
Pages 216–221; 276–277
Chapter 1
Pages 194–200
Pages 232–235
From Chapter 1 on
Light-hearted stories
Pages 158–159
Pages 262–263
Chapter 2
Chapters 5 and 6
Practiced throughout
Chapters 5 and 6
Focus of curriculum
From Chapters 1, 2, 3 on
A major theme in text
From Chapter 1 on
Chapters 6 and 11

A One-hour Presentation with Videos and Slides

Visit http://www.getfocusedstayfocused.org/onehourpresentation/

We've made it easy for you to share information about the Get Focused…Stay Focused!™ *program.*

One of the most important lessons we've learned over the last 10 years of working with the Freshman Transition Initiative is this: **Getting buy-in from stakeholders on your campus, in your district, or across your region is a vital first step.**

This buy-in should be in place before the first day of your Freshman Transition course. When your whole school can see the "big picture" and understand the importance of your *Get Focused… Stay Focused!*™ efforts—from the very beginning—your implementation will progress more smoothly. If the whole staff understands the value of the 10-year planning process, students' individual plans can enrich every classroom and program on campus.

The *Get Focused…Stay Focused!*™ series is a programmatic model of the Freshman Transition Initiative (which you'll learn more about in Section 6). To make the process of getting buy-in from the whole school as efficient as possible, and to help explain the *Get Focused…Stay Focused!*™ program, we've created a one-hour presentation that's perfect for staff meetings, professional development days, and parent, community, or school board meetings.

The work has been done for you. The slides include presenter notes and six short embedded videos, so you can provide a dynamic presentation that will generate enthusiasm for the *Get Focused…Stay Focused!*™ program with just a few hours of prep time.

We know educators are very busy. With this sophisticated prop, you can be ready in a very short time to present a comprehensive *Get Focused…Stay Focused!*™ overview designed to spur your audience to get involved.

Please note: The presentation file includes six short videos, so the file is approximately 1GB. Times will vary, but plan to allow at least 2 hours to download. You may want to start the download at the end of the day.

Section 6

Freshman Transition: Create a Vision of What's Possible

Topics covered in this section include:

- The George Washington University has researched the ingredients of a successful Freshman Transition course and has developed standards to guide schools in developing their programs.

- Explore the Standards for a Freshman Transition Course, along with The George Washington University's 10-step Plan for Implementing a Freshman Transition Initiative.

- Review a checklist for principals/administrators implementing a Freshman Transition Initiative in their school.

- The Lead Teacher is of primary importance to the success of a Freshman Transition program. We've laid out their job description for you.

- The best Freshman Transition programs are those that also implement a school-wide initiative in the 10th, 11th, and 12th grade. When all staff members are trained to help students update their plans each year and the online 10-year plan is used for advisory functions and academic coaching, personalized learning can take place.

- *Get Focused…Stay Focused!* ™ Initiative developed a Progression of Education Model (PEM). Starting with a Dual Enrollment Freshman Transition (DEFT) course for all freshmen at their four feeder high schools, students then complete modules in the 10th, 11th, and 12th grades. Not only do they update their online 10-year plans but students also work on projects that assure they enter college with a career path, an informed declared major, and a preliminary course schedule.

- A brief overview of schools that have achieved commendable results using the *Career Choices* curriculum. More examples can be found on www.whatworkscareerchoices.com.

The George Washington University's Freshman Transition Initiative

How do we get students to take more responsibility for their education? After all, learning is a personal experience. In the end, it is up to an individual whether or not they retain new information or embrace new experiences.

We all know the saying, "You can lead a horse to water, but you can't make him drink." Well, the same holds true for our students today.

You can sit students in the classroom, but you can't make them think!

It's a basic human fact: Most of us are not motivated to work hard until we understand the benefits of our efforts.

So the bottom line is this: Without willing and motivated learners, all our best reform efforts will be in vain.

The Freshman Transition Initiative understands this fact and, along with its partners, has developed the tools and the systems to quickly and efficiently bring ALL students to the realization that not only is an education important to their future happiness, but that future is also attainable.

What is a Freshman Transition Initiative?

This total school reform effort was first reported in 2005 in an article in the National Association of Secondary School Principals' *Principal Leadership* magazine. Dr. Rebecca Dedmond, Director of the Freshman Transition Initiative at The George Washington University, shared a school-wide program model that was designed to impact school retention and college matriculation.

In short, schools that adopt the Freshman Transition Initiative model have:

1) Every 8th or 9th grade student complete a semester or year-long course that is

2) Based on the Standards for a Freshman Transition Course developed through The George Washington University's Freshman Transition Initiative and

3) Culminates with each student creating a meaningful and quantitative 10-year plan

Then, in the 10th, 11th, and 12th grades, students' 10-year plans are **updated in their academic courses AND used by all teachers for advisory purposes and academic coaching**.

Why the 8th or 9th Grade?

The 2007 edition of *Diplomas Count*, published by *Education Week*, reported that more than one third of the students who drop out of high school fail to make the transition from the 9th to the 10th grade. This explains why, for more than two decades, schools and districts across the country have struggled to develop freshman transition activities and courses to address this critical transitional time for students.

Unfortunately, many freshman programs failed to impact school retention because there were no plans, no roadmaps, no guidelines or standards to point the way to success. Teachers were left to their own devices to develop—from scratch—what should be a rigorous, comprehensive course. In far too many cases, due to lack of resources, the outcome did not meet expectations and, eventually, the programs were abandoned. This has been a frustrating cycle, to say the least.

It was this realization and the resulting Standards for a Freshman Transition Course that launched the **Freshman Transition Initiative** in 2004.

In developing the necessary standards it became clear that, in order to achieve the ambitious goal of impacting school retention, the new standards had to go beyond traditional career exploration. Career exploration is only one facet of what motivates students to take ownership of their futures, so additional measures were added, including helping students to:

- Establish and consolidate their identity
- Create a comprehensive 10-year career and life plan
- Master the skills and attitudes of a resilient personality
- And, most important, understand the consequences of dropping out of high school, post-secondary training, or college

A successful Freshman Transition course and initiative requires five key components. They are:

- A 10-year education and career plan for all students by the end of the 9th grade
- A curriculum that meets the Standards
- Well-qualified and enthusiastic teachers
- A School-wide Initiative in the 10th, 11th, and 12th grade
- Leadership continuity over the first 4 years

The key element of a Freshman Transition course is the development of a personalized 10-year plan grounded in each student's career goals and lifestyle expectations.

The outcome? When all students have a comprehensive and meaningful 10-year plan that is updated throughout high school, you'll have more motivated students.

Why? Students now understand **quantitatively** the value of a good education.

- They have a vision of a productive future that matches their own personal goals and dreams.
- They recognize the benefits of working hard to make their desired and personalized future a reality.
- And, perhaps most important, they'll have an understanding of the consequences of giving up and not getting a good education.

How do we get all 13- and 14-year-old students to create 10-year plans that will be personalized and meaningful?

It starts with a course based on the Standards for a Freshman Transition Course.

This semester- or year-long course carries the same rigor, credibility, and status of traditional academic courses. Whether implemented as a stand-alone 8th or 9th grade Freshman Transition class, used as the foundation for Freshman Academies, or integrated into academic courses such as English and math, the goal is to enable students to take ownership of their own learning.

The Standards for a Freshman Transition Course function as the blueprint for these well-designed freshman courses. They provide a roadmap for teachers, administrators, and policy makers. Teachers who incorporate all of the standards into their course have the formula for a class that culminates with each student developing a comprehensive 10-year educational and career plan.

But that is only the beginning. Once the course is complete and the 10-year plans are finished, you'll want students to continue updating and using them throughout high school. This is known as the School-Wide Initiative.

Adolescents need to revisit their plans on a regular basis to update goals and verify that they are on the right track. The more realistic their plans, the more likely they'll be to exert the energy and effort needed to follow through.

Every discipline in the 10th, 11th, and 12th grades should be encouraged to develop at least one lesson each year that provides data, information, or an understanding of the world, which will provide students an opportunity to refine their plans. After orienting your whole school on the 10-year plan, ask each department to identify where they can assist in this project.

In addition, be sure to provide each teacher with immediate access to each of their students' current 10-year plans. You can do this by putting their 10-year plans online. That way, all teachers have increased insight when advising and personalizing their efforts with each student.

For instance, if a student is failing a course that is required for their desired career goal, any academic teacher, upon reviewing the student's online 10-year plan, is in the position to coach that student. Using the student's specific dreams and goals for their future as the starting point of their discussion, teachers can either help them devise a plan to make up the deficit or, if the student is reluctant to exert the energy, rewrite their plan with lowered expectations—and a more modest lifestyle. If a student has taken a course based on the Freshman Transition Standards, they'll fully understand the consequences of that and will be more likely to buckle down and bring their grades up.

How Can I Get Started?

Start your research by visiting The George Washington University's **Freshman Transition Initiative** web site at **www.freshmantransition.org**. There you will find the Standards for a Freshman Transition Course along with a variety of resources. You'll want to sign up for a free membership to receive bulletins on upcoming events and research.

While on the web site, you'll want to review the 10-Step Plan advocated by the **Freshman Transition Initiative**. This provides a leadership plan and system to ensure success. Designed as a bottom-up effort rather than a top-down mandate, this step-by-step system encourages the involvement of the whole school. Because a **Freshman Transition Initiative** is a school-wide reform effort, you'll find ideas and opportunities to develop shared-leadership and responsibility in all departments and all grades.

We all know when implementing a school-wide reform effort that quality, sustained professional development is critical to success. Consider either signing up for one of the various professional development opportunities or hosting one in your district. They include:

- The George Washington University's Freshman Transition Leadership Institute for principals, administrators, or school leadership teams to jumpstart their school-wide reform effort using the 10-step Plan

- A *Career Choices* Lead Administrator and Lead Teacher workshop for instructional leadership teams to help them design quality professional learning communities

- The annual three-day Focus on Freshmen conference sponsored by Academic Innovations each summer

By implementing a Freshman Transition Initiative, you will change the culture of your school and help successfully launch students into their decade of transition. Your students will come away with both the skills and attitudes needed to succeed in the highly competitive 21st century. The insight they glean from a carefully crafted Freshman Transition course culminating in a 10-year plan will provide the incentive they need to help them become self-motivated learners, which is the only surefire formula for personal success.

When you change your students' expectations and attitudes, you change their lives. Let our Curriculum and Technical Support team help you in jump-starting an effective program that will change the life courses of *all* your students.

The George Washington University Freshman Transition Initiative's

10-Step Plan for Implementing a Freshman Transition Course in Your School

Step 1: Gather your resources. Download a copy of the Standards for a Freshman Transition Course and sign up for the Principals' Forum of the Freshman Transition Initiative at www.freshmantransition.org. You'll also want to download your own copy of a PowerPoint presentation to be used in Steps 2 and 4.

Step 2: Create a vision. Present the 10-year education and career plan concept and the Freshman Transition Initiative in a school-wide meeting. Generate interest around what students have to gain from creating a comprehensive 10-year education and career plan, and cast a vision for how the plan can be used by all instructors to motivate students to higher academic achievement (see Steps 8 and 9 below).

Step 3: Form a team of champions. Form a committee of your most innovative teachers to develop a plan for instituting a standards-driven, Freshman Transition course that culminates in the development of a 10-year education and career plan for all incoming freshmen (whether it is completed in grade 8 or 9). Their duties should include formulating and assisting with Steps 4, 5, 6, 8 and 9.

Step 4: Generate community buy-in for the new course and the 10-year plan. With the help of your team, make presentations to parents, community groups, and your school board. Lobby your school board to consider mandating a semester or yearlong classroom-based Freshman Transition course for all students in either grade 8 or 9.

Step 5: Identify a curriculum that will accomplish your course goals. Good curriculum is one with scope and sequence, where it is apparent to the learner what the results are for their efforts (in this case, a comprehensive—yet flexible—10-year plan for students' transition into adulthood). Seek out resources that provide your teachers with the textbooks and materials required. Support your team in finding the best tool they can that meets the Course Standards for Freshman Transition Classes.

Step 6: Recruit your most enthusiastic teachers to conduct the course. This kind of course requires a high level of teaching skills. Ideally, by this time, your team of champions will become your pool of potential instructors. When recruiting, don't make the mistake of assigning the newest teachers or the least skilled. In addition, provide course continuity by identifying a lead teacher who will commit a minimum of four years to the project. Provide him or her with the release time needed to train and to support both the course instructors and the School-wide Initiative (see Step 8).

Step 7: Provide professional development and course planning time. In order for course instructors to develop a comprehensive, rigorous classroom experience they will need professional development and course planning time, particularly during the first year. Arrange schedules so all course instructors have at least one common prep time each week in which to meet and discuss the progress of their efforts. Send the complete team to appropriate workshops and conferences.

Step 8: Make your Freshman Transition Initiative a School-wide Initiative. Provide professional development to all instructors on how to best use and support their students' 10-year plans. Because it is important for students to reassess their goals each year, develop a system in which each student revisits and updates their 10-year plan at least once per year within their sophomore, junior, and senior coursework. Ask each department to identify where they can assist in this project.

Step 9: Share all students' 10-year education and academic plans. Provide teachers with immediate access to each of their students' current 10-year plans. Every teacher then has increased insight when counseling and personalizing their efforts with each student. If a student is failing a course that is required for their desired career goal, any academic teacher, upon reviewing the student's 10-year plan, is in the position to counsel that student and either help them make up the deficit or rewrite their plan with altered expectations.

Step 10: Recognize and reward. To maintain the energy of your best instructors and to keep the enthusiasm of the total school community high, it is important to reward and recognize excellence. One way to do this is to invite your local newspaper and news channel to cover your Freshman Transition Initiative once it is up and running, with periodic updates. Encourage your lead teacher to attend conferences and make presentations about your school's efforts. Ask students to vote each year on the teacher in each grade who most supports their dreams, and then recognize those "dream catchers" at a year-end assembly.

Reprinted with permission from Dr. Rebecca Dedmond.

For additional details, visit
www.freshmantransition.org.

Standards for a
Freshman Transition Course
developed by The George Washington University's Freshman Transition Initiative

The following outlines a Classroom-Based, Comprehensive Guidance
and Career Exploration Course for 8th or 9th Grade Students

Course Goals

Reduce dropout rates for both high school and post-secondary education and training because students learn the value of education and what a diploma means to their future life and career satisfaction.

Increase matriculation rates for college and post-secondary programs because students understand the quantitative life differences (e.g., financial, personal satisfaction, career options) various kinds of post-secondary training and education provide.

Help students acquire the skills necessary to successfully navigate their life/work transitions:

- Middle school to high school
- High school to college or post-secondary training
- Education to a quality workforce
- Adolescence to adulthood
- Dependency to self-sufficiency

The freshman year of high school has been documented as a pivotal time for students. It is during the freshman year that:

- The highest dropout rates are recorded
- Students are asked to make academic choices that either launch them along a trajectory toward college or some other form of post-secondary education, or potentially condemn them to a life of limited career choices
- Students start making lifestyle choices that can either lead to a life of self-sufficiency or one of dependency (e.g., teen parenting, substance abuse, unemployment or under-employment, gang involvement)

To combat these realities, districts and schools across the country have grappled with a variety of solutions and courses in an effort to circumvent the downside possibilities and enhance the opportunities. The results have been mixed. Without a clear vision of what a freshman transition class or freshman academy should address, many schools struggle to reach their ultimate goal of student retention and higher academic achievement. For some, a freshman course is viewed by the school staff as a form of purgatory and, therefore, the newest or least experienced teachers are assigned to teach it—when in reality its imperatives cry out for the most seasoned among us.

The following standards were developed to raise both student and educator expectations and to provide a roadmap and vision of what it takes to make a significant difference at this critical point in the lives of our students. The intent is to outline a rigorous, research-based course from which ALL 8th or 9th grade students will benefit—whether they are entering the workforce following high school graduation or have their sights set on college, a graduate degree, or some other form of post-secondary education.

Course Overview

To meet the requirements of these emerging adults, a freshman transition course must address a combination of personal/social, educational, and career and life skills.

In short, the coursework must:

PERSONAL SOCIAL DEVELOPMENT

☐ Help students **envision a future that is productive, achievable, and stimulating.**

☐ Provide the framework for helping **students learn to project into the future and understand the consequences of today's choices and actions.**

☐ **Expose students to potential stumbling blocks** that could impede their success and help them develop the necessary coping skills and attitudes required for a productive transition into adulthood.

☐ Help **students become identity-achieved**, a necessary developmental process for all adolescents, but particularly necessary for youth at risk of becoming teen parents, substance abusers, or dropouts.

☐ Provide practice in the **communication and interpersonal skills** required for career and personal success.

EDUCATIONAL ACHIEVEMENT

☐ Facilitate students' **recognition of the value of education** and the importance of becoming internally motivated to succeed in school.

☐ Motivate learners and workers who **challenge themselves and strive for higher achievement.**

☐ Help students understand **how education, training, and career choice impact their personal lifestyle.**

☐ **Motivate students to apply themselves,** because once they understand how core subjects (e.g., reading, writing, speaking, computing) impact their future success, **academic achievement will increase.**

CAREER AND LIFE SKILLS

☐ **Teach a life and career planning "process,"** so students can continually adjust their plans throughout their education and adult life.

☐ Help **students become "career focused,"** so every student is prepared to enter the workforce upon completion of their education.

☐ Facilitate the development of a **personalized ten-year plan** that matches each student's career aspirations and commitment to education.

☐ **Teach students the skills, aptitudes, and attitudes** needed to successfully transition into high school, post-secondary education and/or training, the workforce, and adulthood.

Correlations for the *Career Choices* curriculum and the Standards for a Freshman Transition Course

developed by The George Washington University's Freshman Transition Initiative

The following outlines a Classroom-Based, Comprehensive Guidance and Career Exploration Course for 8th or 9th Grade Students

Freshman Transition Standards Correlations

Knowledge and Skills	*Career Choices*	*Instructor's Guide,* 7th Edition	Optional Enhancements at CareerChoices.com
01. The student learns to project into the future and to understand the consequences of their actions and the choices made today. The student is expected to:			
A. Visualize and describe the adult life they envision.	12–14, 63, 76–92, 156–157, 279–280	4/4–4/7, 4/41, 4/47–4/63, 4/92–4/93, 4/140, 4/166	78, 80, 83, 88–89
B. Identify the choices and actions that could impede a successful transition to adulthood.	194–227	4/109, 4/123–4/139	
C. Describe the challenges faced by individuals whose lives were sidetracked due to drug addiction, teen parenting, and/or dropping out (high school or college).	203–207	6/36–6/40, 4/128–4/129	
D. Analyze the impact of education on life satisfaction, by determining what they think the average lifestyle is for individuals who have been out of school at least 15 years for each of the following situations: high school dropout; high school graduate who enters the workplace with no further training or education; community college/industry certification; college graduate; graduate or professional school certification/degree.	97–103, 203–207, 227	4/66–4/67, 4/128–4/129, 4/139–4/140	
E. Develop and analyze a budget for a single parent raising two children whose annual income is below the average in their community.	95–96	4/65	
F. Set goals for wellness practices to maximize present and future health, appearance, and peak performance.	56–59, 64–71, 74–75, 89, 200–202, 208–209	4/43–4/45, 4/60, 4/127, 4/30–4/131	
02. The student completes formal assessments and surveys to help them establish and consolidate their identity, becoming "identity-achieved." The student is expected to:			
A. Reflect on and write a personal definition(s) of success. (To be re-evaluated and re-written throughout the course.)	18–21, 60–61, 282–283	4/10–4/11, 4/39–4/41, 4/167–4/168	
B. Contemplate and list their unique traits (e.g., passions, values and priorities, personality, strengths and weaknesses).	24–49	4/16–4/31	

Knowledge and Skills	Career Choices	Instructor's Guide, 7th Edition	Enhancements at CareerChoices.com
C. Identify any limiting factors that might impede their progression to a successful life and create plans to circumvent limitations.	70–71, 121, 172–174, 183–185, 194–200, 210, 214–221	4/45, 4/77, 4/108–4/09, 4/111–4/112, 4/118–4/119, 4/123–4/126, 4/134–4/136	
D. Develop a plan for overcoming the anxieties and fears that might keep them from succeeding.	210, 216–221, 276–277	4/135–4/136, 4/165	
03. The student analyzes the effect of personal interest and aptitudes upon educational and career planning. The student is expected to:			
A. Complete a formal career interest and aptitude assessment.	24–49	4/16–4/31	
B. Match interests and aptitudes to career opportunities.	57–71, 124–141, 144–165	4/38–4/45, 4/80–4/84, 4/86–4/105	145–150, 158–160
C. Begin a personal career portfolio by conducting an in-depth study of the varied aspects of occupations related to their interest areas.	57–71, 124–141, 144–165	4/38–4/45, 4/80–4/84, 4/86–4/105	145–150, 158–160
04. The student recognizes the impact of career choice on personal lifestyle. The student is expected to:			
A. Prepare a personal budget reflecting future lifestyle desires.	74–121	4/48–4/67	78, 80, 83, 88–89, 93, 120
B. Prepare a subsistence budget (e.g., supported by minimum wage, unemployment insurance, or welfare) and articulate how their ideal lifestyle (described in 04.A) would change at this income level.	95–96	4/65	
C. Use print or online information to determine salaries of at least three career choices in their interest area with varying education requirements (e.g., no high school diploma, high school diploma, and post-secondary education/training).	148–155	4/89–4/90	148–150
D. Develop a chart that graphically demonstrates the difference between the total lifetime wages for each of the career choices found in 04.C, outlining the time commitment for education and training for each.	114–119	4/74–4/75	
E. Prepare a list of the possible rewards and sacrifices (psychological, as well as financial) for each of the career choices researched in 04.C.	104–113	4/69–4/73	
F. Select the career most closely matching both their personal lifestyle budget and their commitment to education and training.	93, 131, 148–155, 227	4/64, 4/129, 4/139–4/140	

Knowledge and Skills	Career Choices	Instructor's Guide, 7th Edition	Enhancements at CareerChoices.com
05. The student recognizes the impact their commitment to education has on their future lifestyle and life satisfaction. The student is expected to:			
A. Develop a chart classifying employment opportunities based on the education and training requirements of careers in their interest area.	211–213	4/132–4/133	
B. Prepare a proportional life-long timeline (until age 78) that graphically shows the amount of time the student plans to commit to education and training and the amount of time they expect to be active in the workforce. Factor the ratio between time spent preparing for their chosen career and time spent working.	114–119, 272–273	4/74–4/75, 4/164	
06. The student demonstrates the skills to locate, analyze, and apply career information. The student is expected to:			
A. Access career information using print and online resources to complete an education and/or training plan for a career pathway.	144–165, 266–283	486–4/105, 4/162–4/169	145–150, 158–160, 267–269, 271, 279
B. Access career information using interviews with business and industry representatives to create a career resource file.	120, 254–255	4/76, 4/94–4/100, 4/155	120, 254–255
C. Complete career critiques gained through a variety of experiences (e.g., shadowing, career study tours, guest speakers, career fairs, videos, CD-ROM, Internet, and simulated work activities).	120, 158–161	4/76, 4/94–4/101, 6/36–6/40	120, 158–160
D. Use career information to apply entrepreneurial skills by developing a small business plan.	38–43, 138–139, 162–165, 238–241	4/22–4/23, 4/83, 4/102–4/105, 4/146–4/147	
E. Identify the key disadvantages of careers/jobs traditionally held by women.	211–213	4/132–4/133	
07. The student knows the process for career planning and educational preparation. The student is expected to:			
A. Identify high school courses related to specific career choices in their interest area.	266–283	4/162–4/169	267–269, 271, 279
B. Select appropriate high school courses and experiences, and develop a graduation plan that leads to a specific career choice in their interest area.	266–283	4/162–4/169	267–269, 271, 279
C. List and explain education and/or training alternatives after high school for a career choice within their interest area.	148–155, 266–283	4/89–4/90, 4/162–4/169	267–269, 271–279
D. Prepare an education and career plan for an occupation within their interest area that begins with entry into high school and continues through a post-secondary education and/or training program. Place this information in the personal career portfolio.	266–283	4/162–4/169	267–269, 271, 279

Knowledge and Skills	Career Choices	Instructor's Guide, 7th Edition	Enhancements at CareerChoices.com
E. Complete a 10-year plan outlining yearly quantitative goals and objectives for education, work, finances, and lifestyle choices.	222–223, 278–280	4/137, 4/166	

08. The student can apply the skill sets required to succeed (both in the classroom and the workforce). The student is expected to:

Knowledge and Skills	Career Choices	Instructor's Guide, 7th Edition	Enhancements at CareerChoices.com
A. List and explain the steps in the decision-making process.	168–179	4/108–4/115	
B. Write quantitative goals and objectives for three personal or classroom projects.	186–191	4/120–4/121	
C. Apply problem-solving strategies to resolve a personal dilemma or that of a friend.	183–185	4/117–4/119	
D. Diagram the steps required to achieve identified short- and long-term goals.	186–191, 278–280	4/120–4/121, 4/123, 4/166	
E. Describe at least five situations common to teens in which delaying gratification would lead to long-term rewards.	183–185, 203–207, 274–275	4/118–4/119, 4/128–4/129, 4/165	
F. Prioritize and manage personal and academic activities using time management strategies.	121, 232–235	4/77, 4/143–4/144	
G. Generate personal strategies for managing stress and tolerating anxiety.	214–221, 226–227, 274–277	4/134–4/136, 4/139–4/140. 4/165	
H. Give and receive constructive criticism.	194–200, 236–241, 260	4/123–4/126, 4/145–4/147, 4/158	
I. Make a persuasive oral presentation about a contemporary teenage problem (e.g., convince an imaginary friend who is contemplating dropping out to stay in school).	172–174, 185, 208–209, 222–223	4/111–4/112, 4/118, 4/130–4/131, 4/137	
J. Explain and demonstrate effective communication in family, community, and career settings.	Practiced throughout text	Practiced throughout text	
K. Apply reading, writing, listening, speaking, and mathematic skills in family and workplace settings.	Practiced throughout text	Projects throughout text	

09. The student demonstrates the importance of productive work habits and attitudes. The student is expected to:

Knowledge and Skills	Career Choices	Instructor's Guide, 7th Edition	Enhancements at CareerChoices.com
A. Conduct interviews with a minimum of two employers to determine the importance of work ethics, such as dependability, promptness, getting along with others, and honesty.	238–241	4/146–4/147, 10/5–10/6	
B. List the characteristics of an effective team member.	38–43, 162–165, 230–235, 238–241	4/22–4/23, 4/102–4/105, 4/115, 4/143–4/144, 4/146–4/147	
C. Work on a team to accomplish an assigned task and complete an "effective team member" profile to be placed in the personal career portfolio.	38–43, 162–165	4/22–4/23, 4/102–4/105, 4/115, 4/127, 4/137, 4/148–4/149	
D. Write job scenarios demonstrating positive and negative employee/customer relations.	232–235, 238–241	4/143–4/144	

Knowledge and Skills	Career Choices	Instructor's Guide, 7th Edition	Enhancements at CareerChoices.com
E. List and explain in the context of a school assignment the traits of those who strive for excellence.	232–235	4/143–4/144	
F. Create systems and strategies for managing personal activities and resources, such as schedules, assignments, school materials, and projects.	121, 186–191, 270–271	4/13–4/14, 4/77, 4/120–4/121 4/150, 4/164	
G. Demonstrate respect for multiple diversities with sensitivity to anti-bias and equity in gender, age, race, culture, ethnicity, socio-economic status, and exceptionalities.	31–37, 196–199, 211–215, 242–247	4/20–4/21, 4/43, 4/123–4/125, 4/132–4/134, 4/148–4/149	
10. The student knows that many skills are common to a variety of careers and that these skills can be transferred from one career opportunity to another. The student is expected to:			
A. Compile a list of transferable skills, along with a corresponding list of possible career options that match their interests and aptitudes. Place the list in the personal career portfolio.	46–48, 132–134, 147, 150–155, 162–165, 246, 272–273	4/13–4/14, 4/27–4/29, 4/150	150
B. Create a presentation portraying transferable skills within their interest area.	246	4/150, 4/162	
11. The student knows the process used to locate and secure entry-level employment. The student is expected to:			
A. Complete a job application form for an employment opportunity in their interest area.	256–257	4/156	256
B. Develop a resume for an employment opportunity in their interest area.	250–253	4/152–4/153	253
C. Role-play appropriate interviewing techniques for an employment opportunity in their interest area.	258–259	4/157	258
12. The student knows the effect change has on society and career opportunities. The student is expected to:			
A. Cite examples of change in our society.	135–137, 211–213, 242–246	4/14, 4/61, 4/90–4/91, 4/139–4/140, 4/148, 4/150	
B. Compose a report explaining positive and negative aspects of one example of societal change.	135–137, 242–246	4/61, 4/148, 4/150	
C. Demonstrate an understanding of the relationship between the changing nature of work and educational requirements.	242–246	4/148–4/150	
D. Develop a timeline that covers the last ten years and depicts the changes in a selected career choice.	150–155	4/90–4/91, 4/139–4/140, 4/150, 4/153	150
E. Use labor market information and knowledge of technology and societal and/or economic trends to forecast a job profile for a career in their interest area ten years from now. Add this profile to the personal career portfolio.	135–139, 148–149, 150–155, 226–227, 242–246	4/90–4/91, 4/139–4/140, 4/150, 4/153	148–149

The above standards were developed using state standards from Texas, Tennessee, Indiana, and Maine, along with research findings and input from various experts and authors. **Career Choices** is a Texas state-adopted textbook for Career Connections and Career Investigation. **Career Choices** is also a recommended textbook for Tennessee's Career Management Success course for 9th graders.

Examples of Freshman Transition Courses

Advancing Student Success, One Connection at a Time
Indio High School, Indio, California

Until quite recently, Indio High stood out for its abysmal test scores. Now, the school is receiving accolades for the exceptional progress its students made academically and behaviorally in just one year from 2009 to 2010. Though dedication alone will not turn around an underperforming school, the Indio administration let their passion for the school fuel efforts to find and apply a tested method for focusing freshmen on school. They then recruited their most gifted teachers to implement the freshman transition program known as Success 101, which has now been in place for several years.

"Success 101 is all about making relationships, all about making connections, all about setting students on a path to their next journey," Margo McCormick assistant principal, says. "It's giving them direction, it's giving them purpose, it's giving them ideas…and actually enabling them to make those choices and take them to the next step."

Results of Indio's efforts include: two thirds fewer freshman expulsions, half as many students with three or more Fs, and seven times more students joining the California Scholarship Federation. The freshmen were responsible for 49 points out of the school's 65-point API (Academic Performance Index) score increase within that first year.

In 2012, Indio was ranked in the top 10% of High Schools in the United States by the prestigious *U.S. News and World Report*.

Watch the documentary and read the whole story at www.whatworkscareerchoices.com/success101doc.html.

The Story of a District-wide Adoption
Kern Union High School District, Bakersfield, California

There truly is strength in numbers. Nowhere is this evidenced more clearly than the work being done at Kern Union High School District. Kern Union serves the county of Kern, located at the southern end of the San Joaquin Valley. It is California's largest high school district with more than 35,000 students and 3,500 employees.

With 18 comprehensive campuses, 5 alternative education campuses, 4 special education campuses, 3 career and technical education sites, an adult education center, and a charter school, District Counselor, Christy Fraley, has the daunting task of ensuring that the *Career Choices* curriculum is taught with fidelity and enthusiasm.

"I look for teachers who not only are experienced in the classroom, but have that overwhelming desire to encourage every student, no matter what their circumstance," she explained. She encourages her teachers to motivate students to dream big and to overcome obstacles. "Those concepts will assist in so many areas of their lives as they continue to mature," said Ms. Fraley.

Before Kern UHSD began using *Career Choices* in 2015, the schools in the district did not have uniform career planning for their students, with some schools implementing certain practices while others did nothing. Given that starting point, when it came to choosing a curriculum for adoption, the career exploration component of *Career Choices* was the major selling point. Infused into a Life Planning class, students that may have been overlooked—the "disconnected youth," as Ms. Fraley called them—now had a purpose and a direction.

Many of the Kern UHSD graduates attend the local community colleges where the *Career Choices* experience and students' 10-year Plans complement the Naviance tools already in place to assist students in identifying the courses they should take. "[*Career Choices*] really has taken away a lot of the anxiety that new students face when the go to college for the first time," according to Ms. Fraley.

Three schools were initially chosen to pilot the program in 2014, and things have grown from there. "Superintendent Dr. Schaefer has been supportive and has channeled funds into the program for additional teachers, training, and supplies all along the way," Mrs. Fraley added. In 2015, eighteen schools in the district implemented the *Career Choices* curriculum successfully, and the program will be expanded to include all freshmen in the Kern Union High School District in the 2016–2017 school year!

District Puts Freshmen Front and Center with Freshmen Academy
Granite School District, Salt Lake City, Utah

College and career readiness is an integral part of Granite School District culture, as evidenced by the district's College and Career Readiness (CCR) department focused specifically on helping students prepare for the next step—whatever it might be.

CCR Director Judy Petersen began utilizing the *Career Choices* curriculum in three of Granite's nine high schools in 2015–2016, actively engaging 1,500 freshmen in pursuit of their dreams at Kearns High School, Granger High School, and Hunter High School. "We want all students to commit to graduate from high school college, career, and life ready," says Ms. Petersen, explaining that Freshmen Academy was a success from the very beginning.

"The *Career Choices* curriculum was exactly what we were looking for! We wanted a research-based curriculum and we found it." Ms. Petersen, in doing her preliminary research, came across the George Washington University Freshman Transition Initiative established by Dr. Rebecca Dedmond. Ms. Petersen made the journey to Los Angeles and attended the annual Focus on Freshmen Conference in the summer of 2014. "I learned so much… saw the possibilities of My10yearPlan, and when I returned to Salt Lake City, I met with my Superintendent, Dr. Martin Bates. He bought in immediately and so we began…"

Recruiting twelve top teachers, including lead teachers Tracy Timothy (Granger HS), Chad Martin (Kearns HS), and Jeff Sillito (Hunter HS), made the implementation of the curriculum nearly flawless. "The staff at Academic Innovations, the publishers of the *Career Choices* curriculum, were there at every step," added Ms. Petersen.

What's next? "We are developing benchmarks to actually measure the results that we feel we are getting from this program. The *Career Choices* curriculum is doing a very good job, in a very direct way, to help students see the link between what they are learning in school and the rest of their lives," concludes Ms. Petersen. And, most certainly, Freshmen Academy will become an even greater part of the district curriculum as Cottonwood High School and Cyprus High School begin implementation in 2016–2017.

GEAR UP Grant Pays Off for Newkirk Tigers
Newkirk High School, Newkirk, Oklahoma

Career Choices—the most important class that a student can take!

This high opinion of the *Career Choices* curriculum is the enthusiastically stated viewpoint of teacher Mary Truitt Newkirk, Oklahoma, home of the Newkirk High School Tigers, where she has been teaching Success 101 for the last two years. Mary, along with teachers Debbie Brazil and Grace Etter, teach a total of 90 freshmen and 90 sophomores each year. "The curriculum makes teachers real people to our students," commented Ms. Truitt. "When we share our own stories, it really does make a difference," she added.

Looking for better ways to motivate students and to improve the graduation rate, the school superintendent, principal, and these three teachers attended the Focus on Freshmen Conference in Los Angeles. "We saw something that was working and came back excited to try it with our students," Ms. Pruitt added.

With the help of a GEAR UP grant, Newkirk began the program in earnest in 2014. Meeting weekly throughout the school year, all three Success 101 teachers go over their lesson plans, prepare for their upcoming guest speakers, discuss their challenges, and the share highpoints they have had with students. "Building those relationships has been monumental," according to Ms. Truitt.

Changes have occurred in administrative positions, with a new superintendent as well as a new principal, but administrative support remains high for the Success 101 program at Newkirk. "Maurisa Pruett, our current principal, backs us 100%," says Ms. Truitt. There is no doubt that having strong of support is a key component to the successful of the *Career Choices* curriculum.

Solid team planning, strong administrative support, and enthusiastic teachers pays dividends in student success. "Our students can see how learning applies specifically to their futures," explains Mary.

One student, Kaitlyn, dreamed of becoming a pediatric oncologist, a specialty requiring a minimum of 6 years of training after medical school. After closely examining the costs, length of training involved, and other factors, Kaitlyn developed a plan for becoming a pediatric oncology nurse. By learning to analyze her choices and adjust her path accordingly, Kaitlyn was able to identify and plan for a rewarding alternative rather than simply giving up on a dream.

Newkirk High School has even found ways to integrate the curriculum into the community. One student's parent, a volunteer with the local domestic abuse shelter program, is advocating for *Career Choices* as an effective tool for assisting individuals of all socio-economic and cultural backgrounds in discovering: (1) their aptitudes and interests; (2) a career path that is keyed to their interests and abilities (and learning specifically what is required to achieve that career goal); and (3) how to simply be better prepared, in general, for the financial realities of adulthood and how those realities may affect their choices for career pathways.

PRINCIPAL'S CHECKLIST

6/17

How to Launch a Successful Freshman Transition Initiative

You'll find most of the resources for this effort in:

- The *Project Planning Guide for Implementing a Freshman Transition Initiative* by The George Washington University's **Freshman Transition Initiative**

- The *Career Choices* **Teachers' Lounge** web site at www.careerchoices.com/lounge

- The *Get Focused...Stay Focused!*™ Initiative web site at www.getfocusedstayfocused.org

PLANNING AND DOCUMENTATION

☐ Attend a workshop to learn about the management and resources required for a successful Freshman Transition effort. If you can't attend, purchase the planning guide along with some individualized consulting from The George Washington University **Freshman Transition Initiative** team.

☐ Review the *Project Planning Guide for Implementing a Freshman Transition Initiative* and choose the planning documents and strategies you wish to incorporate into your program.

☐ Do any necessary editing of those documents or strategies so they match your vision.

☐ Review sample committee job descriptions (Step 3) and edit to match your school's needs and goals.

☐ Make a presentation to your district superintendent/school board to solicit support.

☐ Determine and approve release time for staff for project functions and project leadership.

☐ Recruit a Coordinating Committee Chairperson and with their input recruit the Vice Chair and the Documenter/Archivist.

☐ With this team, finalize the project manuals (using the documents noted above), to be used in training the Executive Committee.

PRESENT THE PROGRAM AND GET BUY-IN FROM YOUR FACULTY AND STAFF

☐ Once you have a clear vision of what the program looks like and what you want to accomplish, start building enthusiasm within your school for the **Freshman Transition Initiative**.

☐ Gather resources and make presentations to the school community about the benefits of the **Freshman Transition Initiative**. You can find resources in the *Career Choices* **Teachers Lounge**.

☐ From the enthusiasm of that meeting, help the Coordinating Committee Chairperson with the recruitment of the other committee chairs.

☐ Oversee the training of the Executive Committee members, (i.e., plan a team retreat).

☐ With the Funding Chairperson, meet with potential contributors to discuss any grant proposal or funding needs.

☐ Chair the Executive Committee meetings, at least through the planning phase.

☐ After planning is complete, approve the final flow chart, responsibility charts, and plans for the **Freshman Transition Initiative**.

LAUNCHING YOUR FRESHMAN TRANSITION COURSE

☐ Purchase *Career Choices* curriculum, at minimum the textbook and a workbook that includes My10yearPlan.com® license for each student.

☐ Review recommendations, approve appointment of a Lead Teacher and finalize an agreement for four years (see Step 6).

☐ Recruit and review final candidates for instructor positions for the Freshman Transition course and decide on assignments.

☐ Approve professional development and technical assistance plans and budget.

LAUNCHING YOUR SCHOOL-WIDE INITIATIVE

☐ Meet with the School-wide Initiative Committee and department heads to begin discussions on strategies for updating the 10-year plans.

☐ Review the *Get Focused...Stay Focused!*™ Initiative as a systematic program to not only update students' 10-year plans in the 10th, 11th, and 12th grade, but to ensure students are college and career ready.

☐ Approve School-wide Initiative plans of each department.

☐ Conduct quarterly evaluations to check on the progress of the institutionalization of the 10-year plan within your school.

ASSESSMENT AND EVALUATION

☐ Review all data of assessments and evaluations and, with the Coordinating Committee chair, make recommendations for upgrades the following year.

☐ Conduct all personnel reviews of project staff, based on input from team members.

The Lead Teacher

Adapted with permission from the Freshman Transition Initiative of The George Washington University

The Role of the Lead Teacher

To facilitate ongoing professional development and leadership of a school's *Career Choices* team, the *Career Choices* Lead Teacher may have to function, at times, in a variety of different roles. For instance, when generating buy-in inside and outside the school, the Lead Teacher functions as the program's most enthusiastic cheerleader. When participating with the team in ongoing troubleshooting and brainstorming, the Lead Teacher functions in the role of coach. When introducing new strategies in capacity-building professional learning community sessions, the Lead Teacher functions as trainer. And, when helping to organize and execute the School-wide Initiative implementation using the 10-year plan as advisory tool, the Lead Teacher functions as manager.

The Lead Teacher may:

- Provide training, support, encouragement, and coaching for the instructors of the course

- Demonstrate various active learning techniques for use in a *Career Choices* course

- Facilitate the customization process as the group develops their detailed lesson plan pacing guide spreadsheets

- Demonstrate how to use the various online resources of the *Career Choices* curriculum

- Monitor use of the optional technology applications of the course

- Generate and maintain buy-in from course instructors and the school community

- Facilitate team building for course instructors and all school staff involved with the 10-year plan

- Chair weekly meetings of the course instructors using a professional learning community format

- Determine how to evaluate the course and assess success

- Troubleshoot and problem solve, making recommendations to the administration regarding adjustments to future plans

- Encourage creative solutions while maintaining the focus required for success

- Develop a plan to involve parents and the community

- Find resources to address the needs of special populations

Other Factors to Consider in Selecting a Lead Teacher

A long-term commitment is desirable. To provide course continuity from year to year, a Lead Teacher should commit a minimum of four years to the project. This is particularly important if your school plans to adopt the School-wide Initiative (see pages 6/22–6/24). During the course of those four years, the Lead Teacher can bring each grade's academic department on board to help with the annual review and revising of students' 10-year plans, and can help to institutionalize the use of 10-year plans for advisory purposes.

A Lead Teacher should have release time during the day to train and support the other course instructors. They can also be a resource person and provide support for the School-wide Initiative for updating and using the 10-year plan as a school-wide advisory tool.

This is not an administrative position. It is important that the *Career Choices* Lead Teacher also teach the course. With their peer Freshman Transition teachers, they'll work to refine the classroom efforts of the team.

There can also be a *Career Choices* Lead Administrator, either at the school level or the district level. This optional position provides a "champion" of the course, someone to work closely with the school and district administration to make sure the course receives the resources and attention required. Some schools are fortunate enough to have a person who (usually because of special funding) can devote most, if not all, of their time to supporting a redesign effort such as a **Freshman Transition Initiative**. While these individuals are not necessarily in the classroom, the duties in the job description of the Lead Teacher could be split between the Lead Teacher and the Lead Administrator.

However, our historical observations tell us that, in addition to a Lead Administrator, one of the instructors of the *Career Choices* course should be designated as Lead Teacher and given the responsibility and authority required on a day-to-day basis for classroom success.

Job Duties for the Lead Teacher
of the Career Choices Course

Note: These duties can be split between a Lead Teacher and a Lead Administrator if the school has both.

Classroom Instructor of the Career Choices Course

- Teaches at least three class periods of the *Career Choices* course

Oversee Classroom Practices of the Team of Instructors

- Provide leadership and support to the team of course instructors
- Make sure the standards are being met, whether they are the Standards for a Freshman Transition Course or state- or district-mandated standards
- Work with Academic Innovations to take advantage of all benefits and resources offered by the publisher
- Help the team finalize a comprehensive pacing guide lesson plan for all sessions
- Conduct weekly lesson planning sessions with the team
- Share best practices among the team
- Monitor classroom performance of team members and make constructive suggestions

Professional Development of the Team

- Train and mentor newly hired instructors in the specifics of the curriculum design
- Provide implementation workshop(s) for the team, using the resources of **The Teachers' Lounge** and the Lead Teacher Manual
- Conduct periodic professional development sessions for the *Career Choices* instructors using the sessions outlined in the Lead Teacher Manual
- Plan yearly professional development opportunities for the whole school related to updating and using the 10-year plan for academic coaching and advisory efforts

Organizational Duties

- Monitor the administration of the pre- and post-course surveys so detailed data can be collected on the success of the class
- Once a year, review data from pre- and post-course surveys and analyze the findings
- Maintain comprehensive records and develop systems so that, when you leave the position, the transition is efficient and seamless
- One year before the end of their tenure as Lead Teacher, recruit, train, and orient your replacement
- Report on the progress of the overall project and individual classes at staff meetings and school board meetings

With the Principal's Approval

- Develop a professional development plan for each Freshman Transition course instructor
- Attend appropriate conferences and make presentations regarding your Freshman Transition program

If the Lead Teacher is also overseeing the School-wide Initiative of the 10-year plan, their duties include:

- Championing the School-wide Initiative
- Working with department heads to develop plans for the yearly updating of students' 10-year plans
- With the principal, monitoring the 10-year plan updating process and evaluating its effectiveness
- Providing the support and professional development to help each teacher in the school learn how to use the 10-year plan to provide personalized instruction and mentoring
- Conducting periodic professional development during staff in-service days on how to use the 10-year plan in an advisory capacity
- Orient new hires on the School-wide Initiative and its goals, systems, and operation

The School-wide Initiative:

Every student has an online 10-year plan that is updated yearly and used for advisory purposes

> *We need to spend time with kids—planning, monitoring, changing, visualizing, and thinking about their long-range plans. We should sit with a kid every four to six months and have him look carefully at himself and his plan.*
>
> — Dr. Mel Levine, bestselling author
> *One Mind at a Time* and *Ready or Not, Here Life Comes*

One way this can be accomplished in a school setting is to adopt the School-wide Initiative outlined in the article "A Personalized Plan for Life" (*Principal Leadership* magazine, November 2005). If you haven't already, you'll want to read this article by Dr. Rebecca Dedmond, Director of the **Freshman Transition Initiative** of The George Washington University. It outlines the 10-step Plan for reducing dropout rates and increasing post-secondary matriculation and completion. The ultimate goal is transitioning students into a self-sufficient adulthood, which is what we want for all students.

We suggest you share this article with your entire faculty. The article will help jumpstart your efforts. It can be found on **www.freshmantransition.org**

My10yearPlan.com®: The Ultimate Tool for Personalization

My10yearplan.com® was developed in response to the recommendations made in this article, providing an online planning area where students can store, update, and save—for the duration of their time in high school—the work and data related to the development of their 10-year plans.

Quick and easy to access, My10yearPlan.com® provides data-driven information about each student's future plans.

For advisory situations to function at the highest level, teachers, counselors, and advisors need quantitative information about each student as it relates to their education and career goals. The best guidance is provided when working from specific examples, rather than from general or vague notions about the student.

If advice and mentoring is based on each student's identifiable goals and lifestyle expectations, it has more meaning. By having this information online, all appropriate stakeholders can quickly access this in-depth information, providing individual guidance easily and efficiently.

Traditional advisory programs pair students with one specific staff member as their advisor for their four years of high school. There are drawbacks to this strategy. We believe that providing every teacher with in-depth information about every student's hopes and dreams empowers all teachers to act in an advisory capacity with every student in their classes.

Storing the 10-year plan information online means students can update their plans throughout their four years of high school. When students' 10-year plans are online and dynamic, each academic department can provide opportunities for students to review and update their plans using the knowledge gathered in their other courses.

For example:

- In 10th grade social studies, students could review their plans once they study globalization and understand how it impacts the workplace. They may discover that the career path they were considering will likely be outsourced to an area providing cheaper labor, or they'll learn about emerging technologies that will create future employment opportunities.

- The 11th grade English department might coordinate the annual re-editing of the plans after students read a literary work in which a character struggles with his or her own life-planning or identity issues.

- Essays that trigger self-reflection and personal reassessment could be assigned. Because the 10-year plan is now an important part of each student's understanding of themselves and their future plans, instructors will find these types of assignments rich in content.

- For an independent study project, seniors could update their 10-year plans to use in college or employment interviews.

- Students could choose a service-learning project related to a specific career interest area they've explored as a part of their most current version of their plans.

This effort requires planning and coordination with academic teams, but embedding this system of challenging students to revisit and update their 10-year plans in the culture of your school will result in more engaged students. Student education and career plans will have more meaning, students will actively practice adapting to change, and at-risk students will have a constant reminder of the consequences of dropping out or not performing at their personal best.

Why is This Important?

The more students are asked to rethink and rework their plans, the more meaningful the plans will become and the more students will value and strive to meet their stated education and career goals. With each "tweak" of their plan as they customize it to better reflect their dreams, hopes, and aspirations, they take more ownership.

In addition, as students get in the habit of updating their plans, they become more comfortable making decisions that involve change—which is a crucial survival skill in the workforce of the 21st century.

Why? Career stability is no longer assured for the vast majority of jobs because of industry changes, globalization, and technological advancements. Knowing how to navigate the ever-changing world of work is crucial. Those that fail to adapt to this new workforce reality could be condemned to a life of subsistence living.

Finally, for those students considering dropping out (whether it's leaving school physically or "checking out" emotionally), and, therefore, not performing to their greatest capacity, this constant reminder of the consequences of dropping out will keep them in school and striving. Because they have completed a *Career Choices* course, they understand the consequences of not following through with their education plans.

How to Facilitate the Updating of 10-year Plans

We recommend that, at a minimum, one academic department per year commits to facilitating the updating process. That department's instructors can develop lessons that integrate their coursework with this process.

Why stop there? Why not stretch as a staff and get a commitment from every department for this effort. With creativity and planning, each department in each grade can choose an area of the 10-year plan for discussion and reassessment.

- The math department could develop a series of real-life case studies or word problems relating to budgeting for a future lifestyle as found in chapter four. Why not study the formulas related to the magic of compounding interest in tax-free pension funds to launch a review of the exercises in chapter nine?

- In English, students could read a work of fiction or nonfiction that provides insights into a career path they are contemplating. Discussions and follow-up essays could ask students to compare and contrast their own lives with what they learned from the characters, analyzing the impact on their own future plans. With this newfound understanding, they can fine tune their own 10-year plans.

- In science, instructors can discuss the benefits of STEM (science, technology, engineering, and math) careers, thereby encouraging more students to choose science majors or career pathways. Our country needs more students getting degrees in the sciences, and these conversations need to start in high school.

Upon completion of these targeted academic activities, students would be directed to revisit and upgrade their online 10-year plan.

Get Focused . . . Stay Focused!™ *Initiative*

The *Get Focused...Stay Focused!* ™ Initiative, in conjunction with Academic Innovations, has developed follow-up curriculum modules for the 10th, 11th, and 12th grades that not only facilitates the systematic updating of students' online 10-year plans but also ensures all students are college and career ready. With Common Core State Standards-based activities providing 16 hours of instruction per year, students will be ready to enter college or post-secondary training with a chosen career, an informed declared major, and a preliminary course schedule. For details, see pages 6/29–6/30 and 4/170 or visit www.getfocusedstayfocused.org.

The opportunities for a School-wide Initiative are limited only by the creativity of your staff. If you and your colleagues devote the time and energy to coordinate the integration of the 10-year plan into the culture of your school, your students and staff will grow in ways you never imagined.

Santa Barbara City College
Discovers the Missing Link Between High School and College: A Dual Enrollment Freshman Transition Course

An affluent Southern California community with beautiful beaches and colonial Spanish architecture, the Santa Barbara area would seem to be the last place that might have an academic achievement problem. And indeed, a 92.7% high school graduation rate, as achieved by Carpinteria High School in 2009, would be the envy of many school districts (SARC, 2010).

An issue lies, however, in the fact that too few of these students actually attend and graduate from college. In an effort to motivate students to put forth a stronger effort in high school and seek post-secondary training afterward, Santa Barbara City College (SBCC) teamed up with the local school districts, Santa Barbara Unified and Carpinteria Unified, to offer a Dual Enrollment Freshman Transition (DEFT) course.

The class facilitates the creation of online 10-year Career and Education Plans that are unique to each of the students' desired career paths, which he or she chooses after carefully examining his or her strengths, interests, and lifestyle requirements. Students discover the tremendous impact that their high school performance can have on the degree of satisfaction or hardship they experience in their lives, so they increasingly value their education. With such personally motivating goals and all the steps laid out to achieve them, they are more likely to successfully complete relevant post-secondary training and live productive, fulfilling lives.

"Santa Barbara City College has always been an entrepreneurial-thinking college with a very 'big picture'-type of leadership," said Dr. Diane Hollems, Dean of Educational Programs at SBCC. "The big picture is that if students as young as 14 years of age learn, in an informed way, what they want to do with the rest of their lives, the benefit is not only to those students but to parents, the high school, the college, and the community."

Students are enrolled at the city college and the high school simultaneously and receive three units on their college transcripts upon completing the semester-long class known as Freshman Seminar, which they attend on their high school campuses. Offering a freshman transition course that also earns college credit has the additional benefit that, not only do students learn who they are and the life skills they will need to achieve their dreams, but they truly begin to see themselves as college students. This increases the likelihood that they will prepare early for college and enroll after high school graduation. Such a program makes great strides toward leveling the playing field for populations currently underrepresented in higher education, as the DEFT program is intended for all students in an entire freshman class.

"Our program is designed to reach all students," asserted Dr. Lauren Wintermeyer, Dual Enrollment Coordinator at SBCC. "We're reaching minority population students that may otherwise not have access to post-secondary education. If we get them experience, and access to people at the college while they're still in high school, hopefully they'll have a more successful transition after high school."

Too Many Students are Not College-Ready

Too often, educators believe that just getting students into college means that the high school has completed its mission. This is evidenced by the commonly used 5-year plan that ends only a year after students graduate from high school and gives little attention to graduating from college or career choice. This frequently results in students who are unprepared for college and who fail to understand why they are there.

"It seems like everything is always talking about how you get to college and they never really talk about what you do after," observed Sierra Saragosa, former Freshman Seminar student at Carpinteria High School. "Freshman Seminar really helped me realize that there's life after college and that everything I'm doing now is working for *after* college and not just *for* college."

Students who do not see the relevance of education to their lives are unlikely to even get to college, much less finish.

"Most of the time, when students complete high school, they still don't have a clear picture of what they want to be or what their major should be," Hollems commented. "They often hear, 'Just explore, you have all the time in the world, make up your mind later.' Well, that doesn't work and it's not realistic. But students that come to college knowing what they want to be and having researched that are going to finish. And that's huge. That's why we invest in the 9th grade dual enrollment course."

A 10-Year Plan Keeps Students on Track

The freshman transition course serves as an important bridge from middle school to high school and paves the way for a successful transition to post-secondary education or a career pathway. The student discovers how hard it is to earn the extravagant salary she imagined but that it is possible to earn a decent living in a career she enjoys. It then ties a student's performance in all of her core academic classes to her chances of living the lifestyle she desires and shows her that putting forth her strongest effort in high school is the wisest first step to achieving her goal.

With a new, more realistic understanding of adult responsibilities and of her own strengths and preferences, the student explores the concepts of identity achievement: who am I, what do I want, and how do I get it. Throughout the course, she builds the self-knowledge and learns the strategies to be able to write her own quantitative 10-year Career and Education plan.

The 10-year plan lays out the steps for each student to get through high school, through post-secondary training, and into his or her chosen career. Even if students decide to change their plans later (as many inevitably will, in today's world), they know how to go about the decision-making process.

"Whether or not the students, down the road, continue with the [plans] they created way back in the 9th grade, they've learned how to set goals and they've learned how to check on those goals, and hopefully they can look back and see that they've completed those goals," Hollems said.

The 10-year plan also becomes an important advisory tool throughout high school. Carpinteria High School has set up designated "touch points" to check in with students on their progress toward their goals. The online 10-year plans are available anytime a counselor or instructor needs to re-engage students who might be faltering on the path to self-sufficiency.

Having the connection between the high school and the community college extends the length of time that students can receive guidance related to their 10-year plans. Instead of hoping that students will remain motivated and keep their plans in mind through all the ups and downs of college, SBCC will have counselors onsite, trained in using the 10-year plan, who can continue to assist students in achieving their goals.

"We're not supposed to do it for the students, we're supposed to empower the students to do it for themselves and I think if we're all on the same page looking at the students' own words then we can best reflect that back to them," Wintermeyer said.

The Results Start to Come In

The program continues to grow. As of Fall 2011, three comprehensive high schools in the SBCC enrollment area required a DEFT course for all incoming freshmen.

Carpinteria High School led the way for this local initiative. School officials report an evident change in school culture over the past three years as this initial cohort and subsequent classes have embraced career and educational preparation.

"Students seem to be more connected to school, are here in the classroom more, and are just not getting in trouble as much," Hansen reported. "I think that relates to the Freshman Seminar course and what they're getting from the class—they understand that they need to be here and why their decisions [now] will affect them in the future."

In the fall of 2011, Santa Barbara High School and San Marcos High School joined SBCC's *Get Focused...Stay Focused!*™ movement by implementing the DEFT course. Both high schools offer the course for all 9th graders, and the introduction to dual enrollment encourages participation in additional dual enrollment courses and career technical pathways. Students will also benefit from follow-up curriculum in the 10th, 11th, and 12th grades at all of the comprehensive high schools in which they will revisit their 10-year plans and re-articulate their self-directed goals.

Carpinteria High School reports that freshman suspensions have decreased significantly since the program was implemented. In addition, a preliminary study at Dos Pueblos Senior High School found that 10th grade students who have taken the DEFT course are absent five fewer days per year than 10th graders who had not taken the course. Such results reported by the high schools have spurred SBCC to expand the DEFT program even further.

A Crucial Step Toward Educational Equality

Implementing a dual enrollment freshman transition course is a key strategy to increase college enrollment and graduation among students that are currently underrepresented in higher education. With a semester-long comprehensive guidance course based on the Standards for a Freshman Transition Course and continual support in the 10th, 11th, and 12th grades, any student is capable of writing and following a 10-year Career and Education Plan. Additionally, early exposure to college enables these students to see themselves as "college material" and enhances the odds that they will adequately prepare for post-secondary education, enroll, and graduate.

Without this knowledge, guidance, and experience, students must put all these pieces together by themselves, and if they do figure it out, it is often too late.

"Unless they have parents that are actively involved and sharing this with them," Hansen observed, "there's nowhere else on our campus where reality is so embedded in the classroom."

Dual enrollment freshman transition promotes equal opportunity for all students and, by helping them to plan where they are going, helps them to make the most of their lives.

Voiced Lauren Mingee, a former Freshman Seminar student at Carpinteria High, "When I was a freshman, I was taking pretty easy classes, doing my homework in the morning, not really trying as hard. After taking [Freshman Seminar], I realized how much applying yourself really matters. Education really matters and the choices you make now really affect your future. This year I'm taking AP classes and a dual enrollment course."

 You'll find the complete article in Section 6 of the online version of this *Instructor's Guide.*

GET FOCUSED

Middle School:
✓ Participate in a transition program to prepare for high school and the Freshman Transition course
✓ Learn career exploration strategies using online resources from the U.S. Department of Labor
✓ Learn study skills and expectations for high school

In 9th Grade:
✓ Take the Freshman Transition course (dual credit optional)
✓ Work through a process that answers the questions:
   ✓ Who Am I?
   ✓ What Do I Want?
   ✓ How Do I Get It?
✓ Create an online 10-year Plan as the culminating project of that comprehensive guidance course

In 10th Grade: **Developing Attitudes & Aptitudes that Promote College & Career Readiness**
✓ Research high-demand/higher-wage careers
✓ Determine appropriate post-secondary options/pathways
✓ Learn about college access and affordability
✓ Continue to envision a productive future through autobiographical writing
✓ Update 10-year Plan

In 11th Grade: **Determining Your Informed Major & Post-Secondary Education Path**
✓ Research STEM-related careers
✓ Reaffirm or change chosen career path
✓ Choose a major/program of study to match chosen career
✓ Identify colleges/post-secondary options that offer your major/program of study
✓ Prepare for college applications
✓ Update 10-year Plan

STAY FOCUSED

In 12th Grade: **Preparing to Act on Your 10-Year Career & Education Plan**
✓ Apply to college/post-secondary training
✓ Apply for scholarships and financial aid
✓ Update resume, cover letter, and portfolio
✓ Mock interview and job applications
✓ Outline a Skills-based Education Plan
✓ Update 10-year Plan

End of High School:
✓ College Ready: No need for remedial coursework upon entering college
✓ Enter college/post-secondary training with an informed declared major
✓ Graduate with a portable, online 10-year Plan and a Skills-based Education Plan
✓ Ideally, graduate with at least 12 college units and portable, online 10-year Plan

Attending College/Post-secondary Training:
✓ Enter with a 10-year Plan or take a Student Success course to create a 10-year Plan
✓ Use 10-year Plan in meetings with advisors and counselors

End of College/Post-secondary Training:
✓ Certificate or degree completion and/or transfer to a 4-year college or university

Goal for End of Post-Secondary Education & Training
✓ Have the skills to be competitive and find work in chosen career field

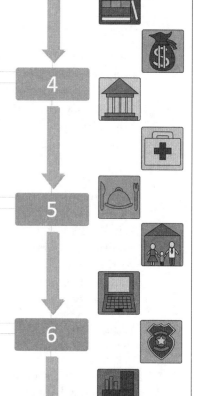

What is the *Get Focused…Stay Focused!* ™ Initiative?

How is it different from other college and career ready programs?

The *Get Focused…Stay Focused!* ™ Initiative, developed through Santa Barbara City College's Dual Enrollment department, is a scalable, cost-efficient program that promotes high school graduation, post-secondary completion, and successful entry into the workforce.

A *Get Focused…Stay Focused!* ™ Initiative (GFSF) starts with a semester or year-long freshman course based on the Freshman Transition Standards of The George Washington University's Freshman Transition Initiative. This standards-based, comprehensive guidance course is the "get focused" part, helping students become identity achieved and career committed.

The freshman course culminates with the development of a 10-year career and education plan. Students' 10-year Plans are updated throughout high school and stored online for use by advisors for counseling and instructors for academic coaching. This important data is portable so students can easily share it with post-secondary counselors and instructors.

During the 10th, 11th, and 12th grade, using the hybrid *Get Focused…Stay Focused!* ™ follow-up module workbooks, students experience the "stay focused" part of the process as they update their online 10-year career and education plan as they:

- Expand their career and education options
- Learn the process for selecting and applying to post-secondary education
- Create a Skills-based Education Plan

Completion of the freshman transition course and the three follow-up modules means students have identified:

- A carefully-considered career path
- An informed major or program of study
- A post-secondary institution or training program that matches their career and life goals and their budget
- A unique Skills-based Education Plan that facilitates successful entry into a highly competitive workforce upon completion of their education

Stakeholders' most important goals are met as a result of this process:

- **Students** gain the knowledge and experience necessary to successfully navigate higher education and enter a competitive workforce.

- **Parents** applaud this reality-based experience that sets their children on a trajectory toward a self-sufficient adulthood.

- **Teachers** appreciate the engaging lessons that support the Common Core Standards and motivate students in their academic studies.

- **Administrators** understand that motivated students have better attendance, and improved attendance rates result in increased funding.

- **Community members** realize that engaged, motivated, and informed young people who "stay focused" on their education and career goals become contributing members of society.

The freshman "get focused" course is the ideal launch for career pathway and career academy programs, and should be delivered before students make a pathway selection. When students make an *informed* pathway choice after carefully examining their personal goals and predilections, lateral movement between pathways is reduced.

This hybrid, classroom-based comprehensive guidance program is unique among educational programs today:

- It is a whole-school effort, touching **every student** on campus rather than a select few in silo programs.

- Every professional on campus (instructors, counselors, administrators, et al) can easily access each student's online 10-year plan to personalize advisement and academic coaching efforts.

- It delivers vital guidance functions in a classroom-setting, supporting the under-staffed, over-burdened counseling team.

- It integrates academics in the guise of a personal development course with Common Core-based lessons and provides opportunities for a "double dose" of English, math, speaking, and technology skills.

It is built on a proven foundation. With a history stretching nearly three decades, the comprehensive and award-winning *Career Choices* series provides chronologically and developmentally appropriate tasks essential to individual student success.

The *Get Focused...Stay Focused!* ™ programmatic model is the "missing link" in education today. If "Guidance is Key to Student Success," as espoused in a 2012 report from the California Community Colleges' Student Success Task Force, yet counselor to student ratios are between 1:400 and 1:1800 (at the secondary and post-secondary levels), new formats for delivering these all-important services must be found.

To assume technology can replace the role of human interaction in helping individuals make some of the most important choices of their lives is naïve and short-sighted. The classroom-based format of the GFSF program mixes high tech with high touch and is both cost efficient and scalable in this era of dwindling resources.

How does the Get Focused…Stay Focused! ™ (GFSF) program differ from other programs designed to help students become college and career ready?

GFSF was designed for **ALL students** rather than a select few or a special population within a school. In the GFSF program, all incoming freshmen take a freshman transition course in which students develop an online 10-year career and education plan. This semester or year-long comprehensive guidance course is as applicable for the highest functioning students as it is for at-risk students.

GFSF is a **whole-school redesign project** with a continuum covering the four years of high school. After the freshman transition course, students continue in the 10th, 11th, and 12th grades updating their 10-year Plans and expanding their career and educational options using the three follow-up module workbooks. The 10-year Plans, easily accessible online, are used by all instructors and counselors for advisories and academic coaching.

GFSF is a curriculum-based effort, with **comprehensive instructional materials** for each of the above classroom efforts.

One of the key ways in which the GFSF program stands apart from other career or college exploration programs is that instructors are not left to their own devices to develop their course content. Using the GFSF recommended course materials, classroom teachers have the tools to deliver, from the first day of class, consistent, content-rich lessons in a meaningful scope-and-sequence fashion.

There are also thorough planning and implementation resources so you can conduct a *Get Focused…Stay Focused!*™ program in a way that assures your students graduate with the attitudes, aptitudes, and plans that research shows encourage college/post-secondary completion.

Upon completion of high school, students graduate with **two vital and unique documents:** their dynamic 10-year Career and Life Plan and their Skills-based Education Plan.

This is only possible because of the comprehensive guidance designed in a careful, scope-and-sequence fashion that is not only developmentally appropriate but also reinforces the critical and creative thinking skills coveted in today's workforce. Through this in-depth planning process, students build the intrinsic motivation necessary to succeed.

The curriculum materials address **rigorous standards**.

The freshman transition course not only meets the Common Core State Standards, but also aligns with the Standards for a Freshman Transition Course from the George Washington University's Freshman Transition Initiative.

To allow for easy integration into English Language Arts classes in 10th, 11th, and 12th grades, the 16 lessons in each of the three *Get Focused…Stay Focused!* ™ modules were developed using the English Language Arts Common Core State Standards as the foundation.

The keystone of the GFSF program is a **10-year career and education plan** that is broader than the four-year education plans commonly used by high schools and colleges.

By the time students complete a GFSF program, they have developed, reassessed, upgraded, and enhanced an online 10-year Plan of their own design. This tool is intended to propel them through high school graduation, into and through college or post-secondary training, and into employment that leads to economic self-sufficiency and life satisfaction.

The process is effective because students who have identified a career pathway that matches their individual drives and life goals enter post-secondary education ready to declare a major or program of study that is a good long-term fit.

> "Research from the Institute for Higher Education Leadership and Policy shows that students who entered a program [of study] in their first year were twice as likely to complete a certificate, degree or transfer as students who entered a program after their first year. First-year concentrators were nearly 50 percent more likely to complete than those who entered a program in their second year, and the rates of completion fell sharply for students entering a program of study later than their second year."
>
> "Advancing Student Success in the California Community Colleges," p. 34,
> California Community Colleges Student Success Task Force

Students' online 10-year Plans can be used by all instructors and counselors for **advising and academic coaching.**

A sophisticated, browser-based tool, use of My10yearPlan.com® creates the opportunity for true personalization with each student. The *10-year Plan Summary Page* can be quickly reviewed by an instructor or counselor, enabling them to provide laser-focused advice and guidance centered on each student's goals, plans, and dreams.

The My10yearPlan.com® mobile app provides portability and just-in-time access to the 10-year Plan. In their coursework, students learn that the 10-year Plan is a lifelong process. Thus the mobile app for My10yearPlan.com®. Students have on-demand access to the information that populates their *10-year Plan Summary Page.* Using the app, students can not only share their plans with advisors, mentors, family, and friends at a moment's notice, but they can also update their plans with new information when inspiration strikes.

GFSF facilitates the development of a **Skills-based Education Plan**, promoting self-directed skill development and successful entry into the workforce.

A traditional Student Education Plan outlines the courses required to complete a specific major or program of study. Unique to the GFSF program, the Skills-based Education Plan helps students create a plan which includes not only skills and knowledge gained in traditional coursework but also strategies to acquire specialized skills required for their identified career path.

In today's workforce, when there are so many experienced workers seeking employment, it is difficult for a recent graduate to be competitive. Employers are looking for individuals who have the specialized job-content skills they require. Except for professional or advanced degrees, most traditional courses cannot deliver the wide range of information required. Students must become self-directed learners who seek out opportunities (internships, mentorships, on the job training, online courses, the best book on the topic) to acquire the knowledge and skills necessary to be competitive.

The GFSF coursework supports **development of the higher-order thinking skills** required in the 21st century workforce.

Too many career exploration programs advise students through online assessments and algorithms, removing critical thinking and caring adult advocates from the equation. After answering a string of multiple-choice questions, the computer magically maps an education or career path for the student. In contrast, the GFSF program was designed to teach students a decision-making process in which they employ their own brainpower to analyze, synthesize, and evaluate life choices before developing their own strategic plan. The learner can use this in-depth model throughout life as they navigate our fast-changing workplace and society.

The GFSF program is the **"missing link"** for career academy and career pathway programs.

Most career academy or pathway students are asked to select their path after attending an assembly or a career fair. Is it little wonder that these important programs are plagued by high dropout rates and "pathway hopping" (i.e., lateral movement between pathways)? Without the benefit of a comprehensive guidance course that takes students through the process of determining not only the career they desire but also the lifestyle they envision, too many young people make uninformed choices and lose interest or focus before completing a program of study.

The GFSF program was designed to include a viable **dual enrollment option**.

Santa Barbara City College (SBCC) has one of the largest and well-respected dual enrollment programs in the country. The GFSF program began with a 3-unit Dual Enrollment Freshman Transition (DEFT) course at four high schools in the SBCC catchment area. The 16-lesson *Get Focused…Stay Focused!* ™ follow-up modules can equate to one unit of college credit for each module.

While the dual enrollment component is optional, it is encouraged, when possible. When freshman students realize that they can tackle college-level material, the overall impact is that students expand their personal vision of what is possible.

Designed so schools can launch quickly and efficiently, GFSF has one of the most **comprehensive professional development** programs available.

The GFSF program has a variety of capacity-building options for schools and districts, including workshops, conferences, online videos and self-directed courses, and technical assistance contracts. Too numerous to inventory here, the following web sites provide additional information:

> www.getfocusedstayfocused.com/conference
> www.aiworkshops.com
> www.careerchoices.com/lounge
> www.focusonfreshmen.com

Also review the professional development resources found in the *Get Focused…Stay Focused!* ™ *Program and Instructional Manual* and the *Instructor's and Administrator's Guide for Career Choices* and My10yearPlan.com®.

The GFSF program changes the culture of the school.

With the online 10-year Plan, every adult on campus can personalize their work with each student.

- Academic instructors can review each student's 10-year Plan so they can recognize and support student goals—both in class and in one-to-one discussions.

- Parent-teacher meetings can be even more productive when the child's 10-year Plan is part of the discussion.

- With training, classroom instructors can support the over-committed guidance staff and become part of the advisory team. After all, guidance is recognized as critical to student success.

- Attendance will increase and academic achievement will increase, while suspensions and dropout rates will decrease. Why? Because when students see a path to a satisfying life, they understand the value of education. Students no longer ask, "Why do I need to learn this?"

The GFSF program **flips the paradigm** of college and career planning.

As a country we've had it backwards for a long time. Most students choose the college they want to attend with little thought of a major, much less a career. It's little wonder that far too many students wander through the educational maze and do not complete.

In reality, it is a career path that dictates which major or program of study to tackle, which in turn dictates which college to attend. The GFSF program exposes students to this reality and, beginning in the freshman year, provides the foundation to help them tackle this more realistic, multi-stage strategy.

Get Focused…Stay Focused! ™ Program and Instructional Manual

This manual provides the necessary resources so you can plan and implement a *Get Focused…Stay Focused!* ™ program that assures your students graduate with the attitudes, aptitudes, and plans that research shows encourage college/post secondary completion.

For more information and to view the table of contents, visit:
http://getfocusedstayfocused.org/gfsf_manual.php

Section 7

Program Planning Resources

Topics covered in this section include:

- Through years of research, we have discovered what makes a *Career Choices* course successful and what doesn't.

- We've prepared a comprehensive checklist for instructors planning a course, including professional development, lesson planning, and best practices.

- Our medal program rubric can help you evaluate how your program compares to the most successful *Career Choices* courses. Medal winning programs are recognized by Academic Innovations at the annual Focus on Freshmen conference.

- Integrating academics and technology into your *Career Choices* course is something to consider as you plan. While touched on here, Sections 8 and 9 provide additional guidance.

- Customizing a pacing guide to fit your goals and program structure is also an important part of program planning. While touched on here, Section 10 provides additional guidance.

The Planning Phase

The five ingredients of a successful *Career Choices* course are that it:

- Culminates with each student writing a quantitative and meaningful 10-year plan
- Provides a minimum of 60 hours of *Career Choices* instruction
- Is taught in sequence from Chapter 1 to Chapter 12
- Is taught by an enthusiastic instructor
- The instructor refers to Section 4 of the *Instructor's Guide* on a daily basis

Research has shown that the most successful Freshman Transition programs share certain attributes. This means you don't have to reinvent the wheel to find what works best.

Before you begin developing your course, become very familiar with The George Washington University's Standards for a Freshman Transition Course and strategies for involving the entire school in updating students' 10-year plans throughout high school. You'll also want to be on the lookout for opportunities for integrating academics and technology. And expand your understanding by learning about other schools' successes in creating programs to fit their unique needs.

Program Design that Supports Success and Sustainability

After years of working with school districts, we know what works and what doesn't. For a succinct overview of the conditions that promote success, review these three key resources:

- The online training video *Five Ingredients of a Successful Career Choices Course* available at **www.careerchoices.com/lounge/success/**
- The hierarchy of needs for a *Career Choices* course that impacts dropout rates
- Medal program rubric for evaluating effective Freshman Transition, dropout prevention, and college readiness programs using *Career Choices*

Next create your plan and then work your plan.

- Review the Quick Start suggestions in Section 1 of this *Instructors Guide*.
- For prompts in developing your plan, create an account and log into Academic Innovation's Program Planning web site **www.academicinnovations.com/programplanning** or see page 7/5. This tool will help you stay on track so you can efficiently and effectively individualize your Freshman Transition course and School-wide Initiative.
- If you follow the recommendations on the *Instructor Success Checklist* and use the resources outlined on page 7/9, you are sure to deliver a life-changing experience for your students.

Hierarchy of Needs

for a *Career Choices* course that impacts dropout rates*

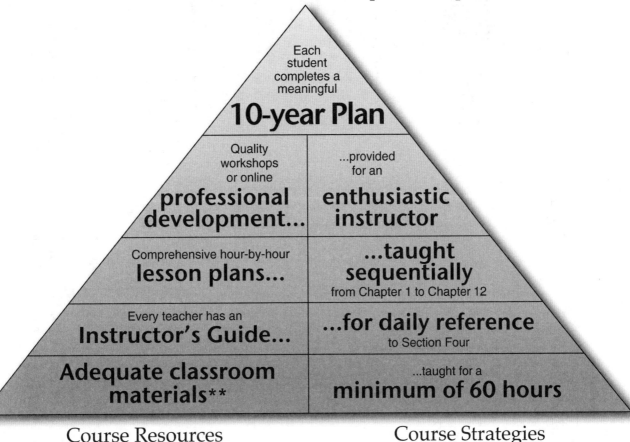

Each student completes a meaningful

10-year Plan

Quality workshops or online **professional development...**	...provided for an **enthusiastic instructor**
Comprehensive hour-by-hour **lesson plans...**	**...taught sequentially** from Chapter 1 to Chapter 12
Every teacher has an **Instructor's Guide...**	**...for daily reference** to Section Four
Adequate classroom materials**	...taught for a **minimum of 60 hours**

Course Resources   Course Strategies

*Both high school and college

**Every student has a copy of the textbook and their own consumable
  workbook so homework can be assigned. Completed workbooks are then
  used as an advisory tool by 10th, 11th, and 12th grade instructors.

REACH FOR THE GOLD

The foundation for a medal-winning program begins with:

✓ Each student having their own *Workbook and Portfolio*

✓ Instructors who are experienced and excited about teaching the course

✓ Giving teachers time prior to the first day of class to customize a lesson pacing guide

✓ Instructors leading students through the textbook in a sequential manner

✓ Students developing a meaningful 10-year Plan

✓ Having students complete the pre-/post-course survey

✓ Involving the entire school in supporting students and their 10-year Plans

START HERE

GOLD

✓ Complete at least 90% of the *Career Choices* activities

✓ Devote at least 90 hours to the content in *Career Choices*

✓ Provide all instructors and administrators with:
  * an *Instructor's Guide* for weekly reference
  * access to The Teachers' Lounge for weekly reference

✓ Integrate *Lifestyle Math* AND *Possibilities*

✓ Integrate My10yearPlan.com®, CareerChoices.com, or LifestyleMath.com

✓ My10yearPlan.com® is used to store, update, and share students' 10-year Plans

✓ Students' plans are available through My10yearPlan.com® for faculty to use for advisory purposes

✓ Lead Teacher is in place and trained

✓ Lead Teacher facilitates regular trainings for the team

✓ A plan is in place to assist students in revisiting and updating their 10-year Plans annually

✓ School Site Executive for My10yearPlan.com® is in place and trained

✓ Principal has attended a school-wide initiative training

✓ Data related to the course is recorded, compiled, and evaluated

SILVER

✓ Complete at least 80% of the *Career Choices* activities

✓ Devote at least 90 hours to the content in *Career Choices*

✓ Provide all instructors and administrators with:
  * an *Instructor's Guide* for periodic reference
  * access to The Teachers' Lounge for periodic reference

✓ Integrate *Lifestyle Math* OR *Possibilities*

✓ Integrate My10yearPlan.com®, CareerChoices.com, or LifestyleMath.com

✓ Have a method for storing, updating, and sharing students' 10-year Plans

✓ Students' plans are available to faculty for advisory purposes

✓ Lead Teacher is in place and trained

✓ Lead Teacher facilitates regular trainings for the team

✓ A plan is in place to assist students in revisiting and updating their 10-year Plans annually

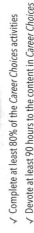

BRONZE

✓ Complete at least 70% of the *Career Choices* activities

✓ Devote at least 60 hours to the content in *Career Choices*

✓ Provide all instructors and administrators with:
  * an *Instructor's Guide* for occasional reference
  * access to The Teachers' Lounge for occasional reference

RECOGNIZING EDUCATIONAL TEAMS WORKING TO PROMOTE STUDENT SUCCESS

Career Choices Medal Schools are committed to increasing student motivation and improving college and career readiness. These exemplary secondary schools foster success—of their *Career Choices* program and, most importantly, of their students—through careful planning and intentional implementation.

Complete the online survey at WWW.CAREERCHOICES.COM/LOUNGE/MEDAL to develop an action plan for making improvements.

Academic Innovations, LLC
(800) 967-8016
support@academicinnovations.com

Step-by-step Program Planning Web Site

www.academicinnovations.com/programplanning

This online resource provides resources for each step in the process of planning a course—conducting research, getting buy-in, designing your program, obtaining funding, implementing the program, and assessing the results.

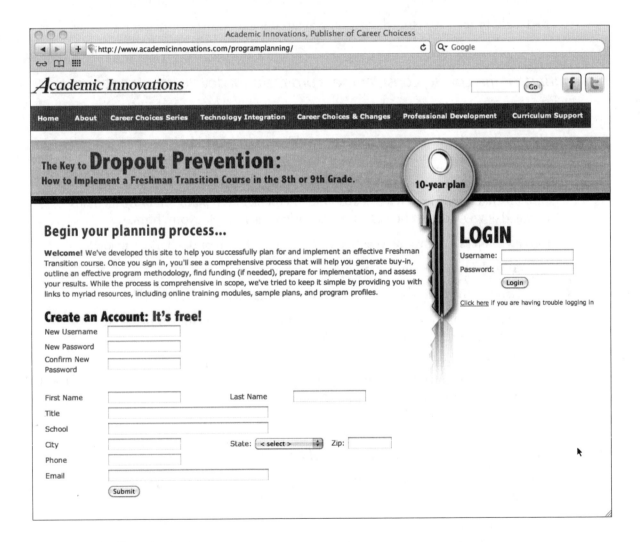

Instructor Success Checklist

This list is an expansion of the Quick Start Checklist in Section 1.

To achieve the desired dropout prevention results, it is important to remember that your *Career Choices* coursework should:

- ☐ Be **comprehensive, with class discussion and active learning as the key delivery methods**; review the appropriate pages in Section 4 of the *Instructor's Guide* on a daily basis

- ☐ Be **sequential, running from beginning to end**—Chapters 1 to 12

- ☐ Devote at least **60 hours** to the lessons from *Career Choices*

- ☐ Culminate with the completion of a written, comprehensive **10-year plan** (Chapter 12)

- ☐ Be taught by an instructor who is **well-prepared** and **enthusiastic** about the course

In preparing for this course, consider these professional development options:

- ☐ Join **The Teachers' Lounge** and spend some time working through the "Getting Started" **online training videos**. You'll come away with tips and strategies to help you make choices about the structure of your course. Visit **www.careerchoices.com/lounge** for additional details.

- ☐ **Lead Administrators or Lead Teachers:** Participate in a *Career Choices* Lead Administrator and Lead Teacher Institute or complete the online training modules outlined at **www.careerchoices.com/lounge/profdev_ceu3dayotm.html**.

- ☐ *Career Choices* **Classroom Teachers:** Choose one (or all) of the options below.

    - ☐ Attend a **two-day implementation workshop**

    - ☐ Request the loan of a set of **two-day workshop DVDs**

    - ☐ Complete the **online training videos for course instructors** available at **www.careerchoices.com/lounge/modules.html**

    - ☐ Your Lead Teacher and team of *Career Choices* instructors meet to begin working through the **introductory workshop agendas** outlined in the *Career Choices* Lead Administrator and Lead Teacher Manual

Between now and the first day of class, finalize your lesson plans.

Based on (1) the time you have to complete your course, (2) your program goals, and/or (3) your academic discipline:

- ☐ **Choose an appropriate pacing guide to use as your starting point.** Created by author Mindy Bingham, these guides will help you meet course goals while providing a challenging and inspiring course. View examples at **www.academicinnovations.com/sample_lesson_plans.html**. Need guidance as you make your choice? Call our Curriculum Support Team at (800) 967-8016.

- ☐ **Study the lesson planning pacing guide spreadsheet** and become familiar with the contents of each page referenced.

☐ Read through the textbooks and thoroughly review Section 4 of the *Instructor's Guide* making note of the content selected. At this point you may choose to edit and enhance the lessons based on your school's particular goals and your student population.

☐ Meet with your school's team of *Career Choices* teachers and your Lead Teacher. Going lesson by lesson, brainstorm and finalize your strategies for delivery. Your *Career Choices* instructional team is a great support system for daily and weekly evaluation. Share what works for you, strategies you may try, and challenges you encounter. Your team will also benefit from ongoing review of the training sessions outlined in the *Career Choices* Lead Administrator and Lead Teacher Manual.

☐ Study My10yearPlan.com®, watch the overview videos, and review the suggested strategies for use by students, teachers, and advisors.

☐ Work with your principal to choose a School Site Executive and activate your site license(s) for the online enhancements.

☐ Grab your copy of the *Workbook and Portfolio* and do a side-by-side walk-through of My10yearPlan.com®. Look at it as if you are a student experiencing this important tool.

☐ Study CareerChoices.com and determine how and when you can incorporate this optional enhancement into your class (given your Internet access).

☐ Reserve time in the computer lab so students can enter the data from their *Workbook and Portfolio* into My10yearplan.com®. The amount of time needed will depend on which level of My10yearPlan.com® you are using.

☐ Review the pre- and post-survey (pages 14/9 to 14/14 in this *Instructor's Guide*) so you are ready to administer these at the appropriate times. The pre-survey is done prior to any work in *Career Choices*. The post-survey is done after students have completed their 10-year plans.

IMPORTANT: Homework assignments are critical to course success.

- As a comprehensive guidance course, it is important to set high expectations from the first day of class. This is a rigorous class. The more students put into it, the more they'll get out of it.

- Homework assignments help to prepare students for the day's discussion and provide the space for reflection of their own thoughts, goals, plans, and attitudes about the lesson for the day. Class time is then used for discussions, energizers, brainstorming, and group activities as noted in this *Instructor's Guide*.

- Student homework assignments from the *Workbook and Portfolio* are noted on pacing guide spreadsheets.

- Be sure to thoroughly review homework at the time it is assigned.

Once your class starts:

First few days of class

☐ Administer the pre-survey before you hand out the books. The pre-survey is available on page 14/11 of this *Instructor's Guide* or through My10yearPlan.com®.

Daily

- [ ] Review your pacing guide spreadsheet.

- [ ] Turn to the corresponding page(s) in **Section 4 of this *Instructor's Guide*** and review the recommendations for that activity or exercise. The course is content-rich and rigorous, while providing relevance and helping students build relationships (with themselves, others, and the world). You'll need to finely tune your delivery and timing for each lesson. See yourself as a discussion leader, mentor, coach, and cheerleader, helping students develop and explore their own vision of a productive future.

- [ ] **Assign homework from their *Workbook and Portfolio* each day,** so students come to class prepared for discussion and group activities.

Weekly

- [ ] **Meet with your team of *Career Choices* instructors and Lead Administrator/Teacher** to review the training sessions outlined in the *Career Choices* Lead Teacher Manual, to discuss presentation of activities, and to brainstorm solutions to challenges. Occasionally invite your principal and district leaders to attend.

- [ ] Visit The Teachers' Lounge (www.careerchoices.com/lounge). Spend time reviewing corresponding online training videos, stories of other successful schools, and the contents of the Resource Cupboard as new material is added as it becomes available.

Throughout the course

- [ ] As you progress through the curriculum, visit The Teachers' Lounge and review the **online training videos providing an overview of each section** (i.e., Who Am I? What Do I Want? How Do I Get It?).

- [ ] **For personalized support and professional development resources,** remember that we are here to help. Contact our Curriculum Support team at (800) 967-8016 or support@academicinnovations.com.

Course final

- [ ] At least two weeks before the end of your class, **assign the completion of Chapter 12 and the 10-year plan as the take-home final.**

- [ ] **Assign the post-survey after students complete their 10-year plans.** Compare students' pre- and post- survey responses in My10yearPlan.com® or using the evaluation tool on The Teachers' Lounge.

At the end of the course or school year

- [ ] **Share your experience** with Academic Innovations by completing an online teacher survey at www.academicinnovations.com/survey.html. We take these evaluations seriously and it helps us upgrade the services we offer you.

- [ ] **Consider sending your pre- and post-survey data to the Freshman Transition Initiative at The George Washington University.** Contact them at www.freshmantransition.org.

- [ ] CELEBRATE a job well done both with your students and with your colleagues! See page 5/18 of this *Instructor's Guide* for ideas.

Essential Course Planning Resources

Other key course planning resources can be found throughout this *Instructor's Guide* and online.

Resource	Instructor's Guide Page(s)	Web Address
Self-Study Guide for a Quick Start	1/20–1/22	www.careerchoices.com/lounge/quickstartguides.html
The 10-step Plan for Implementing a Freshman Transition Initiative	6/6	www.freshmantransition.org/10step.php
Standards for a Freshman Transition Course	6/7	www.freshmantransition.org/fts.php
Principals Checklist for a Freshman Transition Initiative	6/17–6/18	
Integrated Course Structure Options	3/4	
Cross Reference for *Career Choices* and *Possibilities*	8/11–8/14	
My10yearPlan.com® Essentials vs. Interactive	9/7–9/9	www.my10yearplan.com/pdfs/difference_betweenmy10yearplan.pdf
Recommended Models for My10yearPlan.com® Interactive	9/10	www.academicinnovations.com/docs/interactive_program_models-2.pdf
Quick Start Directions for My10yearPlan.com®	9/11	
Sample Lesson Plan Pacing Guides	10/7–10/17	www.careerchoices.com/lounge/cupboard_lesson.html
Project-based Learning Opportunities	11/18	
The Teachers' Lounge	12/5	www.careerchoices.com/lounge
Career Choices Online Training Videos	12/6	www.careerchoices.com/lounge/modules.html
Curriculum and Technical Support Resources	Section 12	
Sample Parent Letter	13/3	www.careerchoices.com/lounge/cupboard_letters.html
Authentic Assessment for Higher Order Thinking	14/2	
Pre- and Post-Course Surveys	14/11–14/12	www.careerchoices.com/lounge/prepost.html
Online Data Tool for Tracking Results	14/16	www.whatworkscareerchoices.com/dataproject
Examples of Best Practices and Results	1/27–1/30	www.whatworkscareerchoices.com

Designing Your Course

The next three sections of this *Instructor's Guide* provide more detail on options you should consider when planning your course.

Section 8 highlights opportunities for incorporating the supplemental texts *Possibilities* and *Lifestyle Math* into a *Career Choices* course or for using *Career Choices* and *Possibilities* in an English course that meets the Common Core State Standards.

Section 9 explains My10yearPlan.com®, the online enhancement that allows students to store and update their 10-year plans throughout high school. Learn about the two levels of access:

- My10yearPlan Essentials is made up of the 25 keystone exercises that form the skeleton of the 10-year plan

- My10yearPlan Interactive replicates each of the activities from the *Workbook and Portfolio* and features automated prompts to help students review work completed earlier in the process when making decisions

Section 10 will help walk you through the critical step of pacing your instruction so you are sure to complete the 10-year planning process in the last chapter. Once you have an idea of what you would like your course to include, visit **The Teachers' Lounge** Resource Cupboard to select an appropriate pacing guide spreadsheet. After you find the one that most closely correlates with your plans (i.e., how long your course will be, which texts you are using, how much technology you are integrating), you can easily edit the spreadsheet to fit the needs of your students. Section 10 covers the process in more detail and features a sample 145-hour interdisciplinary lesson plan pacing guide.

Titling Your Course

While you may be tempted to title your Freshman Transition course something like "Freshman Experience" or "Freshman Seminar," schools have run into problems with those names. Why? Over the years, the Freshman Transition course and the development of a 10-year Plan has become a graduation requirement in some districts. As a result, students who move in as upperclassmen need to take the course. Juniors and seniors will not be happy about taking a course with "freshmen" in the title, no matter how valuable the content.

The title you choose can be used to peak students' interest and increase their motivation. A course title like Success 101 will be universally appealing. Everyone wants to be successful, and the use of "101" reinforces a post-secondary theme.

Secrets of Success for Implementing or Improving a *Career Choices* Series Program

1. **Carefully consider the course name.**

   The name of your course needs to convey to students that the course is important, different, desirable. You also need to look down the road a bit. What if your course becomes a graduation requirement or is offered as an elective to students in upper grades? If you use the word "freshman" in the title, students who take the course as upperclassmen may be put off by the name.

   A few suggestions: Success 101, Get Focused, Post-Secondary & Career Readiness.

2. **Set your sights on the end goal.**

   Begin with the end in mind, and let your end goal guide your planning. For your students, the "end" is a career that matches their aspirations and their aptitudes. As the course instructor, your goal is to make sure your students work through all of the curriculum content in the allotted time and leave class with a self-articulated 10-year Plan.

3. **First impressions are lasting impressions.**

   This course is not like anything else students have experienced. Demonstrate that difference— right from the start—to prepare students for a truly unique class. To really impact students' first impression of the course, do something on the first day of class to set the tone for your journey together.

4. **Watch your phraseology.**

   Vocabulary is important. Sometimes we overuse the word "college" when talking about where students are headed after high school, when what we really mean is "post-secondary." Not every student's plan is going to include college. In fact, many higher-wage/high-demand careers don't require a college degree. What every student should be planning for is some kind of post-secondary education or training.

5. **Give yourself a "cushion" to avoid the last-minute rush.**

   To create your lesson pacing guide, start with the total number of instructional hours you will have to cover the content in the *Career Choices* series text. Don't include any time focused on other topics or testing, field trips, pep rallies, etc. Once you have a total, reduce that by 10% to give yourself some additional flexibility.

6. **Consider a first semester start for ALL students.**

   If possible, schedule all sections of this course for the first semester of the school year. Understandably, schools with semester-long courses may hope to divide the sections across first and second semester. Unfortunately, by the start of the second semester, some students may have already fallen behind or failed required coursework.

7. **Be intentional in your use of My10yearPlan.com®.**

   We've been intentional in our design of **My10yearPlan.com®** and your use of the system should be just as intentional. Once students record their initial (draft) responses to exercises and activities in their *Workbook and Portfolio,* plan to allow some lag time before they input those responses into their My10yearPlan.com® account. The editing and polishing that takes place after that lag will be much more effective because students have had time to process, reflect, and mull over the topics and choices.

8. **Encourage ownership.**

Encourage students to take ownership of their *Workbook and Portfolio*. Ownership of their *Workbook* leads to ownership of the process and the 10-year Plan they develop. The *Workbook* also helps students to stay organized, which fosters responsibility. There are some fun, creative ways for students to establish their ownership. Let them personalize the cover of their *Workbook* with collages or "graffiti" or another artsy-crafty, hands-on project.

9. **Homework will enhance the experience for your students.**

Homework doesn't have to feel like a chore and, with this course, it shouldn't. Assign homework that helps students make additional connections between your class and the "real world." There are any number of opportunities for students to include friends, family, and neighbors in their process. Ask students to conduct a poll on a certain topic or to collect items to help with the budget exercise (Chapter 4). Give students a list of items to price out at the grocery store or have them interview a working adult in their life about their own career path.

10. **Build a *Get Focused…Stay Focused!*™ community.**

Get everyone in your community involved in this game-changing effort—students, parents, all faculty, employers, community members, etc. Make all of your stakeholders aware of the 10-year Plan and encourage them to ask for it when students apply for scholarships, college entry, or jobs. The more people in the community ask about the 10-year Plan, the more students will value the process.

For resources related to these tips, see www.careerchoices.com/lounge/10tipsforsuccess

Section 8

Integrating Academics and Technology

Topics covered in this section include:

- Integrating academics and technology into *Career Choices* is important for motivating students to learn. Students need to understand how academic subjects and technology skills relate to their lives outside of the classroom in order to reach their potential.

- Integrating academics and technology into your *Career Choices* course provides a very progressive way of meeting many of the Common Core State Standards.

- *Career Choices* and the language arts anthology *Possibilities* make is easy to integrate education, career, and life planning themes into an English class that still meets the Common Core State Standards.

- *Lifestyle Math* can be used in secondary math classes to enhance financial literacy and career planning while reinforcing the Common Core State Standards.

- One or both of the academic supplement texts can be used along with *Career Choices* in any course format you can imagine.

Much of the information in this section is also available via the online training videos listed below. All of these videos are accessible through The Teachers' Lounge.

- Integrating Academics and Technology
- *Possibilities*: Integrating Career Exploration into the English Classroom
- *Lifestyle Math*: An Overview
- Strategies for Integrating *Lifestyle Math* into your *Career Choices* Course
- CareerChoices.com
- Strategies for Incorporating an Online Career Exploration Tool

Integrating Academics and Technology

Learning is mostly about creating a context for motivation.
It's about why should you learn things.

— Bill Gates
"10 Questions for Bill Gates"
Time magazine, February 12, 2007

Learning in context provides the meaning and the in-depth understanding of a concept, information, or skill that an individual is required to learn. Learning in context is what bridges the gap between the abstract learning of the classroom and the practical applications outside of formal education.

When you integrate any or all of the enhancements to the *Career Choices* curriculum, you'll provide a powerful opportunity for students to learn academic skills or technological applications in context.

What was once delivered through "drill and skill" will take on new meaning when layered into a *Career Choices* course, because the information has been repackaged in the thematic format of self-discovery and personal planning.

Why it works is very simple. *Career Choices* addresses the individual reader. No matter what his or her circumstance, all young people seek the answers to common questions: Who am I? What do I want? How do I get it? By teaching self-knowledge along with reading, writing, and math, *Career Choices* adds the context that makes basic skills relevant and motivates students to learn. Students are willing to pay attention, to work harder, to stretch themselves because, suddenly, what's going on in the classroom is of urgent personal interest.

There are two optional academic textbooks:

- *Possibilities: A Supplemental Anthology for Career Choices*
- *Lifestyle Math: Your Financial Planning Portfolio*

Possibilities is an anthology with 50 literary classics: short stories, essays, speeches, poems, and plays by renowned writers like James Thurber, Maya Angelou, Langston Hughes, Pat Conroy, Emily Dickinson, O. Henry, Longfellow, and Elizabeth Barrett Browning. Discussion questions, activities, compositions, grammar, and vocabulary lessons all support a literature-based approach to English/language arts while building on the highly motivational themes of *Career Choices*. Suddenly, the classics have more relevance and interest to the adolescent reader, which increases their motivation to learn.

Lifestyle Math is a consumable workbook outlining a 100-page math problem that asks students to create a budget for the life they want when they are 29 years old. Students use real-life formulas, problems, and data to work personalized computations that cover each of the Common Core State Standards for Mathematical Practice:

1. Make sense of problems and persevere in solving them.
2. Reason abstractly and quantitatively.

3. Construct viable arguments and critique the reasoning of others.

4. Model with mathematics.

5. Use appropriate tools strategically.

6. Attend to precision.

7. Look for and make use of structure.

8. Look for and express regularity in repeated reasoning.

Because the math exercises are relevant to their lives, motivation and learning increase. For instance, once students have a figure for the cost of the future lifestyle they envision, they are asked to find a career that will support that lifestyle. Education suddenly takes on new meaning because students understand the need to apply themselves to their academic endeavors.

While *Career Choices* may, at first blush, appear to be lighthearted and fun, it is a rigorous, competency-based curriculum. In order to complete the numerous exercises and activities in the *Career Choices* textbooks, students practice reading, writing, and computation, as well as higher-order thinking skills (i.e., analysis, synthesis, and evaluation). They must also employ critical, creative, and strategic thinking.

There are also dynamic online enhancements available, including:

LifestyleMath.com
CareerChoices.com
My10yearPlan.com®

LifestyleMath.com, the online correction tool for the *Lifestyle Math* workbook, uses technology to make personalized math possible. As students develop a budget for the lifestyle designed in their *Lifestyle Math* workbooks, they can check their individual math computations using this web-based instrument. Developed to support the learner, the program identifies where and when mistakes are made, directing students to retry their calculations. This immediate feedback should increase the learning that takes place by encouraging students to use their own brainpower to correct the error rather than giving them the answer.

CareerChoices.com delivers more than 80 interactive online lessons that enhance the activities and exercises found in *Career Choices*. The links point students to carefully chosen resources that provide the information and research needed to complete activities on the corresponding pages in *Career Choices*. Detailed instructions, learning objectives, lesson plans, and extension ideas are provided for both students and teachers.

My10yearPlan.com® provides an online decision-making tool where students can store, update, and save the data related to the development of their 10-year plans. Designed to work in concert with the *Career Choices Workbook and Portfolio*, this online functionality creates the ultimate guidance tool, empowering all teachers to provide data-driven advisories and interventions that center on a student's personal dreams, goals, and plans.

One of the best things about the *Career Choices* curriculum is its flexibility. Depending on your school's goals, strategies, and student population, a variety of effective formats are possible.

The core structure is provided by *Career Choices* and the *Workbook and Portfolio*. This is a great combination for:

- Freshman Transition courses
- Career education classes
- Freshman academies
- Foundation course for a career academy or cluster

If students can get online easily in either a computer lab or your classroom, we recommend adding My10yearPlan.com® and/or CareerChoices.com.

Incorporating *Possibilities* makes a combination that's ideal for:

- A semester or year-long class in the English department
- A team teaching opportunity for the English department and school counselors, careers instructors, or the family and consumer sciences department
- Two integrated classes—a Freshman Transition class coupled with 9th-grade English

Adding *Lifestyle Math* then provides the content for:

- A semester- or year-long interdisciplinary course taught by the English, math, and social science departments
- A fully integrated academic course taught by one instructor within an academy, career pathway, or special populations program

If students can get online easily in either a computer lab or your classroom, we recommend adding the *optional* LifestyleMath.com.

By integrating these academic and technology enhancements with *Career Choices*, your team can easily provide ample content for:

- Freshman Transition courses
- Smaller learning community or interdisciplinary teaching teams
- Career academy, cluster, or pathway foundation courses
- Advisor/advisee programs
- Career and technical programs that mandate academic integration

As much as we would like students to learn for the love of learning, many young people need the motivation that comes from seeing how the subject at hand relates to the real world and to their place in it. *Career Choices* provides the spark that motivates students while allowing them to practice academic and technological applications. In addition, the 10-year plan that is created graphically illustrates the personal benefits of staying in school and offers ongoing guidance as they apply themselves to bring the plan to fruition.

Integrating Academics to Meet the Common Core State Standards with *Career Choices*

The Common Core State Standards Initiative, coordinated by the National Governors Association Center for Best Practices and the Council of Chief State School Officers, is an exciting step toward making sure students across the country leave high school prepared for college and workplace success.

By standardizing curriculum across state lines, students who relocate can more easily transition to academic life in a new school. These new standards also increase the depth with which students study certain topics, emphasize the use of more informational texts, and rely on additional cognitive skills, requiring less memorization and more analyzing.

And, above all, the Common Core State Standards are:

> ...*designed to be robust and relevant to the real world, reflecting the knowledge and skills that our young people need for success in college and careers.*[1]

An overarching goal of the *Career Choices* series has always been to motivate students to apply themselves by helping them recognize the role academic skills play in their lives outside of the classroom. You could say *Career Choices* was delivering the Common Core State Standards long before they were common.

Used with the *Possibilities* anthology and the *Instructor's Guide, Career Choices* supports the Common Core State Standards for English. You can find examples of how the *Career Choices* curriculum addresses these standards throughout Section 4, or you can download a copy of the document at **www.academicinnovations.com/standards.html** or from the online version of this *Instructor's Guide*.

As students create a detailed budget in , they encounter each of the Common Core State Standards for Mathematical Practice:

1. Make sense of problems and persevere in solving them.

2. Reason abstractly and quantitatively.

3. Construct viable arguments and critique the reasoning of others.

4. Model with mathematics.

5. Use appropriate tools strategically.

6. Attend to precision.

7. Look for and make use of structure.

8. Look for and express regularity in repeated reasoning.

---

1. Common Core State Standards Initiative mission statement. Retrieved from www.corestandards.org 01/04/2013.

You'll find comprehensive correlations for the Common Core State Standards on the online version of this *Instructor's Guide*.

College and Career Readiness Anchor Standards for Reading - Literature

Key Ideas & Details

Grade 8	Career Choices	Possibilities	Instructor's Guide	Grades 9-10	Career Choices	Possibilities	Instructor's Guide
1. Cite textual evidence that most strongly supports an analysis of what the text says explicitly, as well as inferences drawn from the text.		pp. 21-23, 38-39, 41-42, 66-68, 110, 125, 173-177, 208-211, 250-251	pp. 2/10-2/14	1. Cite strong and thorough textual evidence to support analysis of what the text says explicitly as well as inferences drawn from the text.		pp. 21-23, 38-39, 41-42, 66-68, 110, 125, 173-177, 208-211, 250-251	pp. 2/10-2/14
2. Determine a theme or central idea of a text and analyze its development over the course of the text; including its relationship to characters, setting and plot; provide an objective summary of the text.		pp. 54-56, 79, 84-86, 93-94, 101, 160-162, 208-211, 238-239, 260-261, 268-269, 271-272, 274-275	pp. 2/10-2/14	2. Determine a theme or central idea of a text and analyze in detail its development over the course of the text; including how it emerges and is shaped and refined by specific details; provide an objective summary of the text.		pp. 54-56, 88-89, 160-162, 208-211, 215	pp. 2/10-2/14
3. Analyze how particular elements of dialogue or incidents in a story or drama propel the action, reveal aspects of a character, or provoke a decision.	Practiced throughout text	pp. 17-18, 54-56, 84-86, 136-138, 208-211, 268-269, 274-275	pp. 2/10-2/14	3. Analyze how complex characters (e.g., those with multiple or conflicting motivations) develop over the course of a text, interact with other characters and advance the plot or develop the theme.		pp. 54-56, 79, 84-86, 93-94, 101, 160-162, 208-211, 238-239, 260-261, 268-269, 271-272, 274-275	pp. 2/10-2/14

Craft & Structure

Grade 8	Career Choices	Possibilities	Instructor's Guide	Grades 9-10	Career Choices	Possibilities	Instructor's Guide
4. Determine the meaning of words and phrases as they are used in a text, including figurative and connotative meanings; analyze the impact of a specific word choice on meaning and tone, including analogies or allusions to other texts.		pp. 21-23, 25-26, 29-32, 41-42, 58-60, 62-63, 88-89, 125, 136-138, 140, 160-162, 173-177, 213, 219-220, 224, 246-247, 250-251, 278-283	pp. 2/10-2/14	4. Determine the meaning of words and phrases as they are used in a text, including figurative and connotative meanings; analyze the cumulative impact of specific word choices on meaning and tone.		pp. 21-23, 25-26, 29-32, 41-42, 58-60, 62-63, 88-89, 125, 136-138, 140, 160-162, 173-177, 213, 219-220, 224, 246-247, 250-251, 278-283	pp. 2/10-2/14
5. Compare and contrast the structure of two or more texts and analyze how the differing structure of each text contributes to its meaning and style.	Integration of *Career Choices* with *Possibilities*	Follow-up questions throughout text	pp. 2/10-2/14	5. Analyze how an authors choices concerning how to structure a text, order events within it (e.g., parallel plots) and manipulate time (e.g., pacing, flashbacks) create such effects as mystery, tension or surprise.		pp. 11-18, 47-56, 80-86, 87-89, 95-102, 127-138, 142-163, 178-211, 228-239, 254-261	pp. 2/10-2/14

Supporting the Common Core

Why should you make the effort to incorporate these acedemic and technology pieces in your coursework?

Because the Common Core focuses on the application of knowledge in authentic situations, teachers will need to employ instructional strategies that integrate critical and creative thinking, collaboration, problem-solving, research and inquiry, and presentation and demonstration skills.

— *Education Week*, January 2012

The personal planning process required to effectively plan for their future by factoring the costs of the lifestyle they envision is one of the most complex "problems" adolescents and young adults face. Integrating technology with these activities provides an excellent platform for supporting the Common Core State Standards.

As they research, write, and calculate, students are actively engaged in critical, creative, and strategic thinking challenges related to a topic of utmost importance: their future happiness. These lessons offer a variety of opportunities for collaboration, communication, and authentic assessment of their findings and plans.

Using the optional LifestyleMath.com and CareerChoices.com will contribute a valuable new dimension to your course—effective use of technology in the classroom. Many researchers and experts agree that effective use of technology in the classroom is a critical element in preparing students for the information age. Turning a computer on isn't enough. Integrated activities need to focus on three things: content, critical thinking, and computer skills.

The project-based learning experience outlined on page 11/18 provides content and critical thinking. If you utilize LifestyleMath.com to check calculations, you enhance computer skills as students build their math competency. Adding CareerChoices.com addresses all three components again. Better yet, it exposes students to the types of real-world tools and calculators they can use online throughout their lives—even once they leave your campus.

Two high tech classroom ideas from teacher Cathie Klein of Topeka, Kansas, that support the Common Core

A Modern-day Collage: After students have completed their Bull's Eye chart, have students create a digital Voice Thread of each section. Those are then emailed to the instructor and shared. This is an opportunity for students to see commonalities and differences. Students could share in small group setting (perhaps groups of 4) then rotate, or in a video presentation format where each VT pops up and moves to the next. You'll need computers or iPads using the app Voice Thread. Students will need to share with their instructor, but not public usage. They are short, quick, and students love the technology.

QR Code Activity: This can be part of their research required to meet a number of the Common Core Standards. Students create a QR Code for three schools which have a program of study in their researched Career Interest Survey (pages 150 to 155 of Career Choices). We then take time and have each student present their three careers using their QR Code program of study as the backdrop of the presentation. This activity will require computers using a QR Code Generator web site—an iPad or iTouch appcan scan to reveal the code.

Possibilities: Integrating Relevant Themes into the English Language Arts Classroom

The work for building a thematic course that combines literature with directed reading and writing opportunities has been done for you. An in-depth cross-reference, found on pages 8/11 to 8/14, will help you decide when to incorporate the works found in *Possibilities* with the corresponding activities and exercises in *Career Choices*.

Possibilities employs an "into, through, and beyond" format to help students relate what they read in the text to their own lives. The "into" activity for each piece is a journaling prompt that gets students thinking about what they'll be reading about in a personalized way. The journal entry questions can also be used for brainstorming as a class.

After reading "through" the assigned material, students go "beyond" the piece with questions and activities that help them uncover the meaning of the work and explore topics standard in most English/language arts courses. Students apply the information, themes, and advice from the stories to their lives in an affective manner.

Here's how *Career Choices* and *Possibilities* create synergism.

The first short story in *Possibilities* is "The Secret Life of Walter Mitty" by James Thurber. This brief tale portrays a middle-aged man who daydreams his way through the mundane tasks of his life. Walter's imagination may whisk him to the middle of a courtroom drama or a harrowing battle where the guns rage around him. It's clear that Walter Mitty wants to be anyone but himself.

Before reading the story, students are asked to write a journal entry about their own daydreams. After the story, a series of questions take students through multiple tasks. They're put in the shoes of the story's characters and asked critique their choices. The end result: increased awareness of the importance of choosing a career and life that will lead to personal happiness.

Take a look at page 17 of *Possibilities* and see how the questions after "The Secret Life of Walter Mitty" relate to and reinforce the material in *Career Choices*.

Questions 1 to 4 focus on comprehension and interpretation of the components of the story, questions that are common to basal English texts.

Question 6 asks students to imagine what one minute on the job in a chosen industry might be like. They're asked to write a dialogue between people working in the ideal environment they've chosen, much like how Walter Mitty dreams up a conference between a doctor version of himself and a cadre of other esteemed physicians. Doing this gives students permission to fantasize about a role to which they aspire, an important first step in career exploration. They are creating—with words—a "vision" of what their future might be like.

Question 7 refers students to the Envisioning Your Future activity on page 14 of *Career Choices*. They are directed to use the dialogue they created for Question 6 as a prompt to imagine their ideal careers. This helps students visualize, perhaps for the first time, a career they might find interesting. It stretches their imagination, something necessary not only for great writing, but also for career and life planning.

Question 9 asks students to review the text of the story and outline the different career roles Walter Mitty imagined for himself. Military officer. Marksman. Physician to America's rich and famous. These are the kinds of roles Walter pines for but doesn't have. Students are asked to imagine Mitty as a teenager and to think through what he could have done at school and at work to work toward a career he desires. Students then complete a chart for him like the one found on page 13 of *Career Choices*. This is the first of many times throughout the course that they'll be asked to project into the future and understand the consequences of choices made as a young person.

As you review the activities and questions at the end of each work, you'll see the progressive use of higher order thinking skills, such as analysis, synthesis, and creativity. While the culmination of the *Career Choices* text is the development of the students' 10-year plan, the final project in *Possibilities* is developed around Linda Pastan's poem "25ᵗʰ High School Reunion." In this class-wide project, students "form" their own publishing company to produce a high school reunion booklet filled with idealized stories outlining the lives they hope to live.

This writing project reinforces all they've learned and, more important, gives them an opportunity to continue to articulate a vision of a productive future.

Your class may decide to put this booklet in a time capsule to open at their 25ᵗʰ reunion, or you may suggest they keep a copy of their essay in a special place and review it annually.

You may be asking yourself how you can integrate this material into our English program.

Consider using *Career Choices* and *Possibilities* as a semester- or year-long thematically-driven class in the English department. Because of the high level of interest a course with this theme engenders, student motivation increases and performance on reading and writing assignments improves.

Teachers who use these books in their English/language arts classes tell us they're grateful to see students excited about and responding to literature for, perhaps, the first time in their lives.

It's also possible to use the two books for a team teaching opportunity involving an English teacher and an instructor from another discipline teaching the same students in two separate classes. For example, English teachers may join forces with technology instructors, Freshman Transition teachers, family and consumer sciences teachers, business educators, or school counselors, to name a few.

The reading of [Possibilities] was enjoyed by even the most difficult-to-engage students.

— Ellen Kamau, English Teacher
Waiakea High School, Hilo, HI

I found these materials adaptable to both my gifted and talented students and to my non-motivated students.

— Kathryn T. Harcum, English Chairperson
North Caroline High School, Ridgely, MD

[Possibilities] is a most helpful approach to teaching "required" literature…The questions at the end of each selection were thought-provoking and stimulated the students to think critically.

— Stacy Raley, Language Arts Teacher
Louisville High School, Louisville, GA

I loved the journal entries [in Possibilities] because they were theme-oriented/values-oriented rather than literary-oriented, and we English teachers need a different approach at times.

— Stacy Raley, English Teacher,
9ᵗʰ & 10ᵗʰ grade Drop-Out/At-Risk Program
Louisville High School, Louisville, GA

You'll find a comprehensive case study of how one school integrated the *Career Choices* curriculum into their English courses on the online version of this *Instructor's Guide*.

How to Integrate Career Development into the English Classroom

Ohio District Adopts *Career Choices* in Multiple Schools

" I could have been talking to the wall,"

said Career Coordinator Liz Lamatrice, referring to her early efforts to infuse a careers theme into the academic curriculum of high schools in Jefferson County, Ohio. "Because, until teachers see it for themselves, they don't believe it."

And that is exactly what happened in the Jefferson County Joint Vocational District—a model careers program spread from school to school as a pair of English teachers taught their colleagues how to develop lessons and deliver the new subject to 1,500 students in their academic classes.

Download the complete 11-page profile of this successful program at
www.academicinnovations.com/library/howtoeng.pdf

Career Choices / Possibilities
Cross-reference

The following cross-reference guide is designed to assist you in deciding when in your *Career Choices* process to incorporate the stories, poems, essays, plays, or speeches found in *Possibilities*.

Career Choices is a sequential curriculum. This outline assumes you are working through the *Career Choices* textbook from beginning to end in the order presented.

Work in *Possibilities*	*Career Choices* Chapter 1: Envisioning Your Future
"The Secret Life of Walter Mitty" (page 11)	Read after reading pages 10–13 in *Career Choices*
"Psalm of Life" (page 19)	Read after completing page 14 in *Career Choices*
"Dreams" (page 24)	
"I Have a Dream…" speech by Martin Luther King, Jr. (page 27)	
"Work," an excerpt from *The Prophet* (page 33)	Read after completing pages 15–17 in *Career Choices*
"Richard Cory" (page 37)	Read after completing pages 18–21 in *Career Choices*

Work in *Possibilities*	*Career Choices* Chapter 2: Your Personal Profile
"Sonnet 43" from *Sonnets from the Portuguese* (page 40)	Read after completing pages 18–21 in *Career Choices*
Excerpt from *Alice in Wonderland* (page 43)	Read after completing pages 28–45 in *Career Choices*
Excerpt from *I Know Why the Caged Bird Sings* (page 47)	Read after completing pages 28–49 in *Career Choices*
"Sympathy" (page 57)	
"Life" (page 61)	Read after completing page 52 in *Career Choices*
Excerpt from *Self-Reliance* (page 64)	Read after completing page 53 in *Career Choices*

Work in *Possibilities*	*Career Choices* Chapter 3: Lifestyles of the Satisfied and Happy
"Growing Older" (page 69)	Read to introduce the "Looking into the Future" exercise on page 4/41 of this *Instructor's Guide*
"I Shall Not Pass This Way Again" (page 72)	Read after completing pages 60–61 in *Career Choices*
"Red Geraniums" (page 74)	Read after completing pages 66–69 in *Career Choices*

Work in *Possibilities*	*Career Choices* Chapter 4: What Cost This Lifestyle?
"The Mills of the Gods" (page 76)	Read after Ivy Elms's story on pages 74–75 in *Career Choices*
"The Savings Book" (page 80)	Read after completing page 103 in *Career Choices*
"Miss Rosie" (page 87)	
"Christmas Day in the Workhouse" (page 90)	
"The Gift of the Magi" (page 95)	Read before assigning Money Isn't Everything on pages 104–105 in *Career Choices*
"A Legacy for My Daughter" (page 103)	Read after completing pages 114–121 in *Career Choices*

Work in *Possibilities*	*Career Choices* Chapter 5: Your Ideal Career
"I Decline to Accept the End of Man" (page 108)	Read after completing Chapter 5 in *Career Choices*

Work in *Possibilities*	*Career Choices* Chapter 6: Career Research
"The Boys' Ambition" from *Life on the Mississippi* (page 112)	Read after completing page 146 in *Career Choices*
"Lego" article from *The New Yorker* Magazine (page 118)	Read after completing page 147 in *Career Choices*
"I Hear America Singing" (page 124)	Read after completing page 165 in *Career Choices*

Work in *Possibilities*	*Career Choices* **Chapter 7: Decision Making**
"The Monkey's Paw" (page 127)	Read after completing pages 168–174 in *Career Choices*
"The Road Not Taken" (page 139)	Read after completing page 139 in *Career Choices*s
"To Build a Fire" (page 142)	Read after completing page 179 in *Career Choices*

Work in *Possibilities*	*Career Choices* *Chapter 8: Goal Setting*
"Uphill" (page 164)	Read before beginning Chapter 8 in *Career Choices*
"The Myth of Sisyphus" (page 166)	Read after completing pages 182–185 in *Career Choices*
Excerpt from *The Prince of Tides* (page 178)	Read after completing pages 182–191 in *Career Choices*

Work in *Possibilities*	Career Choices **Chapter 9: Avoiding Detours and Roadblocks**
"Hope" (page 172)	Read after completing pages 194–199 in *Career Choices*
"A Dream Deferred" (page 212)	Read after completing pages 214–215 in *Career Choices*
"Mother to Son" (page 214)	Read after completing pages 196–197 in *Career Choices*
"A Noiseless Patient Spider" (page 216)	Read after completing pages 216–217 in *Career Choices*
Excerpt from *All I Really Need to Know I Learned in Kindergarten* (page 216)	
"Over the Hill to the Poor-House" (page 221)	Read after completing pages 208–209 in *Career Choices*
"George Gray" (page 225)	Read after completing pages 216–221 in *Career Choices*

They showed me how much they really know and that they are further ahead than we usually give them credit for.

— Jose E. "Tito" Chavez, English Department Chair
West Las Vegas High School, Las Vegas, NM

Work in *Possibilities*	*Career Choices* Chapter 10: Attitude is Everything
"The Necklace" (page 228)	Read after completing page 228 in *Career Choices*
"Tonia the Tree" (page 240)	Read after completing pages 242–245 in *Career Choices*
"To Be of Use" (page 249)	Read after completing pages 238–241 in *Career Choices*
"Be the Best of Whatever You Are" (page 252)	Read after completing page 246 in *Career Choices*

Work in *Possibilities*	*Career Choices* Chapter 11: Getting Experience
"Looking for Work" (page 254)	Read after completing pages 250–259 in *Career Choices*
"The Bridge Builder" (page 262)	Read after completing pages 262–263 in *Career Choices*
"Thank You, M'am" (page 264)	

Work in *Possibilities*	*Career Choices* Chapter 12: Where Do You Go from Here?
"If" (page 270)	Read after completing pages 270–273 in *Career Choices*
"Ex-Basketball Player" (page 273)	Read before beginning to work on Your Plan on pages 279–280 in *Career Choices*
"25th High School Reunion" (page 277)	Read after completing Your Plan on pages 279–280 in *Career Choices*

I feel the usage of these materials helped my students to see the relevance of English to their lives and helped them formulate a more mature career plan. These materials, I think, have also caused them to be more conscious of the quality of their assignments and the importance of doing well in school.

— Amy S. Heaton, Applied Communications/Creative Writing Teacher
Horn Lake High School, Horn Lake, MS

Lifestyle Math: Real World Math Integration

As you design your course, you'll want to decide how and where you are going to incorporate *Lifestyle Math* and LifestyleMath.com.

Where to Incorporate Lifestyle Math

Lifestyle Math is most commonly used as a supplementary module in a math course or as an interdisciplinary unit within a *Career Choices* class.

While you may look to the math department for support, this part of the *Career Choices* curriculum can be taught by any enthusiastic instructor who has good math skills and enjoys personal finance. Many programs incorporate *Lifestyle Math* into their year-long *Career Choices* course. For a detailed example, see the preview of the 145-hour lesson plan pacing guide beginning on page 10/9 of this *Instructor's Guide*, or visit The Teachers' Lounge Resource Cupboard and click on the Lesson and Pacing Guide link. If you need more information than what's provided in this section of the *Instructor's Guide*, contact the Curriculum and Technical Support team at Academic Innovations at (800) 967-8016 for additional suggestions on integrating *Lifestyle Math* into your *Career Choices* course.

If you are working with an interdisciplinary team or in an academy setting, the math instructor on your team could infuse *Lifestyle Math* into their lesson plans. For a sample interdisciplinary lesson plan pacing guide, visit The Teachers' Lounge.

If your math department chooses to use *Lifestyle Math* as a supplemental activity to support your *Career Choices* course, students at all math levels will benefit.

For pre-algebra students, the review of basic math skills will be valuable, as will the application of math concepts related to their daily lives. This project-based math activity can be incorporated into the school year over 20 to 40 sessions.

For algebra or higher-level students, launch your course with *Lifestyle Math* to expose students to a variety of ways math is used in daily life. This one activity will help increase their motivation to work harder in their traditional math course as the important role math will play in making life choices will become abundantly clear to them.

You may use *Lifestyle Math* as an incentive, allowing time for students to work on their budgets once they finish other work. Students with solid basic math skills will view this project as a reward.

For high-achieving students, you may provide *Lifestyle Math* as an independent study project. Students could come together periodically to share their insights and figures. Encourage these students to focus on STEM (science, technology, engineering, and math) careers, pointing out how these careers usually pay salaries that allow for more choices in lifestyle.

If working with instructors from another department, you'll want to share information about student progress, detailing what is giving them trouble or what topics are most appealing to them.

As you thumb through your *Lifestyle Math* workbook, you'll see a variety of energizers, project-based activities, and group brainstorming problems. These activities provide opportunities to differentiate instruction for students with a variety of learning styles. And, because these problems and case studies relate to their own personal issues, the activities effectively demonstrate how numeracy, financial literacy, and solid math skills can be used to craft a life of their choosing.

Turn to the What is Your Math Education Worth to You? activity on page 98 of *Lifestyle Math* for a good example of how you can use this workbook to change students' attitudes about math, even if they are reluctant learners.

Integrating Technology

Get Focused...Stay Focused! ™ *Curriculum Modules*

Take a look at the *Get Focused...Stay Focused!* ™ curriculum modules for the 10th, 11th, and 12th grades. Most of the class sessions are done online, using the U.S. Department of Labor's O*NET Online web site. Working with Academic Innovations, *Get Focused...Stay Focused!* ™ Initiative developed these follow-up lessons to ensure that students graduate from high school with an updated, online 10-year plan and arrive at college with an informed, declared major, a career path, and an outline of the coursework required to meet their career goals. For details, review the chart on page 4/170 of this guide.

Helping students learn to use these no-cost, public web sites is an important life lesson and skill set. Then, when students leave your school, they'll still have easy access to resources they'll benefit from throughout their lives.

LifestyleMath.com and CareerChoices.com are two *optional* Internet-based tools that you may find valuable. Even if you don't have Internet access in your classroom, you'll want to seriously consider incorporating these tools if students can get access at home, at the library, or in a computer lab at school.

CareerChoices.com

For students to really embrace their budgets as real and believable, you'll want them to research options related to their choices so the data is really their own. CareerChoices.com can help.

Throughout the *Lifestyle Math* workbook, you'll find a logo indicating that there are resources or calculators available at CareerChoices.com. These online activities will help students find current costs related to their choices so they can determine their best course of action.

If you've adopted *Lifestyle Math* and don't have a school ID and password for either LifestyleMath.com or CareerChoices.com, contact Academic Innovations for a temporary one so you can determine if these are resources you can use. Depending on your order size, you may even qualify for a free site license.

LifestyleMath.com: The Online Correction Tool for Lifestyle Math

Traditionally, math textbooks have been designed with one static answer for each problem. This allowed instructors to check student work easily using an answer key, but limited math to answering "someone else's" problem. Not very interesting for the average student.

Lifestyle Math personalizes mathematics by allowing students to dictate the variables used in their own calculations, giving the work they are doing more personal meaning. LifestyleMath.com makes correcting that work quick and easy, sparing teachers the sizable task of poring over each student's unique calculations and answers.

Here's an example. One student in your class may choose a home in another part of the country for $280,000, while another may choose to purchase a two-bedroom condo near their hometown for $185,000. Each student's math calculations and answers relating to the mortgage payments, interest, and utilities will be very different. The LifestyleMath.com online correction tool delivers a straightforward and simple way to check answers at school or at home, anywhere there is an Internet connection.

LifestyleMath.com is easy and intuitive.

Here's how it works!

Students begin by working through a mathematical problem in their workbook the old fashioned way, with pencil, paper, and their own brainpower.

Once students factor each budget line item, they can go online to **www.lifestylemath.com** and login using your school's access information.

They'll choose the page they want to correct from the listing to access an online worksheet that looks like the page in their workbook.

Students enter their own calculations in the appropriate fields and click "Check Answers!" The computer program reviews their work, notes any incorrect figures or incomplete information, and highlights it.

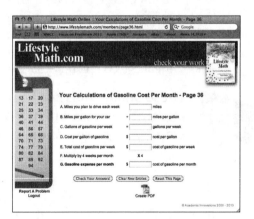

If the program finds inaccuracies, students can rework their mathematical calculations, go back online, and enter their amended figures. Once they successfully complete the assignment and all calculations are correct, they can print out their work and turn it in to their instructor for credit.

You'll find even reluctant math students are eager to pursue the correct answer because the final product—their budget—has meaning to them. What was once drill and drudgery will be attacked with newfound enthusiasm and curiosity. Students receive instant feedback on whether their mathematical calculations are correct. The end result of all this is confident students with increased career goals and, therefore, increased educational aspirations!

Strategies for Incorporating an Online Career Exploration Tool with the *Career Choices* Curriculum and My10yearPlan.com®

If your school has access to a commercial or state-sponsored online career exploration tool that provides digital surveys and post-secondary planning resources, this can enhance your ***Career Choices*** course when used strategically.

Most government-sponsored online surveys and career assessments were originally designed for adults. Without the necessary experience, awareness, understanding, and skills, they have little meaning for the average 13- or 14-year-old. For these digital prompts to have real meaning for most early adolescents, you need to take the time to prepare them for the experience.

Before students make education and career choices, it is important that they consider how the choice and the probable consequences of the choice relate to their vision of the future—how it correlates with who they are, what they want, and how they can get it. This formula for success is as important to learn as any quadratic equation or scientific theory they'll encounter in their academic courses.

You'll want to expose your students to this self-discovery process **before** using the short cuts available through online career exploration tools and surveys. Placing students behind a computer and assuming they are going to successfully make the second most important decision of their lives after a few hours of taking surveys and getting lists of appropriate careers could be naïve.

These online tools may be adequate for a small percentage of your students, those who are going to succeed in college no matter what you do. But far too many students lack the life experience, the family support, or the maturity level required to make these sophisticated decisions. Relying on online tools for these students runs the risk of not capturing their attention with this important information and will not have the desired outcome of dropout prevention, whether it is high school or college completion you seek.

 These online tools can be used effectively if you consider the 5-step strategy for integrating them with the personalized format of *Career Choices*. You'll find this step-by-step process on the online version of this *Instructor's Guide*.

In summary, online tools are good but it is important to be strategic about where and when to use them, particularly with early adolescents. When asked in a *Time* magazine interview if **there is better learning through technology, Bill Gates responded:**

> *It's important to be humble when we talk about education. Because TV was going to change education and videotape was going to change it and computer-aided instruction was going to change it. But until the internet exploded 10 years ago, technology really hadn't made a dent in education at all. Learning is mostly about creating a context for motivation. It's about why should you learn things. Technology plays a role, but it's not a panacea.*

Section 9

My10yearPlan.com®

Topics covered in this section include:

- What My10yearPlan.com® is and how it works.

- How having students write their initial responses in the *Workbook and Portfolio* before entering their answers into My10yearPlan.com® encourages contemplation, improves the online experience, and more.

- My10yearPlan Essentials or My10yearPlan Interactive—deciding which version is best for your class.

- Responses students input from the *Workbook and Portfolio* are used to populate documents that students can share to demonstrate their strengths, interests, achievements, and career aspirations.

- Along the way, the My10yearPlan.com® system prompts students to review answers to past activities, reinforcing the decision-making process.

- Unlike other online career planning tools, My10yearPlan.com® gives students a process for considering all aspects of a potential career and for making informed career and lifestyle decisions.

- When all instructors and counselors are trained in the use of My10yearPlan.com®, they can use students' personal education and career goals to advise and motivate them.

- Easy steps for setting up student and teacher accounts in My10yearPlan.com®.

Introduction to My10yearPlan.com®

Personalization has been shown to be one of the most successful reform efforts in high schools today.

How can we personalize the high school experience for students and, at the same time, help them develop a vision of a productive and attainable future? How can we, their teachers, act as advisors and use their dreams and plans to motivate them to academic and personal success?

My10yearPlan.com® provides an online planning area where students can store, update, and save—for as long as they are in school—the work and data related to the development of their 10-year plans.

It starts with *Career Choices* and the *Workbook and Portfolio*. Students work through the books in a sequential format, gathering the data and understanding required for their comprehensive and meaningful 10-year plan. Once students have completed the activities and exercises in their *Career Choices Workbook and Portfolio*, they are ready to access their own password-protected My10yearPlan.com® account and enter the information they've collected about themselves. This can be done in a school computer lab, in the library, or at home.

From their My10yearPlan.com® home page, students can easily navigate to the activity page or *My 10-year Plan Summary Page*. This is a snapshot of the data they've created throughout the course. This summary page is the key to personalized instruction and advisory options. This is where teachers and counselors can get a quick overview of a student's goals, plans, and dreams.

Online Advisory Tool

Once students enter all their data online and their 10-year plans are complete, every teacher and administrator with a school-issued My10yearPlan.com® account can access this important data from their computer. Information that once would've required 20–30 minutes of reading through a student's completed *Workbook and Portfolio* is now available in seconds. Any teacher, counselor, or administrator with a school-issued My10yearPlan.com® account can gain a thorough understanding of a student's goals and ambitions by quickly reviewing the summary page.

This is particularly valuable in advisory and counseling situations. Now at the beginning of each grading period teachers can quickly peruse students' plans. Then, if academic efforts don't correlate with career choice or lifestyle vision, this reality can be pointed out to the student in a caring conversation. Students who have completed a *Career Choices* course understand the lifelong consequences of not applying themselves to their studies and will correct the behavior.

Archives to Assess Growth

My10yearPlan.com® archives each version of an activity. Students and teachers can refer back to any project they may have modified during their time in high school, providing an historical record of their growth and changes over this important developmental time.

Any archived activity is only a mouse click away. This function allows students to see and analyze their progress. For example, a 12th-grade English teacher could ask her students to compare the most recent data in their 10-year plans to the original information they entered as freshmen. The resulting essay exploring how their plans changed and the factors that influenced those changes could be a powerful affirmation of their growth.

Financial Planning Increases Educational Impact

My10yearPlan.com® includes a sophisticated budget calculator that corresponds to the budget exercise found in Chapter 4 of *Career Choices*. This tool makes it possible for students to explore a wide range of financial scenarios during their time in high school. This is especially effective as students determine the amount of effort they want to put into preparing for a career because it will soon become apparent to the graduate of the *Career Choices* program that salaries usually match educational commitment. The more you learn, the more you earn.

Career Portfolio—A Life-Long Habit

My10yearPlan.com® supports the development of a career portfolio. This important life-long process can be helpful when preparing for college, scholarship, or workplace interviews. Individuals who get into the habit of updating their portfolios on a regular basis are more aware of how necessary it is to keep their skills current and to acquire new skills for success in the 21st century workplace.

The *My 10-year Plan and Portfolio Report* feature in My10yearPlan.com® is a multi-page narrative that provides a detailed picture of the student and his or her plans. This personalized in-depth report is a collection of all the work the students entered online. As information in the activities is updated, revised, or polished, this dynamic report is seamlessly revised at the same time. An authentic assessment that can be graded as the final project, it provides a wonderful foundation on which students can create a professional-looking career portfolio.

A Place for Everything: Staying Organized with My Portfolio

Students can upload up to 1 MB of documents to the My Portfolio area of My10yearPlan.com®. This gives them a consistent place to store things like resumes, letters of recommendation, projects, and any writing samples that students may need for job interviews or post-secondary applications.

Internet-Based Planning Tools Support Successful Decision-Making

Students also have access to a number of career and college-prep web sites by clicking on the Internet Resources link in the side navigation.

The Internet is rich with free government and business web sites that support this process. Using this function, your students can access some of the best online resources available today. And when they leave school and begin to navigate the global workplace, they'll still have access to these powerful tools.

It's easy to see what students stand to gain from My10yearPlan.com®.

- With online access at school or at home, students are able to update their personal plans throughout high school. With their goals and dreams available online, every teacher and administrator is then able to access this important data and provide the highest level of personalized advisory support.
- Students begin to understand the need for ongoing planning, developing career portfolios, and using online planning and research tools to maximize their efforts.
- Your students' meaningful and personalized 10-year plans help them through their decade of transition—from high school through college or post-secondary training and into a productive self-sufficient adulthood.

This is the gold standard of personalization. This is comprehensive guidance at its best.

My10yearPlan.com®: Different from Other Online Career Exploration Tools

Most online career exploration tools provide a series of questions and then suggest various careers based on the user's answers. Such questionnaires invariably fail to account for *all* aspects of choosing a career, including personal strengths, work environment preferences, and desired lifestyle.

More important, they also fail to educate students on the process for achieving a career goal through proactive planning. Learning you should be a carpenter or an engineer is one thing; it's an entirely different thing to develop a plan and manage your life as you pursue the education and training necessary to become a carpenter or an engineer.

To develop the intrinsic motivation and follow-through necessary to prepare for most careers, the career exploration process must be based on each learner's personal vision of their future. For most of your students, a couple hours with computerized inventories is just not enough to set them on the path to making the second most important decision of their lives: how they'll spend 40 hours per week for the next 40 years.

In addition, it is important that *all* students have the skills and information necessary to change direction when they choose to—or are forced to. Rather than relying on lab-based software that is unavailable once they graduate, help them use *Career Choices's* self-discovery and planning process, the U.S. Department of Labor's real-world research tools, and My10yearPlan.com®'s decision-making coaches. With the confidence to plot their own productive work-life course and the skills to manage their own education plan and career trajectory, students won't have to rely on survey-based tools that "magically" assign a career choice or direction.

My10yearPlan.com® was built on the premise that educational technology can be a powerful catalyst for growth, but not when it supersedes a student's own brainpower. This is especially true when the task is as individual as plotting the course for their own unique future.

The Dynamic Documents Created by My10yearPlan.com®

Once students enter their answers from the *Career Choices Workbook and Portfolio* activities into My10yearPlan.com®, the following documents are seamlessly populated.

For both the Essentials and Interactive versions:

The *My 10-year Plan Summary Page* provides a snapshot of the student's dreams, goals, and plans. This overview of who the student is, what he or she wants, and how he or she plans to go about getting it is designed to be used in advisory and academic coaching settings. Anyone reviewing the *My 10-year Plan Summary Page* will quickly gain an understanding of the student so their advising and support efforts can be personalized. See pages 9/2 and 9/6 for details.

The *My 10-year Plan and Portfolio Report* feature in My10yearPlan.com® is a multi-page narrative that provides a detailed picture of the student and his or her plans. This personalized in-depth report is a collection of all the work the students entered online. As information in the activities is updated, revised, or polished, this dynamic report is seamlessly revised at the same time. An authentic assessment that can be graded as the final project, it provides a wonderful foundation on which students can create a professional-looking career portfolio. (Note: an abbreviated version of the report is created in My10yearPlan Essentials.)

For the Interactive version only:

My Skills Inventory provides a technological solution for maintaining an inventory of the skills students have identified as those they have and those they want to acquire. Skills can be sorted and selected based on the career paths they've identified and researched.

My Education Plan is developed from *My Skills Inventory* entries students identify as those skills they need to acquire. As students explore a chosen career path and the skills they need to cultivate become apparent, this feature helps students build an appropriate education plan.

These four dynamic documents help students easily share their plans with advisors, counselors, instructors, family, friends, and mentors. In the event that academic effort and plans don't correlate with vocation choice or lifestyle vision, supporters can more readily identify discrepancies, point out related realities, and aid in developing strategies to correct deficiencies. Students who complete a *Career Choices* course using My10yearPlan.com® understand the life-long consequences of not applying themselves to their studies and will be open to this feedback.

In addition, because the 10-year plan is online, students can update it as they learn more about themselves and the world, and their vision of the future grows. The careers they choose in the first iterations of their 10-year plan are meant for the duration of the course, **not necessarily for the rest of their lives. Most people will change careers five to seven times. As students discover careers that hold even more interest, they'll be able to easily revise their plans just by going online and revisiting some of the key activities.**

My10yearPlan.com® and the School-wide Initiative

You'll want to instruct every teacher, counselor, and administrator in your school on the use of My10yearPlan.com®. That way, staff will be better equipped to:

- Advise students on their best educational path
- Provide support when academic effort doesn't match lifestyle aspirations
- Help students update their education and career plans throughout high school
- Keep at-risk students from dropping out of school

Here's how My10yearPlan.com® can help your faculty maximize their opportunities to provide personalized student support:

- ✓ *Identifying the Problem*—Marcus is failing algebra II. While meeting with him, his advisor, Ms. Hernandez, logs into My10yearPlan.com® and, in five minutes or less, reviews his *My 10-year Plan Summary Page*. She discovers that Marcus wants to be a high school teacher and baseball coach.

- ✓ *Motivation for Academic Achievement*—Ms. Hernandez meets with Marcus and mentions that she's reviewed his goals and dreams, and she sees a problem if he doesn't pass algebra II. It's required for a four-year college degree, which is required to become a teacher.

- ✓ *Understanding the Consequences*—After highlighting the discrepancy, she suggests strategies for getting him back on track. When Marcus resists, Ms. Hernandez suggests that he rewrite his 10-year plan, revising his aspirations to match his effort. Because Marcus has completed a ***Career Choices*** course, he fully understands the consequences of that action and is far more likely to buckle down and do the work required to pass algebra II.

- ✓ *The Gold Standard of Personalization*—When approached in this manner, education takes on new meaning for even the most ambivalent students. Putting this tool in the hands of all instructors and providing staff development so they are confident in its use is a giant leap in personalization. When advice, counseling, and academic support is provided in the context of a student's concrete hopes, dreams, and lifestyle goals, real personalization is possible.

My10yearPlan.com® Essentials or Interactive?

The cornerstone of the *Career Choices* experience is the development of a 10-year education, career, and life plan. My10yearPlan.com® provides an online planning area where the learner can enter the personal information from their *Career Choices Workbook and Portfolio*, making it easy to store and update the data related to the development of their 10-year plan.

An optional enhancement to the planning process, My10yearPlan.com® has two different levels of online student access: My10yearPlan Essentials and My10yearPlan Interactive.

My10yearPlan Essentials

 The My10yearPlan.com® logo seen throughout *Career Choices* identifies the activities that provide the data **essential** to the development of an online 10-year plan and portfolio.

Once the learner inputs the information completed in *Career Choices*, the My10yearPlan.com® system uses it to populate the *My 10-year Plan Summary Page*. This overview provides a snapshot of the key goals and plans the learner has set for their education, finances, and lifestyle choices over the next decade. This easily accessible document is valuable for advisors and teachers as they personalize their work with each student.

By putting these essential artifacts from the planning process online, the learner also has the core pieces of their 10-year plan in a digital format that can streamline the process of compiling, editing, and producing a career portfolio.

My10yearPlan Interactive

The level of access available with My10yearPlan Interactive takes the digital planning experience a step further by providing an online home for all 98 of the activities in *Career Choices*. Each step of the learner's own unique self-discovery, decision-making, and personal planning process is outlined in My10yearPlan Interactive, so they have a complete, mobile record of who they are, what they want, and how they plan to get it.

While much of My10yearPlan Interactive mirrors the activities from *Career Choices*, the learner will also encounter some enhancements. These functions within the My10yearPlan.com® system coach and prompt the learner through a contemplative process while providing a forum for practicing critical and strategic thinking skills.

Functions and Features of My10yearPlan.com® Essentials vs. Interactive

	Essentials	Interactive
My 10-year Plan Summary Page	✓	✓
10-year Plan Summary Page access can be granted to appropriate support or instructional personnel (password required)	✓	✓
Can print results from completed activities	✓	✓
Revisions to activities are saved in Archives so the learner can review the growth they've achieved	✓	✓
Supports a hardcopy portfolio process	✓	✓
Pre-/post-survey assessment tool	✓	✓
Checks computations for accuracy and alerts learners to errors so they can be reviewed, re-worked, and corrected	✓	✓
Includes Chapter Checkpoint self-assessments to gauge student progress	✓	✓
School can add customized links to approved Internet resources	✓	✓
Provides My Portfolio area for storing resumes, awards, work samples, etc.	✓	✓
My College Plan	✓	✓
My Skill Inventory: Dynamic, sortable list of skills that is populated and grows as the student works through the program	✓	✓
Vocabulary words and definitions for each chapter	✓	✓
Transferable Skills chart: Provides sortable list of transferable skills related to up to five careers or job titles	✓	✓
Back-up career planning tool	✓	✓
Technology skills survey		✓
Dynamic decision-making process that requires the learner to gather and evaluate information, facilitating an informed and considered decision		✓
Review Stop wizards featuring the C.A.S.T. (Critical And Strategic Thinkers) that teach and promote the critical thinking process		✓
Integrated with CareerChoices.com activities		✓

Requirements and Recommendations for My10yearPlan.com® Essentials vs. Interactive

	Essentials	Interactive
Basis of program	Student can store, update, and share their 10-year plans online. Program compiles a 10-year plan summary page for quick review by advisors and counselors and for the purpose of academic coaching.	Dynamic, interactive program that automatically updates data and activities as students understanding of themselves and their goals grows. Program provides automated prompts that facilitate critical thinking, decision making, and goal setting as the learner progresses through their 10-year education, career and life planning process. Students can store, update, and share their 10-year plans online. Program compiles a 10-year plan summary for quick review by advisors and counselors and for the purpose of academic coaching.
Scope of project	Students enter their data from 20 of the keystone activities in *Career Choices*.	Students enter data from all 98 activities and exercises in *Career Choices*, including new enhancements and extensions.
Equipment required	Computer linked to the Internet and current web browser	Computer linked to the Internet and current web browser
Time required (online)	Five to ten hours for entry of students' responses from their Workbooks	Computer lab availability once per week for one class period (minimum)
Computer access needed	Computer lab availability for five to ten one-hour sessions (minimum)	Computer lab availability once per week for one class period (minimum)
Student can complete work from home?	Yes	Yes
STUDENT: Skills required	Beginner with basic typing skills and experience using an Internet browser	Beginner with basic typing skills and experience using and Internet browser
INSTRUCTOR: Skills required	Basic experience with computers, such as word processing, navigating the Internet, and managing passwords	Basic experience with computers, such as word processing, navigating the Internet, and managing passwords
Textbooks required	*Career Choices* textbook	*Career Choices* textbook
Student requires personal copy of consumable workbook	Yes	Yes

Recommended Operational Models for a *Career Choices* Course Using My10yearPlan.com® Interactive

Operational Model	Description	Considerations
Course held in computer lab: Every student has their own computer for independent work during class	The *Career Choices* class is held within a computer lab rather than a traditional classroom.	Student time on the computer should be 30% or less. The strength of the experience is the personal interaction between teacher and students. Discussion, reflection, and brainstorming are important components of the *Career Choices* pedagogy.
Class visits computer lab at least once per week	Class visits computer lab **at least** once per week. Depending on student familiarity with computers, increased frequency may be needed.	Each student must have their own computer to work on within the lab. The online portion of the course is about their own personal plan and, therefore, more solitary and thoughtful. More than one person on each computer does not contribute to this and may be frustrating.
One-to-one laptop classroom	Each student has their own laptop computer to use in class and at home.	Student time on the computer should be 30% or less. The strength of the experience is the personal interaction between teacher and students. Discussion, reflections and brainstorming are important components of the *Career Choices* pedagogy.
Classroom rotation model: 1/3 on computers, 1/3 in project/group work setting, 1/3 working directly with instructor (lecture/mentor)	This classroom includes enough online computers for one third of the class, an area of round tables for group projects and an area conducive to teacher-lead discussions and lectures. Ideally, students rotate between all three settings in each class period.	Best used with block scheduling for longer class periods. This model requires careful planning by instructor so clear directions are given each day for each group.
Traditional classroom: Online assignments are completed as homework or after class in available computer lab/library	The *Career Choices* course proceeds as outlined in Section 4 of the Instructor's Guide. Homework can include the assignment to complete the corresponding activity online at My10yearPlan.com®.	This would work with student populations where the instructor can be sure that students have access to an online computer either at home or easily accessible at a public computer lab (e.g., local library).
Distance learning: Outside of the traditional classroom setting	Self-paced course where a student reads the main *Career Choices* textbook, completes their work in their *Workbook*, and then enters their work online, completing the related operations at My10yearPlan.com®. Regular meetings with instructor would provide the best results for the majority of students.	Not ideal for the majority of 8th and 9th graders. Not only does this model require self-discipline and motivation, it also requires an understanding of the world around them. At this young age, the majority of students require the mentorship and experience of an adult leader/teacher.

All of these models assume:

- Each student has a copy of the main textbook *Career Choices* to refer to and their own consumable copy of the *Workbook and Portfolio* developed specifically for the Interactive version of My10yearPlan.com®.
- After class discussions, students are completing their work in their workbook BEFORE going to the computer and logging in to My10yearPlan.com®.

Quick Start Directions for My10yearPlan.com®

System Requirements

You must have an up-to-date web browser and an Internet connection.

Setting Up Accounts

If your school has designated you as the School Site Executive (SSE), you will be charged with the task of setting up accounts for your *Career Choices* teachers and students so they can begin working in My10yearPlan.com®.

To log in, you will need to enter the username and password you created during the account activation process. If you have any questions, call (800) 967-8016 and speak with one of our technical support associates.

Visit Section 9 of the online version of this *Instructor's Guide* for step-by-step directions on:

- How to add teacher accounts
- How to add student accounts
- How to add other accounts (counselors, advisors and other teachers in your school)
- How to easily import student information to create accounts

Navigation in the Student Level of My10yearPlan.com®

Orientation & Support

This program is designed to be intuitive. However, we've created online video tutorials to help users orient themselves so they can easily navigate the menus. The tutorials can be accessed using the link on the home page under Quick Tips.

Using the Top Menu

- Click on the Home button to access any of the dynamic documents, Internet Resources, and these tutorial videos. Each time you log in, you'll see a link to the activity you most recently viewed at the top of the page along with Dain Blanton's chapter introduction video for that chapter.

- The Table of Contents button displays all of the chapter names. Hovering over a chapter name displays all of the activities in that chapter.

- The numbers 1–12 represent each of the book's chapters. This is typically the quickest navigation method. You can select the chapter title to access a landing page for that chapter. Select an activity within each chapter. If you want the menu to stay open, just click on the number at the top.

- The "Select an activity…" drop-down menu lists all of the activities in **My10yearPlan.com®** in the order they appear in the book. Alternatively, you can select to view activities by name. Simply click on the "OR View Activity By Alphabetical Order." This is useful when you remember the title of an activity but not which chapter it was in.

Using the Left Menu

- *My 10-Year Plan Summary* provides a brief summary of the student's 10-year plan, including links to the personal profile, budget narrative, and 10-year action plan.

- *My Online 10-year Plan & Portfolio Report* open the student's portfolio with all of the information he or she has entered to date that builds to the 10-year plan. (See also *Online 10-year Plan & Portfolio* below).

- *Career Portfolio* contains links to the key activities that document the student's career exploration process and resulting plans. This information would be of interest to a potential employer. Students can upload resumes and other relevant documents here, too. See page 9/3 to read more about the *Career Portfolio*.

- *My Skills Inventory* helps students to easily track the skills they have and the skills they need to acquire for their chosen and back-up careers. (Not available in **Essentials**.)

- *Internet Resources* contains links to the best online sources of career information.

- *Update Profile* allows the user to update account information.

- *Email My Instructor* gives students an easy way to send you an email.

- *Report a Problem* sends a message to our development team so students and teachers can easily report any problems they may encounter within the system.

- *Online 10-year Plan & Portfolio Report* open the student's portfolio with all of the information he or she has entered to date that builds to the 10-year plan.

Completing an Activity

- After typing in the boxes provided or selecting the appropriate radio buttons, be sure to click the Save button at the bottom of the page before navigating away from the page.

- After saving work on an activity, you should see "Successfully saved" at the top of the page and a date and time stamp under Archives at the bottom of the page.

- To move on, click the Next Activity button at either the top or the bottom of the page.

- You can come back to an activity as many times as you want to make changes. Just be sure to click the Save button to save any changes before moving one.

- If you make a mistake or otherwise want to erase changes you've made since the last save, click the Undo Changes button. This will only undo any changes that you made since you last saved the page.

Sticky Notes with Helpful Information

- Sometimes "sticky notes" will appear on the right side of an activity. These contain helpful information, web links, or links to information you've already entered that will help you complete that activity.

My Skills Inventory

- The Skills Inventory helps students to easily track the skills they have and the skills they need to acquire for their chosen and back-up careers. The system guides students in filling it out as they progress through the course, but here are the general guidelines:

    Step 1–Along the top row are the careers the student has identified as having the greatest interest. To add careers to this list, students must first complete a Career Interest Survey (see pages 4/89 for details). To change their chosen career they must revisit Make a Career Choice (*Career Choices*, page 177) and work through the decision-making process. However, they can alter the order of their back-up careers using the *Change* drop-down buttons.

    Step 2–If a student needs a skill for a particular career and it is not currently listed, they can add that skill to the inventory by typing it in either the *Add a skill you already have* box or the *Add a skill you want to have* box at the top of the chart.

    Step 3–In the column under each career title, the student checks boxes to indicate which skills match that career.

    Step 4–What is the plan for learning each skill? In the *My Plan For Learning* column, students indicate how they plan to acquire each skill. It can be in school, on the job, as an intern or volunteer, self-taught, from a mentor, in the military, online, reading a book, etc.

- Note that the Skills Inventory updates automatically. If a student edits a skill, they should immediately see the word "saved" appear in the bottom corner of the box. To instantly remove a skill, click on the trash can to the left. But be careful though, since deleted skills are not recoverable.

Answering Students' Questions about My10yearPlan.com®

Your students will likely have some questions about **My10yearPlan.com**®, so we've developed a guide to help you answer them. Some of the questions are technical while other questions are more theoretical and deal with the pedagogy behind the system and the process. If you can respond to these issues when they arise, you'll find that your course will run smoothly.

 This information can be found on My10YearPlan.com® under FAQ and Help as well as the online version of this *Instructor's Guide*.

Many of these issues are common to online learning in general, and your students will benefit from understanding these basics as they prepare for post-secondary success.

How to Use the Workbook & My10yearPlan.com® Together

Even with the optional access to My10yearPlan.com®, secondary students will want to use it in conjunction with their *Workbook and Portfolio* for maximum benefit. Students might have access to computers in class every day, or maybe only in the computer lab periodically. The frequency with which computers are needed will depend on if you are using Essentials or Interactive. The *Workbook and Portfolio* helps to make either situation work.

1. **Students should always complete the activity in the *Workbook and Portfolio* first.**

   Just like most writing assignments, students' responses to the activities in *Career Choices* will go through a few different editorial stages. Think of the *Career Choices Workbook and Portfolio* as the place where students will create a **draft** for each activity, and think of My10yearPlan.com® as the place where they will **review, edit, and polish their draft**.

2. **After students complete the activity in the *Workbook*, they can log in to My10yearPlan.com® and enter the information online.**

   This can happen whenever students have access to a computer—whether it's during class time, after school in the library or career center, or at home during the evening.

3. **Before just typing away, students should take a moment and read through the response written in their *Workbook and Portfolio*.**

   Maybe students have given the activity some more thought since they completed it in class. They'll want to ask "Does my answer still seem like the best possible response?" If so, they can go ahead and enter it into My10yearPlan.com®. If not, they might want to update the answer as they type it in.

   Instructors report that students often upgrade or change their responses once they've had time to think about them. This is a very important step to teaching critical, creative, and strategic thinking.

4. **Either way, this is also a chance to pay attention to spelling, check for typos, and make sure they are answering in complete sentences when appropriate.**

   Keep in mind that the information students input in the activity pages of My10yearPlan.com® will flow to the *My 10-year Plan Summary Page* and to portfolio pages that students will want to print and use for assignments, grading, job interviews, scholarship interviews, and more. Students might also share these pages with an advisor, counselor, parent, or mentor, so this process gives students an opportunity to make sure they are always putting their best work into My10yearPlan.com®.

Why Students Need Both the Workbook and the Online Experience

Students may be tempted to skip writing in their *Workbook and Portfolio* in favor of just entering their responses directly into the online version of the activities on My10yearPlan.com®. Urge them not to take this shortcut. They want to give themselves the best opportunity possible to create 10-year plans that will start them on the path of personal fulfillment and life satisfaction.

This important two-step process was designed:

- **For in-depth learning**

  This course was designed with a print version of the content as well as the online tool because this combination facilitates a deeper, more comprehensive understanding of this life-defining, multi-step process.

- **For ease of learning this life-defining complex process**

  Making career, education, and lifestyle choices based on one's own goals, aptitudes, and attitudes is probably one of the most important skills for anyone to develop. But the process is also complex, which is probably why so many people don't consciously make these choices, instead floating from one job, relationship, or life situation to the next. Young learners would find it challenging to keep the entire sequential, step-by-step process in their heads without the ability to flip through a print copy, visualize the steps, and understand where they've been and where they are going.

- **To be more user-friendly**

  The online activities and worksheets were designed to be as user-friendly as possible. Adding all the content/text required for the background understanding of the concepts presented would have made the online experience too cumbersome and overwhelming.

- **To promote growth through contemplation, reflection, and adaptation**

  As students read the important content in the text and participate in class discussions, they'll want to jot down their initial thoughts in the *Workbook and Portfolio*. They should consider this their first draft. They'll discover that when they finally sit down to enter their work online, they'll have had a chance to reflect and think about their responses, and they'll probably want to expand or even change their initial thoughts. Even if their feelings haven't changed, having their ideas already written out will make the data entry process much easier.

- **To encourage critical, creative, and strategic thinking**

  Students will discover that going back and reviewing their choices multiple times will help to build their confidence that they are making the right choices for themselves. They'll want to give this two-step process the time and attention it deserves, because they are, after all, making one of the most important choices of their lives.

- **To provide support as students face changes and transitions throughout their lives**

  The *Workbook and Portfolio* is something students will want to keep on their shelf with their important papers where they can pick it up and refer to it as they face life-altering decisions.

Section 10

Lesson Planning and Pacing

Topics covered in this section include:

- Ensuring that students complete the entire book in sequence is important to the creation of 10-year plans.

- Pacing guide spreadsheets on **The Teachers' Lounge** can be helpful in keeping your course on track.

- Tips for making the lesson planning process easy and efficient.

- Pacing guides are formatted as spreadsheets and can be easily edited to include the Lesson Plan Suggestions you choose to include from Section 4.

- Meeting the Common Core State Standards with the *Career Choices* suite of curriculum.

The Importance of Teaching the Curriculum in Sequence

The 10-year plan students develop outlines a personal vision and pathway, providing a reason to learn! Getting your students to this important culminating project is critical for the success of your course and your students. To be meaningful, the planning process can't be short-circuited; the curriculum needs to be taught in sequence, from beginning to end, not jumping between activities or presenting the material piecemeal.

Scope and sequence is an important component of all successful learning experiences. The learner wants to know where they are going and what outcome to expect. Skills are built incrementally, so what is learned early on is used later to increase a person's capacity and build new skills. For instance, the toddler learns to crawl, then to walk, then to run. The progression of basic math instruction (addition, then subtraction, then multiplication, then division) is another good example of scope and sequence.

Career Choices was carefully developed with this in mind. The insights and skills learned in the beginning chapters are used again and again in the later chapters as students develop their 10-year plans.

When instructors first open *Career Choices*, they are intrigued by the variety of exercises and activities. Some immediately begin thinking, "Okay, I can use this exercise here and this one there." In the past they may have been forced to pick and choose from a variety of resources without the benefit of the proper tool in the form of a complete curriculum, so this is a natural inclination.

Please resist this urge. It's essential to understand that what's being taught is a **process**, a crucial decision-making process that will be valuable not only when choosing a career, but also when contemplating other important life decisions.

Once they've learned the process, they can step back and analyze most life-defining decisions by reconsidering three core questions: Who am I? What do I want? How do I get it? Using the problem-solving models and prompts taught in *Career Choices* and referring to their 10-year plans, students can infer how particular choices will impact those plans. This empowers them with a skill set they can use to build successful and satisfactory lives.

Your Lesson Plan Pacing Guide:
The Key to Success

We all know the saying, "It is far easier to edit than it is to create." Our goal is to make success as easy to reach as possible, so Academic Innovations provides sample lesson plan pacing guides in spreadsheet format. These draft documents can save you countless hours, providing the foundation and structure of your course as you develop your day-by-day, hour-by-hour lesson plans.

Over the years, we've observed that instructors who complete this planning process *before the first day of class* are much more likely to experience success with their students and feel satisfied with their course. After all, the theme of this curriculum—vision plus energy equals success— imparts the message that *planning is critical* to a life of personal satisfaction. The same holds true for any successful course.

Your Mission: Create a detailed, session-by-session lesson plan pacing guide that is easily managed.

Let's begin with the end in mind. You need to develop a customized, day-by-day lesson plan pacing guide that:

- Fits the parameters of your course
- Follows the scope and sequence of the *Career Choices* textbook, starting in Chapter 1 and working through Chapter 12
- Empowers every student to develop a meaningful 10-year education and career plan

An example of the recommended format is on pages 10/9–10/10 in this *Instructor's Guide* and there are a variety of sample lesson plan pacing guides online.

Step 1: Outline Your Vision and Course Parameters

An important first step is assessing your program's needs. In order to develop the best customized lesson plan pacing guide possible, you'll need to look at your proposed program, population, time limitations, educational goals, and district or state requirements. The **Needs Assessment Survey** available on **The Teachers' Lounge** may help focus this process.

You'll want to answer the survey questions in as much detail as you can to reveal where more planning and discussion may be necessary. Once you've completed the first draft of this questionnaire, you may want to share copies with your instructional team and any administrators supporting your efforts. Their comments and suggestions will help as you continue the detailed work of customizing your day-by-day, hour-by-hour lesson plan pacing guide.

Step 2: Consider Your Curriculum Enhancement Options

Remember to keep the ultimate goals for your course in mind. What motivated you to adopt/or consider adopting the *Career Choices* curriculum in the first place?

- Was it for reducing your high school or college dropout rates?

- Are you meeting a particular district or state mandate for career exploration, dropout prevention, or freshman transition?

- Are you looking to support the Common Core with academic materials with a motivational thematic format, so that students can practice their reading, writing, and math skills while they are also developing a 10-year education and career plan?

- Were you intrigued by the real-world technology applications offered by the Internet enhancements My10yearPlan.com®, CareerChoices.com, and/or LifestyleMath.com? Do these reflect your notion of how online materials should be incorporated into coursework?

Answering these questions will help you determine if and how you are going to integrate any or all of the supplemental academic or Internet-based content in your *Career Choices* course.

You'll want to carefully review the following resources for different options:

- Your *Instructor's Guide*, Sections 2, 3, 4, 8, 9, and 11

- The online training modules listed under Integrating Academics and Technology on The Teachers' Lounge

Once you've completed the survey and reviewed the information in this guide and on The Teachers' Lounge, you'll have a clearer idea of how these supplements may fit within your course parameters.

Step 3: Choose the Lesson Plan that Most Closely Meets Your Needs and Your Time Constraints

We suggest the format you'll want to use for your task of developing your pacing guide is the same as the format used for the sample lesson plan pacing guides available on The Teachers' Lounge.

Remember, these samples are only a starting point. Using one of the existing spreadsheets makes the customization process efficient and easy, because you can add, enhance, or change the pacing of your lessons.

For students to develop real insights and produce a meaningful 10-year plan, please keep two key points in mind as you work on customizing your own lesson plans. We recommend that you:

- Dedicate at least 60 hours to the exercises in the main *Career Choices* textbook and *Workbook & Portfolio*

- Work through the main text in sequence (Chapters 1–12)

On The Teachers' Lounge you'll find a variety of sample lesson plans for integrating academics and/or technology. How you choose to incorporate each enhancement will depend on the number of hours you have for your course. If you are incorporating *Career Choices* into a 90- to 180-hour course, your options are wide open.

You'll also find these three online training videos on the topic of lesson planning:

- Five Ingredients of a Successful *Career Choices* Course
- Integrating Academics and Technology
- *Instructor's Guide*: Section 4

For additional assistance, call our Curriculum and Technical Support team at (800) 967-8016.

Step 4: Edit Your Plan to Customize Your Course

Don't look at this as a daunting task but an energizing, creative effort. The customized lesson plans that you develop, rich in content and active learning opportunities, will change the lives of your students, by changing their attitudes about their education and their futures.

Good luck, and don't hesitate to call our Curriculum and Technical Support team if we can answer any questions for you.

Tips for Managing Your Spreadsheet Editing Process

Let's say you have a semester course (or 90 sessions). You've reviewed the options available on **The Teachers' Lounge** and chosen to start working from the basic 60-hour lesson plan pacing guide. This will allow you to add 30 hours of coursework. You may decide to include some readings from *Possibilities*, the periodic entry of work into My10yearPlan.com®, or online research using CareerChoices.com.

You've downloaded your foundation pacing guide spreadsheet and you're ready to start customizing!

 You can find a variety of lesson plans to edit on the online version of this *Instructor's Guide* and on the Teacher's Lounge.

An Interdisciplinary Opportunity to Meet Common Core State Standards

The Common Core State Standards Initiative, coordinated by the National Governors Association Center for Best Practices and the Council of Chief State School Officers, is an exciting step toward making sure students across the country leave high school prepared for college and workplace success.

By standardizing curriculum across state lines, students who relocate can more easily transition to academic life in a new school. These new standards also increase the depth with which students study certain topics, emphasize the use of more informational texts, and rely on additional cognitive skills, requiring less memorization and more analyzing.

And, above all, the Common Core State Standards are:

> …*designed to be robust and relevant to the real world, reflecting the knowledge and skills that our young people need for success in college and careers.*[1]

An overarching goal of the *Career Choices* series has always been to motivate students to apply themselves by helping them recognize the role academic skills play in their lives outside of the classroom. You could say *Career Choices* was delivering the Common Core State standards long before they were common.

Used with the *Possibilities* anthology and the *Instructor's Guide*, *Career Choices* supports the Common Core State Standards for English. You can find an examples of how the *Career Choices* curriculum addresses these standards throughout Section 4 or at www.academicinnovations.com/standards.html or from Section 8 in the online version of this *Instructor's Guide*.

As students create a detailed budget in *Lifestyle Math*, they encounter each of the Common Core State Standards for Mathematical Practice:

1. Make sense of problems and persevere in solving them.
2. Reason abstractly and quantitatively.
3. Construct viable arguments and critique the reasoning of others.
4. Model with mathematics.
5. Use appropriate tools strategically.
6. Attend to precision.
7. Look for and make use of structure.
8. Look for and express regularity in repeated reasoning.

---

1. Common Core State Standards Initiative mission statement. Retrieved from www.corestandards.org 01/04/2013.

145-Hour Lesson Plan Pacing Guide:

An Interdisciplinary Course that Meets the Common Core State Standards

Designed for a course that involves:

- One instructor
- All four textbooks and My10yearPlan.com®
- Daily 50-minute periods
- One complete school year

Ideal for:

- Freshman academies, freshman seminar, or freshman transition courses
- A career exploration course
- Academic classes with a self-discovery theme
- Motivational courses for at-risk students

This specialized lesson plan pacing guide assists you in your daily planning by showing how the textbooks work together, detailing some of the activities you might use, and outlining the order of the activities. It is our hope that this lesson plan will save you time and present you with proven strategies for classroom success.

This plan also supports the Common Core and the goal of motivating students by helping them recognize the role academic skills play in their lives outside of the classroom.

The Goals of this Lesson Plan Pacing Guide

This pacing guide is designed to facilitate a guidance and planning process that gives students an understanding of the importance of education and the role it plays in their future satisfaction. This experience should impart a strong sense of direction and the skills to adapt as circumstances change and students grow.

This is a competency-based course. Students will understand how acquiring basic skills will increase their chances at a satisfying adult life. Never again will they ask, "Why do we have to learn this?" While the activities outlined in this pacing guide will give students practice in reading, writing, speaking, and mathematical computation, the self-exploration, career awareness, and planning activities are the focus. More of the academic exercises may be added at the instructor's discretion.

Because this curriculum teaches an important decision-making process that students will use throughout their lives, it has a strong scope and sequence. Skipping around is not recommended. While some activities may be deleted or substituted, it is important to note that certain exercises are critical to the success of the course. Since skills are built incrementally, what is learned in early chapters is used again later to increase the student's capacity and understanding of other, more complex concepts.

This lesson plan requires each student to have a copy of or license for:

- *Career Choices: A Guide for Teens and Your Adults: Who Am I? What Do I Want? How Do I Get It?* (text)
- *Workbook and Portfolio for Career Choices* (consumable)
- *Possibilities: A Supplemental Anthology for Career Choices*

- *Lifestyle Math: Your Financial Planning Portfolio* (consumable)
- CareerChoices.com
- My10yearPlan.com®

As the instructor, you will also use this *Instructor's Guide* on a daily basis.

Getting Started

Have a copy of each textbook and this *Instructor's Guide* handy so you can refer to the pages and exercises noted in the lesson plan pacing guide.

It is strongly recommended that, as the instructor, you actually work through your own copy of the *Career Choices* textbook, completing the activities yourself. This will help you understand the scope and sequence and provide you with discussion material or examples based on your own experience. Students love to hear the teacher's responses! You might want to pretend you are searching for a second career when you retire from teaching. As an adult, this task should take 20 hours or less. Most educators find this an enjoyable and enlightening experience.

How to Use This Pacing Guide

- The first column provides an hour-by-hour count

- The second column notes which book(s) the students will use for that lesson, along with the specific pages. This is the reading material covered that day. In the case of *Career Choices*, you may want to assign all or a portion of the next day's reading as homework. Students will come to class somewhat familiar with the topic and ready to discuss and complete the activities.

  - Flipping the classroom: By assigning the reading and the activities for homework the night before, your discussions will be richer and students will be able to do more in-depth learning in class.

- The third column shows the title of the activity or exercise in the texts. If the title is in parenthesis, it is a description of the lesson instead of an official title.

- The fourth column directs the instructor to the pages in this *Instructor's Guide* for that particular lesson. It also notes the sections suggested for that page. For example, if it says "Presentation suggestions" you will read and execute the directions under that topic on that particular page. The same is true for other topics such as Activities, Energizers, Resources, etc. This does not mean you shouldn't use other information on the page if you have the time or inkling. The listing is just the minimum recommendation.

- The fifth column presents any Special Directions that may not be included elsewhere in this *Instructor's Guide*. You will want to combine the information in this column with the directions detailed in the fourth column. Or augment the special directions with some of your own ideas for enhancements.

- The sixth column provides an estimate of the amount of time you should allow for each activity.

- The seventh column lists suggested homework assignments.

- The final column suggests additional activities to integrate other academic subjects into the curriculum.

First Page of an Example of a 145-hour Lesson Plan

WHEN ASSIGNING HOMEWORK: Students should complete the reading in Career Choices and the written work in their workbooks the evening before those topics are addressed in class. Students will then come to class prepared for the activities and discussions noted in this guide. The "Homework Assignment" column provides some suggestions for assignments you will want completed outside of class time.

IF WORKING IN INTERDISCIPLINARY TEAMS: If you are working as an interdisciplinary team with other academic instructors or if you are hoping to integrate academics and/or technology into your class, make note of opportunities to share assignments and activities in the "Interdisciplinary/Technology Opportunities" column.

Session # (50 min.)	Textbook and/or Workbook	Lesson or Activity	Instructor's Guide Pages or Other Instructor Resource	Special Directions (beyond those given in the Instructor's Guide)	Approx. Minutes	Homework Assignment	Interdisciplinary Opportunities
1	Pre-assessment Activity	Pre-/Post-Survey	Section 14	Have each student complete the survey found on page 6/12 of the Instructor's Guide. Save these for comparison at the end of the course. This survey will measure attitudinal change toward the value of education and students' expectations for their future self-sufficiency and productivity. Hand out the parent letter and the project sheet for the Visualizer activity.	10	Bring something that flies. (for introduction, Career Choices, p. 6-7).	Review Section 8 in the Instructor's Guide for additional information and ideas.
1	Chapter Intro Video	Introduction to Career Choices	The Teachers' Lounge	Olympic Gold Medalist Dain Blanton introduces your class to the course, fuels the excitement for the topics, and helps them to understand the real-life importance of what they will learn.	10		
1	Course introduction	Course introduction		Review the syllabus, course disclosure, and any other "housekeeping" items that need to be taken care of at the start of the course. Be sure to share an example of a completed 10-year Plan Summary page (in My10yearplan.com®) so your students can see what they'll create in this course. If you don't have time to complete your own sample 10-year Plan, request a populated sample account code from Academic Innovations.			
1	Workbook, p. 4	(Vocabulary)	Section 11	To help with student mastery of the vocabulary for each chapter, there are quizzes and crossword puzzles available through The Teachers' Lounge at http://CareerChoices.com/lounge/cupboard_list.html.		Vocabulary should be assigned as homework due to time constraints in the classroom. Consider teaming with your English department to cover this aspect of the course.	
CHAPTER ONE							
2	Career Choices, pp. 6-7	Introduction	p. 4/2, Presentation suggestions	Have students report out on what they brought that flies. In reading the introductory material, emphasize the last paragraph of the introduction. It is not the purpose of this course to make a final career choice. Students will, however, learn a process for making rewarding life choices in the future.	30		
2	Chapter Intro Video	Chapter 1: Envisioning Your Future	The Teachers' Lounge	Dain discusses how having a plan and following that plan were essential to his success.	5		
2	Workbook, p. 4	(Vocabulary)	Section 11	To help with student mastery of the vocabulary for each chapter, there are quizzes and crossword puzzles available through The Teachers' Lounge at http://CareerChoices.com/lounge/cupboard_list.html.	15		
3	Discuss homework reading of Career Choices, pp. 10-14; Workbook, pp. 5-6	Vision + Energy = Success; Envisioning Your Future	pp. 4/4-4/6, Presentation suggestions	Brainstorm as a class the charts on page 13. Explain the rules of brainstorming (see page 6/30 of Instructor's Guide).	30		
3	Possibilities, p. 24	"Dreams" by Langston Hughes		Read Hughes' poem to the class.	5	Assignment: Workbook, pp. 7-9	
3	Possibilities, pp. 27-32	"I Have a Dream..." by Dr. Martin Luther King, Jr		Read Dr. King's speech to the class.	15	Compare and contrast the tone of Hughes poem and Dr. King's speech.	
4	Possibilities, pp. 11-17	"Secret Life of Walter Mitty" by James Thurber	Read in class (silent or aloud)	Discuss question 5 in class. Students write dialogue for question 7. As a class discuss question 8.	50	Assignment: Edit Envisioning Your Future assignment (p. 6, Workbook) from the previous evening, after learning more about themselves.	
5	Career Choices, pp. 10-13; Workbook, p. 5	(Visualizer activity)	p. 4/7, Instructor brings items	Divide students into groups of three to develop, design, and build their Visualizer. Have groups "model" and explain their Visualizers for the rest of the class. Leave Visualizers hanging in the room with permission to use if needed at any time.	50		
6	Video Book Club	October Sky	Section 11	Viewing guide available on The Teachers' Lounge web site (http://www.careerchoices.com/lounge/cupboard_viewing.html).	50	Assignment: Workbook, pp. 7-9	
7	Video Book Club	October Sky	Section 11	Viewing guide available on The Teachers' Lounge web site (http://www.careerchoices.com/lounge/cupboard_viewing.html).	50	Writing assignment: Students are to start writing their definition of success. Workbook, p. 9	
8	Discussion: Career Choices, pp. 15-21; Workbook, pp. 7-9	Why People Work; Everybody Works, Defining Success	p. 4/8-4/10, Presentation suggestions; Activity; p. 4/10, Activity (1st half)	Have students brainstorm how they think well-known individuals would define success. Students will be updating the Defining Success statement throughout the course.	25		
9	Possibilities, pp. 37-39	"Richard Cory" by Edwin Arlington Robinson	p. 4/11, Writing the last page of Richard Cory's diary	Pre-reading discussion topic: Journal entry p. 37. After reading discussion: Questions 5, 8.	25	Assignment: Question 7, Possibilities, p. 39	
9	Possibilities, pp. 40-42	Excerpt from "Sonnets from the Portuguese" by Elizabeth Barrett Browning	p. 4/18 Activity	Discussion topic: Second paragraph of Journal entry p. 37, use this as a lead in to the activity in the next class session.	25		English/Language Arts: Write an Essay describing a student's ideal day. Instructor's Guide, p. 4/18
10	Workbook, p. 132	Checkpoints: Chapter 1	p. 4/20, Presentation suggestions	Students complete a series of "I" statements as a self-assessment of mastery of key concepts from the chapter they have completed.	5	Checkpoints could be assigned as homework.	Checkpoints for each chapter are available on My10yearplan.com®.
				Provide students with the opportunity to enter information from this chapter's KEYSTONE activities and Checkpoints into My10yearplan.com®.			
CHAPTER TWO							
11	Chapter Intro Video	Chapter 2: Your Personal Profile	The Teachers' Lounge	Dain outlines the process for learning more about yourself and creating the personal profile.	5		
11	Career Choices, p. 24	(James and Letitia)		Choose three students who are able to confidently read aloud to be (1) a narrator, (2) James, and (3) Lettia. Their story is told throughout chapter 2 of Career Choices (pp. 24-50). Each time the class arrives at a portion of their story, ask the "actors" to read their parts.	10		
11	Discussion of homework			Vocabulary can also be assigned as homework.	10		
12	Career Choices, p 27; Workbook, p. 11	(Your Personal Profile); (Bulls Eye Chart)	p. 4/16, Presentation suggestions	Have students try to complete their own bulls eye chart in class. This is a preliminary attempt.	25		
12	Career Choices, p. 28	(James and Letitia)		Dramatic Reading	5		
12	Career Choices, p. 29; Workbook, p. 12	Identifying Your Passions	p. 4/18, Presentation suggestions, Activities	Give students time to edit and update their definitions of success. Then ask for volunteers to share their definitions of success (so far). Remind students these will grow and change over the course.	30	Assignment: Workbook, pp. 12, 13-16.	
12	Career Choices, pp. 31-37; Workbook, pp. 13-16	Work Values Survey (introduction)	p. 4/20, Presentation suggestions	Review the survey together and discuss any words or concepts they don't understand. Be non-judgmental about the statements read.	15		
13	Review homework: Workbook, p. 12			Ask for volunteers to share their passions. As a class begin brainstorming possible careers that address each student's passions.	20		
13	Career Choices, p. 30	(James and Letitia)		Dramatic Reading	5		
13	Review homework: Workbook, pp. 13-16			Review each values category. Check to see that each student scored it correctly.	25		

First 2 Pages of an Example of a Year-long Course

Session # (50 min.)	Textbook and/or Workbook	Lesson or Activity	Instructor's Guide Pages or Other Instructor Resource	Special Directions (beyond those provided in the Instructor's Guide)
1	Career Choices, pp. 6-7	Introduction	p. 4/2, Presentation suggestions, Activities	Give students a piece of 8½" × 11" white paper and ask them to "create" something that flies. Responses will vary greatly.
	Pre-assessment activity	Pre/Post Survey	Section 14	Have each student complete the survey found in Section 14 of this Instructor's Guide. Save these for comparison at the end of the course.
2	Career Choices, pp. 10-13; Workbook, p. 5	Vision + Energy = Success	p. 4/4, Presentation suggestions	
3	Career Choices, pp. 10-13; Workbook, p. 5	(Visualizer activity)	p. 4/7	Divide students into groups of three to develop, design, and build their Visualizer. Have groups "model" and explain their Visualizers to the rest of the class. Leave Visualizers hanging in the room with permission to use if needed at any time.
4	Career Choices, pp. 14-17; Workbook, p.6	Envisioning Your Future	p. 4/6, Presentation suggestions	Visual Assessment: Videotape students presenting their Envisioning Your Future essay during the first week of class. Then, during the last week of class, have students rewrite their essays and videotape the new responses. Compare the two videotapes. Share the final production not only with the students but with administrators and funders. This is powerful!
5	Possibilities, p. 24	"Dreams" by Langston Hughes		Read Hughes' poem to class then discuss the questions in the journal entry on p. 24
6	Video Book Club	October Sky	Section 11	
	Video Book Club (continued)	October Sky	Section 11	
7	Career Choices, pp. 15-16	Why People Work	p. 4/8, Presentation suggestions	
	Career Choices, p. 17; Workbook, p. 7	Everybody Works	p. 4/9, Presentation suggestions	
8	Career Choices, pp. 18-21; Workbook, pp. 8-9	Defining Success	p. 4/10, Presentation suggestions	
9	Career Choices, pp. 18-21; Workbook, pp. 8-9	Defining Success (continued)	p. 4/10, Activities	
10	Possibilities, pp. 37-39	"Richard Cory" by Edwin Arlington Robinson	Read poem to class	Have the Simon and Garfunkel song "Richard Cory" playing as the students enter the classroom. Read story aloud. Have students discuss journal entry and question 5.
11	Possibilities, p. 38	"Richard Cory" (continued); Question 7		Present the project: Choose an outcome. For example, present findings to the school newspaper or submit to a community paper's editorial page.
		How to gather data and conduct an interview		Where to find people to interview. How to take notes. Homework: Conduct interviews.
12	Possibilities, p. 38	"Richard Cory" (continued); Question 7		Students report out on findings from their interviews. Group decides how to compile findings.
		How to analyze data		

Session # (50 min.)	Textbook and/or Workbook	Lesson or Activity	Instructor's Guide Pages or Other Instructor Resource	Special Directions (beyond those provided in the *Instructor's Guide*)
13	*Career Choices*, p. 20 Workbook, p. 9	Making Career Choices	p. 4/13, Presentation suggestions	After you've discussed as per *Instructor's Guide*, make a chart for classroom wall with the characters' names and a descriptive title. For example, Eric/Wishful Thinker, Louisa/Escape Artist, etc. Throughout the course, let students identify the decision-making patterns of friends, characters in stories, and themselves. "I'm reacting like Harold (procrastinator) when I wait until the night before to start my social studies report."
14		(Identity activity)	p. 4/6, Activity	Personal Collage: Who am I? What do I want? What are my dreams? On a very large sheet of paper, mark off a quarter section to be used for this assignment. Other parts of the collage can be added later, after they complete other activities that help them identify their dreams and goals.
15	*Career Choices*, p. 24 *Career Choices*, pp. 25-27; Workbook, p. 11	(James and Letitia) Your Personal Profile (Bulls Eye Chart)	p. 4/16, Presentation suggestions, Energizer	Choose three students who are able to confidently read aloud to be (1) a narrator, (2) James, and (3) Letitia. Their story is told throughout chapter 2 of *Career Choices* (pp. 24-50). Each time the class arrives at a portion of their story, ask the "actors" to read their parts.
16	*Career Choices*, p. 28 *Career Choices*, pp. 28-29; Workbook, p. 12	(James and Letitia) Identifying Your Passions	p. 4/18, Presentation suggestions, Activities	Dramatic Reading
17	*Career Choices*, pp. 28-29; Workbook, p. 12	Identifying Your Passions (continued)	English/Language Arts	Break into small groups and have each group member help the others describe their ideal day. Ask each person to report out. Note: Follow-up statement on p. 4/19 of *Instructor's Guide*.
18	*Career Choices*, p. 30 *Career Choices*, pp. 31-37; Workbook, pp. 13-16	(James and Letitia) Work Values Survey	p. 4/20, Presentation suggestions	Dramatic Reading Review the survey together, discuss any words or concepts they don't understand. Be non-judgmental about statements read.
19	*Career Choices*, pp. 31-37; Workbook, pp. 13-16	Work Values Survey (continued)		Students take the survey. They must take it alone, not in groups. Note: Follow-up suggestion on p. 4/21 of *Instructor's Guide*.
20	*Career Choices*, pp. 31-37; Workbook, pp. 13-16	Work Values Survey (continued)		Students score the survey. Have a discussion of to review each category.
21	*Career Choices*, pp. 31-37; Workbook, pp. 13-16	Work Values Survey (continued)		As a class, brainstorm careers for each student, given his or her top three work values. Ask each student to write his or her top three values on the board. Open the discussion up to the floor so classmates can make suggestions. This is an introductory activity and will need a lot of support from teachers and adults. You might even invite two or three other individuals (career counselor, guidance counselor, principal, etc.) to help brainstorm.
22	*Career Choices*, pp. 31-37; Workbook, pp. 13-16 *Career Choices*, p. 38	Work Values Survey (continued) (James and Letitia)	p. 4/20, Gender Equity Activity	Reading and discussion of the story *My Way Sally*. Invite a special guest to read (drama student or teacher, favorite adult or teacher, principal). Call (800) 967-8016 to order. Dramatic reading
23	*Career Choices*, pp. 38-42; Workbook, pp. 17-19	Strengths and Personality	p. 4/22, Presentation suggestions	Review the definitions on p. 39 of *Career Choices* before students complete the activity. Complete the activities individually.
24	*Career Choices*, p. 43	(How personality impacts career choices)	p. 4/22, Presentation suggestions	Discussion of styles. Brainstorm the types of careers in which each style might be happiest.

Special Lesson Plans

Visit **The Teachers' Lounge** and review the variety of special lesson plans available. If you have a lesson plan you would like to share, please send a copy to Academic Innovations.

15-hour Interdisciplinary Lesson Plan for a Successful Launch

Strategies to help you successfully launch your *Career Choices* course with 15 interactive, interdisciplinary sessions, thereby setting a rigorous tone for your entire course.

The fifteen opening sessions outlined in this lesson plan will help you launch your students into their ***Career Choices*** course and a successful, self-sufficient life. Using this lesson plan during the first few weeks of your course—along with the ***Workbook and Portfolio***, activities in the ***Instructor's Guide***, and readings from ***Possibilities***—you'll provide a rich interdisciplinary experience for your students. You'll stretch even the most resistant student to think beyond their typical "next Saturday" timeframe and learn the important skills of long range thinking and envisioning. In addition, you'll provide activities for a variety of learning styles grounded in academics.

If you have any questions, do not hesitate to contact us at (800) 967-8016. We'll happily brainstorm strategies with you. Remember, we are here to support you throughout the school year, not just during the first few weeks.

 You'll find the 15-hour interdisciplinary lesson plan on The Teachers' Lounge at www.careerchoices.com/lounge/files/lessonplan.pdf or the online version of this *Instructor's Guide*.

Section 11

Instructional Strategies

Topics covered in this section include:

- This curriculum encourages the instructor to help students learn through dialectic instruction utilizing questioning and discussion (Socratic method) rather than through a didactic lecture style.

- "Flip" your classroom by having students read assigned content and complete exercises in the *Workbook and Portfolio* for homework so class time can be spent on discussion and group activities.

- An involved student is an engaged student, and there are a number of strategies instructors can use to create an interactive, engaging classroom.

- It's important to cultivate a supportive atmosphere within your class, so be sure to review tips for facilitating effective groups.

- Distance learning presents many challenges, especially for a course of this nature. Success hinges on planning sufficiently, students' computer skills, and communication.

- Sharing appropriate movies and songs with your students can reinforce the themes presented in *Career Choices*.

- The vocabulary in *Career Choices* may be challenging for some students. Encourage your students to study the vocabulary of success.

The Socratic Method: Engaging students through self-discovery and questioning

To become college and career ready, students must have ample opportunities to take part in a variety of rich, structured conversations—as part of a whole class, in small groups, and with a partner—built around important content in various domains. [1]

Think back to one of the most profound discoveries you've made in your life. Did someone else teach you this information? Was it the result of something someone told you? Or did you discover this truth on your own? Often, the things we hear from well-meaning friends, acquaintances, and even teachers don't mean as much to us as the things we come to realize for ourselves.

This curriculum was developed around the Socratic method of teaching, which, in simple terms, is questioning versus lecturing. Questions are posed and students then seek to answer those questions for themselves. As you thumb through *Career Choices*, you'll find that a large portion of the content is devoted to questions, activities, and problems designed to challenge learners to find their own answers rather than text outlining what the author feels they need to know.

The process is propelled by questions that the learners must explore as they develop their own plans for their futures. Dialectic rather than didactic, this is an ideal vehicle for a learning experience where students rely on the textbook for the foundational or background information and complete follow-up questions in the *Workbook and Portfolio* to jump-start their thinking. In class, the instructor will facilitate discussions that promote more in-depth understanding. The online component, My10yearPlan.com®, is initially for completing and refining their thinking on each activity and, later, for easy updating and enhancing as they discover more about themselves and clarify their plans.

This process of posing, investigating, and discussing questions helps develop students' critical thinking skills by prompting them to think for themselves, create their own ideas, and solve their own problems rather than relying on someone else's plan for the future. It will require the use of analysis, evaluation, and creativity to synthesize the information they've discovered—about themselves and their future options—and to create a meaningful 10-year plan.

The curriculum's progressive format doesn't position the instructor as an authority who tells them what to learn or what to believe. As a result, students come to view the instructor as an advisor, a mentor, or a coach, which leads to a more satisfactory learning relationship for student and teacher alike.

In keeping with the spirit of the curriculum, be careful not to dictate "realistic" occupations or budgets, or to give too many opinions on the choices students make. Trust the process. The carefully designed scope and sequence of the curriculum leads students through thought-provoking questions that allow them to discover for themselves which options might truly be best for them. **This is why it's important not to skip around in the curriculum but to work through it from beginning to end.**

This is a very personalized process that requires such in-depth thinking and research that students come to "own" their plans. Ownership increases the personal value of the process and the product (the 10-year plan), and also increases the likelihood they will follow through with their plans. Once students complete meaningful personalized 10-year plans, high school and college completion will follow. Not only will they have a vision of a productive future and a plan for making it a reality but they will understand the consequences of not following through with their plans.

Flipping the Classroom
Using technology to enhance in-depth learning

As video lectures and online learning have surged in popularity, the concept of the "flipped" classroom has received much attention. In this model, instead of instructors using class time to lecture on a topic and sending the students home to do the work, students typically study the content at home using technology.

How does a flipped classroom work?

Prior to class time, students either watch a video of the lecture on the topic or work online using interactive activities that present the material. They arrive at class with a basic understanding of the topic and, as a result, precious time with the instructor does not have to be spent in passive lecture format.

By completing the content delivery prior to class, students can learn at their own pace, spending as much time as they need on topics they find difficult with the freedom to move more quickly though topics that come easily to them. Most important, the instructor can maximize valuable class time by helping students as they work through the assignment rather than sending them home to struggle with it on their own. The instructor can also provide tutorial support and facilitate more in-depth discussions, collaborative or project-based work, and other activities that are only possible when the class is together, all of which enhances students' understanding and grasp of the material.

Flipped Classroom Strategies for Your *Career Choices* Course

The "flipped" classroom is an ideal fit for a **Career Choices** class. Assign reading, videos, and **Workbook and Portfolio** activities for homework prior to the class devoted to the topic or chapter. These exercises are very personal in nature and this format gives students the time and space to contemplate their initial responses independently. They will arrive in class with a basic understanding of the topic, ready to go into more detail in discussions or request help from the instructor if they struggle with any concepts. What makes this course so powerful is the individual guidance an instructor can provide, exposure to various viewpoints, and input from peers.

When instructors "flip the classroom", precious face-to-face time with students can be used to provide the classroom-based, comprehensive guidance experience that studies validate is critical to student success. The role of the instructor will change from lecturer to advisor, and both instructor and student satisfaction will soar.

When students complete the reading and workbook activities before class, obtain new perspectives from thought-provoking interaction in class, and then refine their own thinking as they enter and edit their initial responses in **My10yearPlan.com®**, they will have thoughtful, meaningful 10-year plans. They will also have firsthand experience with the best methodology for problem solving and utilizing critical and creative thinking.

Tips and Ideas to Involve Learners

Rather than sticking to a didactic format—"read and remember"—the *Career Choices* curriculum is organized around a series of exercises, activities, questionnaires, and models that challenge learners to find their own answers. When you thumb through the main text, you'll see interactive exercises throughout. Recognizing that learning takes place when the learner is involved, this *Instructor's Guide* includes hundreds of suggestions to keep your class time challenging yet exciting, informative yet fun.

If you are just starting your *Career Choices* course, you are about to embark on an odyssey that may very well change the way you teach. Time invested in studying these classroom strategies will surely pay dividends in student engagement and achievement, not only in your *Career Choices* class, but in any course you teach from this point forward.

Energizers

Energizers ask students to get fully involved and make good use of their own creativity! They're called energizers because they increase the energy level for the task at hand. We all know that when this happens, real learning takes place.

Energizers can take the form of art projects or utilize computer skills as students share their ideas with one another. With some energizers, students get physically involved in learning. Energizers will be the activities that your students will talk about and remember long after your class is over. Take a moment to flip through **Section 4** of this guide and you'll find energizers scattered throughout (e.g., pages 4/81, 4/102, 4/157).

Teamwork and Cooperative Learning

Individuals who can work effectively and efficiently as part of a team are valued in the workplace. To support students as they strive to be college and career ready, the *Career Choices* curriculum was designed to provide opportunities to practice and perfect the skills required for teamwork, team-building, and cooperative learning.

Formalized cooperative learning strategies increase your chances of success with your group discussions and projects. You'll find a range of resources in this *Instructor's Guide* on pages 11/7–11/17 from guidelines for behavior to setting up your classroom to subtly influence the way students act.

Project-based Learning

Project-based learning is based on the idea that students retain more information when their learning is tied to a project, but it is particularly effective when that project is truly valued by the individual. A project that is relevant to students' lives generates more enthusiasm, which drives them to work harder, increases retention, and promotes skill development.

It's important that we de-compartmentalize learning. After all, isn't life just one big project? Project-based learning gives students a context for problem-solving, investigation, decision-making, and project management, and the *Career Choices* curriculum provides a variety of opportunities for ready-made projects that can be easily incorporated into your lessons. Review page 11/18 for examples.

Integrating Technology

Integrating technology into your coursework is increasingly critical. In order to succeed in the workplace, students should leave school possessing basic technology literacy and skills. They need to type quickly and accurately. They need proficiency with Internet browsing and searching. They also need familiarity with a variety of computer applications, such as word processing, spreadsheets, and basic graphic design. *Career Choices* presents a number of ways for students to practice these skills, and the optional *Career Choices* online enhancements present additional opportunities (see pages 8/3–8/4).

Engaging and easy to implement, the online 10-year planning process is enjoyable for students and instructors alike. This hybrid course allows the instructor to act as a facilitator, coach, and mentor rather than simply a lecturer, and class discussions segue naturally to the online program. Once online, the system guides students through empowering activities that teach the "habits of mind" common among those who regularly experience personal and professional success. For more in depth information, review Section 8 of this *Instructor's Guide*.

> *Technology itself is changing quickly, creating a new urgency for students to be adaptable in response to change.* [2]

Optional Enhancements:

Guest Speakers

Guest speakers are the perfect way to get relevant information "straight from the horse's mouth." Guest speakers can help you bring the highest level of reality to your *Career Choices* course.

Because so many topics are covered throughout the course, there are plenty of opportunities for you to bring in someone from the community to elaborate on what your students are learning. Counselors, retired persons, community leaders, business people, and family members are all good choices for guest speakers (see pages 11/21–11/22 for details).

Job Shadowing

Job shadowing is a great way to give students new insights and a healthy dose of reality as they conduct career research. How can you aspire to a specific career you've never seen in action? For most students, their only exposure to the working world is what they see in their own sphere of family and friends, on TV, and in the movies. It's no wonder that the majority of students, when left to their own devices, articulate a career goal that falls within a narrow range of job titles.

Job shadowing provides students firsthand experience with careers they might find interesting. Being at work with someone experienced in a career, even for just a day, exposes students to the reality of that work and the excitement of the working world.

Share Your Ideas

As demonstrated by the suggestions on pages 11/4–11/5 of this guide, there are myriad opportunities to enhance and enliven this course. The solid scope and sequence of *Career Choices* provides a proven framework ready for your creativity.

When you try a great new idea and it works, don't forget to share your strategy with Academic Innovations. We have several avenues for passing your innovations along to instructors across the country, with your permission, of course.

TIPS (Teaching Insights, Practices, & Solutions) Newsletter

Throughout each school year, our Curriculum and Technical Support team sends out a bi-weekly email newsletter with helpful reminders, tips, and strategies to help keep your *Career Choices* course on track.

The Teachers' Lounge

This online professional development site provides on-demand access to a variety of planning, training, support, and classroom resources related to the *Career Choices* curriculum. If you don't already have access to The Teachers' Lounge, learn more at www.careerchoices.com/lounge/whyjoin.html.

Career Choices Online Professional Learning Community

This moderated forum was launched so instructors could connect online to discuss their use of *Career Choices*, share ideas, and create a virtual professional learning community. All visitors are invited to follow the discussions and learn from the strategies that are shared, but full participation is limited to registered members of The Teachers' Lounge. Learn more at www.careerchoices.com/lounge/plc_home.html.

Best Practices: Freshman Transition in Action at the Focus on Freshmen Conference

We are always on the lookout for successful *Career Choices* models we can share. In fact, we dedicate an entire institute at our annual three-day conference to showcasing best practices from across the country. We also recognize all medal-winning *Career Choices* programs during the conference's awards luncheon. Learn more about becoming a medal-winning school at www.whatworkscareerchoices.com/bestpractices.html.

Best Practices & Award-Winning *Career Choices* Programs

Cooperative Learning and Team-Building

Working efficiently and effectively as a member of a team is a prized skill in the 21st century workplace. In addition, research indicates that group learning has positive effects on student learning and achievement, self-confidence, and relationships with peers.

A classroom that incorporates a variety of cooperative learning opportunities into the coursework helps students learn important lessons.

- They develop essential life skills, including speaking, listening, negotiating, compromising, and cooperating.

- They increase their ability to accept others' points of view, receive constructive criticism, and work within a team.

- They learn to view problems as challenges and arrive at creative solutions.

- They take responsibility for their own learning by actively participating in the process.

To become college and career ready, students must have ample opportunities to take part in a variety of rich, structured conversations—as part of a whole class, in small groups, and with a partner—built around important content in various domains. They must be able to contribute appropriately to these conversations, to make comparisons and contrasts, and to analyze and synthesize a multitude of ideas...[3]

Classroom Management Techniques for Active Learning

An instructor's most important—and challenging—role is to create a classroom environment that ensures success for all students. Using proven classroom management techniques for the active learning classroom, you can help your students stay focused and productive.

The success of group discussions can depend largely on the class environment. Every student must feel important, cared for, and supported. It is helpful if students can see each other. Arrange desks in a circle or have students sit around a table, if possible.

Before you begin, set simple guidelines for the class, including these essential ones:

- Every student must be allowed to give his or her own opinion on a topic

- No one is allowed to interrupt or discount anyone else's opinion

- The personal nature of topics requires that everyone is allowed to "pass" if called on in discussion

You'll want to point out that these same basic ground rules apply when working as a team to accomplish anything.

Basic Ground Rules for Active Learning Classroom

The personal nature of some discussions may lead students to reveal serious problems requiring professional help. In these situations, show concern; however, avoid giving the impression that anything's "wrong" with the individual. Meet with the student after class, suggest options for getting help, and then offer any assistance he or she may need.

Make yourself available between classes or after school, and let students know you are willing to listen and lend support. This provides students who may be reluctant to share with the entire class a more private forum in which to discuss their concerns. Likewise, if a student seems to be upset during the class discussion period, suggest that he or she see you after class.

Just as there are sensitive subjects, there are sensitive students who may feel uncomfortable sharing their innermost thoughts with the class or even with you. Their privacy should be respected. Allow students to hand in written work rather than participate in group discussions if they prefer. On particularly personal or sensitive points, they may indicate that you are not to read an assignment by turning it in folded in half or by folding down those pages in the workbook. As you establish an atmosphere of trust in the class, these students should gradually become less fearful.

The curriculum is appropriate for team teaching with the school guidance counselor. You may ask him or her to participate, in particular, with your presentation of the topics Chapters 2 and 9.

Evaluating Your Group

Is your group operating effectively?

Take time periodically to consider this question. The following checklist may be helpful. In an effective group:

- ✓ Members participate somewhat equally
- ✓ Members are involved and stimulated by group discussions
- ✓ The environment is warm and supportive
- ✓ Ideas and emotions are effectively communicated and accepted by others
- ✓ Stated tasks are completed (or not completed by group agreement)
- ✓ Group accomplishments are easily discernible by all members

Effective Group Facilitation Strategies

For those instructors who have more practice with a traditional lecture style of teaching, we offer a brief review of effective group facilitation.

- Group participation is essential, but students must be motivated to participate. They will generally be motivated when they:

  ✓ Have input on discussion topics

  ✓ See the discussion topics or exercises as relevant to their own lives

  ✓ Solve a problem or make a decision as a group

  ✓ Have an opportunity to voice their opinion and hear a variety of other viewpoints

  ✓ Are given tasks with a clearly defined beginning and end

- An informal atmosphere is key. Arrange desks or chairs in a circle rather than rows so that students can see each other.

- An atmosphere of trust is of utmost importance and an honest, respectful process ensures the best discussions. It is important to build a cohesive group in which all opinions are validated and accepted.

- Practice active listening skills and instruct the group to do the same. You may want to devote at least one class session to discussing and practicing this communication tool. In active listening, the person who is not speaking takes an active role in the dialogue. He or she never interrupts the speaker, but paraphrases what's been said when the speaker has finished. In this way, the speaker knows that he or she has been heard.

Example:

Speaker: "I like this book very much. I can really relate to the main character."

Active listener: "I'm pleased you like the book and can identify with the main character."

It is also appropriate for an active listener to ask about the speaker's feelings.

Example:

Speaker: "I don't like stories with unhappy endings."

Active listener: "How do they make you feel?"

Effective group facilitation and active listening will involve:

1. Restating what's been said.

2. Asking how the speaker feels.

3. Letting the speaker complete his or her statement without interruption.

4. Addressing students by name so they know they are important, you're interested in them, and you care about them.

5. Establishing a dialogue by asking questions rather than lecturing. Before offering your opinion, ask students if they want to hear it.

6. Giving students your full attention and making eye contact with the group.

7. Using humor in appropriate situations.

8. Establishing an atmosphere of trust within the group by respecting students' privacy and being honest. If you make a mistake, admit it.

9. Being clear about class rules and insisting that they be honored. State the consequences for breaking these rules and enforce them. Threats are not effective.

10. Pointing out cause and effect. Hold students accountable for their actions. Ask them to think of consequences, both immediate and long-term. This will increase their sense of autonomy and responsibility.

11. Asking for and listening to students' opinions. This will help to increase their self-esteem. Use their suggestions when you can. Let students know you believe in them.

12. Celebrating the accomplishments of the group or individuals within the group. Mentioning positive traits or behaviors, especially those of resistant or reluctant students.

13. Letting the group get to know you. Be aware of your feelings at the beginning of each class period and, if you are angry or distracted about something, let the group know that they are not the cause of your negative feelings.

14. Redirecting the discussion or taking a short break if you sense too much tension in the room.

15. Communicating your approval. When a student does or says something that pleases you, let him or her know with a word, look, smile, or nod.

16. Reminding students of the ground rules. If one or more students tend to be judgmental or try to impose their values and ideas on the group, speak with them outside the group regarding everyone's right to speak without fear of ridicule from others. You might mention that being able to get along with others and working effectively within a group are skills that are valued in the workforce.

17. Recognizing students' growing sense of self-identity.

18. Expecting students to be enthusiastic about the course. They will probably live up to your expectations as attitudes are contagious.

19. Being patient when the inevitable setbacks occur. Group learning often proceeds in a "two steps forward, one step back" fashion.

20. Never concurring with a student's disparaging remarks about family or friends. His or her ties to these people are likely strong in spite of what they say, and your remarks will not be well received.

21. Encouraging empathy by asking students to imagine how other people feel. Your example as an empathetic facilitator will help students understand the importance of empathy.

These strategies will set the tone for effective classroom discussions and will help students acquire key college and career readiness attributes, including:

Students appreciate that the twenty-first-century classroom and workplace are settings in which people from often widely divergent cultures and who represent diverse experiences and perspectives must learn and work together. Students actively seek to understand other perspectives and cultures through reading and listening, and they are able to communicate effectively with people of varied backgrounds.[4]

Getting Acquainted

If most of your students are unacquainted, you may want to use several group warm-up exercises during the first week of class. We suggest dividing students into pairs and having them interview each other briefly (2.5 minutes each). Bring the class back together and have students introduce their interview subject to the others. If the group seems unsure of what to ask, you might suggest some of the following questions:

If you could have any job in the world, what would it be?

If you could be any person in history, who would it be and why?

Where would you most like to live? Why?

What would you consider the ideal vacation?

Who is your hero? Why?

What do you like most about school? What do you like least?

What are your favorite hobbies? Books? Movies? Sports?

Name a famous person you'd like to have lunch with. What would you talk about?

Energizer

Later in your course, after students complete Chapter 2 and update their Personal Profile (on page 27), post the bulls eye charts around the classroom. These can easily be printed from My10yearPlan.com®. As the course proceeds, students will learn more about themselves and make updates to their charts. Encourage them to print out and post these updates.

Typical Problems and How to Handle Them

No matter how well you facilitate your group, some students will have problems. We've listed a few common difficulties and some suggestions for dealing with them.

If a student doesn't get an opportunity to talk:

To make sure everyone gets an opportunity to be heard, break the group into pairs and have each duo come up with a certain number of ideas, answers, or suggestions. Bring the class back together and have team members take turns sharing their responses.

If someone else has already presented a student's idea or answer:

Ask him or her to rephrase the response or to elaborate.

When self-conscious students are embarrassed to speak:

Working in small groups can help these students feel safe enough to speak up. As they gain confidence, they'll be more likely to participate in larger group discussions. Don't push it, but encourage shy students with words, smiles, or nods.

When the class isn't paying attention:

A less formal atmosphere requires students to adapt to new rules and may encourage some to act up. Calmly state your own feelings of frustration and help students recognize their behavior as a response to change. Allow students to discuss their feelings and brainstorm ideas for making the group feel more comfortable and, therefore, more focused.

When the class is bored:

Boredom can be a sign that students don't understand the material or don't find it relevant. The better you know your group, the better able you will be to tailor your presentation of the materials. Breaking into smaller groups is another way to get more students active and involved.

When no one seems able to concentrate:

Lack of concentration may be due to tension or fatigue. A short stand-up break might be helpful. Alternatively, ask students to sit quietly, close their eyes, and concentrate fully on the source of their distraction for two or three minutes. When you bring their attention back to the classroom, ask them to note what they see, hear, and feel. This will help to re-focus their attention.

When there are conflicts or bad feelings in the classroom:

Conflicts between individuals should be settled out of class. The student who simply wants to complain about something should be asked to elaborate on his or her feelings and explain what, exactly, should be done about the situation. Sometimes the resolution can be as simple as placing students in different groups. But it is important that all students understand that conflicts will not be tolerated in class. In the workplace, people get fired for that sort of behavior, whether is it overt or covert.

Group Size

Whatever the size of your class, dividing into smaller groups can be advantageous. Group size varies with the task to be completed. In general, we've discovered the following:

Pairs of students:

These are ideal for sharing personal information or for encouraging students to voice personal opinions or ideas.

Groups of three:

This is a great size for discussion, especially at first, when some students may feel uncomfortable speaking in front of larger groups. Groups of three feel relatively safe. They are also good at accomplishing tasks. However, if group members are close friends, there may be too much socializing. If you use trios regularly, assign students to different groups from time to time.

Groups of four or five:

As students become more experienced and confident communicators, they can move effectively into a slightly larger group. This size is good for meetings, making decisions, or completing tasks. It also allows students to practice group problem-solving skills. Be sure the task or goal is clearly understood.

Groups of six:

To be most effective, groups of six need an appointed or elected leader, a student who is a good communicator. It might be helpful, too, to have a secretary or recorder. An easel or oversized pad can help groups of this size to stay on track. Generally, they are most effective as the course nears its end. Note: Groups of this size can easily break down into pairs or trios, which may derail completion of the assigned task. However, these smaller subsets are good for situations in which personal feedback is required.

Groups of seven or more:

As groups reach this size, they tend to become less effective. It's too easy for individuals to sit back and let others do the work.

Mixing groups:

Depending on the task, it may be appropriate for group members to know each other well or be less well-acquainted. When you want to mix the composition of groups, you might base groups on numbers or names pulled out of a hat.

Or you might give half the class questions written on 3" x 5" cards, and the other half of the class answers to the same. Have students partner with the person holding the question/answer matching their card.

One instructor kept a fish bowl by the door of their classroom. Each day as students entered they pulled a number from the fish bowl and that was their seat assignment for the day. That way, when groups were formed, the composition was always different.

Strategies for Active Learning

There are many techniques that encourage learning by stimulating enthusiasm, motivation, and group participation. Below we've listed several strategies that work particularly well with the *Career Choices* materials.

Brainstorming

A topic is introduced to the group using a phrase such as, "Think of as many ways as you can to…" or "What are some possible solutions for…" Class members then respond verbally and suggestions are written on the board. There is no comment or criticism from the group. When all ideas have been expressed, class discussion, ranking, or prioritizing may follow.

Buzz Groups

Groups of six or fewer students share their opinions or reactions to a speaker, an article, a question, or a statement. A time limit (short in duration) should be stated at the outset to stimulate participation and competition.

Case Studies

A situation that illustrates a point or problem is presented and analyzed. Case studies are easy to relate to and can be less threatening than dealing with the same topic on a personal level. Cases may come from newspapers, magazines, TV shows, movies, books, or students' past experiences.

Debates

Debates allow students to express their opinions or examine the other side of an argument. A debate can match two individuals or two panels of students. Allow each side to present its case and respond to the other arguments, then follow with class discussion. You might set up a debate in which participants argue the position opposite their own. This is a valuable job skill.

Dialogues

Two students discuss a particular topic in front of the class. Class discussion follows.

Exercises

These can be done individually or as a group to stimulate discussion or teach skills.

Fishbowls

Group six (or fewer) students in the center of the class and have them discuss an issue or case study while the rest of the class observes from the perimeter. A class discussion may follow.

Interviews

Asking questions of people outside the class allows students to collect and synthesize data and reach conclusions concerning their topic of investigation.

Journals

This is an important ongoing activity for use with *Career Choices*. By keeping a journal, students can review their growth process now and in years to come.

Lectures or Panels

An outside speaker or group of speakers can offer detailed information, new perspectives, personal experiences, and opinions on a topic. Time should be allowed for the class to ask questions of the speaker(s).

Models

Models promote understanding by providing visual representations of certain concepts, processes, or events.

Peer Learning Groups

This is an advanced technique utilizing the leadership skills of particular students. Peer leaders must be trained for their tasks. They then lead teams of their peers through an exercise.

Role-playing

Students are asked to act out the roles in a particular situation, saying what they think their character would say. This can be an emotional experience for some individuals, so be sure to ask each role player how he or she feels both before and after the exercise.

Skits

Groups of students prepare, practice, and present short plays dealing with a given situation.

We presented a play based on the Prince of Tides *selection in* Possibilities, *and the students loved it. Many wanted to be "Luke." While not totally professional, everyone dressed as a character. We even made a dolphin and stuffed it.*

— Julie Delrusso, SLD Instructor
Lake Brantley High School, Altamonte Springs, FL

Examples of Group Learning

To get you started planning cooperative learning experiences for your class, we've listed some examples of activities and exercises that lend themselves to the active learning strategies discussed on the previous pages. This list is by no means complete and you may find a different technique works just as well (or better) with your students.

What we've heard over and over again is that it is important to use different strategies and techniques to maintain students' interest. Try not to get stuck in the rut of using only brainstorming or small work groups.

Many of these cooperative learning experiences also provide students with opportunities to practice teambuilding. This might not be obvious to them, so you'll want to remind them periodically that learning to work effectively as part of a team will pay off in the workplace.

Brainstorming

Lifestyle Math: page 31, Affording Home Ownership on One Income

Possibilities: page 213, "A Dream Deferred," Question 6

Career Choices: page 4/145 in this *Instructor's Guide*

Buzz Groups

Lifestyle Math: page 38, Group Think, Questions 4 and 5

Possibilities: page 224, "Over the Hill to the Poor-house," Questions 1, 2, 3, and 4

Career Choices: pages 4/118–4/119 in this *Instructor's Guide*

Case Studies

Lifestyle Math: page 42, Case Study

Possibilities: page 85, "The Savings Book," Activity A, B, or C

Career Choices: pages 204–205, Detours and Roadblocks

Debates

Lifestyle Math: page 83, Making Choices

Possibilities: page 22,"A Psalm of Life," The Formal Debate

Career Choices: page 4/32 in this *Instructor's Guide*

Dialogues

Lifestyle Math: page 89, Computing Salaries in Your Head—Quickly!

Possibilities: page 208, excerpt from *The Prince of Tides*, Question B

Career Choices: page 4/33 in this *Instructor's Guide*

Exercises

Lifestyle Math: pages 60–63, Planning a Party

Possibilities: pages 279–283, Your 25th High School Reunion Booklet

Career Choices: page 4/26 in this *Instructor's Guide*

Fishbowls

Lifestyle Math: page 26, Group Think, Questions 4a, 4b, 4c

Possibilities: page 88, "Miss Rosie," Question 4

Career Choices: page 4/20 in this *Instructor's Guide*

Interviews

Lifestyle Math: page 52, Hints for Stretching Your Food Dollar

Possibilities: page 215, "Mother to Son," Question 10

Career Choices: page 4/30 in this *Instructor's Guide*

Lectures and Panels

Lifestyle Math: page 92, Group Brainstorm

Possibilities: page 31, "I Have a Dream…" Question 10

Career Choices: page 4/67 in this *Instructor's Guide*

Models

Lifestyle Math: pages 102–106, Developing an Action Plan

Possibilities: pages 44–45, from *Alice's Adventures in Wonderland*, Acrostic Poetry

Career Choices: page 27, Bulls Eye Chart

Peer Learning Groups

Lifestyle Math: pages 98–99, What is Your Math Education Worth to You?

Possibilities: page 247, "Tonia the Tree," Writing an Allegory for Children

Career Choices: page 4/118 in this *Instructor's Guide*

Role Playing and Skits

Lifestyle Math: pages 96–97, Using Charts and Graphs to Understand Statistics

Possibilities: page 269, "Thank You, M'am," Create a Dialogue

Career Choices: pages 4/102–4/105 in this *Instructor's Guide*

Project-based Learning

Studies have found that students retain more when their learning is tied to a project. The more relevant the project is to students' lives, the more enthusiasm it generates and the more the student retains information and skills related to the experience.

Life is one big project! It is important that we de-compartmentalize learning, particularly for the adolescent. Students can analyze, synthesize, problem solve, and manage resources all within the context of project-based learning. These models also provide opportunities for effective teamwork. You'll find a variety of activities in the *Career Choices* curriculum that are ideal for group projects.

Career Choices

On page 4/26 of this *Instructor's Guide*, you'll find four scenarios that challenge student teams to develop creative solutions.

On pages 4/102–4/105 of this guide is a project where students "develop" a company and design jobs within the company that utilize each team member's aptitudes and work profile.

Possibilities

Students develop their own 25th High School Reunion Booklet (pages 279–283). Team members learn important workplace skills along with organizational skills.

For your creative thinkers and future authors, review the Writing an Allegory for Children project (page 247).

Lifestyle Math

Everyone loves to plan a party, but do students realize how much math this entails? On pages 60–63, students will find a spreadsheet for planning a spaghetti feast.

What is Your Math Education Worth to You? (pages 98–99) is a project that demonstrates the use of SCANS skills and provides eye-opening results.

Assessing Students' Readiness for Hybrid Learning

Most students will find My10yearPlan.com® to be an enriching, intuitive experience. However, some students may lack the prerequisite characteristics and skills to be successful in a course with a significant online component. This is one of the main reasons My10yearPlan.com® was designed to enhance the *Career Choices* classroom experience rather than as a distance-learning course.

That is not to say that you couldn't use *Career Choices* and My10yearPlan.com® in a hybrid format with independent study students.

The information below will help you evaluate a student's readiness for successful online learning.

Personal Attributes and Behaviors for Successful Online Learning

Students need to:

- ✓ Have the self-discipline to complete the course work on time
- ✓ Have the intrinsic motivation for in-depth learning rather than just completing
- ✓ Practice good time management strategies
- ✓ Have good follow-through, see problems as challenges, and not give up easily
- ✓ Have the ability to focus without being easily distracted or taken off task
- ✓ Ask for help from instructors and peers

Academic and Technical Skills Required for Successful Online Learning

Students need to:

- ✓ Type 30–40 words per minute
- ✓ Read at a proficient level
- ✓ Write and compute at proficient levels
- ✓ Have sufficient technical skills to work independently without frustration
- ✓ Confront technical issues proactively and troubleshoot on their own
- ✓ Be competent at Internet research and aggressively seek answers to their questions

Distance Learning Dos and Don'ts

The *Career Choices* curriculum can be paired with My10yearPlan.com® Interactive for a distance learning course. Because the leadership and mentorship of the instructor is a vital part of the course, this is not an ideal delivery method for a comprehensive guidance course. However, for some populations this is the only way they can access this vital experience.

Distance learning can be as effective as learning in a traditional classroom setting, but it is essential that the course use methodologies known to deliver the best possible experience for both student and instructor. The following best practices for distance instruction will help. You can also contact Academic Innovations for support at (800) 967-8016.

First, you'll want to ensure that the students have mastered basic computer skills. If students in your class are unfamiliar with Internet searches, navigating web sites, and communicating through email, they are likely to struggle with this course or any online course.

Preparation prior to the first class is a key ingredient to success. Before class starts, you'll want to set up your online classroom on your course management system (e.g., Blackboard®, Moodle®, etc.).

You'll also want to select an appropriate pacing guide to ensure the course ends with each student completing an online 10-year plan in Chapter 12. For sample pacing guides, see pages 10/9 and 10/11 of this guide or download a sample from **The Teachers' Lounge**.

Communication is paramount to the success of a distance learning course, especially this one. Sometimes you might communicate with the group; much of the communication will be with individual students. Let your students know when you are available and how quickly you can likely respond to them so expectations are realistic.

The career and life planning process requires guidance and thought-provoking feedback, so the lack of a physical classroom requires that you double your efforts in email communication and online discussion. Consider setting up an online forum where students can share their experiences with the materials? You can monitor the conversations to provide input as needed. If you are using **My10yearPlan.com®**, a discussion feature is already available for your use.

Grading students' online work and truly assessing their development can be time consuming. Be sure to allow enough time. See Section 14 in this guide for assessment suggestions.

Distance learning has its pros and cons. With careful planning and continuous feedback, you can make a difference in students' lives even without face-to-face contact by helping them identify and plan for their ideal careers and lifestyles.

Speakers Bureau

Many of the discussion topics in *Career Choices* can be made even more meaningful by involving guest speakers. You'll need to determine who to use and how to use them, and it's unlikely you are personally acquainted with experts and resource people in all these areas. To make tracking down appropriate guest speakers a bit easier, we've compiled a list of suggested topics and general speaker descriptions. The list can be easily tailored to reflect your community or the needs of your students. Use this list to get some help; you might:

- Distribute copies of the list to friends and co-workers who might be able to supply some names and phone numbers.

- Pass a copy around at the next Kiwanis, Soroptimists, or Rotary meeting, especially if you are a member.

- Make a brief presentation about your class to some of these community organizations, asking for help from the members.

- Get other community people involved by bringing your request before the school improvement team.

Page 4/96 of this guide provides a description of a "Director of Mentors." Perhaps the person who holds this volunteer position could assist in locating and scheduling guest speakers.

If you teach several sections of this class, it may be difficult to find speakers who can devote a full day or two. You may try scheduling your guest speakers in the morning before the school day begins or as a special morning assembly. For most working adults the early morning won't interfere too much with their workday.

Arrange for the presentations to be held in the school auditorium so many classes can be accommodated. Students may groan about coming to school early, so point out that schedule adjustments are common in the world of work and flexibility is required of most jobs. The expectations should be clear and this should be seen as part of their homework.

Be sure to advise the other faculty members of your scheduled presentations. Perhaps they would like to attend. Filming the speakers would be a good project for a video production class and would allow you to build a library of presentations for future use.

It might be helpful to lend each speaker a copy of the *Career Choices* text so they can review the appropriate section and be familiar with the concepts the students are studying. To help your speaker, supply a list of questions they should address in their presentation.

Note: Include plans for speakers in your pacing guide so you don't run short on time. Remember that the ultimate goal is development of the 10-year Plan.

 For forms that you can distribute among your network to solicit volunteer speakers, visit Section 11 in the online version of this *Instructor's Guide*.

Parents came in to speak to classes about how they started in their chosen field. They brought slides, videos, etc. Since many students knew these speakers personally, it was highly relevant and interesting to them.

— Mary Turella, 8th Grade English and Communications Teacher
North Royalton Middle School, North Royalton, OH

References for Speakers' Bureau

	Corresponding page(s) in *Career Choices*
Chapter 3	
Successfully retired individuals (3–5)	60–61, 208–209
Chapter 4	
Real estate professional	78
Travel agent	87
Insurance agent	89
Parents on welfare (2–3)	102–103
Person who gave up an opulent lifestyle to do something meaningful	104–105
Chapter 5	
Psychologist	135–137, 218–221
Entrepreneur	138–139
Chapter 9	
Physically-challenged individual who has persevered	197–199
Individuals who overcame adversity:	
High school dropout	203–209
Teen mother	203–209
Recovering substance abuser	203–209
Individuals still struggling:	
High school dropout	207
Teen mother	211–213
Recovering substance abuser	208–209
Women successful in:*	
Balancing career and family	211–213
Professional career	
Nontraditional career	
Immigrant entrepreneur	222–223
Community social service resource specialist	226
United Way staff person	226
Chapter 10	
Bank manager	242–245
Stockbroker	242–245
Chapter 11	
Human resources manager	250–253, 258–259
Chapter 12	
Career counselor	267–269
Vocational counselor	
College placement officer	
Military recruiter	
Union director	
Employment developing director	
Owner of recruiting firm	

*Be sure they meet the criteria of the exercise

Video Book Club

Being literate in contemporary society means being active, critical, and creative users not only of print and spoken language but also of the visual language of film and television, commercial and political advertising, photography, and more.

— International Reading Association and the National Council of Teachers of English

As forms of communication change, our societal focus is shifting from reading, writing, and speaking to include electronic communications—video, audio, computerization—it is imperative that we teach students to be media-conscious consumers who analyze electronic mediums with the same skills required in analyzing traditional forms.

The Common Core State Standards for English spell out a series of anchor standards in which the college-and-career-ready student is expected to integrate, evaluate, gather relevant information from, and make strategic use of "content presented in diverse formats and media."

To help students gain these skills, we suggest you form a Video Book Club to introduce literary themes, provide practice in analysis, and encourage lively discussion.

You'll want to make sure that all students have access to a DVD player or computer. You may need to sponsor a showing of the film after school or during the lunch break for those students who cannot rent or get access to the film. Students could also form groups, meeting at one member's house and splitting the cost of the movie rental.

Assignments should be made far in advance, so students have ample time to see the film. You might pass out a list early in the course with film titles and dates of discussion so students can schedule accordingly.

After discussing several videos, you may assign a novel or play for the next meeting. Students are more likely to complete the assignment enthusiastically and participate in the discussion once they have experienced success in the Video Book Club.

Then, encourage students to watch the movie version of the literary work that was read. At some point, discuss how the book and movie were different and ask students which they preferred. People generally prefer the book; ask students why.

 You can view summaries of suggested movies and access viewing guides on the online version of this *Instructor's Guide.*

Top Movie Suggestions

The movies we've listed illustrate topics or concepts raised in the text. Many of these suggestions came from *Career Choices* instructors and originated as novels or plays that could also be assigned for reading.

Please preview selections before showing them to your class. You will want to make sure they are appropriate for your students, fulfill your classroom goals, and adhere to school policies.

Bend It Like Beckham (2002) PG-13—Starring Parminder Nagra, Keira Knightley, and Jonathan Rhys-Meyers

Jess aspires to become a professional football (soccer) player, but her traditional Indian parents disapprove and have other ideas for her future. This film deals with the themes of stretching established gender roles and following one's own dreams rather than parents' wishes. (*A viewing guide is available on* The Teachers' Lounge.)

Blind Side, The (2009) PG-13—Starring Sandra Bullock, Tim McGraw, and Quinton Aaron

An inspiring story based on the life of Michael Oher, a homeless boy who went on to become an All-American college football player and a first-draft NFL pick after being taken in as a high school student by a woman and her family. This movie exemplifies success as a result of hard work and can lead into a discussion of the importance of academics even for students aspiring to become professional athletes. (*A viewing guide is available on* The Teachers' Lounge.)

Little Red Wagon (2012) PG—Starring Chandler Canterbury, Anna Gunn, Frances O'Connor

This docudrama explores the story behind the Little Red Wagon Foundation, a charity Zach Bonner started at the age of eight. In 2004 aftermath Hurricane Charley, Zach used his little red wagon to gather truckloads of supplies for homeless children.

McFarland, USA (2015) PG—Starring Kevin Costner, Maria Bello, Ramiro Rodriguez

Based on a true story, Jim White is struggling to deal with the consequences of his choices. He winds up coaching and teaching in one of the poorest cities in California, where he sees untapped potential all around him. Coach White starts a cross country team that quickly becomes competitive against bigger programs across the state.

October Sky (1999) PG—Starring Jake Gyllenhaal

When Sputnik takes flight in October 1957, so do the dreams of Homer Hickman, a boy growing up in a small mining town. Homer is inspired to learn about rockets, hoping to build one of his own. Just about everyone in town, including his father, thinks his efforts are a waste of time. After all, his future is already decided—to work in the local coal mine like his father. Homer and his friends keep working toward their dream anyway, with the encouragement of one of their high school teachers. The movie is based on the memoir *Rocket Boys*. (*A viewing guide is available on* The Teachers' Lounge.)

"October Sky was GREAT for visions and dreams!! The best yet!"

— Kim Smith, Special Resource Teacher
Ewing Township, Lawrenceville, NJ

Mr. Holland's Opus (1995) PG—Starring Richard Dreyfuss

This film is about a passionate musician who takes up teaching in order to pay the rent. His true goal is to compose one piece of music for which he will be remembered. As the years go by, Mr. Holland finds his own personal definition of success. A great film to help students understand the concepts discussed with the bulls eye chart activity (page 27, *Career Choices*). *(A viewing guide is available on* The Teachers' Lounge.*)*

Suggested by Julie Gergen, Teacher, Dover-Eyota High School, Eyota, MN

Pursuit of Happyness, The (2006) PG-13—Starring Will Smith and Jaden Smith

This film is based on the true story of Chris Gardner, who, while raising a young son, worked his way out of extreme poverty and homelessness to become a stockbroker. This film is an excellent example of delaying gratification and achieving success as a result of sacrifices and hard work despite valid "excuses" for not succeeding. *(A viewing guide is available on* The Teachers' Lounge.*)*

At the end of Chapter 3 show the movie The Pursuit of Happyness *in its entirety. Have students draw a triangle that fills a notebook page and label the levels of the triangle according to Maslow. As students watch the movie, they are instructed to identify a scene from the movie that represents each level. The triangle acts as a graphic organizer. Students then write a paper teaching me about Maslow's Triangle.*

I reference this movie throughout the curriculum. It's very powerful. For instance when working on the hard times budget on pages 55 and 56 of Career Choices, *I reference the movie from a budgeting standpoint. What about pouring undrunk tea into the pitcher, yet money is spent on cigarettes. Reinforce the difference between wants and needs.*

Another opportunity to reference the Pursuit of Happyness *is when reviewing the character traits of successful individuals found in the activity, the Six E's of Excellence, on pages 232–233 in* Career Choices.

– Cathie Klein, College & Career Readiness Coordinator
Seaman High School, Topeka, KS

Rudy (1993) PG—Starring Sean Astin and Ned Beatty

Rudy wanted to play football at Notre Dame, something the folks in the steel town where he grew up thought was impossible. After all, most people in the town ended up working at the steel mill. Rudy had some other barriers: his grades were a little low and he was only half the size of the other players. People told him he'd never play for Notre Dame, but Rudy had drive, spirit, and determination.

Rudy [is] great for showing how to pursue a goal, a dream, and not letting others say you can't accomplish something.

— Roseann Reynolds, Teacher, 9th Grade Foundation Class
Moreno Valley High School, Moreno Valley, CA

For Rudy, *I have my students write a response to "what could have happened to Rudy if he believed what everyone else thought he should do: quit," and then we have an open discussion.*

— Kim Smith, Special Resource Teacher
Ewing Township, Lawrenceville, NJ

Using Music to Trigger Discussion and Generate Energy

Song of the Day

Music is an integral part of our culture, especially for teens. With a little bit of planning, music can play a role in motivating students, generating positive energy, and as a trigger for discussion.

In 1983, author Mindy Bingham, attended a week-long institute sponsored by the IBM Corporation. At the time, IBM was known as one of the most sophisticated training providers in the country and they sponsored intensive business management for executive directors of community service organizations. Each morning participants arrived for class and were greeted by music. It soon became apparent that the songs being played were chosen not only to enliven the experience but also to subtly introduce the topic to be addressed during that session.

Consider adding a "song of the day" project to your course. Choose music that reinforces topics or concepts introduced that day. As students arrive for class, have music playing. When the bell rings, fade it out and begin class.

You can find song ideas that correspond to *Career Choices* activities in Section 11 on the online version of this *Instructor's Guide*.

Better yet, ask students to suggest appropriate songs to create your own class playlist. Be sure to share your suggestions with us so we can pass them along to *Career Choices* teachers across the country.

Vocabulary Lists and Definitions

Vocabulary words are included for each *Career Choices* chapter in the *Workbook and Portfolio*. Printable lists of the vocabulary words and their definitions are available on **The Teachers' Lounge** at www.careerchoices.com/lounge/cupboard_vocablists.html. The vocabulary lists and definitions are available to students using **My10yearPlan.com®** by clicking on the Vocabulary link on the left menu.

You can find a list of vocabulary words in Section 11 on the online version of this *Instructor's Guide*.

Resources

1. National Governors Association Center for Best Practices, Council of Chief State School Officers, Common Core State Standards for English Language Arts & Literacy in History/Social Studies, Science, and Technical Subjects, (Washington, DC: National Governors Association Center for Best Practices, Council of Chief State School Officers, 2010) p. 48. Retrieved from www.corestandards.org 04/19/2013.

2. ibid

3. ibid

4. ibid, p. 7

Section 12

Curriculum Support and Professional Development Options

Topics covered in this section include:

- A vast array of professional development options—from workshops to phone support to online resources.

- All online course planning resources can be found on **The Teachers' Lounge** at www.careerchoices.com/lounge.

- Online training videos are available to walk you through various aspects of the curriculum and preparing to launch a course.

- Our free e-newsletter provides timely teaching advice related to *Career Choices* and shares ideas submitted by *Career Choices* teachers across the country.

- Complimentary curriculum support is available by phone at (800) 967-8016 during business hours (9:00 AM to 4:00 PM MST). Referrals to technical assistance contractors can be made for customized onsite professional development.

- Opportunities for students to update their 10-year plans throughout high school as part of a school-wide initiative will provide the best results for your *Career Choices* program.

Academic Innovations: Your Partner in Professional Development

Providing high-quality instructional material is only a part of our responsibility to you, your teachers, and your students. Helping you make the most of those materials is a big part of what we do.

To meet your very specific needs, we have a comprehensive menu of professional development services and resources developed with the understanding that everyone learns differently, on different time schedules, and at a different pace.

Online Professional Development

- The Teachers' Lounge
- 40 Online Training Videos
- Courses for Teachers and Administrators
- Online Professional Learning Community
- Webinars
- Online courses for CEU credits

Workshops and Institutes

- One- and Two-day Workshops
- Two- and Three-day Institutes
- Focus on Freshmen Conference (annual)
- Freshman Transition Leadership Institutes
- Workshops and Institutes in our St. George, Utah Training Center
- Onsite Workshops at Your School
- Technical Assistance Contracts
- Hands-on Lab-based Workshops

Call (800) 967-8016 or visit www.aiworkshops.com for information on any of the professional development options offered by Academic Innovations.

 View a sample professional development plan on page 12/16 and develop your own using a blank template found on the online version of this *Instructor's Guide* or on The Teachers' Lounge.

Checklist of Professional Development Considerations

As you're planning, consider the many factors that instructors may need for program success: release time, credit, substitutes, travel, recognition, and opportunities to share their new knowledge.

With that in mind, you can determine how you'll achieve your professional development goals.

Time is an important consideration—common prep period or release time

- ☐ Arrange schedules so instructors have at least one common prep period each week to meet, participate in quality training, and discuss their progress
- ☐ If a common prep period isn't possible, provide substitutes or use in-service days so teams can meet for longer blocks of time (half days and whole days) to complete their training
- ☐ Conduct the bulk of your training over the summer and prior to the start of class to eliminate the need for substitutes; participants may need to be compensated for time outside their regular contract

Coordinate activities and develop a professional development calendar

- ☐ Introduce the Freshman Transition course and school-wide initiative to all faculty
- ☐ Train the *Career Choices* classroom teachers on the course materials and standards
- ☐ Introduce the Freshman Transition course and school-wide initiative to parents and community members
- ☐ Hold a school-wide training entitled "Every Teacher an Advisor: Using Students' 10-year Plans to Personalize Instruction and Mentoring"

Consider including these strategies/tasks in your professional development plan

- ☐ Follow the workshop session schedule included in the Lead Administrator & Lead Teacher Manual
- ☐ Use the online training modules and the online course options at www.careerchoices.com/lounge/modules.html
- ☐ Attend a workshop or an institute sponsored by Academic Innovations
- ☐ Contact the Curriculum Support team at Academic Innovations for sample meeting agendas, presentations, videos, and other resources to help your staff conduct effective professional development at your school
- ☐ Recommend outside professional development opportunities (e.g., conferences and conventions) and determine which staff members would benefit most by attending
- ☐ Remember that "reporting out" to all stakeholders is an important step
- ☐ Promote capacity building by encouraging successful instructors to make presentations at state and regional conferences
- ☐ Plan implementation workshops prior to the start of class so new *Career Choices* teachers can be up and running quickly
- ☐ Identify your best instructors and arrange for them to mentor other *Career Choices* instructors
- ☐ Carve out time for instructors to watch colleagues presenting the *Career Choices* materials
- ☐ Determine budget requirements for the above plans; submit the plan and proposed budget for approval

Online Instructor's Guide

Develop your own professional development plan using a blank template available through The Teachers' Lounge at www.careerchoices.com/lounge. See page 12/16 for an example.

AIWorkshops.com: Your *Career Choices* Professional Development Source

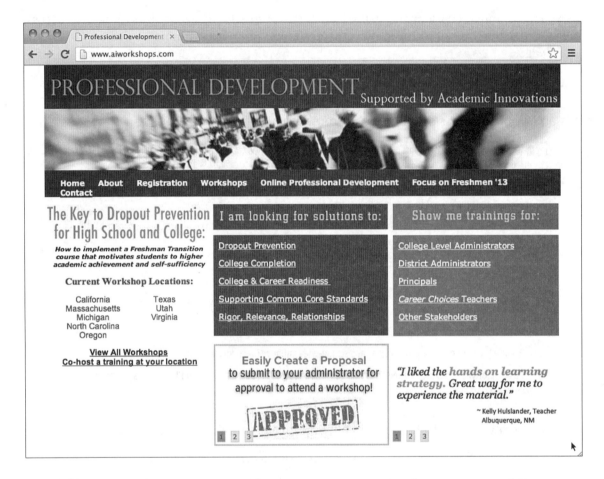

AIWorkshops.com has information on all professional development events offered by Academic Innovations.

If you know which workshop, institute, or conference you're interested in attending, you can register online for the most convenient date and location. You can also create a proposal for your administrator to request approval to attend. Once you attend a workshop, you can work to earn graduate elective units through Brandman University, and AIWorkshops.com provides information on that opportunity, as well.

If you're interested in hosting a workshop at your site, there's an online survey to help determine if your facility would be a match for our workshop set-up.

AIWorkshops.com is also where our webinar schedule is updated. These online sessions and courses cover a variety of topics related to implementation of *Career Choices* and the online enhancements. Sessions are presented by Curriculum and Technical Support staff, *Career Choices* trainers, and special guest experts.

Online Professional Development: The Teachers' Lounge

www.careerchoices.com/lounge

This online professional development web site for the *Career Choices* curriculum puts all of our resources right at your fingertips in one convenient place. It includes:

- Motivational chapter introduction videos with Olympic Gold Medalist Dain Blanton
- Over 40 online training videos (with optional assessments)
- Online professional learning community of *Career Choices* teachers
- Video footage of Best Practice sessions presented by *Career Choices* educators
- An online evaluation tool for scoring students' pre-/post-surveys
- Grading resources and lesson planning materials to enhance your course

…and countless other tools and tips to ensure a successful *Career Choices* course

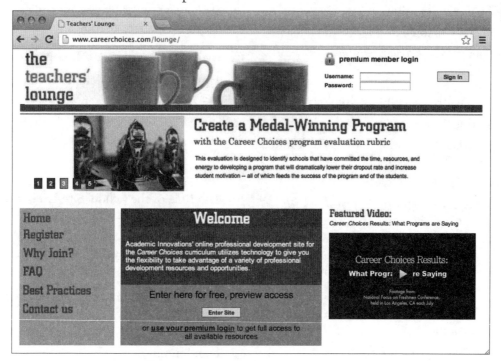

Basic membership is free and includes limited access to online training videos, lesson planning materials, funding and buy-in resources. Premium membership is available for an annual fee and allows unlimited access to The Teachers' Lounge, including grading resources and the professional learning community discussion.

Your initial **12-month site licensing fee** is calculated on a sliding scale based on your largest order of *Career Choices* materials to date. Annual re-orders are used to determine the licensing for subsequent years.

Please call (800) 967-8016 for a fee quote or complete the "Do I qualify?" form at www.careerchoices.com/lounge/membership.html and we'll contact you.

Online Professional Development: Training Videos

www.careerchoices.com/lounge/mod_vieworder.html

Viewed in the order listed below, these videos provide the most complete picture of how the *Career Choices* curriculum can be used to deliver a Freshman Transition course and school-wide initative.

Curriculum Overview

- What is a Freshman Transition Initiative?
- The Key to Success for Dropout Prevention Programs
- *Career Choices*: Why It Works
- Why the *Career Choices* Curriculum was Developed
- Success 101 (documentary)
- Five Ingredients of a Successful *Career Choices* Course
- The School-wide Initiative
- From Clueless to Focused (documentary)
- Overview of the *Career Choices* Curriculum

Integrating Academics and Technology

- Integrating Academics and Technology
- *Possibilities*: Integrating Career Exploration into the English Classroom
- *Lifestyle Math*: An Overview
- Strategies for Integrating *Lifestyle Math* into your *Career Choices* Course
- In-Depth Overview of My10yearPlan.com®

Using *Career Choices* for your Freshman Transition Initiative

- Every Teacher an Advisor: Strategies for Personalization
- Tips for Getting Buy-in From All Stakeholders

Online Professional Development

- The Teachers' Lounge: An Overview
- How to Use the Online Training Videos

Customizing your Lesson Plans

- The *Instructor's Guide*: An Overview
- Section Four of the *Instructor's Guide*
- Customizing Lesson Plans Using Microsoft Excel

Course Planning Strategies

- Who Am I?: Chapters 1 – 2
- What Do I Want? Chapters 3 – 7
- How Do I Get It? Chapters 8 – 12
- Chapter 12: The Take-Home Final Exam Option
- How to Use the Pre- and Post-Surveys to Assess *Career Choices*' Impact
- How To Develop the Career Portfolio Notebook
- Strategies for Incorporating an Online Career Exploration Tool

Classroom Management Techniques

- Tips and Ideas to Create an Involved Learner
- Cooperative Learning and Teambuilding
- Strategies for Active Learning

My10yearPlan.com® How-Tos

- The Role of the School Site Executive
- Tips for Selecting Your School Site Executive
- Getting Started Guide for the School Site Executive
- How to Set up *Career Choices* Teacher Accounts
- How to Search for Students and View their Plan Summaries
- How to E-mail Students
- Managing Your School Site License Quotas

Modules vary in length from 3 minutes to 15 minutes.

Other Online Professional Development Options:

Courses for Instructors and Administrators

Wouldn't it be great if you could earn graduate level credit as you prepare for your upcoming course or Freshman Transition program? With Academic Innovations and Brandman University, you can!

Academic Innovations has developed several courses that instructors or administrators of *Career Choices* classes can take for graduate elective units. Once you've registered with Brandman University, courses involve viewing online videos, completing online assessments, and reflective written assignments. All of the courses we offer meet Brandman University's standards for graduate level professional development units.

Some course work can be completed through attendance at an Academic Innovations workshop, while the content for other offerings is delivered completely online.

Course listing and additional details can be found at www.careerchoices.com/lounge/profdev_ceucourses.html.

Webinars

www.aiworkshops.com/webinars.html

We schedule online sessions covering a variety of topics related to implementation of *Career Choices* and the online enhancements. Sessions are presented by Curriculum and Technical Support staff, *Career Choices* trainers, and special guest experts.

Professional Learning Community Forum

www.careerchoices.com/lounge/plc_home.html

This **moderated** forum stimulates discussion and facilitates the sharing of information and ideas related to the use of the *Career Choices* curriculum. Participating members can get feedback on issues they're facing and/or share their expertise with others. All visitors to The Teachers' Lounge are invited to follow the discussions and learn from the ideas shared, but participation in this community is a privilege granted only to **registered members** of The Teachers' Lounge.

TIPS Newsletter

www.careerchoices.com/lounge/subscribe.html

Throughout each school year, our Curriculum and Technical Support team sends out a bi-weekly email newsletter with helpful reminders, tips, and strategies to help keep your *Career Choices* course on track. The TIPS (Teaching Insights, Practices, and Solutions) newsletter is a free, valuable resource featuring timely advice and unique ideas from *Career Choices* educators.

Workshops and Institutes

From a motivational standpoint, nothing beats face-to-face contact with trainer and learners. To that end, Academic Innovations workshops and institutes include:

- One- and two-day workshops
- Two-and three-day insititutes
- Annual *Focus on Freshmen* conference
- **Freshman Transition Leadership Institutes**
- *Get Focused...Stay Focused!*™ workshops and conferences
- Summer institutes in **Academic Innovations's Training Center** in St. George, Utah
- Onsite workshop at your school
- Hosted and co-sponsored workshop with your district or college
- Ongoing technical assistance contracts
- Hands-on computer lab-based workshops

For details and brochures about these professional development opportunities, visit www.aiworkshops.com or the online version of this *Instructor's Guide*.

Academic Innovations' Training Center in picturesque and historic St. George, Utah provides the best in high-tech/high-touch professional development.

High-Tech: Our onsite computer lab allows participants to get hands-on experience with the *Career Choices* online enhancements: My10yearPlan.com®, CareerChoices.com, LifestyleMath.com, and the online Teachers' Lounge. Our state-of-the-art use of video enhances the learning experience with real-world examples.

High-Touch: Workshop groups are kept small (15 to 25 participants) so you get personalized attention and customized solutions. Special one-to-one or small group strategy sessions can be arranged with members of our Curriculum and Technical Support team.

A great opportunity to visit one of the prettiest communities in the southwest, step away from your school duties, revitalize, and immerse yourself in the learning process with educators from all over the country.

Ideal for First-time *Career Choices* Instructors

For the current implementation workshop schedule, visit www.aiworkshops.com/career-choices.html.

Lead Administrator and Lead Teacher Institute and Online Courses

Develop your own in-house team leader for your *Career Choices*/Freshman Transition course effort; someone with the training and the tools to easily:

- Provide implementation workshops for new teachers
- Lead content-rich *Career Choices* professional learning community workshops throughout the year
- Create buy-in strategies for the rest of the school personnel
- Facilitate the school-wide updating of students' 10-year plans in grades 10–12 that also supports the Common Core State Standards

To address the need for quality, ongoing technical assistance, the *Career Choices* Lead Administrator and Lead Teacher Institute equips you to deliver capacity-building workshops for your school teams at your own site.

Institute participants receive the *Career Choices* Lead Administrator and Lead Teacher Manual, which includes:

- A step-by-step agenda for 22 hours of professional development that include 22 training videos that make workshops easy to conduct with confidence and minimal preparation
- Strategies and tools for getting buy-in for the Freshman Transition Initiative from staff and parents
- Innovative classroom teaching strategies that create involved learners

This institute provides the tools and knowledge to guide your colleagues in implementing:

- *Career Choices* coursework successfully
- *Optional* academic and technology integration strategies that incorporate the literature anthology *Possibilities*, the math supplement *Lifestyle Math*, and the online tools My10yearPlan.com®, CareerChoices.com, and LifestyleMath.com
- My10yearPlan.com® not only in the *Career Choices* classroom but throughout high school as an advisory tool for academic coaching and advisory functions

---

Please Note:

This institute is designed for experienced *Career Choices* teachers and administrators responsible for coordinating the efforts of a team of *Career Choices* instructors. To benefit fully from the Lead Administrator and Lead Teacher Institute, it is recommended that the participant complete at least one of the following prior to attending:

- Teach the *Career Choices* course for at least one year
- Attend a two-day *Career Choices* implementation workshop
- Watch the *Career Choices* implementation workshop DVDs

First-time *Career Choices* teachers will benefit most from attending a two-day implementation workshop (see page 12/9 for details).

Freshman Transition Leadership Institute and Online Courses

Principals or district administrators who share our goal of increasing school retention and student success won't want to miss this professional development opportunity.

This institute delivers a **10-Step Plan** for initiating a Freshman Transition course, based on the Standards for a Freshman Transition Course developed through The George Washington University's Freshman Transition Initiative, and for implementing a school-wide program that provides data-driven advisory opportunities.

Participants leave the Freshman Transition Leadership Institute with:

- The tools, templates, and training to develop a comprehensive plan for their Freshman Transition efforts
- The necessary data and resources to generate buy-in from teachers, parents, school board members, and community partners
- A complete manual of resources that includes planning committee job descriptions, teacher recruitment rubrics, timelines, curriculum correlations, and planning checklists
- Strategies for implementing a school-wide initiative that takes advisory functions to a new level through the interdisciplinary efforts of all departments

This sponsored institute is open to all but will be of particular interest to principals and administrators whose schools are working to meet the Standards for a Freshman Transition Course and have adopted, or are considering adopting, the *Career Choices* curriculum for their 8th or 9th grade students.

Get Focused…Stay Focused! ™ Initiative Conference and Webinars

A grade 8–14 model for college and career readiness

One very successful school-wide initiative model is the *Get Focused…Stay Focused!* ™ Initiative. In collaboration with local high schools and other partner organizations, *Get Focused…Stay Focused!* ™ provides every student with the necessary information and experiences to:

- Develop college and career readiness skills
- Facilitate the development of an online 10-year career and education plan

Once students develop their initial 10-year plans in 9th grade, targeted classroom-based lessons in the 10th, 11th, and 12th grades ensure students stay focused on their goals. Each 16-hour *Get Focused…Stay Focused!* ™ module provides a "touch-point" to help students transition seamlessly to their post-secondary goal. The content for each module aligns with the Common Core State Standards, making integration into academic courses an easy process.

For more information, visit **www.getfocusedstayfocused.org**.

Annual Focus on Freshmen Conference

Both the Lead Administrator and Lead Teacher Institute (see page 12/10) and the Freshman Transition Leadership Institute (see 12/11) are offered as a part of our annual Focus on Freshmen Conference.

Held each July in Los Angeles, this dynamic, three-day leadership conference provides strategies to change the culture of your school and transform your students' attitudes about the future.

With myriad institutes and breakout sessions offered each year, teams find ample opportunities to explore new innovations, gain inspiration, and work in collaboration to improve their Freshman Transition and *Career Choices* efforts.

What Participants are Saying
ABOUT THE FOCUS ON FRESHMEN EXPERIENCE

"I am completely thrilled. I've gone to literally hundreds of conferences at this point in my career, but I had never felt the level of energy and commitment from the people that were part of the organizing committee…but then also the participants. I saw that there were a lot of people here that are visionaries and that have the same kind of passion and mission that I have…it was very exhilarating for me to be here."

Josefina Canchola, Associate Director, Regional Centers
Puente Project, Diamond Bar, CA

"The conference continues to be very well organized and interesting. Great food, too! And, the participants are a wealth of information."

Barnaby Gloger, Assistant Principal
Carpinteria High School, Carpinteria, CA

"I am very impressed that the entire staff is available between sessions. This program is life-altering, not only for students, but should be for all stakeholders. Thank you! We'll be back!"

Scott Walker, Assistant Principal
Foothill High School, Henderson, NV

"I loved the entire experience…I came wanting to gain ideas, info, and strategies to improve what we do with our students to ensure success. I came away with so much more than I hoped for!"

Ramona Ketcher, Vice Principal
Stilwell High School, Stilwell, OK

"The institute is powerful for any school of any level. This program works for students who are struggling and it also works for students who are very successful."

Beverly Strickland, Director of High School Programs
Duval County Schools, Jacksonville, FL

"This was the most professionally organized and presented seminar I have ever attended. There was something for everyone."

Roger Haserot, Teacher
Mt. Diablo High School, Concord, CA

"The Course Standards are a priceless gift to us! Not having to recreate the wheel will save us hours."

Pat Murray, Counselor
Nevada R-5 High School, Nevada, MO

"Listening to the guest panel brought a sense of reality, positivity, and confirmation that this program can be a success if used as intended."

Rochelle Bell, Assistant Principal
Cahokia USD, Cahokia, IL

"We really enjoyed discussing solutions to our time barrier with the presenters and other teachers. We are now equipped with great resources and contacts to make this program a success at our school."

Khrystal Boudreaux, Teacher
Bay High School, Bay St. Louis, MS

"This program is for everybody's population. And, it's just so comprehensive that everything you need to know is answered…I've never had such personal attention!"

Jaunice Woodall, Teacher
Maynard Jackson High School, Atlanta, GA

"That was what was so wonderful: I was able to sit down and talk with others. We just had ample opportunity to pick their brains."

Sue Bond, Teacher
Nevada R-5 High School, Nevada, MO

"This seems to tie everything together that we've been striving toward for nine years, and I'm extremely, extremely excited."

Betty Myers, Dean
Streamwood High School, Streamwood, IL

"The presentations were great, and now I can effectively plan and implement my lessons in a more efficient and effective manner."

Cetresa Freeman, Teacher
Southwest Magnet High School, Macon, GA

Current dates and strand offerings at **www.FocusonFreshmen.com**

Onsite Workshops

If you have a group of educators in need of training, consider bringing a one- or two-day *Career Choices* workshop to your site.

Academic Innovations has conducted workshops around the country and trained more than 30,000 educators. Let our trainers energize your instructors and provide tips and tools for classroom success.

Contact our Curriculum and Technical Support team to learn more, or visit www.aiworkshops.com/onsite-workshops.html.

Consider Co-hosting or Co-sponsoring a Workshop

Co-hosting a workshop may be another option for bringing training to your site. A co-hosted workshop is held at your location (e.g., school, district office, college, professional development center) for your teachers, but you agree to allow people from other districts to attend.

Co-hosting a workshop can benefit your program in many ways.

- You'll receive multiple complimentary spots in the workshop.
- Your team gets training without the need to travel.
- Our exceptional staff supports and helps execute the planning and coordination of the event.
- It's a wonderful opportunity to "show off" your site to educators from around your region.

As our co-host, you can request additional time with the workshop trainer to discuss your district's/school's specific needs.

For details on how to co-host or co-sponsor a workshop call (800) 967-8015.

Technical Assistance

Technical Assistance Contracts

Studies clearly show that school redesign requires ongoing and consistent professional development. This is usually provided through a technical assistance contract.

Academic Innovations has identified, trained, and certified technical assistance professionals from across the country. They are available to contract with schools and districts to provide ongoing support as you develop your Freshman Transition efforts. These independent consultants contract directly with schools/districts to help plan, implement, and sustain Freshman Transition courses that utilize the *Career Choices* curriculum.

Contact us for a referral or visit www.whatworkscareerchoices.com/TA for details.

Computer Lab-based Workshops

If your plan includes use of the *Career Choices* online enhancements, especially My10yearPlan.com®, our trainers and technical assistance contractors can provide hands-on experience at your site in your own computer lab. This type of training will enable your faculty to use My10yearPlan.com® effectively for advisory or academic coaching purposes and to facilitate the annual review and updating of the 10-year plans.

Technical Assistance Experts Provide Specialized Training

The technical assistance contract can be expanded to include specialized topics that support the goals of the Freshman Transition Initiative's 10-Step Plan model, such as Caring And Responsive Educators: Starting the CAREing Conversation.

Caring And Responsive Educators: Starting the CAREing Conversation

Educators in all disciplines can play a significant role in making classroom learning relevant to students' lives and futures. Students will integrate this learning into their own lives and reflect the meaningful decisions they come to in the updating of their plan. **The CAREing Conversation serves as a guide to facilitate this critical relationship between educators and students.**

The CAREing Conversations training is intended for use with educators who will oversee and/or directly participate in the school-wide initiative, including but not limited to teachers, administrators, counselors, and paraprofessionals.

For more information, visit www.freshmantransition.org/care.php.

Assistance Launching a School-wide Initiative

Embedding the *Career Choices* course and the annual updating of 10-year plans into school culture has made a remarkable impact on many schools. This broader, school-wide effort requires training for all school staff and frequent collaboration among program leaders, and Academic Innovations' technical assistance contractors can help.

Suggested School-wide Initiative Launch Package

Onsite visitations (one day each at a minimum)

- Prior to course start
  - Implementation training for course instructors (two days is best)

- During first semester
  - Morning: My10yearPlan.com® hands-on workshop
  - Afternoon: School-wide motivational orientation—What is a 10-year plan and why is it important for every student to have and use?

- After first semester
  - Morning: Course instructors' team meeting
  - Afternoon: School-wide meeting—Advisories/academic coaching using the 10-year plan

- Prior to year end
  - Morning: Team wrap-up and assessment
  - Afternoon: Whole-school meeting—Updating the 10-year plan in grades 10, 11, and 12

During the morning of each day, the technical assistance contractor works with the instructional team of the *Career Choices* course, providing professional development workshops (on the topics outlined above).

Each afternoon is spent conducting (or assisting the lead teacher in conducting) school-wide meetings (as outlined above). Bringing the entire school into the project at this point ensures that the school-wide initiative will be ready to launch.

Monthly Team Meeting by Webinar (up to 9 hours per school year)

The technical assistance contractor will provide an hour-long team meeting (via conference call or online meeting) each month. All instructors and administrators directly involved with the project will be in attendance. It is suggested that this recurring conference call is scheduled for the same time on the same day (e.g., the first Thursday of the month at 3:00 PM) for efficiency.

Individualized Support and Mentoring

The technical assistance contractor will provide individualized support and mentoring via phone and email (up to 20 hours per school year) for the lead teacher, course instructors, the principal, any other lead administrators, and the School Site Executive.

Sample Professional Development Plan

Professional Development Event	Approx. Date(s)	Principal	Career Choices Lead Teacher	Career Choices Instructors	Counselors Advisors	Academic Chairs	All Staff	Parents/ Partners
Attend a one-day The 10-year Plan: The Key to Dropout Prevention workshop	Fall 20__	X	X	X	X	X		X
Attend Freshman Transition Leadership Institute to learn more about the Freshman Transition Initiative and the 10-Step Plan	Late 20__/ Early 20__	X	X			X		
Attend *Career Choices* Lead Teacher Institute to gather resources and prepare to conduct ongoing training the *Career Choices* teaching team	Summer 20__		X					
Implementation workshop: Attend a 2-day *Career Choices* implementation workshop presented by Academic Innovations or completes using the appropriate online training modules	Fall 20__ / Spring 20__, Fall 20__		X	X	X	X		
Conduct short "buy-in" workshop for counselors and academic chairs to generate support for new class and vision of school-wide initiative	Early Spring 20__	X	X	X	X	X		
Conduct short "buy-in" assembly for all staff to generate support for new class and vision of school-wide initiative	Spring 20__	X	X	X	X	X	X	
Back-to-school night, conduct short "buy-in" workshop for parents and community partners to generate support for new class and vision of school-wide initiative	Early Fall 20__	X	X	X				X
Technical Assistance: Implementation begins; conduct workshops/strategy sessions with Lead Teacher and *Career Choices* teaching team using a professional learning community framework	Ongoing		X	X				
Attend summer **Focus on Freshmen** conference in CA, participating in professional development strands that match school's goals	Yearly	X	X	X				

The FLIPPED Workshop

Go Deeper & Get More Value from Your Professional Development Experience with
The FLIPPED Workshop Model

With a little technology and some pre-workshop, self-directed study, maximize your capacity-building efforts and workshop satisfaction using the "FLIPPED" Workshop model. This progressive professional development delivery model can be added to your onsite implementation workshop.

What is The FLIPPED Workshop?

The FLIPPED Workshop, like the flipped classroom, has a key trait: It inverts the traditional relationship between the workshop participants and the workshop presenter. Instead of passively receiving content during the workshop session, the participants take the time to digest the information **prior to their workshop attendance** following a carefully designed self-study process made up of online videos, archived webinars, and print materials. Then, during the workshop session, the instructor can spend more time helping participants process what they've learned, presenting advanced information and strategies, working in small groups, facilitating hands on-activities, and answering questions.

This method supports learning science. At its root, the flipped workshop model puts the learner at the center of the course instead of the instructor, and is a more effective technique than the traditional lecture model. The result, according to a growing body of research, is deeper, more connected learning, which will mean more satisfied instructors and better implementation of your freshman transition course.

How does it work?

Once a participant is registered for a flipped workshop, they receive an email outlining the preliminary coursework. This includes registration for their Self-Study Guide for a Quick Start and the delivery of any print materials (within 7 to 10 days).

Following the online Self-Study Guide for a Quick Start, the participant watches the online videos, taking a short multiple-choice assessment after each. When the self-study is complete, the participant prints their Assessment Certificate, which they provide to their workshop instructor. This certifies the necessary work has been completed and the attendee is ready to be an active workshop participant.

As part of the self-study process, participants will download any necessary pacing guides or checklists so they are prepared to efficiently complete their implementation plans. If the workshop includes instruction regarding My10yearPlan.com®, participants will also receive instructions for activating their own dynamic Populated Trial Account (PTA). This live, complete, sample student account allows participants to familiarize themselves with this exciting tool prior to the workshop.

What happens if a participant is unable to complete the necessary work prior to the workshop?

Life happens! If a participant is unable to complete their self-study work prior to their scheduled workshop, they will be identified as a workshop guest. As a guest, they will audit the workshop session but, because they have not studied the foundational information, they won't be expected to participate in the discussions and hands-on activities.

For more information on The FLIPPED Workshop model, contact Academic Innovations at (800) 967-8016.

Section 13

Getting Parents and the Community Involved

Topics covered in this section include:

- You'll want to connect with students' parents so they understand what their children will be working on in your class. In our experience, parents are supportive of the course when they understand how it will expose their children the realities of life and help them develop plans for the future.

- Getting service organizations, local businesses, and corporations involved is generally well worth the effort. You may be able to find financial support for your program or adult volunteers to work with your students.

Strategies for Involving Parents

If you're teaching a standalone freshman seminar or career exploration course, parents may see the class on their child's schedule without really understanding what it is. You'll want to reach out to parents at the beginning of the course and communicate that this is a rigorous process rooted in academics. A letter home (similar to the one on the following page) would provide an excellent introduction to your course goals.

In a time when kids take increasingly longer on average to become economically independent, parents will welcome a process that helps their children map out a plan for a self-sufficient future.

Your letter can also serve to give parents a "heads-up." Their students may come home with new questions about money, careers, and education, and may develop a new level of respect for the sacrifices their parents have made. Parents will want to be ready to field the questions and respond to their student's changing attitudes.

Continue to communicate with parents throughout your course, perhaps through a newsletter or inviting them to various class events. Cathie Klein of Seaman Freshman Center in Topeka, Kansas, maintains a blog to keep parents and the community informed about the progress her class is making and the activities they are doing.

On pages 13/4, you'll find a great suggestion for a project in which students coach their own parents through the *Career Choices* process.

However you decide to involve parents in your program, if you educate them on the process and keep them informed, you're sure to find them overwhelmingly supportive of your efforts.

> *So many parents say, "I'm so happy that you're doing this because my child is understanding the difference between wants and needs and stops to think instead of badgering me for more money.*
>
> — Cathie Klein, College & Career Readiness Coordinator
> Seaman High School, Topeka, KS

Other Ways to Involve Parents

- Gather a list of parents who are willing to speak on a topic in the curriculum. See pages 11/21–11/22 for resources to help you start a Speakers Bureau.

- A word of caution: Students have a lot of material to get through in the curriculum as they prepare to develop their meaningful 10-year plan. If your class lasts a semester, you'll want to make sure that any scheduled speakers are directly supporting the topic at hand.

- Recruit a parent to take on the role of Director of Mentors. See page 4/96 for details.

- Some parents might work for businesses that support community youth programs or local schools either by providing funding (which could be used for field trip or other extra course expenses) or volunteers.

- Do any of your students' parents work for local media outlets? If so, see if you can get publicity for your course.

Review Section 4 of this manual for additional ideas on how parents can participate with their student or to support the class as a whole.

Sample Parent Letter

Please note: This is only a sample. You'll want to edit the details to fit your program's structure and goals. You might also consider personalizing each letter to refer to each student by name.

Dear Parent:

Where will [insert student name] be in 10 years? Surely you've asked yourself this question a time or two, but how much thought has your child given to the future? In 10 years, will they be thriving in a career that supports their desired lifestyle or will they be asking you for handouts and free rent while struggling to figure out who they are, what they want, and what they will do with their life?

These are all valid questions, and I'm happy to tell you that your student is spending the next [insert time period] thoughtfully considering what their life will look like in 10 years.

You may be thinking, "My child can barely see past Saturday night, let alone what their life will look like in 10 years!" Not to worry. Our class, using the *Career Choices* curriculum, will be exploring a step-by-step decision-making process and enabling all students to articulate the answers to three questions: Who am I? What do I want? How do I get it?

Through this process, your student will be challenged to envision a future that includes:

- Graduation from high school
- Matriculation and graduation from post-secondary education or training
- Workforce entry with the training and skills necessary for economic self-sufficiency

Career Choices is designed to help ALL teens deal with the two major tasks of adolescence: establishing and consolidating their identity and deciding what they want to do with their lives. Each of the more than 100 active-learning exercises builds on the ones before and, using the *Workbook and Portfolio* and My10yearPlan.com®, students can easily compile their plans and store them online to review, modify, or update for the duration of their time in school.

As we work through the *Career Choices* material, you can expect your child to come home with a lot of questions and comments about their own self-discovery process and what "reality" looks like for a self-sufficient adult. We'll be discussing everything from job interviews to mortgage payments to how to feed a family of four on a tight budget—so don't be surprised if, at some point, you hear "I had no idea how much money I cost you!" Please be prepared to listen and offer your insight, as your input and support will add a great deal of meaning to this process.

I hope you're as excited as I am about witnessing this journey of self-discovery. Your child is about to learn how their high school experience will impact their future life satisfaction and how setting goals and staying true to their passions will lead to the achievement of all they desire.

Thanks for your support!

Parent-Student Project

After your students have completed the *Career Choices* program, consider sponsoring a weekend workshop where your students teach their parents the *Career Choices* process. It's a great way to facilitate parent-child communication.

The process of making wise life choices is the same no matter the age. The college/adult edition, *Career Choices and Changes*, mirrors the original text, but provides examples and stories geared for a more mature audience. It also features three additional chapters that provide more guidance on building a Skills Inventory, the importance of life-long learning, and the challenges of making career changes.

Capitalize on the fact that often parents are experiencing mid-life challenges as their children are moving through adolescence. Organizing your students to host a workshop for their parents could prove to be one of the most powerful experiences of your teaching career.

To receive a 60-day examination copy of the *Career Choices and Changes* workbook, call (800) 967-8016.

Anytime I mention this class to anybody, they say, "I wish we had that class when I was in school. I wish I could take your class. Can I take your class?" It's amazing. A lot of people don't know this stuff.

— Chris Pulos, Teacher
North Valley Charter Academy, Granada Hills, CA

Parent-Student Workshop Project

This activity can be accomplished during a weekend workshop (Saturday and Sunday, 9:00 AM to 4:00 PM each day) or a series of evening sessions (five weekly evening sessions, from 7:00 PM to 9:00 PM).

Texts:

- For parents—*Career Choices and Changes: A Guide for Discovering Who You Are, What You Want, and How to Get It* (Academic Innovations, 2012)

- For instructors—*Instructor's and Administrator's Guide for Career Choices* (Academic Innovations, 2013)

Lectures:

Your secondary school students will provide the lectures. To be successful, the student instructors must have completed *Career Choices* and developed their own 10-year plan.

During the workshop, the student instructors will introduce their parents to the process of career and life planning. Ideally, teams of students can be assigned different lecture topics to prepare ahead of time using the content from *Career Choices and Changes*.

Small Group Discussions:

These will be completed by pre-assigned groups that stay together for the whole 10 hours. We recommend that each group consist of three or four parent-student pairs.

You can find a sample agenda for the Parent Student Workshop Project in Section 13 on the online version of this *Instructor's Guide*.

Getting the Community Involved

Career Choices is an ideal vehicle for getting community members and organizations involved with your school. Many people have a vested interest in helping the young people of their community prepare for the future, especially local employers.

Community Help with Funding

More and more, large businesses and corporations are focusing their philanthropic efforts on education. Because of the nature of this curriculum, it makes sense to approach a local business, industry, or community service organizations for funding assistance.

When seeking such support, it is important to know your audience.

Consider their needs, goals, and overarching philosophy or mission, and communicate how your program can support those goals—with a well-prepared future workforce, a lower dropout rate, a reduction in anti-social behavior, more focused part-time workers, etc.

Organizations prefer to fund tangible items or events, such as materials or books, special events, and student scholarships. They usually do not like to fund salaries and infrastructure, and requests that lack specifics or don't align with the business or organizational objective will not work.

Section 15 of this guide has additional ideas and information on finding funding for your *Career Choices* program. If you would like further assistance with your grant request, contact Academic Innovations at (800) 967-8016.

Working with Community Service Organizations

If you haven't already considered it, think about recruiting one of the service organizations in your community to sponsor your school's program.

Finding the Right Service Organization to Approach

If you aren't familiar with the different service organizations in your community, contact your local Chamber of Commerce. They will have contact information for each organization in your community.

Consider contacting a local chapter of one of the following:

- Altrusa International
- American Association of University Women
- ASPIRA Association
- Association of Black Women in Higher Education
- Business and Professional Women International
- Elks Lodge
- Kiwanis International
- Lions Clubs International
- National Black Chamber of Commerce
- Rotary International
- Soroptimist International
- United States Hispanic Chamber of Commerce
- Zonta International

These organizations are made up of professional-, career-, and service-oriented individuals, people who have a vested interest in readying young people for the workforce.

Learn what you can about each organization before you make contact. Use your network of friends, parents, and professional acquaintances to find out if they support youth or education programs. If your school or department has an advisory board or community council, ask for help with this task.

Recruiting the Service Organization

Once you have determined which organization(s) might be interested in supporting your program, contact the organization's program chair and offer to give a presentation at one of their meetings. Many organizations have weekly meetings (usually at lunch or dinner), and program chairs are always on the lookout for interesting presentations about the community. Your call will be most welcome.

Your Presentation

Once you have scheduled a presentation, plan and practice what you want to say. Be sure to ask the program chair how much time you have. Leave time for questions and be careful not to go over that limit. These suggestions might be helpful as you plan your presentation.

- Give the Startling Statement Quiz (*Career Choices*, page 201) to warm up the audience.

- Tell success stories about students. Find course graduates willing to speak in front of groups and bring them with you to provide testimonials. If the course turned a student's life around—from apathetic to motivated learner—your audience will want to hear that story.

- If you have sample student work, supporting videos, or articles, bring these along and set up a display in the back of the room. You may want to record students talking about the course and create a short video presentation to share.

- Take along at least one set of the *Career Choices* books to pass around the audience while you are speaking.

Asking for Support

Toward the end of your presentation, be sure to ask for support or assistance from the members. As their name implies, community service organizations are dedicated to giving service to the community. They organize primarily for that purpose and are often looking for projects in the community that will make a difference. Helping students become productive citizens should appeal to the members of the organization.

What Kinds of Support Can You Ask for?

Speakers Bureau

At the minimum, be sure to take a copy of the Speakers Bureau recruitment forms found in Section 11 of the online version of this *Instructor's Guide*. Ask the audience to help you identify individuals who would be good guest speakers for your group. Pass the form around the room as you speak.

You may find you have more volunteer speakers than you have time for. If so, ask them to come to school and present their topic while the video production class films them. The video production class could also conduct on-camera interviews with each volunteer speaker as a project. The resulting videos could be posted on a class blog, an area of the school's web site, or a YouTube channel so students with a particular interest in the topic can watch them.

Shadowing Mentors

Provide copies of the Shadow Program Mentor Survey form (*Instructor's Guide*, pages 4/98–4/99) and ask individuals to volunteer as mentors for your program. Be sure to add your name and address at the bottom of the form so people can fill it out and send it to you.

Director of Mentors

If you are looking for a Director of Mentors (*Instructor's Guide*, page 4/96), mention that fact and ask any interested individuals to see you after the meeting. There may be individuals in the audience who have good contacts in the business community and would like to be involved with a project that can make a difference in the lives of young people.

Funding for Books

Most community service organizations raise funds throughout the year for projects in the community. After your presentation, if you feel there was a lot of interest in your program and the organization's members support the concepts, contact the president of the organization and ask about the process for submitted a funding request.

Follow the procedure and suggest that the organization fund the purchase of a *Career Choices Workbook & Portfolio* for each student. This is something "concrete" that the service organization can take pride in providing.

Once you receive funding for the books, design a sticker and affix it to the cover of each book. Your local print shop can print custom stickers and may be willing to donate their services, or you can design and print the stickers from your computer.

Keeping Your Supporters Involved

Book Presentation Ceremony

You may want to ask representatives of your sponsoring community service organization to attend a ceremony where each participant of your class is presented with their own consumable *Career Choices Workbook & Portfolio*. The sticker on the cover will be a more meaningful reminder of the community supporting them if students have an opportunity to actually meet the people responsible for the gift.

At the End of the Course

At a meeting of the service organization, share copies of students' 10-year plans (*Career Choices*, pages 279–280) and mission statements (page 281). You could also print their 10-year Plan Summary reports from My10yearPlan.com®. When service organization members see young people making an effort, you'll find they are willing to take a more active role in seeing that these students succeed.

Thank You—Say It Early; Say it Often

Remember to say thank you often. Cards made by students or letters written by students are always appreciated.

Solicit media attention for your program throughout the year (newspaper articles, TV news stories, etc.). Anywhere your *Career Choices* program is mentioned, be sure to add the tagline "Graciously funded by the local chapter of the _____." The more you do this, the more likely the organization is to fund your program year after year. A group that knows it is appreciated will become a committed group.

Presentations Throughout the Year

If you keep your sponsoring organization informed and involved, you'll increase your chances of continued support. In coordination with the community service organization's program chair, schedule two or three mutually beneficial events throughout the year. Here are some ideas:

Career Exploration Brainstorming Session

Schedule this session to take place after your students have completed Chapter 5 in *Career Choices*.

Prep meeting: Make a presentation about the *Career Choices* career decision-making process to the service organization membership. Include a description of the bulls eye chart, the budgeting process, and the career characteristics in Chapter 5. Because you are going to ask them to work directly with students, give them some guidelines and prospective outcomes.

Brainstorming session: A week or so after the prep meeting, have students brainstorm career possibilities with a panel of two or three service organization members. The students will provide each member of their panel with a completed copy of the following worksheets from *Career Choices*: the bulls eye chart (page 27), a copy of their budget (page 92), and a copy of their desired career characteristics (page 134). Because the panel members have real-world experience, they can present career options and strategies for getting the education and training necessary to get a job.

This should be a noisy and lively session that everyone will enjoy. Allow enough time for the groups to report out. Some of your students may receive offers for shadowing or internships from their group members. You may find that your sponsors enjoy this activity so much they will want to repeat it with more students from your program.

Job Interview Night

After the students complete Chapter 11, ask your service organization to sponsor a job interview night. You may want to hold this at the school so you have plenty of classrooms for breakout rooms.

The service organization members will break into three-person panels and conduct mock job interviews. Each panel should provide a fictitious job description for the position for which they will be interviewing. Give students copies to study as they prepare for the interviews.

At the end of each mock interview, the panel should critique the interviewee and give suggestions to help students increase their interviewing prowess.

Encourage students to interview for at least three different "jobs." Suggest they pay particular attention to the areas the panelists identify as "needing practice" so they can try to improve in each subsequent interview.

A reception for all participants could be held in the cafeteria at the end of the evening. Recruit parents to organize that event.

Consider holding a training session for your volunteer interviewers before this activity, especially if you feel they need to be sensitive to certain issues. This can be done the hour before the event or at a club meeting prior to Job Interview Night.

Motivational Guest Speakers

If you contract with notable motivational speakers to provide assemblies on topics related to your *Career Choices* course, consider asking your guest to extend their visit to include a luncheon or evening reception for your community service organization membership. For example, Olympic Gold Medalist Dain Blanton travels the country as a motivational speaker and has visited several *Career Choices* programs to share his message that "vision coupled with energy and perseverance lead to success." Dain is often asked to participate in an event for community members as a way of promoting community involvement and to recognize the efforts and support the school has already received.

My inbox just keeps filling up with positive feedback. We are basking in the glow after Dain's speech!

— Rebecca Simmons, Lead Teacher
Marquette Senior High School, Marquette, MI

Olympic Gold Medalist Dain Blanton

Academic Innovations was very fortunate to team up with Dain Blanton for the production of the *Career Choices* chapter motivational videos. Dain works with schools nationwide to increase student engagement and academic achievement through the most overlooked method of school reform: **direct student motivation.**

Through school assemblies and classroom visits, Dain imparts his personal story of triumph through challenge. Dain's presentations demonstrate to students in grades 7 – 12 that personal success will come through increasing their tolerance of the struggle to stay focused and do good work, applying a greater effort, and building up the tenacity required to succeed in school and beyond. After listening to and participating with Dain, students are filled with a new level of motivation for higher personal achievement. They start getting engaged in their own education; they see the reasons for completing high school and planning to attend a post-secondary institution—not because of adults telling them to do so—but from a newly heightened sense of personal agency.

Dain's presentations always cover these motivational themes.

- Creating a vision and setting goals
- Establishing self-discipline and managing a balanced life
- Checking your attitude; how you treat yourself—and others—determines character
- The importance of leadership—leading yourself and others

Why not solicit a business or community organization to sponsor a presentation at your school?

For more information about how to bring Dain Blanton to your school, visit **www.GoldSparkSuccess.com** or call (800) 655-7187.

Section 14

Assessment

Topics covered in this section include:

- Authentic assessments are ideal for measuring student growth by reviewing work and products students have created.

- The 10-year plan students develop is a great final exam, and My10yearPlan.com® Interactive compiles student work from each section into a report that can be used for midterm assessments.

- To assess the 10-year plan, consider how goals and plans relate to work completed earlier in the course, and if goals and plans are realistic and measurable.

- If weekly quizzes are a part of your grading strategy, we've developed sample discussion and multiple-choice questions to get you started.

- Pre- and post-course surveys assess the impact and overall success of your course.

- Provide feedback and share ideas to help us improve our products and services by completing the survey at www.academicinnovations.com/gettingstarted. You may also earn recognition for your school's success.

- Our online data reporting tool can help you track and report quantitative changes in student achievement related to use of the *Career Choices* curriculum.

Authentic Assessments to Promote Higher-Order Thinking

The *Career Choices* curriculum is unlike any other teaching tool used today. Other textbooks use didactic prose to communicate information to the learner in a passive, "tell-me" way. The *Career Choices* and My10yearPlan.com® model delivers a series of interactive rubrics, activities, questions, and surveys in a carefully developed scope and sequence. Written in a dialectic style that encourages dialogue and discussions, teachers comfortable with the Socratic Method—teaching through questioning rather than lecturing—will effectively foster the development of the critical thinking skills required in the workplace.

The text, consumable workbook, and online material walk students through a step-by-step process that provides the foundation for confidently determining the life, career, and education plans that match their personal goals and ideals. Students learn a decision-making process that can be used throughout their lives when making any life-defining choices.

Understandably, this is a complex process that requires higher-order thinking: analysis, synthesis, and critical, creative, and strategic thinking. As they make important life decisions, learners are prompted to continually review the information and personal data collected in Sections 1 (Who Am I?) and 2 (What Do I Want?) and apply that knowledge and understanding in Section 3 (How Do I Get It?) while developing their quantitative and meaningful 10-year career, lifestyle, and education plans.

Assessing students' learning by simply reviewing their work is the best method for this course. My10yearPlan.com® makes this process even easier by compiling the data students input throughout the course and transforming it into a variety of valuable documents that can be used for assessment and grading.

- *My 10-year Plan Summary Page* can be quickly reviewed by instructors and advisors to personalize their work with each student.

- The student's *My 10-year Plan and Portfolio Report* can serve as an authentic assessment for grading, midterms, finals, and can provide rich content and background information for interviews, college admissions, and workforce recruiting.

- My Skills Inventory is a dynamic digital chart that helps students recognize and organize their skills so they can develop skills-based learning plans.

- The skills-based Education Plans ties directly to chosen career paths.

- The Lifestyle Budget Plan details the adult lifestyle the student envisions, which must match with the commitment to education and training the student is willing to make.

- Career Interest Surveys help the learner research and analyze personal and career-specific data as a part of the systematic process of finding careers that match their skills, aptitudes, goals, and dreams.

- Career Back-up Plan provides a flexible, industry-specific roadmap and teaches that adaptability is required in today's ever-changing workplace.

Each of these documents can be graded as an authentic assessment (as noted in the infographic that follows) for assessing increases in critical thinking according to Bloom's Revised Taxonomy.

You'll notice that the most important aspects of this course—the budget, the Career Interest

Surveys, the career choice, the back-up plan, and the creation of the 10-year plan—require thinking skills at the upper end of Bloom's Taxonomy. Evaluating the thought and consideration students have dedicated to these activities is the best way to gauge a student's success in the course.

Important: Multiple-choice quizzes utilize remembering, the most basic of the lower-order thinking skills. This type of assessment is a poor measure of the fundamental growth that has transpired during the course. If quizzes are used, discussion questions are preferable as they require understanding, although they are still are not ideal as a stand-alone assessment.

These tools provide a unique opportunity to not only evaluate students' understanding of the concepts and processes taught, but also to assess their ability to use the higher-order thinking skills required in the workforce.

Below you'll find some sample recommendations.

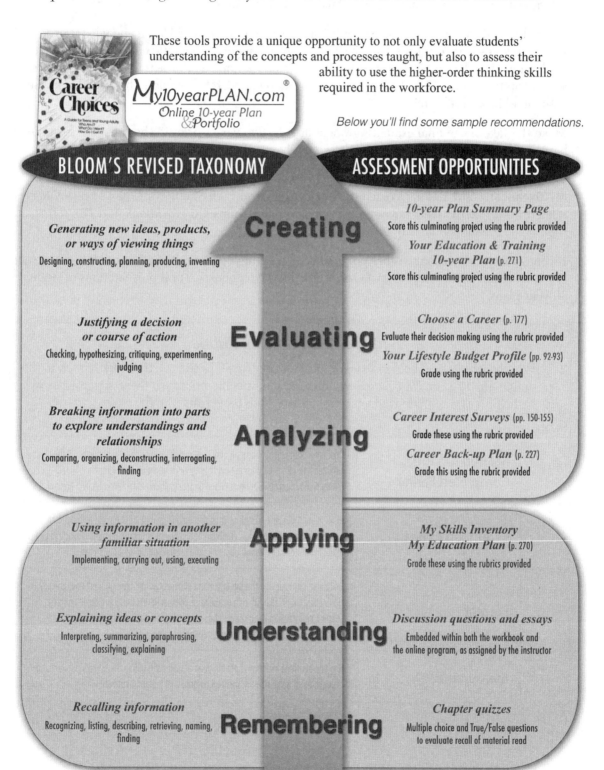

BLOOM'S REVISED TAXONOMY

Creating
Generating new ideas, products, or ways of viewing things
Designing, constructing, planning, producing, inventing

Evaluating
Justifying a decision or course of action
Checking, hypothesizing, critiquing, experimenting, judging

Analyzing
Breaking information into parts to explore understandings and relationships
Comparing, organizing, deconstructing, interrogating, finding

Applying
Using information in another familiar situation
Implementing, carrying out, using, executing

Understanding
Explaining ideas or concepts
Interpreting, summarizing, paraphrasing, classifying, explaining

Remembering
Recalling information
Recognizing, listing, describing, retrieving, naming, finding

ASSESSMENT OPPORTUNITIES

10-year Plan Summary Page
Score this culminating project using the rubric provided
Your Education & Training 10-year Plan (p. 271)
Score this culminating project using the rubric provided

Choose a Career (p. 177)
Evaluate their decision making using the rubric provided
Your Lifestyle Budget Profile (pp. 92-93)
Grade using the rubric provided

Career Interest Surveys (pp. 150-155)
Grade these using the rubric provided
Career Back-up Plan (p. 227)
Grade this using the rubric provided

My Skills Inventory
My Education Plan (p. 270)
Grade these using the rubrics provided

Discussion questions and essays
Embedded within both the workbook and the online program, as assigned by the instructor

Chapter quizzes
Multiple choice and True/False questions to evaluate recall of material read

For more information, call (800) 967-8016 or visit www.academicinnovations.com.

14/3

Evaluating the 10-year Plan

In the final chapter of **Career Choices**, students call on all the skills and knowledge they've acquired throughout the course to develop a meaningful 10-year education and career plan. This process provides an excellent opportunity for what is known as "authentic assessment," or the opportunity to demonstrate learning and skills in a real-world context. We recommend using the activities found within Chapter 12 as a take-home final exam.

As you begin the course, provide students with a vision of what they'll learn and what is expected. Let them know early on that Chapter 12—the development of their 10-year plans—will be their final exam. Emphasize that students who diligently complete the activities and assignments leading up to Chapter 12 will have all the information needed to complete these final worksheets without additional research.

Make the take-home final exam assignment at least two weeks prior to the due date so students have ample time to thoughtfully complete the Chapter 12 activities.

When students have completed Chapter 12, you can evaluate their work by going online to My10yearPlan.com®, linking to each student's *My 10-year Plan Summary Page* and reviewing the related work. Alternatively, have students turn in their completed **Workbook and Portfolios** and then grade the individual activities.

If time permits, incorporate other project-based learning opportunities into students' final exam grade by requiring development of Career Portfolio Notebooks or oral presentations of students' 10-year plans.

10-year Plan Grading Rubric

Whether the course final assesses all of the work from Chapter 12, the work related to the online *My 10-year Plan Summary Page*, or just specific exercises, these suggestions will be helpful as you grade students' work. Score each topic from 1 to 5.

Score		
	Related to Work Completed Earlier	Does the plan reflect carefully considered decisions made throughout the course? You can easily ascertain this by reviewing each student's *My 10-year Plan Summary Page* or *My 10-year Plan and Portfolio Report*.
	Grounded in Reality	How much thought has gone into the development of the plan and does this plan seem realistic for this student? If a student requires remedial work to get on track for his or her chosen career, is that reflected in his or her plan?
	Format	Does the student use the systems and rubrics taught throughout the course? Have they taken the time to make sure their written work is grammatically correct and easy to read? Have they produced something they'd be proud to share with a future employer or mentor?
	Measurable	Has the student written their 10-year action plan using measurable goals and objectives or have they defaulted to broad general statements?

Final and Midterm Exam Options

Using an authentic assessment of what students have learned will more accurately reflect students' ability to analyze, synthesize, and create information and data.

Products for Authentic Assessment

- Chapter 12 in the *Workbook and Portfolio*
- *My 10-year Plan Summary Page*
- *My 10-year Plan and Portfolio Report* (from My10YearPlan.com Interactive)

My 10-year Plan and Portfolio Report has three sections, just like the *Career Choices* text (Who Am I? What Do I Want? How Do I Get It?). These reports compile the information students enter in the online activity pages for each section.

If your school does not use My10yearPlan.com®, you can assess students' work in their *Workbook and Portfolio* for midterm or final grades.

Midterms

Option 1: Assess the first two sections of the *My 10-year Plan and Portfolio Report* in My10yearPlan.com® (after Chapters 2 and 7) to determine midterm grades.

Option 2: Assess students' completed *Workbook and Portfolio* activities through Chapter 2 and again through Chapter 7 to determine appropriate midterm grades.

Course Final

Option 1: The final section of *My 10-year Plan and Portfolio Report* (after Chapter 12) is a culmination of all that the student learned during the course and makes an excellent final exam.

Option 2: The *My 10-year Plan Summary Page* is another document that can be graded as a final exam. It reflects the keystone activities of the course and will provide an overview assessment of what the student has learned.

Option 3: Whether or not you are using My10yearPlan.com®, Chapter 12 of *Career Choices* can be assigned as a take-home final examination. Allow at least two weeks to finish it as several assignments require that earlier work be reviewed and contemplated.

A word of caution:

Resist the urge to assess students' ability to memorize career- or industry-specific information. Multiple-choice and true-false tests do not measure the higher-order skills (critical thinking, problem-solving, analysis, and synthesis) that students learn and use in this course.

Assessing the application of principles is a better measure of mastery than simply recalling them. This is what is essential for student success: the ability to apply the skills and information they learn to their own lives. Their 10-year plans will not only function as an authentic assessment of the process they've learned, but will also act as an important product they can use as a touchstone and a valuable habit they'll embrace throughout their lives.

Post-Course Assessment Essay

At the end of the course, a simple way to measure each student's personal growth is to ask students to rewrite their essay/narrative from the "Envisioning Your Future" exercise (*Career Choices*, page 14).

Compare each student's end-of-course essay with the version completed at the beginning of the course. Do you see any growth? Are their horizons broader? Perhaps their goals are tied more closely to their capabilities and commitment. Have young women considered non-traditional careers? Do you sense better self-knowledge? Do plans include appropriate preparation for their chosen career—college graduation or completion of a certificate program?

If you have access to video equipment, consider recording each student presenting the Envisioning Your Future essay at the beginning of the course. Then also record them reading their rewritten essay at the end of the course. Match up the two video files for each student—before and after—and share these at a celebration event during the last class meeting. Students may be surprised by their growth, their increased knowledge and direction, and their increased self-confidence.

This video project can also be shared at parent meetings and presentations to the school board.

Weekly Quizzes and Discussion Questions

Multiple-Choice Questions

We do not necessarily recommend multiple-choice and true-false assessments; we find them to be contrary to the higher-order teaching and learning opportunities of the *Career Choices* and My10yearPlan.com® pedagogy. At the same time, we realize that education systems often require these types of weekly or periodic assessments. For that reason, we have written multiple-choice questions for each chapter of the book to assist in the development of your own quiz questions. You can download these documents from The Teachers' Lounge.

Review of the *My 10-year Plan Summary Page*

Another weekly assessment option is to grade the corresponding area(s) of the *My 10-year Plan Summary Page*. The summary page compiles work as it's completed, so each section demonstrates students' understanding of a portion of the material.

Grade Keystone Activities

Choose (perhaps randomly) one of the keystone activities in each chapter to grade. The keystone activities (those that carry to the *My 10-year Plan Summary Page*) are noted in the drop-down menu of activities by a graduation cap logo.

Short Essay or Discussion Questions

You can also gauge students' comprehension by assigning essays to measure acceptance and understanding of the topics in the curriculum. You'll find sample questions on The Teachers' Lounge. You may assign written responses to these types of questions as homework, or you may choose to award points for participation in class or online discussion of the topics.

Grading

Understanding how assignments and assessments impact their final grade is always helpful for students. Hand out a grading outline on the first day of class so students can see all graded assignments and how the points are broken down. Students can then keep their own running tally and know exactly how they are doing.

Since the main goal of this course is to get students actively involved in planning a satisfying future for themselves, anyone who shows enthusiasm, participates in classroom activities, and completes the assignments should do very well.

There are several different grading strategies that you can use with this course. You may grade some exercises on the amount of effort that went into their completion, or you may offer points for class participation or attendance.

Development of the 10-year plan (Chapter 12 of *Career Choices*) makes a good final exam. Assigned as a "take-home" exam, allow students at least two weeks to complete it. To assess a student's plan, evaluate its thoroughness, how realistic and well researched it is, and how well goals and objectives are defined. See the 10-year Plan Grading Rubric on page 14/4 of this guide for details.

My students' semester exam grade was their career research papers. Each unit complemented the stage of their paper. For example, Chapter 5 helped them make their choices of topic; a unit on using resources helped them with their bibliography cards; Chapter 6 helped them with their rough draft and composition; Chapter 7 helped them process their information and decide if it was a good career choice for them; Chapters 8 and 9 helped them implement a proper plan.

— Julia S. Forbus, Occupational Specialist
Fort Pierce Westwood High School, Fort Pierce, FL

The following page provides a sample grading form. A customizable version is available on **The Teachers' Lounge** or the online version of this *Instructor's Guide* so you can easily edit topics and values to match your own course requirements.

Sample Grading Form

		Total Points Possible

Attendance: Participation in discussions is important.
You can earn up to [5] points per class; we meet
[45] days (which totals to [225] points). To
receive points for the day's attendance, you must also *complete
assignments in the workbook* <u>*prior to class,*</u> *come prepared to
participate in class discussions about those assignments, and be
supportive of the class goals and your fellow students.*

Total Points Possible: **225**

Text assignments: Complete all assignments for a total of
[175] points.

Assignment	Points	Total
Envisioning Your Future (p. 14)	10	
Definition of Success (p. 21)	5	
Your Personal Profile (p. 27)	10	
Components of Lifestyle (p. 63)	10	
Budget Activities (p. 77-92)	30	
My Ideal Career (p. 134)	10	
3 Career Interest Surveys (p. 150-155)	30	
Make a Career Choice (p. 177)	15	
Your Lifestyle Goals (p. 190)	10	
Alternative Career Ladder (p. 227)	15	
Your Resume (p. 253)	10	
Your Education 10-year Plan (p. 270-271)	10	
My Mission Statement updated (p. 282)	10	175

Journal: — 75

Writing: [3] essays or writing projects at [25]
points each for a total of [75] points. — 75

Vocabulary: [12] vocabulary quizzes at [10]
points each for a total of [120] points. — 120

Final — 100

Total [770] **possible points** — **770**

A =	693	or more points
B =	616	or more points
C =	539	or more points
D =	501	or more points

How to Use Pre- and Post-Course Surveys to Assess Class Impact

Motivation is built on success. The feeling that accompanies success propels us to strive for more success. But how do you know if your efforts with the *Career Choices* and My10yearPlan.com® course are successful?

One obvious way is to look at quantitative data. This includes evaluating high school and college completion rates. Are more students staying in school and graduating? Is the dropout rate for students who have completed the course lower than for students of similar backgrounds and ability? Do students who go on to college stay there and graduate?

Do you see an increase in students' academic achievement? Are test scores and/or grade point averages rising? As the relevance of reading, writing, speaking, and computing becomes clear, is proficiency increasing?

In addition to quantitative data, it's also important to look at behavioral and attitudinal changes. Upon completion of the course, do students' 10-year plans reflect higher or more realistic personal, education, career, and life goals?

What about educational engagement? Are students more engaged with their education? Do they seek out opportunities to learn new skills, gain new knowledge, and better prepare for the future?

Finally, consider self-esteem and self-reliance. Is self-esteem high enough for students to cope with challenges as they arise? Do they feel competent to move into the adult world as emotionally and economically self-sufficient individuals?

We've all heard the saying: *Attitude is everything*. This is a simple but profound statement. Why? Because being motivated to learn and understanding why education is important are key indicators of student success in school. Changing reluctant learners' attitudes about the value of education results in higher grades, decreased attrition rates, and increased test scores.

How can you measure students' attitudinal shifts? The pre- and post-course surveys for the *Career Choices* curriculum are a good place to start. Timing is important. Administer the pre-survey before you start delivering any of the *Career Choices* content and give the post-survey at the end of the course. Comparing students' pre- and post-survey responses provides a measure of progress you can analyze at the individual, class, or program level.

This tool measures each student's change in:

- Attitude about the value of school/education
- Education goals
- Plans for the future once they complete school
- How realistic those plans are, given the effort they are willing to exert to get an education

The pre- and post-surveys can be administered using paper and pencil or online at My10yearPlan.com®. For the hardcopy format, see pages 14/11–14/12 in this *Instructor's Guide* or visit the Resource Cupboard of The Teachers' Lounge.

Directions for the Pre- and Post-Survey

On the first day of class, before you've done much more than welcome students and introduce yourself, you'll provide each student with a copy of the one-page pre-survey.

Once the pre-surveys are completed, keep them in a secure place until the end of the course.

At the end of the course, as soon as your students complete the ***Career Choices*** text material, provide each student with a copy of the one-page post-survey to complete.

Tips for Administering the Surveys

- Before handing out the surveys, make sure students have a pen or pencil in front of them.

- If you feel it's necessary to read the survey aloud for the class, go ahead. Just be sure to provide no commentary or editorializing that might influence their individual responses.

- Allow no discussion during the survey.

- You want students to be truthful and open, so don't tie their responses to any kind of grade or class assignment.

- Some questions may be difficult for your students. They've probably never thought about these issues before. If you wait for all students to "finish" you may be waiting a long time.

- Do expect each student to at least try to answer every question.

- For the post-surveys, you'll want to allow more time for completion. By that time your students should have a lot more to write about, particularly in questions 3, 5, and 6.

Brief Introduction for the Pre-survey

Please get out a pen or pencil. I'm handing out a short survey. This will NOT be graded so say what you think. You may not have thought about some of these things before, but please try to respond to all of the questions—even if you respond with "I don't know." or "I haven't thought about this." I want your thoughts only. No discussion or talking. Be sure to include your name and class information before starting. You have 10 minutes.

Pre-Course Survey

Name: _____ School: _____

Instructor: _____ Course name: _____

1. Select the one statement that best reflects your attitude about school.
   a) I really could care less about school. The sooner I get out, the better.
   b) My family and/or society require that I go. Otherwise, I wouldn't be here.
   c) All I want to do is graduate. I do only what I have to in order to get by.
   d) I want to be self-sufficient, so I do what it takes to achieve that goal.
   e) A good education is important to my future; therefore, I will strive to learn as much as I can.

2. Thinking about your future, select the highest level of education you plan to finish before leaving school.
   a) I plan to leave school before I graduate.
   b) I plan to attend one year of college and then enter the workforce.
   c) I plan to complete at least two years of college or trade school.
   d) I plan to graduate with a four-year college degree.
   e) I plan to get an advanced degree (something beyond a four-year college degree).

3. Imagine yourself 10 years from now. What career do you plan to have at that time?

4. Complete this sentence with numbers:
   I am _____ years old. Between now and the time I retire, I expect to work _____ years at a full-time job outside the home.

5. Describe the life you envision for yourself 10 to 15 years from now. (Use the back of this paper for more space).

6. What are your plans to make the life you just described a reality?

Post-Course Survey

Name: _____ School: _____

Instructor: _____ Course name: _____

1. Select the one statement that best reflects your attitude about school.

   a) I really could care less about school. The sooner I get out, the better.

   b) My family and/or society require that I go. Otherwise, I wouldn't be here.

   c) All I want to do is graduate. I do only what I have to in order to get by.

   d) I want to be self-sufficient, so I do what it takes to achieve that goal.

   e) A good education is important to my future; therefore, I will strive to learn as much as I can.

2. Thinking about your future, select the highest level of education you plan to finish before leaving school.

   a) I plan to leave school before I graduate.

   b) I plan to attend one year of college and then enter the workforce.

   c) I plan to complete at least two years of college or trade school.

   d) I plan to graduate with a four-year college degree.

   e) I plan to get an advanced degree (something beyond a four-year college degree).

3. Imagine yourself 10 years from now. What career do you plan to have at that time?

4. Complete this sentence with numbers:

   I am _____ years old. Between now and the time I retire, I expect to work _____ years at a full-time job outside the home.

5. Describe the life you envision for yourself 10 to 15 years from now. (Use the back of this paper for more space).

6. What are your plans to make the life you just described a reality?

Scoring the Pre- and Post-Surveys

Once both surveys are completed, the instructor will want to paperclip each student's pre- and post-survey together.

If being scored by an outside evaluator, which may be necessary for programs with foundation or grant funding, the instructor will also want to include an outline indicating which *Career Choices* activities were completed by the class.

Questions 1 and 2 are quantitative calculations based on the multiple-choice responses by the students. The pre- and post-survey responses are compared to review the changes in students' attitudes about school and their education goals. Have they increased, decreased, stayed the same, or continued to remain high?

Questions 3 through 6 are qualitative questions and require an evaluator, usually the class teacher, to compare the pre- and post-survey answers and evaluate the goals and any change demonstrated.

Electronic Scoring Tool

Academic Innovations has created an electronic scoring tool to help streamline this process. If using the online scoring tool through **The Teachers' Lounge** or **My10yearPlan.com®**, the instructor can analyze student responses using an online rubric. See page 14/14 of this guide for the rubric.

Call Academic Innovations at (800) 967-8016 for information about **The Teachers' Lounge**. Depending on your school's order history, you may qualify for a free annual membership.

Pre-/Post-Course Survey Evaluation Rubric

Question	Pre-survey vs. post-survey	Criteria
1. Choose the one statement that best reflects your attitude about school.	Quantitative data that the computer can assess.	
2. Thinking about your future, choose the highest grade level you plan to finish before leaving school.	Quantitative data that the computer can assess.	
3. Imagine you are 30 years old. What career do you plan to have at that time?	After completing the *Career Choices* course, the student's career goals…	• Required significantly less education and/or training • Required marginally less education and/or training • Required a similar amount of education and/or training • Required marginally more education and/or training • Required significantly more education and/or training
4. Complete this sentence with a number. Between the ages of 18 and 65, I expect to work _____ years at a full-time job outside the home.	After completing the *Career Choices* course, the student's plans for years spent in the workforce…	• Seem significantly less realistic • Seem marginally less realistic • Remained the same • Seem marginally more realistic • Seem significantly more realistic
5. Describe the life you envision for yourself when you are 35 years old.	After completing the *Career Choices* course, the student's vision of their adult life is…	• Significantly less realistic; significantly less detailed • Marginally less realistic; marginally less detailed • Realistic; detailed • Marginally more realistic; marginally more detailed • Significantly more realistic; significantly more detailed
6. What are your plans to make the life you just described a reality?	After completing the *Career Choices* course, the student's plan for achieving the adult life they've envisioned (see #5) is…	• Significantly less realistic; significantly less detailed • Marginally less realistic; marginally less detailed • Realistic; detailed • Marginally more realistic; marginally more detailed • Significantly more realistic; significantly more detailed
	After completing the *Career Choices* course, the student's plan for achieving the adult life they've envisioned (see #5)…	• Demonstrates significantly lower understanding of the need for appropriate education and/or training • Demonstrates marginally lower understanding of the need for appropriate education and/or training • Demonstrates a similar understanding of the need for appropriate education and/or training • Demonstrates a marginally higher understanding of the need for appropriate education and/or training • Demonstrates a significantly higher understanding or the need for appropriate education and/or training

Educator Survey and Program Evaluation

We invite your feedback and input. Your observations and suggestions help us continue to update and improve our curriculum and services. The majority of the ideas and input in this manual came from completed surveys and interviews triggered by those surveys.

If you are a *Career Choices* instructor or administrator, completing our educator survey gives us valuable feedback and helps us provide the recognition you deserve. For example, we use this survey to identify potential master teachers, conference presenters, and educators willing to be interviewed for our newsletter, *Instructor's Guide* updates, and online teacher resource spotlights.

You'll want to go to www.academicinnovations.com/gettingstarted to complete our *Career Choices* educator survey.

We appreciate your input and so do your colleagues using the curriculum around the country, so each instructor completing our survey receives a thank-you gift.

You'll also want to review and complete our Medal Chart Rubric (see page 7/4 in this guide) to gauge your program's effectiveness. You could join the ranks of our bronze, silver, and gold medal schools. Learn more at www.careerchoices.com/lounge/medalwinners.html.

Online Data Reporting Tool

Writing a grant or evaluating your program's impact?

You'll need a narrative report to explain your data. Thanks to federal regulations of the last decade school educational data is readily available, but writing the resulting report can still be challenging. Academic Innovations' online data reporting tool can help you compile and analyze your data and create automated reports.

Our team is here to support your pursuit of key student achievement and behavior indicators that may have been positively impacted by a *Career Choices* course. For help documenting and sharing information that demonstrates the role your *Career Choices* course has played in student success, visit **www.whatworkscareerchoices.com/dataproject.** You'll find:

- Guidelines for collecting pertinent data related to key dropout prevention and student achievement factors

- References for rigorous evaluation methodology

- An online tool that facilitates the creation of a report highlighting your *Career Choices* program's impact on student learning and behavior

How does it work? Use the data collection worksheet to gather information using public sources or with assistance from your district or school administrators. Then enter the data points and write your own brief narrative about the program.

The resulting report can be a powerful part of your decision-making and planning process. And, by updating your information from one year to the next, you'll have a valuable resource for supporting:

- Presentations to school boards, administrators, community partners, and faculty members

- News releases to the press

- Newsletters for students and parents

Learn more about this digital data tool on page 15/3 of this guide or in the online version of this *Instructor's Guide.*.

Section 15

Sustainability and Funding

Topics in this section include:

- Funding is one of the more challenging aspects of starting or sustaining your *Career Choices* course, but a number steps can be taken to bolster the sustainability of your program.

- An online tool provided by Academic Innovations can help you gather and report data related to your program. Track quantitative program results to inform stakeholders of your successes and to pinpoint areas needing improvement.

- Writing your project proposal doesn't need to be an overwhelming task. To help, templates are provided within this guide and online.

- Making sure school and district leaders are on board and supportive is critical to the longevity of your program.

- Getting publicity for your program is easier than you think and it plays a huge role in generating community support.

- There are opportunities for federal, state, or grant funding if you're willing to do the research and leg work. Suggestions and resources are provided.

- Enlisting support from businesses, foundations, and organizations in your community is a viable way to raise funds and find volunteers.

- Showing your appreciation for the efforts of your staff and key stakeholders maintains morale and encourages continued support.

Sustainability

One of the greatest challenges to any education redesign effort is sustainability; it requires keeping a new program going by maintaining the support of key stakeholders and securing ongoing funding. This section provides advice and resources to help in this effort.

There are some tried and true program planning steps that will ensure the work you invest during the start-up phase will pay dividends down the road in program continuity. Then, when the time comes to review your program, whether at a school board meeting or in the court of public opinion, it will fare well and won't end up on a list of cuts to be made.

These steps may not seem obvious but are critical to sustainability:

1. Gather data and report results to your school, district, community, and local media in a format that clearly communicates the impact your program is having on students.

2. Develop a program proposal that articulates program goals and methodology. Post highlights on your school web site for all stakeholders to see.

3. Keep school and district leaders informed and "on board."

4. Work with your local media to publicize your efforts.

5. Be on the lookout for funding sources that can support your program.

6. Explore local funding options or sources not normally tapped by your school.

7. Celebrate successes—big and small—with all stakeholders, including students.

Step 1: Gather data and report results to your school, district, community, and local media in a format that clearly communicates the impact your program is having on students.

Data: Why It's Important and How to Manage It

Before writing your proposal or starting your search for funds, gather your data. Whether it is a foundation, a government entity, a local source, or your school board, all funding sources require metrics pointing to program goals and success. Data also helps make your request compelling—numbers speak volumes.

Data Required for Establishing New Career Choices Courses

You probably already have ideas about the student outcomes you want to improve. Do you want to boost the 9th to 10th grade promotion rate? Do you want to improve attendance, raise GPAs and test scores, or reduce suspension rates? Do you want to impact high school and college completion rates over the long term?

Whatever your goals, gathering current measurements of key indicators provides baseline data. Getting the information you need shouldn't be hard given the reporting requirements of No Child Left Behind. The online data tool noted below can help you compile and store this information, and can build a simple-to-read report that can be submitted to your governing or funding bodies.

Data Required to Sustain an Existing Course or Program

Since you introduced your *Career Choices* course, have you seen improvements in dropout rates, test scores, attendance, and suspension rates? By comparing the baseline data and data collected after your program has been in place for at least a year, you'll know if your program is succeeding in targeted areas. If your program is achieving significant positive results, you'll want to be sure to share that information with stakeholders and community partners to ensure that support for your course continues. On the flip side, if your program isn't meeting expectations, you can determine what isn't working and make adjustments to improve results.

Online Data Management Tool for Your Career Choices Course

Academic Innovations has developed an online tool to help you analyze your program data, document the role your *Career Choices* course has played in student success, and create a customized report. This online tool:

- Recommends guidelines for collecting data related to key dropout prevention and student achievement factors

- Provides references for rigorous evaluation methodology

- Facilitates the creation of a report regarding the impact of your *Career Choices* program on student learning and behavior

The resulting report can be a powerful part of your decision-making and planning process. And, by updating your information from one year to the next, you'll have a valuable resource for supporting:

- Presentations to school boards, administrators, community partners, and faculty members

- Releases to the local media and press

- Newsletters for students and parents

Visit **www.whatworkscareerchoices.com/dataproject** to get started or to view a sample report.

Step 2: Develop a program proposal that articulates program goals and methodology. Post highlights on your school web site for all stakeholders to see.

Writing Your Project Proposal

Whether you are trying to secure funding or solicit support from decision makers, follow this tried and true format:

1. **Introduction:** Establish your credibility.

2. **Problem Statement:** Outline why this program is needed and provide statistics and data to support your position.

3. **Program Goals and Objectives:** Make them measurable (see page 5/2 of this guide for suggestions).

4. **Program Design:** Describe your methodology for achieving the goals and objectives.

5. **Evaluation:** Spell out how you plan to assess and evaluate your program (see Section 14 of this guide).

6. **Funding:** Describe how you plan to maintain the program once the initial funding cycle is over.

7. **Budget:** Include your program budget (not for public documents).

8. **Appendix:** Include documents that support your credibility and claims.

It's far easier to edit than it is to create.

Why reinvent the wheel? You'll find a variety of resources on our web site that can be downloaded and customized as you develop your proposal. These can streamline your research, reduce your typing, and help you create a fundable proposal. Download text to create the skeleton of your proposal and then edit it to more accurately reflect your school's goals and methodology.

The sample narrative on the following pages is a good starting point. The graphic on page 15/8 might be adapted and included in your proposal. Cost efficiency is critical in today's funding environment.

Our program planning site at **www.academicinnovations.com/programplanning** also provides relevant, valuable information in an actionable sequence.

Sample Narrative:
Overview Text You Can Edit When Developing Your Project or Funding Proposal

What is the Freshman Transition Initiative model developed by the Freshman Transition Initiative at The George Washington University, and why does it work?

The Freshman Transition Initiative model is a school-wide, systemic redesign model where:

- ✓ Every 8th or 9th grade student completes a semester- or year-long standards-based Freshman Transition course

- ✓ The course culminates in the creation of a comprehensive and meaningful online 10-year plan

- ✓ The plan is updated in academic classes in the 10th, 11th, and 12th grades

- ✓ And is used by all instructors for advisory and academic coaching purposes

The Freshman Transition Course

When young people have a productive vision of their future (a vision that matches their goals, identity, aptitudes, personalities, lifestyle expectations, and passions) and a quantitative 10-year plan of their own making, the value of applying themselves to their education becomes abundantly clear. Students will leave the Freshman Transition course motivated to achieve because they not only understand the benefits of their efforts in school but, more important, they also understand the consequences of not getting a good education. The process taught in this standards-based course helps each student quantify the many reasons they should apply themselves to their academic studies.

The School-wide Initiative

The intervention cannot stop at the end of the freshman year. During the Freshman Transition course, students put their 10-year plans online so that, with the guidance of their instructors and counselors, they can continually update their growing and changing plans.

To maintain motivation and direction, students revisit their online 10-year plans in each of their academic classes during the 10th, 11th, and 12th grades. All instructors are trained to use students' individualized online 10-year plans as a tool to inform advisory and academic coaching functions, continuing the motivation to graduate and reach the goals that will lead to an economically self-sufficient adulthood.

The online 10-year plans provide educators with important information for data-driven advisories.

Because each student has an online 10-year plan for quick review, academic instructors and counselors can easily examine individual plans. This allows educators to better personalize their instruction, using students' lifestyle goals as the "carrot" for the purpose of academic coaching and remediation. Academic instructors throughout the high school are trained to use the online 10-year plan for data-driven advisory purposes at all grades. This comprehensive and cost-efficient strategy puts the goal of a successful transition from high school to college within reach.

Why is a Freshman Transition course, based on the Standards for a Freshman Transition Course from The George Washington University's Freshman Transition Initiative, a critical piece in any dropout prevention or college readiness program?

All early-adolescents benefit from a comprehensive guidance course.

- For young people raised in privation, this course explores developmental and self-sufficiency topics that may be missed at home.

- For teens on a college track, early interventions provide a vision of a productive future and an understanding of the consequences for dropping out. The fact that only 61% college students graduate within six years points to the need for this type of support.

- For the highest functioning students, learning the process for career decision-making provides a skill set and an awareness that empowers them to make the best choices. When individual career choice matches ability and personality, productivity increases along with life satisfaction.

All students, no matter their backgrounds, crave a clear sense of direction for their lives. Based on research and a strong belief that all students deserve an excellent education, a Freshman Transition course guides students through a crucial self-discovery process and transforms them into self-motivated learners. Students develop knowledge, skills, and attitudes to successfully examine their own lives, evaluate a wide range of educational options, explore career and life paths, and establish reasoned and researched goals for their future.

What does a Freshman Transition course entail?

Commonly known as a comprehensive guidance course, students in the 8th or 9th grade engage in the process of answering three fundamental questions:

Who am I?

What do I want?

How do I get it?

These questions drive the standards-based *Career Choices* curriculum, making it relevant, rigorous, and effective at increasing engagement and motivation. The course culminates with students developing an individualized, online 10-year plan that charts their journey through high school and post-secondary education or training and into the workforce.

The *Career Choices* curriculum aligns with The George Washington University's Freshman Transition Initiative whole-school redesign model and its accompanying set of standards. *Career Choices* also supports the Common Core State Standards for English and delivers the U.S. Department of Education's six recommendations for effective dropout prevention programs. (See pages 6/7 for the Standards for a Freshman Transition Course and pages 6/9–6/13 for correlations to the Common Core State Standards.)

What makes the Career Choices *curriculum unique and effective?*

Simply put, it is an academically-based curriculum—repackaged in a thematic format to address the developmental needs of the early adolescent. How?

- It teaches a critical-decision making process for life-defining decisions

- It culminates in a 10-year career and education plan that helps young people envision a productive life of their own choosing

- It helps students grapple with a pressing and crucial question: Why do I need a good education?
- It is "different by design" so it's less threatening for all students
- It melds high tech with high touch, increasing student buy-in of the content and concepts presented

The bottom line: By changing attitudes, it changes lives.

Whether students are headed for an Ivy League college or an entry-level job, they all crave a clear sense of direction for their lives. A required class, based on the Standards for a Freshman Transition Course from The George Washington University, can help students develop a personalized, career-inclusive 10-year education plan.

As they work through the coursework, students learn a self-discovery and planning process that culminates with a plan to:

- ✓ Make high school graduation a reality
- ✓ Enter and **complete** post-secondary education or training
- ✓ Help them transition into a productive and self-sufficient adulthood

This interactive course captures the attention of ALL students because it deals with their most critical issues: themselves and their futures.

In addition, this semester- or year-long course can integrate academics and technology in meaningful ways so students see these skills as relevant to their lives.

The decade between ages 14 and 24 is one of the most critical decision-making times in anyone's life. In this "decade of transition," young adults start making choices that impact the rest of their lives. Some of these choices have far-reaching consequences:

- To stay in school or not
- To become sexually active or not
- To invest time, money, and energy in their education or not

When young people have a productive vision of their future that matches their goals, identity, aptitudes, personality, lifestyle expectations, and passions, along with a quantitative 10-year plan of their own making, the value of applying themselves to their education becomes abundantly clear. The process taught in this standards-based course provides the reason to learn.

Scalability and Cost Effectiveness

In today's environment of shrinking resources, new programs must be scalable (easily expanded and cost effective). A Freshman Transition course using the *Career Choices* materials delivers a quality comprehensive guidance experience to all students easily and affordably. The infographic that follows could be used in a proposal to demonstrate this fact.

Freshman Transition/Comprehensive Guidance Course:
A Cost-Effective Strategy

Compare the overall return on investment of
One Dropout Coach vs. One Freshman Transition Course Instructor

Traditional Counseling Model

One Dropout Coach or Counselor
Caseload of 45 students
Each student receives an average of 20 hours of one-on-one counseling or support

Freshman Transition Course Model

One Freshman Transition course instructor
Five periods a day with 30 students per class
- Semester course (taught two semesters) = 300 students, each receiving 90 hours of comprehensive guidance
- Year-long course = 150 students, each receiving 180 hours of comprehensive guidance

So, get out your calculator, and you'll see that
one full-time professional educator
can provide comprehensive guidance using either model, but...

Traditional Counseling Model

45 students x 20 hours of guidance
= 900 student impact hours

Freshman Transition Course Model

150 students x 180 hours of guidance
= 27,000 student impact hours
300 students x 90 hours of guidance
= 27,000 student impact hours

WhatWorksCareerChoices.com

An important part of your program or funding proposal is to provide decision makers and prospective partners with information supporting the probability of success. In this case, the tool you've chosen is the *Career Choices* curriculum. For a variety of supporting documents, and statistics to round out your project proposal, visit www.whatworkscareerchoices.com.

This web site provides easy access to evidence relating to *Career Choices*—both statistical and anecdotal—that you'll need to support your grant writing process.

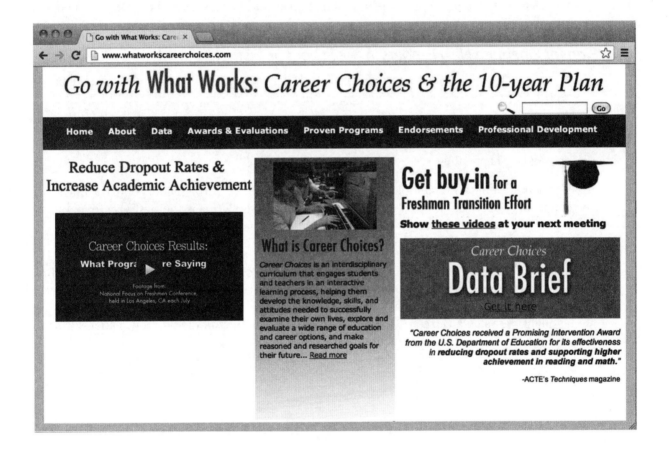

Step 3: Keep school and district leaders informed and "on board."

This is critical if you want to keep your program going and growing. Keep your school and district leaders informed on all aspects of your program's progress. Their decisions drive what happens, so you want their decisions to be informed decisions.

What about when leadership changes?

We've been working with schools and districts for more than two decades, and there is one event that seems to catch educators unaware: What happens to a program if school or district leadership changes? What about the school board? For most districts, membership changes every couple of years.

Too often, leadership changes result in existing programs getting scrapped in favor of programs brought in by the new leadership. These changes don't always mean the existing program didn't provide results. In too many cases the program's impact and success hadn't been documented and effectively communicated to decision makers.

A Plan for Orienting New Leaders in the School or District

1. As soon as a new administrator comes aboard, deliver your project proposal, your data report, and the types of items you would put in a media kit (see page 15/11 of this guide).

2. Schedule a meeting to discuss your *Career Choices* program. Lunch is good; everyone has to eat. If it seems appropriate, invite team members who can enthusiastically report on program happenings.

3. If you are dealing with multiple new committee members (e.g., the school board), arrange one-to-one meetings before a group meeting. Studies show this is the best way to lobby for any outcome. That way, you can deal with individual resistance before the decision-making body meets. You'll also identify those willing to actively support your efforts.

Without this active intervention, any project runs the risk of being displaced by new leadership. The business world calls it the not-invented-here syndrome. New leaders want to put their own stamp on projects, and projects that may be seen as expendable are at greater risk. It is your job to highlight the value a *Career Choices* course provides in pursuit of your new leader's goals so your program is seen as indispensable rather than expendable.

Step 4: Work with your local media to publicize your efforts.

Getting Publicity

Building a Freshman Transition program that's institutionalized and accepted by the community requires a partnership with your local media. Working with media outlets to start a dialogue about what local young people need to become self-sufficient will garner support from parents, businesses, and the community at large.

Getting good publicity is not as hard as you think. You have a compelling story to tell—helping students become economically and emotionally self-sufficient—and your local media will be receptive.

A media kit is an effective means of presenting the key points and information about your program to TV, newspaper, and radio journalists. Providing print materials organized in a folder or as a downloadable "packet" on your school web site allows you to easily communicate key details and helps you deliver a clear and consistent message.

The information in your media kit should conform to media norms and should be concise.

 Visit Section 15 of the online version of this *Instructor's Guide* for a list of suggested media kit contents and a guide to writing a press release.

Developing an Issue-Oriented Campaign: Generating Long-Term Media Interest

Articles that have a local angle will have a higher probability of being published. Include statistics, school data, quotes from administrators, teachers, parents, and students (with permission), and stories highlighting individuals involved in the program to increase interest in the piece. Referencing local, state, and national research also helps validate the issues.

Feature Story Ideas

- Innovative Class Designed to Reduce Dropout Rate
- Keeping Students on the Track to Success Starts in the 9th Grade at [insert school]
- Teachers at [insert school] Enthusiastic About Freshman Transition Initiative
- Students at [insert school] Discover More Than Diploma Needed for Self-Sufficiency

Here are topics that could be included in a series of issue-oriented articles:

- Make Sure Your Child Doesn't Become a Boomerang Kid
- Why Every Freshman Needs a 10-year Plan
- Student Success in College: What Studies Show
- Tomorrow's Electricians, Nurses, Engineers are Today's Students and They Need to Start Planning Now
- Your Child is Going to College. What's Next?

Step 5: Be on the lookout for funding sources that can support your program.

Securing Funding to Sustain Your Course

Based on educator feedback, it seems that finding funding and maintaining that funding are among the most challenging aspects of starting and sustaining this course. Funding is constantly changing and state and local education agencies have different mandates and priorities to address with federal and state funding. One of the major benefits of a *Career Choices* course is that the long-range planning process embedded in the 10-year plan promotes both high school and college completion. Focus on that priority as you research possible funding streams.

Start with Your District Office

Contact the grant writers at your district office to see if they know of any funding opportunities for initiatives related to your goals. Consider how your goals align with the goals of programs focused on dropout prevention, at-risk students, smaller learning communities, individualized education or graduation plans, career and life planning, comprehensive guidance, freshman transition or orientation, advisor/advisee, and academy or house programs. You may also discuss your district's Tech Prep, Career and Technical Education, and Title I funding.

You'll want your grant writer to be familiar with the goals of the Freshman Transition Initiative (see Section 6 of this guide) and the goals of your particular program, so share as much relevant information as you can. Update them as you receive media coverage and remind them about the program's needs on a regular basis. When a possible funding opportunity crosses their desk, they'll think of your program.

Funding Research

You may research funding before you develop your project proposal or you may outline your program methodology first. Either way, you eventually need to find funding to implement this essential program. Even if you have no experience in securing monies for programs, you'll find the process doable and rewarding.

A *Career Choices* course or Freshman Transition program is commonly funded through:

- Federal programs
- State funding
- Corporate funding
- Student-funded workbook purchases
- Community organizations

What follows is a brief overview of these options. For more in-depth information, including links to current and proposed federal programs, visit our funding section of **The Teachers' Lounge** at **www.careerchoices.com/lounge/funding.**

In addition, you'll want to:

- Research funding sources listed online
- Visit your state department of education web site to identify current priorities your program may match. If you find a match, call the state administrator responsible for that program to get more information
- Contact your mayor's office; your program may support a community priority
- Check with your local Chamber of Commerce regarding resources or interest in the business community
- Contact community service organizations to see if you can speak about your program at one of their upcoming meetings
- Get publicity through your local media

Funding Research Worksheet

Internet research

Locate all options available using the keywords: dropout prevention, college and career readiness, college completion, education or graduation plans, funding. Record your findings below, including URLs of web sites, contact people and titles, phone numbers, and email addresses.

Federal initiatives

Foundation and corporate funding

State and regional funding

Local funding (e.g., business partners, community services organizations, local foundations)

Name, phone number, and email address of the person responsible for grant writing in our district.

_____

Name   Title

_____

Email   Phone

Federal Funding

U.S. Department of Education grants may be possible funding sources for schools hoping to plan and implement a Freshman Transition course and school-wide initiative. Each grant has unique eligibility requirements and funding timetables. New funding can become available throughout the year, so conduct a regular check for upcoming funding competitions.
www.ed.gov/grantapps

Most federal grant competitions are announced in Federal Register Notices, so reviewing that resource on a regular basis is another strategy that may lead to funding.
www.federalregister.gov/agencies/education-department

Current Federal Programs

Following are current and proposed federal programs. This information was accurate at the time of printing. Be sure to visit The Teachers' Lounge and watch your newsletters for updates.
www.careerchoices.com/lounge/funding

College- and Career-Ready Students
(ESEA, Title I, Part A)
www2.ed.gov/programs/titleiparta

School Turnaround Grants
(formerly School Improvement Grants)
www2.ed.gov/about/offices/list/oese/ost

High School Redesign
(competitive grant proposed in FY2014 budget)
www.ed.gov/highschool

Career and Technical Education
www2.ed.gov/about/offices/list/ovae/pi/cte

21st Century Community Learning Centers
www2.ed.gov/programs/21stcclc

Upward Bound Program
www2.ed.gov/programs/trioupbound

GEAR UP
www2.ed.gov/programs/gearup

Talent Search Program
www2.ed.gov/programs/triotalent

Small, Rural School Achievement Program
www2.ed.gov/programs/reapsrsa

College Pathways and Accelerated Learning
(proposed to replace High School Graduation Initiative)
www2.ed.gov/about/overview/budget/budget14

Major Federal Funding Opportunities

Title I of the Elementary and Secondary Education Act (ESEA) is aimed at improving the academic achievement of disadvantaged students. If your school receives Title I funds this may be another possible funding source for your Freshman Transition efforts. You'll also want to research the proposed **Title I School Turnaround Grants**.

If your state has been awarded **Race to the Top Funding,** you'll want to make sure your state educational leaders consider a state-wide initiative built around the Freshman Transition model and school-wide initiative.

A Freshman Transition course can help your school and district meet the six Core Indicators required to receive funding from the Carl D. Perkins and Technical Education Act of 2006.

 For in-depth information on how *Career Choices* meets the requirements of these federal programs, review the details on the online *Instructor's Guide.*

State Funding

How to Research State Funding for Your Program

www.careerchoices.com/lounge/funding

Each state has different challenges, mandates, and priorities. The best place to start your research is with your principal. Advise him/her of your plans and ask for the names of individuals at the district office who are responsible for grant writing. Contact them to discuss your project and funding opportunities. Ask if special funding is available for:

- Freshman transition programs
- At-risk or dropout prevention programs
- Tech Prep or Career and Technical Education programs
- Career and college readiness efforts
- Dual enrollment
- Guidance and career planning
- Advisor/advisee programs

Be sure your district grant writers are familiar with your program and its goals. RFPs (requests for proposals) come across their desks daily. If the grant writers are familiar with your program and a suitable RFP arrives, they will be much more likely to contact you and write a proposal for your program. It's a good idea to write a brief summary of what you'd like your program to accomplish and send it to the district office.

> *After utilizing* Career Choices *as a counseling instrument and a career cluster selection, less than 5% of our students are changing programs. This evidence supports our belief that the program is a key to career decision-making.*
>
> — Jim Campbell, Ed.D, Executive Director (Retired)
> Delaware Tech Prep, Recipient of the Dale Parnell Outstanding
> Tech Prep Program Award

How Career Choices *Addresses the Requirements of Other Common Funding Sources*

Career Choices meets the goals and requirements of several funding streams that might be used to fund Freshman Transition courses. The details you need to start formulating a winning grant proposal are available at **www.careerchoices.com/lounge/funding**.

Learn more about the funding available through the following programs:

- High Schools that Work—Key Practices for Accelerating Student Achievement
- Jobs for America's Graduates (JAG) Competencies
- Workforce Investment Act's 10 Essential Elements

Step 6: Explore local funding options or sources not normally tapped by
your school.

Funding Ideas for Corporate or Local Business Partners

Many companies focus their corporate philanthropic efforts on education. Members of the business community are very aware that they need educated and motivated workers—now and in the future. Because *Career Choices* helps students prepare for the workplace, it is a wonderful vehicle for soliciting corporate sponsorship. Here's one plan for researching and executing a corporate funding campaign.

Find out which corporations do business in your community, and what local businesses are prominent. The best place to start your research is with the Chamber of Commerce or the Better Business Bureau. Keep an eye on the local media to see which companies are in the news.

Once you've narrowed your choice to two or three prospects, use your own network of peers, parents, and friends to see if you can get an introduction to the CEO, director of public relations, or director of community relations. If you cannot get an introduction, make an appointment to see the director of community relations anyway.

When you pay your first visit, take along a complete set of the *Career Choices* textbooks, a copy of the Standards for a Freshman Transition Course, and a short PowerPoint presentation. Show the online video *The Key to Dropout Prevention: The 10-year Plan*, found on **The Teachers' Lounge**. These items are wonderful "props" for your presentation because the funding source can quickly see what you intend to accomplish in your program.

Besides talking about the program, be sure to ask questions and listen carefully to what the funder has to say. You'll want to incorporate his or her ideas into your written proposal, which should arrive on their desk within a few days of your interview.

In developing your proposal, don't be shy. Remember, you are not asking for a lot of money by most corporate standards, and most businesses make donations in the community. However, they are also looking for publicity and an opportunity to generate good public relations. It is imperative that you solicit media attention for your program throughout the year (newspaper articles, TV news stories, etc.). Anywhere your *Career Choices* program is mentioned, be sure to add the tagline "Funded by the XYZ Corporation." The more you do this, the more likely the business or corporation is to fund your program year after year.

Some of your presentation strategies will parallel what we suggest for Community Service Organizations in Section 13 of this guide.

Other Local Funding Sources

Foundation Funding

While the first thing that comes to mind may be the large foundations we all hear about in the news, such as the Bill and Melinda Gates Foundation or the Carnegie Foundation, they are unlikely to fund a local effort. A local or regional foundation whose mission is education is more likely to support efforts helping local students become college and career ready and economically self-sufficient.

The process for securing local foundation funding is very similar to corporate funding. Ask an attorney to identify the local legal professionals most likely to help manage family foundations. Once you've identified a possible local foundation, follow their requirements for submitting a request. Sometimes it's as simple as submitting a letter of proposal with supporting documentation.

Community Service Organizations

Community service organizations are often an untapped source of financial support and a source for volunteers to mentor students, provide internships, or speak to your classes. Once you find a community service organization supportive of your goals, ask them to consider funding your *Career Choices* workbooks each year. For more information, see pages 13/6–13/8 in this guide.

Student Funding

Many districts allow for student lab fees to cover the purchase of consumable supplies. As a result, some schools have students purchase their own copies of the *Workbook and Portfolio*. If your district has a similar provision, you might use this strategy to fund part of your *Career Choices* program.

Consider seeking supplemental funding from a community service organization to purchase copies of the *Workbook and Portfolio* for students who can't afford to buy their own.

Many students commented that this class (vocational studies using Career Choices*) was their favorite class. The reasons included their ownership of their workbook and questions and activities about themselves.*

— Deborah Back, Vocational Studies Teacher
Knott County Schools, Litt Carr, KY

Our freshmen were very excited to start putting their work in their workbooks. It's amazing what ownership they take over their work and how a workbook validates all their thoughts and efforts.

— Diane Goncalves, Assistant Superintendent
Region One School District, Falls Village, CT

Step 7: Celebrate successes, big and small, with all stakeholders and students.

Celebrate!

Thank your staff and other supporters of your program throughout the year. Successful projects don't happen without a great deal of energy from a lot of people, and it's important to acknowledge their efforts.

Recognize those willing to assume new roles and tasks. Any new project has challenges, and time and effort is required to achieve success. Outgoing and visionary workers may be driven by a desire to achieve the ultimate goal of a project, but they also desire—and deserve—recognition, even if only in a small, personal way.

Recognition is an endorsement of their professionalism and can take many different forms.

- Share a smile
- Treat them to a coffee or soda
- Ask for an update or report, verbal or written
- Remember a birthday
- Plan for benchmark group meetings
- Include them in emails, memos, or brainstorming
- Accommodate personal needs and problems
- Ask for help in an emergency situation
- Share successes publicly
- Respect their ideas and wishes
- Keep challenging them
- Greet them by name
- Provide ongoing training and guidance
- Take time to explain issues as they arise
- Give them additional responsibility
- Send newsworthy information to local media
- Help create pleasant working situations
- Enlist their help to train new team members
- Have a public reception
- Take time to talk

- Defend them if needed
- Commend them to the administrative staff
- Send them to outside conferences and workshops
- Utilize their discipline
- Write thank-you emails or notes
- Surprise them with a cake or treat
- Nominate them for state, district, school, community, awards
- Praise them to colleagues and friends
- Accept their individuality
- Send impromptu fun cards
- Promote Freshman Transition Champion of the week/month
- Report on successes in newsletters or at board/staff meetings
- Send commendatory letter to elected and local officials
- Have a something printed or engraved that identifies their role and the project
- Award special citations for extraordinary achievements
- Have a picnic
- Be familiar with their assignments and roles

Be sure to do something extra special (e.g., a potluck dinner or other event) at the end of the year to celebrate the successes and the hard work. Invite parents, community supporters, district office staff, etc.

And don't forget your students. At the end of the course, celebrate their hard work as well.

Biographical Sketches

Mindy Bingham

Fostering innovation and excellence in education is Mindy Bingham's mission. As a part-time college professor, author, publisher, and community activist, Mindy has traveled around the country conducting workshops for educators and curriculum specialists. In 1985, she was named one of the outstanding women in education by the Santa Barbara County Commission for Women. In 1991, she was named an honorary life member to the Vocational Education Equity Council (VEEC) of the American Vocational Association. In 2001, Mindy was honored with the Woman of Distinction Award by the Santa Barbara Associates and the Breaking Traditions Award of the Equity Council of the Association of Career and Technical Education.

Mindy's educational spirit is matched by her entrepreneurial drive. She was honored as the Entrepreneur of the Year for Santa Barbara for 1998 by the South Coast Business Network and recognized by the Santa Barbara chapter of the National Association of Women Business Owners as the 2012 Spirit of Entrepreneurship Rock Star.

To date as author or co-author, Mindy Bingham's titles have sold over two million copies. Her award-winning textbook, *Career Choices*, is used in over 5,000 secondary schools, along with the interdisciplinary companion books, *Lifestyle Math* and *Possibilities*. Her children's picture books include the Ingram number-one bestseller, *Minou*; *My Way Sally*, the 1989 Ben Franklin Award winner; and *Berta Benz and the Motorwagen*, inspiration for a soon-to-be-released animated movie.

Sandy Stryker

Sandy Stryker, co-author of the first edition of this guide, is also co-author of the bestselling *Choices: A Teen Woman's Journal for Self-awareness and Personal Planning*. Her first children's book, *Tonia the Tree*, was the 1988 recipient of the merit award from the Friends of American Writers.

Tanja Easson

Along with her duties as editor of this guide, Tanja has helped educators around the country initiate and expand their educational programs as Academic Innovations' Vice President of Curriculum and Technical Support. Her creativity and talent is evident in her work with author Mindy Bingham on the development of My10yearPlan.com®, CareerChoices.com, LifestyleMath.com, and The Teachers' Lounge.

Kelly Gajewski

Kelly Gajewski has written and edited a number of curriculum support materials for Academic Innovations and is well-versed in career education and life planning topics. She also played an integral role in production of the most recent editions of *Career Choices*, *Career Choices and Changes*, and the *Instructor's Guide for Career Choices and Changes*.

Cathie Klein

Catherine Klein began her career teaching Language Arts and Social Studies at the middle school level. Obtaining a Masters in Organizational Studies opened up new opportunities, including a position as an online adjunct instructor for Fort Hays State University. She also tackled the exciting challenge of helping to implement a new curriculum, *Career Choices*, at Seaman Freshman Center in Topeka, Kansas. Cathie is currently the College & Career Readiness Coordinator for Seaman High School, building a senior internship program that acts as an extension of the Success 101 Freshman Transition course.

Becky Simmons

Becky Simmons has taught for four years, all at Marquette Senior High School in Marquette, Michigan. She teaches science and Transitions, and has served as the Transitions Lesson Coordinator for the Freshman Academy teachers. Becky has a bachelor's degree from Northern Michigan University, and is currently working on her master's degree there. Becky calls on her experience in a variety of other careers, including cosmetologist, salon owner, mine tour guide, and geological technician for an exploration geology team, to provide a rich classroom experience.

Acknowledgments

We would like to thank Chris Nolt, owner of Cirrus Book Design in Santa Barbara, California, for her wonderful work on the design, typesetting, and production of this guide. Chris' skill and artistry is apparent in each of the books in the *Career Choices* series.

We would also like to thank the following individuals for contributions to the current edition and earlier editions of this guide: Lynn Anderson, Kathy Araujo, Janice Blair (art), Kyle Brace, Jim Campbell, Ed.D., Deb Teeken, James Comiskey, Shirley Cornelius, Rebecca Dedmond, Ph.D., Rochelle S. Friedman, Ed.D., Janet Goode, Carol Lee Hawkins, Diane Hollems, Ph.D., Michelle Jackman, Ph.D., Jim Johnson, Michele Julien, Diana Lackner (art), Amanda Lake, Pat Lewis, Laura Castle Light, M.Ed., Carl Lindros, Kristen Lunceford, Sara Lykken, M.Ed., Itoko Maeno (art), Nancy Marriott, Shirley Myers, M.Ed., Edward Myers, Susan Neufeldt, Ph.D., Brad Owen, Penelope Paine, Georgette Phillips, Chris Pulos, Patrick Roberts, Russ Rumberger, Ph.D., Robin Sager, Betty Shepperd, Betty Stambolian, Phyllis Stewart, Chas Thompson, Linda Wagner, Lauren Wintermeyer, Ed.D., Merri Ellen Wright.

This guide is rich with practical advice and inspiration because of the hundreds of educators using the *Career Choices* series who have graciously shared their ideas. Our warmest thanks to you all.

And, finally, a very special thanks to Kenneth B. Hoyt, Ph.D., for the hours spent reviewing the original manuscript, giving constructive criticism, and challenging our assumptions. His advice, guidance, and contributions were invaluable. We remember you well, Dr. Hoyt, as a steadfast pioneer to whom we dedicate our ongoing efforts to infuse career education into the core curriculum.

Index

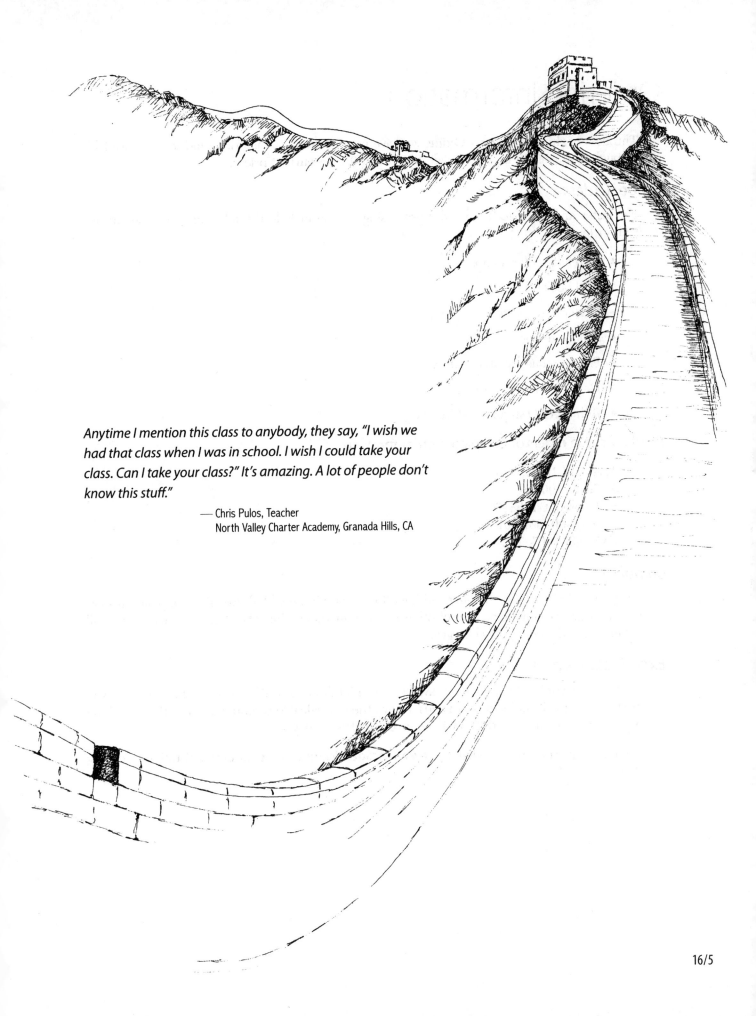

Anytime I mention this class to anybody, they say, "I wish we had that class when I was in school. I wish I could take your class. Can I take your class?" It's amazing. A lot of people don't know this stuff."

— Chris Pulos, Teacher
North Valley Charter Academy, Granada Hills, CA

Ordering Information

Throughout this *Instructor's Guide*, we have noted resources, materials, and services available through Academic Innovations. Call (800) 967-8016 for current prices.

School Orders

For faster and more accurate order processing, please include the following when submitting your order:

- Purchase order number
- Full book title
- Quantity requested
- School and/or district
- Person requesting the materials
- Date the materials are needed
- Billing AND shipping addresses

Send purchase orders or completed order forms to:

Academic Innovations
59 South 100 East
St. George, UT 84770
Phone (800) 967-8016
FAX (800) 967-4027

Shipping

Shipping is FOB origin; shipping and handling costs will be added. Regular shipping rates are based on ground shipment. Use of other delivery methods (2nd Day Air, Overnight, etc.) will result in additional shipping charges.

Examination Copies

Examination copies of materials are available on a 60-day approval basis. If you find the titles you are reviewing will not meet your needs, return them in saleable condition prior to the end of the 60-day examination period. You will be invoiced after 60 days.

You may request a 60-day review set at **www.academicinnovations.com/60day.html** or by calling (800) 967-8016.

Other Books by Mindy Bingham and/or Sandy Stryker

Career Choices: A Guide for Teens and Young Adults: Who Am I? What Do I Want? How Do I Get It?, by Bingham and Stryker. 288 pages. Hardcover, ISBN 978-1-878787-41-5. Softcover, ISBN 978-1-878787-38-5.

Workbook and Portfolio for Career Choices, by Bingham and Stryker. Softcover, 144 pages. ISBN 978-1-878787-37-8.

Possibilities: A Supplemental Anthology for Career Choices, edited by Goode, Bingham, and Mickey. Softcover, 288 pages. ISBN 978-1-878787-14-9.

Lifestyle Math: Your Financial Planning Portfolio, A Supplemental Mathematics Unit for Career Choices, by Bingham, Willhite, and Myers. Softcover, 112 pages. ISBN 978-1-878787-36-1.

Career Choices and Changes: A Guide for Discovering Who You Are, What You Want, and How to Get It, by Bingham and Stryker. Softcover, 382 pages. ISBN 978-1-878787-17-0.

My10yearPlan.com® Essentials (seat license). ISBN 978-1-878787-43-9.

My10yearPlan.com® Interactive (seat license). ISBN 978-1-878787-44-6.

CareerChoices.com + Instructor Access for The Teachers' Lounge (annual site license). ISBN 978-1-878787-42-2.

LifestyleMath.com (annual site license). ISBN 978-1-878787-45-3.

Things Will Be Different for My Daughter: A Practical Guide to Building Her Self-Esteem and Self-Reliance, by Bingham and Stryker. Softcover. ISBN 978-0-14-024125-9.

Choices: A Teen Woman's Journal for Self-awareness and Personal Planning, Bingham, Edmondson, and Stryker. Softcover, 240 pages. ISBN 978-0-911655-22-3.

Challenges: A Young Man's Journal for Self-awareness and Personal Planning, by Bingham, Edmondson, and Stryker. Softcover, 240 pages. ISBN 978-0-911655-24-7.

More Choices: A Strategic Planning Guide for Mixing Career and Family, by Bingham and Stryker. Softcover, 240 pages. ISBN 978-0-911655-28-5.

Changes: A Woman's Journal for Self-awareness and Personal Planning, by Bingham, Stryker, and Edmondson. Softcover, 240 pages. ISBN 978-0-911655-40-7.

Instructor's Guide for Choices, Challenges, Changes, and More Choices, by Edmondson, Bingham, Stryker, et al. Softcover, 272 pages. ISBN 978-0-911655-04-9.

Mother Daughter Choices: A Handbook for the Coordinator, by Bingham, Quinn, and Sheehan. Softcover, 144 pages. ISBN 978-0-911655-44-5.

Women Helping Girls With Choices: A Handbook For Community Service Organizations, by Bingham and Stryker. Softcover, 192 pages. ISBN 978-0-911655-00-1.

All of the following children's full-color picture books are 9" x 12", hardcover with dust jacket and illustrations by nationally acclaimed artist Itoko Maeno.

Minou, by Mindy Bingham, 64 pages. ISBN 978-1-878787-88-0.

Tonia the Tree, by Stryker, 32 pages. Winner of the 1989 Friends of American Writers Merit Award. ISBN 978-0-911655-16-2.

My Way Sally, by Bingham, 48 pages. Winner of the 1989 Ben Franklin Award. ISBN 978-0-911655-27-8.

Berta Benz and the Motorwagen, by Bingham, 48 pages. ISBN 978-1-878787-91-0.

Mother Nature Nursery Rhymes, by Stryker and Bingham, 32 pages. ISBN 978-0-911655-01-8.

You can order these books directly from Academic Innovations

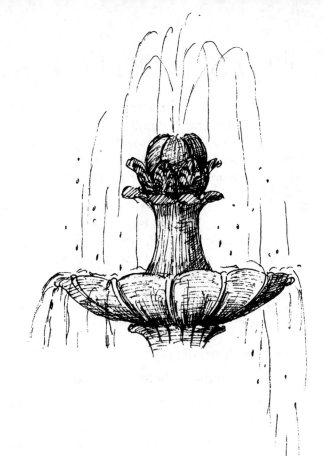

A journey of a thousand leagues begins with a single step.

—Lao-tzu

Online *Instructor's Guide* Account Registration

Each purchase of the *Instructor's and Administrator's Guide for Career Choices and My10yearPlan.com* included with a school adoption comes with a two-year license to an online version of this manual. This convenient new resource provides easy access to the *Instructor's Guide* wherever and whenever you need it as well as added information not included in the textbook edition. Topics that are expanded in the online *Instructor's Guide* are noted in the print version with this small computer symbol.

You can access the easy-to-navigate *Instructor's Guide* on your computer, tablet, or phone, so lesson plans and buy-in talking points will always be right at your fingertips. Once you login to use the *Instructor's Guide*, you can choose to view an entire section at a time or navigate right to the page you're looking for with just a few clicks. Whether you are a technology pro or novice, you'll find the online *Instructor's Guide* to be a valuable, time-saving companion in your busy day.

An access code provided inside a purchased *Instructor's Guide* will allow you to activate that license and access this enhanced information.

Activate Your Account:

1. Go to **www.careerchoices.com/lounge**.

2. In the login area, click on the link below the login boxes to activate your access code.

3. Enter your **Access Code** into the text field and click "Verify Code."

    Please Note: Each access code can only be used once, so make sure you have time to complete the activation process before you start. (The process takes the average user less than 5 minutes.)

4. Follow the on-screen directions to set up your account and create your username and password. (You may choose to record your login information below.)

    My username: _____

    My password: _____

Access the *Online Instructor's Guide*:

Go to **www.careerchoices.com/lounge**, click on the *Online Instructor's Guide* icon, and sign in using your username and password.

Support:

While the design of the *Online Instructor's Guide* is intuitive, online help is available if you have questions.

System Requirements:

Access to the *Online Instructor's Guide* is browser based, so you must have an Internet connection and up-to-date web browser.

** Access to the **Online Instructor's Guide** can be purchased separately if you already have a seventh edition print copy. Visit www.careerchoices.com/store to purchase a two-year license.*